SEXUAL DISSIDENCE

Sexual Dissidence

Augustine to Wilde,
Freud to Foucault

JONATHAN DOLLIMORE

CLARENDON PRESS · OXFORD

Oxford University Press, Walton Street, Oxford OX2 6DP
Oxford New York Toronto
Delhi Bombay Calcutta Madras Karachi
Petaling Jaya Singapore Hong Kong Tokyo
Nairobi Dar es Salaam Cape Town
Melbourne Auckland
and associated companies in
Berlin Ibadan

Oxford is a trade mark of Oxford University Press

Published in the United States
by Oxford University Press, New York

First published 1991
Paperback edition reprinted 1991, 1992

British Library Cataloguing in Publication Data
data available

Library of Congress Cataloging in Publication Data
Dollimore, Jonathan.
Sexual dissidence : Augustine to Wilde, Freud to Foucault / Jonathan
Dollimore.
Includes bibliographical references and index.
1. Sexual deviation.   2. Sexual deviation in literature.
I. Title.
HQ71.D49   1991
306.76'6—dc20   91–8339
ISBN 0–19–811225–4 (HB)
ISBN 0–19–811269–6

Printed and bound in Great Britain by
Butler & Tanner Ltd, Frome and London

For Alan, Niki, and my parents

Two friends who met here and embraced are gone,
Each to his own mistake; one flashes on
To fame and ruin in a rowdy lie,
A village torpor holds the other one,
Some local wrong where it takes time to die:
This empty junction glitters in the sun.

So at all quays and crossroads: who can tell
These places of decision and farewell
To what dishonour all adventure leads,
What parting gift could give that friend protection,
So orientated his vocation needs
The Bad Lands and the sinister direction?

W. H. Auden, 'The Quest'

Foreword

An outline of this book, and how it proceeds, is given in Chapter 2. It can by all means be read first, but Chapter 1 offers a more immediate and engaging point of departure, concerning as it does a remarkable chance encounter between Oscar Wilde and André Gide in Algiers in 1895. I begin with that encounter because what then and subsequently occurred not only suggested this book, but continued to shape it throughout.

Acknowledgements

I worked on this book first at the Humanities Research Centre, Canberra, and then at the National Humanities Center, North Carolina. My gratitude to all who made both trips possible, and to those who befriended me in both places.

Thanks also to the following who helped me in different ways with the writing: Leo Bersani, Homi Bhabha, Rachel Bowlby, Joe Bristow, Peter Burton, Roger Cardinal, Elizabeth A. Clark, Graeme Clarke, Brian Cummings, John Fletcher, Henry Louis Gates, Jr., Jonathan Goldberg, Jim Greeve, Michael Hawkins, Barbara Hodgdon, Ann Jones, Larry Jones, Ian Littlewood, Ania Loomba, Percival Mars, Kobena Mercer, Michael Moon, Tony Nuttall, Pratap Rughani, Jacqueline Rose, Angus Ross, Eve Sedgwick, Kaja Silverman, Alan Sinfield, Peter Stallybrass, Jeremy Tambling, Godfrey Tanner, Colin Thompson, Cedric Watts, Jeffrey Weeks, Allon White, Max Wilcox.

Different drafts of some parts first appeared in the following: *Oxford Literary Review*, *Textual Practice*, *Genders*, *LTP*, *Renaissance Drama*, *Critical Quarterly*.

Contents

Part 8. *Transgressive Reinscriptions, Early Modern and Post-modern*

Part 9. *Beyond Sexual Difference*

PART 1

An Encounter

1 *Wilde and Gide in Algiers*

Encounter

In Blidah, Algeria in January 1895 André Gide is in the hall of a hotel, about to leave. His glance falls on the slate which announces the names of new guests: 'suddenly my heart gave a leap; the two last names . . . were those of Oscar Wilde and Lord Alfred Douglas' (Gide, *If It Die*, 271). Acting on his first impulse, Gide 'erases' his own name from the slate and leaves for the station. Twice thereafter Gide writes about the incident, unsure why he left so abruptly; first in his *Oscar Wilde* (1901) then in *Si le grain ne meurt* (*If It Die*, 1920/1926). It may, he reflects, have been a feeling of *mauvais honte* or of embarrassment: Wilde was becoming notorious and his company compromising (*If It Die*, 271, 273). But also Gide was severely depressed, and at such times 'I feel ashamed of myself, disown, repudiate myself' (p. 271). Whatever the case, on his way to the station he decided that his leaving was cowardly and so returned. The consequent meeting with Wilde precipitated a transformation in Gide's life and subsequent writing, and through the latter, exerted a far-reaching influence on modern literature.

Gide's reluctance to meet Wilde certainly had something to do with previous meetings in Paris four years earlier in 1891; they had seen a great deal of each other across several occasions, and biographers agree that this was one of the most important events in Gide's life. But these meetings had left Gide feeling ambivalent towards the older man and not only does Gide say nothing in *If It Die* about Wilde's obvious and deep influence upon him in Paris in 1891, but, according to Jean Delay, in the manuscript of Gide's journal the pages corresponding to that period—November–December 1891—are torn out (Delay, *The Youth of André Gide*, 290). As Ellmann remarks, 'The main document about the psychic possession of Gide by Wilde is an absent one—a truly symbolist piece of evidence . . .' (*Oscar Wilde* (1987), 336).

Undoubtedly Gide was deeply disturbed by Wilde, and not surprisingly since the remarks of Gide in his letters of that time suggest that Wilde was intent on undermining the younger man's self-identity, rooted as it was in a Protestant ethic and high bourgeois moral rigour and repression which generated a kind of conformity which Wilde scorned. Wilde wanted to encourage Gide to transgress. It may be that he wanted to re-enact in Gide the creative liberation—which included strong criminal identification—which his own exploration of transgressive desire had enabled nine years earlier. (Wilde's major writing, including that which constitutes what I shall call his transgressive aesthetic,[1] dates from 1886, with, according to Robert Ross, his first experience of homosexuality; see Wilde, *Artist as Critic*, ed. Ellmann, p. xviii.)

But first Wilde had to undermine that lawful sense of self which kept Gide transfixed within the law. So Wilde tried to decentre or demoralize Gide—'demoralize' in the sense of liberate from moral constraint rather than dispirit; or rather to dispirit precisely in the sense of to liberate from a morality anchored in the very notion of spirit. ('Demoralize' was a term Gide remembers Wilde using in just this sense, one which, for Gide, recalled Flaubert.) Hence perhaps those most revealing of remarks by Gide to Valéry at this time (4 December 1891): 'Wilde is religiously contriving to kill what remains of my soul, because he says that in order to know an essence, one must eliminate it: he wants me to miss my soul. The measure of a thing is the effort made to destroy it. Each thing is made up only of its emptiness.' And in another letter of the same month: 'Please forgive my silence: since Wilde, I hardly exist anymore' (*Correspondence*, ed. Guicharnand, 90, 92). And in unpublished notes for this time Gide declares that Wilde was 'always trying to instil into you a sanction for evil' (Delay, *André Gide*, 291). So despite his intentions to the contrary, Wilde at that time seems indeed to have dispirited Gide in the conventional sense of the word. Yet perhaps the contrary intention was partly successful, since on 1 January 1892 Gide writes: 'Wilde, I think, did me nothing but harm. In his company I had lost the habit of thinking. I had more varied emotions, but had forgotten how to bring order into them' (*Journals*, 1 January 1892). In general though, Gide reacted, says Delay, in accordance with his Protestant

---

[1] Those aspects of Wilde's transgressive aesthetic which concern me here derive mainly from work published across a short period of time, the years 1889–91. My exploration of this aesthetic rests on a reading of Wilde which is avowedly partial, concentrating on what has hitherto been excluded. Too often, readings of Wilde merely re-present a certain consensus—hence, presumably, Wilde's usual exclusion from certain 'impartial' versions of 'English' studies. More important is his exclusion from cultural criticism and literary theory. What Richard Ellmann said of Wilde nearly twenty years ago is still true today: he 'laid the basis for many critical positions which are still debated in much the same terms, and which we like to attribute to more ponderous names' (*The Artist as Critic*, ed. Ellmann, p. x). Thomas Mann compared Wilde with Nietzsche; Ellmann in 1968 adds the name of Roland Barthes. In 1990 we could add several more. It is in relation to the renewed interest in Wilde generated by Ellmann's recent biography that I want to acknowledge that there is of course more to be said: about those of Wilde's works discussed here, about other works not discussed, about Wilde himself, and indeed about other of his ideas which intersect with and contradict the transgressive aesthetic explored here. I also concur with Regenia Gagnier's contention that a figure as paradoxical as Wilde, and an art as self-contradictory as his, can only be understood in relation to his audiences and the social institutions in which art forms are developed and distributed (*Idylls of the Market Place*, 3).

instincts, reaffirming a moral conviction inseparable from an essentialist conception of self (cf. *Journals*, 29 December 1891: 'O Lord keep me from evil. May my soul again be proud . . .').

Even so, this earlier meeting with Wilde is to be counted as one of the most important events in Gide's life: 'for the first time he found himself confronted with a man who was able to bring about, within him, a transmutation of all values—in other words, a re-volution' (Delay, *André Gide*, 289–91, 295). Richard Ellmann concurs with this judgement, and suggests further that Wilde's attempt to 'authorize evil' in Gide supplies much of the subject of *The Immoralist* and *The Counterfeiters*. (The former work contains a character, Ménalque, who is based upon Wilde.) More generally, the 'momentous association' between these two men was, he suggests, rather like that in *Dorian Gray* between Dorian and Lord Henry Wotton—'in effect, Wilde spiritually seduced Gide'. For Ellmann, the most important document about the 'psychic possession of Gide by Wilde' is those missing pages from Gide's journal. In speculating on what they contained Ellmann argues that Gide's aesthetic and intellectual debts to Wilde were greater than he ever subsequently acknowledged.[2]

With What a Choking Voice

It is against the background and the importance of that earlier meeting, together with the ambivalence towards Wilde which it generated in Gide, that we return to that further encounter in Algeria four years later. If anything, the ambivalence seems even stronger; in a letter to his mother Gide describes Wilde as a terrifying man, a 'most dangerous product of modern civilisation' who had already depraved Douglas '*right down to the marrow*' (Delay, *André Gide*, 391, my emphasis). A few days later Gide meets them again in Algiers, a city which Wilde says he means to demoralize (Gide, *Oscar Wilde*). It is here that there occurs the event which was to change Gide's life and radically influence his subsequent work, an event for which, in retrospect, the entire narrative of *If It Die* seems to have been preparing. He is taken by Wilde to a café: 'in the half-open doorway, there suddenly appeared a marvellous youth. He stood there for a time, leaning with his raised elbow against the door-jamb, and outlined on the dark background of the night' (p. 280). The youth joins them; his name is Mohammed; he is a musician, a flute player. Listening to that music 'you forgot the time and place, and who you were' (p. 281). This is not the first time Gide

[2] *Oscar Wilde: Critical Essays*, 4; see also Ellmann's 'Corydon', 84–5, 90, and *passim*.

has experienced this sensation of forgetting. Africa increasingly attracts him in this respect (pp. 236–7, 247–9, 251, 252, 258–9); there he feels liberated and the burden of an oppressive sense of self is dissolved: 'I laid aside anxieties, constraints, solicitudes, and as my will evaporated, I felt myself becoming porous as a beehive' (p. 264). Now, as they leave the café, Wilde turns to Gide and asks him if he desires the musician. Gide writes: 'how dark the alley was! I thought my heart would fail me; and what a dreadful effort of courage it needed to answer: "yes", and with what a choking voice!' (p. 281; Delay, *André Gide*, 394, points out that the word 'courage' is here transvalued by Gide; earlier courage was needed for self-discipline—now it is the strength to transgress).

Wilde arranges something with their guide, rejoins Gide and then begins laughing: 'a resounding laugh, more of triumph than of pleasure, an interminable, uncontrollable, insolent laugh . . . it was the amusement of a child and a devil' (p. 282). Gide spends the night with Mohammed: 'my joy was unbounded, and I cannot imagine it greater, even if love had been added'. Though not his first homosexual experience (probably his second), it confirmed Gide's sexual 'nature'—what, he says, was 'normal' for him: 'There was nothing constrained here, nothing precipitate, nothing doubtful; there is no taste of ashes in the memory I keep.' Even more defiantly Gide declares that, although he had achieved 'the summit of pleasure five times' with Mohammed, 'I revived my ecstasy many more times, and back in my hotel room I relived its echoes until morning' (pp. 284–5; this passage was one of those omitted from early English editions).

At this suitably climactic moment I postpone further consideration of Gide and turn to the anti-essentialist, transgressive aesthetic which Wilde was advocating and which played so important a part in Gide's liberation—or corruption, depending on one's point of view. And I want to begin with an indispensable dimension of that aesthetic, yet one for which Wilde is hardly remembered—or, for some of his admirers, which is actively forgotten—namely, his political radicalism.

The Soul of Man

> If I do live again I would like it to be as a flower—no soul but perfectly beautiful. (Wilde, *Letters*, 181)

Wilde begins 'The Soul of Man under Socialism' (1891) by asserting that a socialism based on sympathy alone is useless; what is needed is to *'try and reconstruct society on such a basis that poverty will be impossible'* (p. 256, his emphasis). It is precisely because Christ made no attempt to reconstruct society that he had to resort to pain and suffering as the exemplary mode of self-realization (p. 286). The altern-ative is to transform the material conditions which create and perpetuate suffering (pp. 286–8). One might add that if the notion of redemption through suffering has been a familiar theme within English studies this only goes to remind us of the extent to which, in the twentieth century, criticism has worked in effect as a displaced theology or as a vehicle for an acquiescent quasi-religious humanism. So Wilde's terse assertion in 'Soul' that 'Pain is not the ultimate mode of perfection. It is merely provisional and a protest' (p. 288) may still be an appropriate response to those who sanctify suffering in the name not of Christ, but of the tragic vision and the human condition (sainthood without God, as Camus once put it).

Wilde also dismisses the related pieties, that humankind learns wisdom through suffering, and that suffering humanizes. On the contrary, 'misery and poverty are so absolutely degrading, and exercise such a paralysing effect over the nature of men, that no class is ever really conscious of its suffering. They have to be told of it by other people, and they often entirely disbelieve them' (p. 259). Against those who were beginning to talk of the dignity of manual labour Wilde insists that most of that too is absolutely degrading (p. 268). Each of these repudiations suggests that Wilde was fully aware of how ex-ploitation is crucially a question of ideological mystification, and the subjective internalization of ideology, as well as of outright coercion: 'to the thinker, the most tragic fact in the whole of the French Revolution is not that Marie Antoinette was killed for being a queen, but that the starved peasants of the Vendée voluntarily went out to die for the hideous cause of feudalism' (p. 260). Ideology reaches into experience and identity, re-emerging as 'voluntary' self-oppression. But ideology also informs the consciousness of the rulers, preventing them from seeing, for instance, that it is not sin that produces crime but starvation; that punishment of the criminal escalates rather than dimin-ishes crime; that such punishment brutalizes the society which adminis-ters it even more than the criminal who receives it (p. 267).[3]

There is much more in this essay but I have summarized enough to indicate its tough materialist stance; in modern parlance one might call it anti-humanist, not least because for Wilde a radical socialist pro-gramme is inseparable from a critique of those ideologies of selfhood which seek redemption in and through the individual, especially the

---

[3] In a letter to the Home Secretary, written from Reading prison, Wilde was to write of prison life that it 'hardens their hearts whose hearts it does not break, and brutalises those who have to carry it out no less than those who have to submit to it' (*Letters*, 404).

idea of a deep authentic subjectivity. Wilde shows how, in being true to that self, his contemporaries were more often than not simply being true to their social identification. A literary case in point would be Dickens's treatment of Stephen Blackpool in *Hard Times* (Wilde made a point of disliking Dickens); another might be Arnold's assertion in *Culture and Anarchy*: 'Religion says: "The Kingdom of God is within you"; and culture, in like manner, places human perfection in an internal condition, in the growth and predominance of our humanity proper' (p. 8). But isn't a category like anti-humanism entirely inappropriate, given Wilde's celebration of individualism? The term itself, anti-humanism, need not detain us; I have introduced it only to indicate just how different is Wilde's concept of the individual from that which has prevailed in idealist culture generally and English studies in particular. It is this difference which the next section considers.

Individualism

In Wilde's writing, individualism is less to do with a spiritual essence, Arnold's 'internal condition', than a social potential, one which implies a radical possibility of freedom 'latent and potential in mankind generally' ('Soul', 261). Thus individualism as Wilde conceives it generates a 'disobedience [which] in the eyes of anyone who has read history, is man's original virtue. It is through disobedience that progress has been made, through disobedience and through rebellion' (p. 258). Under certain conditions there comes to be a close relationship between crime and individualism, the one generating the other—something which Wilde reiterates elsewhere.[4] Already then Wilde's notion of individualism is inseparable from transgressive desire and a transgressive aesthetic. Hence of course his attack on public opinion, mediocrity, and conventional morality ('Critic', 341; 'Soul', 271–4), all of which forbid both the desire and the aesthetic.

The public voice which Wilde scorns is that which seeks to police culture; which is against cultural difference; which reacts to the aesthetically unconventional by charging it with being either grossly unintelligible or grossly immoral ('Soul', 273). Far from reflecting, or prescribing for, the true nature or essence of man, individualism will generate the cultural difference and diversity which conventional morality, orthodox opinion, and essentialist ideology disavow. Wilde affirms the principle of differentiation to which all life grows (pp. 284–5) and

---

[4] See e.g. his 'Pen, Pencil and Poison', 338, and 'The Critic as Artist', 360, and cf. Ellmann's formulation of Wilde's position: 'since the established social structure confines the individual, the artist must of necessity ally himself with the criminal classes' (*Oscar Wilde: Critical Essays*, 3).

insists that selfishness is not living as one wishes to live, but asking others to live as one wishes to live, trying to create 'an absolute uniformity of type'. Individualism not only recognizes and respects cultural diversity and difference, but positively enjoys them (p. 285). Individualism as an affirmation of cultural as well as personal difference is therefore fundamentally opposed to that 'immoral ideal of uniformity of type and conformity to rule which is so prevalent everywhere, and is perhaps most obnoxious in England' (p. 286).

Uniformity of type and conformity to rule: Wilde despises these imperatives not only in individuals but as attributes of class and ruling ideologies—as which they powerfully persist in England today. Because Wilde's Irish identity is a crucial factor both in his specific critiques of England and for his oppositional stance generally, it is instructive to consider in this connection a piece written two years earlier, in 1889, where he addresses England's exploitation and repression of Ireland (it is a review of J. A. Froude's novel, *The Two Chiefs of Dunboy*). In the eighteenth century, says Wilde, England tried to rule Ireland 'with an insolence that was intensified by race-hatred and religious prejudice'; in the nineteenth, with 'a stupidity ... aggravated by good intentions'. Froude's picture of Ireland belongs to the earlier period, and yet to read Wilde's review now makes one wonder what if anything has changed in Tory 'thinking' except that possibly now the one vision holds for both Ireland and the mainland:

Resolute government, that shallow shibboleth of those who do not understand how complex a thing the art of government is, is [Froude's] posthumous panacea for past evils. His hero, Colonel Goring, has the words Law and Order ever on his lips, meaning by the one the enforcement of unjust legislation, and implying by the other the suppression of every fine natural aspiration. That the government should enforce iniquity, and the governed submit to it, seems to be to Mr Froude, as it certainly is to many others, the true ideal of political science ... Colonel Goring ... Mr Froude's cure for Ireland ... is a 'Police at any price' man ... ('Mr Froude's Blue Book', 136–7).

Individualism joins with socialism to abolish other kinds of conformity, including, says Wilde, family life and marriage, each of which is unacceptable because rooted in and perpetuating the ideology of property ('Soul', 265). Individualism is both a desire for a radical *personal freedom* and a desire for *society itself* to be radically different, the first being inseparable from the second. So Wilde's concept of the individual is crucially different from that sense of the concept which signifies the private, experientially self-sufficient, autonomous but ultimately quietist, bourgeois subject; indeed, for Wilde 'Personal experience is a most vicious and limited circle' ('The Decay of Lying', 310) and 'to know anything about oneself one must know all about others' ('The Critic as Artist', 382). Typically within idealist culture, the experience of an essential subjectivity is inseparable from knowledge of that notorious transhistorical constant, human nature. This is Wilde on human nature: 'the only thing that one really knows about human nature is that it changes. Change is the one quality we can predicate of it' ('Soul', 284). To those who then say that socialism is incompatible with human nature and therefore impractical, Wilde replies by rejecting 'practicality' itself as presupposing and endorsing both the existing social conditions and the concept of human nature as constant, each of which suppositions his own radical politics would contest: 'it is exactly the existing conditions that one objects to . . . [they] will be done away with, and human nature will change' (p. 284). Elsewhere Wilde accepts that there is something like human nature, but, far from being the source of our most profound being, it is actually ordinary and boring, the least interesting thing about us—matter rather than nature. It is where we differ from each other that is of definitive value ('Decay', 297).

Art versus Life

Key concepts in Wilde's aesthetic are protean and shifting, especially when paradoxically and facetiously deployed. When, for example, he speaks of life—'poor, probable, uninteresting human life' ('Decay', 305)—or reality as that to which art is opposed, he means different things at different times. But one of the most interesting and significant referents of concepts like life and reality, as Wilde uses them, is not so much the pre-social, or what transcends the social, as the prevailing social order. Even nature, conceived as the opposite of culture and art, retains a social dimension (e.g. 'Critic', 394, 399), especially when it signifies nature as ideological mystification of the social; that is why, for Wilde, anyone trying to be natural is posing, and embarrassingly so, since they are trying to mystify the social as natural (*Dorian Gray*, 10–11).

Nature and reality signify a prevailing order which art wilfully, perversely, and rightfully ignores, and which the critic negates, subverts, and transgresses. Thus, for example, the person of culture is concerned to give 'an accurate description of what has never occurred', while the critic sees 'the object as in itself it really is not' ('Critic', 343, 368; Wilde is here inverting the proposition which opens Arnold's famous essay 'The Function of Criticism at the Present Time'). Not surprisingly then, criticism and art are aligned with individualism against a conservative social order; a passage which indicates this is important also in indicating the basis of Wilde's aesthetic of transgressive desire: 'Art is Individualism and Individualism is *a disturbing and disintegrating force.* Therein lies its immense value. For what it seeks to disturb is monotony of type, slavery of custom, tyranny of habit' ('Soul', 272, my emphasis). Art is also self-conscious and critical; in fact, 'self-consciousness and the critical spirit are one' ('Critic', 356). And art, like individualism, is orientated towards the realm of transgressive desire: 'What is abnormal in Life stands in normal relations to Art. It is the only thing in Life that stands in normal relations to Art' ('Maxims', 1203). One who inhabits that realm, 'the cultured and fascinating liar', is both an object and source of desire ('Decay', 292, 305). The liar is important because he or she contradicts not just conventional morality, but its sustaining origin, 'truth'. So art runs to meet the liar, kissing his 'false beautiful lips, knowing that he alone is in possession of the great secret of all her manifestations, the secret that Truth is entirely and absolutely a matter of style'. Truth, the epistemological legitimation of the real, is rhetorically subordinated to its antitheses—apearance, style, the lie—and thereby simultaneously both appropriated, perverted, and displaced. Reality, also necessarily devalued and demystified by the loss of truth, must imitate art, while life must meekly follow the liar (p. 305).

Further, life is at best an energy which can only find expression through the forms which art offers it. But form is another slippery and protean category in Wilde's aesthetic. In one sense Wilde is a proto-structuralist: 'Form is the beginning of things . . . The Creeds are believed, not because they are rational, but because they are repeated . . . Form is everything . . . Do you wish to love? Use Love's Litany, and the words will create the yearning from which the world fancies that they spring' ('Critic', 399). Here form is virtually synonymous with culture, and the supposed natural cause shown to be cultural effect. Moreover, it is a passage in which Wilde recognizes the priority of the social and the cultural in determining not only public meaning but 'private' or subjective desire. This means that for Wilde, although desire is deeply at odds with society in its existing forms, it does not exist as a pre-social authenticity; it is always within, and informed by, the very culture which it also transgresses.

Transgression and Subjectivity

Returning now to Gide, we are in a position to contrast his essentialism with Wilde's anti-essentialism, a contrast which epitomizes one of the most important differences within the modern history of transgression.

In a way perhaps corresponding to his ambivalence towards Wilde, Gide had both submitted to and resisted the latter's attempts to decentre him, to undermine his sense of self. Both the submission and the resistance are crucial for Gide's subsequent development as a writer, and through Gide's influence, for modern literature.

The submission is apparent enough in the confirmation of his homosexual desire and the way this alters his life and work. Gide's experience in Africa is one of the most significant modern narratives of homosexual liberation. He at last throws off that 'worn-out ethical creed, which I had ceased to approve, but on which my moral reflexes still depended'; a creed which had driven him into 'nothing but a frightful desert, full of wild unanswered appeals, aimless efforts, restlessness, struggles, exhausting dreams, false excitement and abominable depression'; he also rejects the furtiveness of his previous homosexual encounters, and his attempts to 'normalize' himself, asserting that in such attempts his 'normal propensity . . . was increased by resistance' (*If It Die*, 290, 283, 251–2). In 1924 he published *Corydon*, a courageous defence of homosexuality which he later declared to be his most important book (*Journals*, 19 October 1942). In *Corydon* he did not just demand tolerance for homosexuality but also insisted that, far from being contrary to nature, it was intrinsically natural; that heterosexuality prevails merely because of convention; that historically homosexuality is associated with great artistic and intellectual achievement while heterosexuality is indicative of decadence. About some of these provocative and suspect claims I would only observe that the fury they have generated in commentators is as significant as, and related to, Gide's reasons for making them in the first place. Gide was exactly right when he said: 'we are accepted if we are plaintive; but if we cease to be pitiable we are at once accused of arrogance' (*Journals*, February 1918, ii. 247).

Two years after *Corydon* Gide published the equally controversial commercial edition of *If It Die* which, as already indicated, contained for that time astonishingly explicit accounts of his homosexuality, and for which, predictably, Gide was savagely castigated. Later still, Gide was to write to Ramon Fernandez, confirming that 'sexual nonconformity is the first key to my works'; the experience of his own deviant desire leads him first to attack sexual conformity and then 'all other sphinxes of conformity', suspecting them to be 'the brothers and cousins of the first' (Delay, *André Gide*, 438). At the end of his life he reiterates the point in *So Be It* (p. 42).

Given all this, in what sense did Gide resist Wilde's seduction? Mainly in that, having allowed Wilde to subvert an identity which had hitherto successfully, albeit precariously, repressed desire, Gide does not then substitute for it the decentred subjectivity which animates Wilde's own aesthetic. Instead he reconstitutes himself as an essentially new self. Michel in *The Immoralist* (1902) corresponds in some measure to Gide in Algiers. For Michel, as for Gide, transgression does not lead to a relinquishing of self but to a totally new sense of self; Michel throws off the culture and learning which, up to that point had been his whole life, in order to find himself: that 'authentic creature that had lain hidden beneath . . . whom the Gospel had repudiated, whom everything about me—books, masters, parents, and I myself had begun by attempting to suppress . . . Thenceforward I despised the secondary creature, the creature who was due to teaching, whom education had painted on the surface.' He composes a new series of lectures in which he shows 'Culture, born of life, as the destroyer of life'. The true value of life is bound up with individual uniqueness: 'the part in each of us that we feel is different from other people is the part that is rare, the part that makes our special value' (pp. 51, 90, 100); it is a self understood in terms of a pre-social, individuated essence, nature, and identity; and on that basis invested with a quasi-spiritual autonomy. Culture has repressed this authentic self and the individual embarks on a quest to uncover it, a quest which is also an escape from culture.

Whereas for Wilde transgressive desire leads to a relinquishing of the essential self, for Gide it leads to its discovery, to the real self, a new self created from liberated desire. As he writes in *If It Die*, it was at that time in Algiers that 'I was beginning to discover myself—and in myself the tables of a new law' (p. 298). He writes to his mother on 2 February 1895: 'I'm unable to write a line or a sentence so long as I'm not in complete possession (that is, WITH FULL KNOWLEDGE) of myself. I should like very submissively to follow nature—the unconscious, which is within myself and must be true' (Delay, *André Gide*, 396). Here again there is the indirect yet passionate insistence on the naturalness, the authenticity of his deviant desire. With that wilful integrity—itself a kind of perversity?—rooted in Protestantism, Gide not only appropriates dominant concepts (the normal, the natural) to legitimise his own deviation, but goes so far as to claim a sanction for deviation in the teachings of Christ (*If It Die*, 299). Compare his journal entry for 1893 (detached pages): 'Christ's saying is just as true in art: "Whoever will save his life (his personality) shall lose it."' He later declared, after reading Nietzsche's *Thus Spake Zarathustra*, that it was to this that Protestantism led, 'to the greatest liberation' (Delay, *André Gide*, 467). Delay contends, plausibly, that some of the great Gidean themes, especially those entailing transgression, can be found in the rebellious letters that he wrote to his mother at that time, especially in March 1895 (p. 407), letters inspired by his self-affirmation as a homosexual.

Paradox and Perversity

The contrast between Gide and Wilde is striking: not only are Wilde's conceptions of subjectivity and desire anti-essentialist but so too—and consequently—is his advocacy of transgression. It is as if deviant desire, rather than creating a new integrity of self, actually decentres or disperses the self, and the liberation is experienced as being, in part, just that. Wilde's experience of deviant desire, though no less intense than Gide's, leads him not to escape the repressive ordering of society, but to a reinscription within it, and an inversion of the binaries upon which that ordering depends; desire, and the transgressive aesthetic which it fashions, reacts against, disrupts, and displaces from within.[5]

For Gide transgression is in the name of a desire and identity rooted in the natural, the sincere, and the authentic; Wilde's transgressive aesthetic is the reverse: insincerity, inauthenticity, and unnaturalness become the liberating attributes of decentred identity and desire, and inversion becomes central to Wilde's expression of this aesthetic—as can be seen from a selection of his *Phrases and Philosophies for the Use of the Young* (1894):

If one tells the truth, one is sure, sooner or later to be found out.

Only the shallow know themselves.

To be premature is to be perfect.

It is only the superficial qualities that last.

Man's deeper nature is soon found out.

To love oneself is the beginning of a lifelong romance. (pp. 433–4)

In Wilde's writings a non-centred or vagrant desire is both the impetus for a subversive inversion, and what is released by it. Perhaps the most general inversion in his work operates on that most dominating of binaries, nature/culture; more specifically the attributes on the left are substituted for those on the right:

---

[5] Ellmann suggests that inversion, or the turning of things inside out, was also crucial for Gide, this being the most important lesson that he learned from Wilde as a result of the latter's spiritual seduction of him ('Corydon and Ménalque', 100). But Gide contains inversion within the same kind of essentialist conviction which Wilde uses inversion to displace, while at the same time of course radically redefining the referent of that conviction.

X	for	Y
surface		depth
lying		truth
change		stasis
difference		essence
persona/role		essential self
abnormal		normal
insincerity		sincerity
style/artifice		authenticity
facetious		serious
narcissism		maturity

For Michel in *The Immoralist* and to an extent for Gide himself, desire may be proscribed but this does not affect its authenticity or its naturalness; if anything it confirms them. It is society which is inauthentic. In a sense then, deviant desire is legitimated in terms of culture's opposite, nature, or, in a different but related move, in terms of something which is pre-cultural and so always more than cultural. So Gide shares with the dominant culture an investment in the Y column above; he appropriates its categories for the subordinate. In contrast, for Wilde transgressive desire is both rooted in culture and the impetus for affirming different/alternative kinds of culture (X column). From an essentialist point of view, Wilde's position might seem to rest on a confusion: how can the desire which culture outlaws itself be thoroughly cultural? In fact it is because and not in spite of this shared cultural dimension that Wilde can enact one of the most disturbing of all forms of transgression, namely that whereby the outlaw turns up as inlaw, and the other as proximate proves more disturbing than the other as absolute difference. That which society forbids, Wilde reinstates *through and within* some of its most cherished and central cultural categories—art, the aesthetic, art criticism, individualism. At the same time as he appropriates those categories he also transvalues them through perversion and inversion, thus making them now signify those binary exclusions (X column) by which the dominant culture knows itself (thus abnormality is not just the opposite, but the necessarily always present antithesis of normality). It is an uncompromising inversion, this being the (perversely) appropriate strategy for a transgressive desire which is of its 'nature', according to this culture, an 'inversion'.

Of inversion's specific targets, perhaps the most important is *depth*. As can be seen from the *Phrases and Philosophies* just quoted, Wilde insistently subverts those dominant categories which signify subjective depth. Such categories (Y column) are precisely those which ideologically identify (inform) the mature adult individual. And they too operate in terms of their inferior opposite: the individual knows what he—I choose the masculine pronoun deliberately—is in contrast to what he definitely is not or must not be. In Wilde's inversions, the excluded inferior term returns as the now superior term of a related series of binaries. Some further examples of Wilde's subversion of subjective depth:

A little sincerity is a dangerous thing, and a great deal of it is absolutely fatal. ('Critic', 393)

All bad poetry springs from genuine feeling. ('Critic', 398)

In matters of grave importance, style, not sincerity is the *vital* thing. (*Importance*, 83, my emphasis⁶)

Only shallow people . . . do not judge by appearances. (*Dorian Gray*, 29)

Insincerity . . . is merely a method by which we can multiply our personalities. Such . . . was Dorian Gray's opinion. He used to wonder at the shallow psychology of those who conceived the Ego in man as a thing simple, permanent, reliable, and of one essence. To him man was a being with myriad lives and myriad sensations, a complex, multiform creature . . . (*Dorian Gray*, 158–9)

At work here is a transgressive desire which makes its opposition felt as a disruptive reaction upon, and inversion of, the categories of subjective depth which hold in place the dominant order which proscribes that desire.⁷ As Wilde himself remarked, there was here an intimate connection between perversity and paradox: 'What the paradox was to me in the sphere of thought, perversity became to me in the sphere of passion' (*De profundis*, 466). It was a connection to have far-reaching cultural effects.⁸

In *The Importance of Being Earnest* there is a wonderful repudiation of the depth model, and with a rather different effect:

CECILY. How dare you? This is no time for wearing the shallow mask of manners. When I see a spade I call it a spade.

GWENDOLEN. I am glad to say that I have never seen a spade. It is obvious that our social spheres have been widely different. (II. 675–9)

Cecily tries to take over what we might call the high ground of the straightforward as opposed to the low ground of the shallow, the

---

⁶ In matters of grave importance: at the risk of being laborious we might spell out the way the proposition works: there is a simultaneous fourfold procedure: (1) sincerity is displaced by style; (2) the natural link between gravity and sincerity is undermined; (3) gravity and vitality are appropriated *for* style; and, (4) in the process, transvalued.

⁷ Wilde exploited that confusion—often paranoia—consequent upon a breakdown of Victorian 'sincerity' deriving in part from the social mobility and emergence of a consumerist economy described by Regenia Gagnier in *Idylls and the Market Place*. See also Bowlby, 'Promoting Dorian Gray'.

⁸ On the importance of this connection for the so-called gay sensibility, see below, Ch. 20.

mannered and the duplicitous. But if being natural is only an infuriating pose (*Dorian Gray*, 10–11), so too is being straightforward, and especially since it too masquerades as naturalness. Gwendolen, in a response which shows so memorably that there may be more to snobbery than ignorant condescension, repudiates the implied opposition and kicks Cecily straight back into the domain of class, into the 'social sphere'. Never has a spade been so effectively 'defamiliarized'. Compare Wilde's use of the same idea in May 1892, when an alderman had praised him for calling a spade a spade. Wilde replied: 'I would like to protest against the statement that I have ever called a spade a spade. The man who did so should be condemned to use one' (Ellmann, *Oscar Wilde* (1987), 347).

Parting

I began with the encounter between Wilde and Gide in Algiers in 1895. Gide, dispirited in the sense of being depressed and unsure of himself, sees the names of Wilde and Douglas and erases his own name, pre-empting perhaps the threat to his own identity, social and psychic, posed by Wilde's determination to demystify the normative ideologies regulating subjectivity, desire, and the aesthetic. Nevertheless the meeting does occur, and Gide does indeed suffer an erasure of self, a decentring which is also the precondition for admitting transgressive desire, a depersonalization which is therefore also a liberation. Yet for Gide, transgression is embraced with that same stubborn integrity which was to become the basis of his transgressive aesthetic, an aesthetic obviously indebted to, yet also formed in reaction against, Wilde's own. Thus liberation from the self into desire is also to realize a new and deeper self, belief in which supports an oppositional stand not just on the question of deviant sexual desire, but on a whole range of other issues as well, cultural and political. Integrity here becomes an ethical sense inextricably bound up with and also binding up the integrated self, with the result that this self becomes a powerful source of oppositional strength at once psychic, ethical, and political.[9] And since Gide is less read now than was once the case, we should not forget how complex, vital, and unconventional the existential and humanist commitment to sincerity of self could be in his writing, especially when contrasted with its facile counterpart in English studies, or indeed (a

[9] It is also true that his conception of individualism changed, especially during his involvement with communism, when he became critical of his own earlier views. But he did not so much renounce individualism, as reformulate the principle into what might be called a self-less form. He also argued for the compatibility of this kind of individualism with communism. See Harris, *André Gide and Romain Rolland*, esp. 140–8.

counter image) with the reductive ways in which it is sometimes represented in contemporary literary theory. The following entries in Gide's *Journals* are especially revealing: 21 December and detached/ recovered pages for 1923; January 1925; 7 October and 25 November 1927; 10 February and 8 December 1929; 5 August, September 1931; 27 June 1937.

So the very categories of identity which, through transgression, Wilde subjects to inversion and displacement, Gide reconstitutes for a different transgressive aesthetic, or as it might now more suitably be called, in contradistinction to Wilde, a transgressive ethic, which remains central to the unorthodoxy which characterizes his life's work. We might see the essentialist basis of that ethic acknowledged in two important events: in 1946 Gide was awarded the Nobel prize for literature; six years later, the year after his death, his entire works were entered in the Roman Catholic Index of Forbidden Books. If the significance of Gide's essentialist ethic in earning him the award is readily apparent, it is only marginally less so in the religious ban. His real blasphemy was, after all, adherence to—the Church would say perversion of—an essentialist ethic rooted in his Christian past; there was a proximity within their differences impossible to ignore. Likewise with Gide and Wilde: I have emphasized here the essentialism of the one, the anti-essentialism of the other. These are indeed divergent paths, for them and for us. But as we shall see in subsequent chapters, these are paths which cross and reconverge: historically, conceptually, and experientially. As will become apparent in subsequent chapters, all the main issues explored in this book arise directly or indirectly from that 1895 encounter between these two writers. Here it remains only to point out how different was Wilde's fate from Gide's: within weeks of returning from Algiers to London he was embroiled in the litigation against Queensberry which was to lead to his own imprisonment. He died in Paris in 1900, three years after his release. So whereas Gide lived for fifty-seven years after that 1895 encounter, Wilde survived for less than six.

PART 2

Perspectives

2 *Some Parameters*

This book emerges at the intersection of diverse perspectives, including biography, literary and cultural theory, theodicy, social history, psycho-analysis, philosophy, feminism, and the emerging field of lesbian and gay studies. I also regard it as cultural materialist, though it repudiates some of the orthodoxies of the materialist tradition of cultural critique, and takes it in directions hitherto largely ignored. So it might more accurately be described as written at the points at which the above perspectives intersect with, but sometimes also contest each other.

Several interrelated issues recur, two especially: one is the complex, often violent, sometimes murderous dialectic between dominant and subordinate cultures, groups, and identities; the other concerns those conceptions of self, desire, and transgression which figure in the language, ideologies, and cultures of domination, and in the diverse kinds of resistance to it. One kind of resistance, operating in terms of gender, repeatedly unsettles the very opposition between the dominant and the subordinate. I call this sexual dissidence. The literature, histories, and subcultures of sexual dissidence, though largely absent from current debates (literary, psychoanalytic, and cultural), prove remarkably illuminating for them.

Equally illuminating is the history of the early modern period, to which this study repeatedly turns. More exactly it moves between the post-modern and the early modern. Here's why.

Post/modern to Early Modern

> All they that may not abide the word of God, but, following the persuasions and stubbornness of their own hearts, *go backward and not forward* . . . they go and turn away from God. (*Sermon: Of the Declining From God*, 1562)

> 'Oh!' the sculptor would whisper, seeing a young railwayman with the sweeping eyelashes of a dancing girl at whom M. de Charlus could not help staring, 'if the Baron begins making eyes at the conductor, we shall never get there, the train will start going backwards'. (Proust, *Remembrance of Things Past*, ii. 1075)

The second of these epigraphs nicely articulates a specifically modern, sexual instance of an old and enduring fear that things might be put into reverse, the world turned upside down, subverted through the inversion of right order. My project, being in part about the long, complicated, and revealing history of such fears, does go backward, or follows a backward chronology. This project goes back to the early modern period, finding there the lost histories of perversion, including the theological antecedents of the sexual pervert's backward tendency—antecedents exemplified in the first epigraph—and much more besides. In this and other respects the post-modern is read through the early modern.

Theories of the post-modern are typically premissed on either a simplified conception of the modern, or a suspect retrospective reconstruction of it. The more adequate the history of the diverse modernisms, the less plausible is the representation of the post-modern as a break into the radically new or different. Relatedly, the concept of the post-modern also runs the risk of overvaluing the contemporary and investing it with a significance it does not possess: the imagined radical break is in fact a development more or less compatible with, or at least predictable from, what has gone before. In this intense preoccupation with what has presently and, by implication, dramatically, occurred, the post-modern (like intellectual fashion more generally) may only be reproducing an academic version of the consumerist ethic whereby the latest, despite—or rather because of—being little different from the last, renders the latter obsolete. Something like this occurred within the academy with the shift in theoretical concern from structuralism to post-structuralism. Occasionally, so strong was the wish to abandon the structuralist ship that certain movements once called structuralist were simply renamed post-structuralist without any change whatsoever. Some have even survived into the post-modern, again little changed. So the '/' which I shall henceforth install between 'post' and 'modern' registers the provisional aspect of each of the categories modern and post-modern, and also the confused, unresolved, but always significant dimensions of their relationship. The category of the early modern will be found to relate as much to this confusion between the two, and the presuppositions they share, as it does to each separately.

Despite such reservations, this study remains critically sympathetic to the concept of the post/modern in so far as it has become the focus for a range of contemporary debates attempting to identify what *is* different about the present.[1] In his critical defence of the concept Fredric Jameson rightly observes that 'the history of the preceding few years is always

---

[1] Two informative recent accounts of post/modern debates are Connor's *Postmodernist Culture* and the collection of essays *Universal Abandon*, edited by Ross.

what is least accessible to us', and 'the grasping of the present from within is the most problematical task the mind can face' ('Marxism and Postmodernism', 371, 384). To the extent that the critical debates around post/modernism help us in either or both of these related tasks, they are important. Of course it may well be that this restless attempt to make the present and the recent past reveal the truth of who we are/ were, and where we are going, is itself an aspect of modernity and, in historical retrospect, will be shown to be very much of its time.

As for 'early modern', this is useful primarily to avoid the idealist implications of 'Renaissance'. In English studies there has always been an association of the Renaissance and the modern. Some critics have read the Renaissance as the origin of the present, in particular the origin of modern man, 'he' who threw off the shackles of the dark ages, triumphantly affirming and discovering himself, and so beginning that long march forward to humanism, enlightenment, and progress. For such critics, incipient in the Renaissance is much that we value about Western civilization as it subsequently developed, and the present is linked to the past via the powerful and reassuring idea of a teleological unfolding of the one into the other. Of course not all critics have regarded the present as an improvement; some have celebrated the Renaissance as both the beginning and a flourishing of culture from which the modern is in important respects a decline. In different ways the work of T. E. Hulme, T. S. Eliot, and some in the *Scrutiny* school advanced this view, while studies of Shakespeare sometimes assume it as a subsidiary 'background' explanation of his unrivalled 'genius'.

I approach the early modern neither as origin of the present nor as that from which the present has declined, but as a range of cultural antecedents which can simultaneously problematize and illuminate their subsequent modern forms, especially the post/modern. Michel Foucault, refusing the teleological connection of past and present, remarks (in relation to Nietzsche), that 'What is found at the historical beginning of things is not the inviolable identity of their origin; it is the dissension of other things. It is disparity' (*Language, Counter-Memory, Practice*, 142). This study traces dissension and disparity in both periods, and in a way is intended to give new perspectives on each. To learn from the strangeness inherent in historical precedent is thereby to make it relevant even while recognizing that the past as object shifts as strangely as does time itself.

History Reading Theory

Moving between the post/modern and the early modern is an organizing principle partly consequent upon using history to read theory as well as vice versa. Let me explain that.

This book is an exercise in reading culture, by which I intend much more than identifying this or that post/modern trait of the contemporary. Reading culture involves trying to read the historical process within the social process, and in a way adequately aware of the complexity and discriminations of both, and with as much sensitivity and intelligence as possible. Lives and freedoms literally depend on it, especially where cultural discrimination is concerned—by which I mean both violent repression (as in racial or sexual discrimination) and that which passes as cultural discernment. I also mean to imply that the first sense is often closer to the second than adherents of the second usually admit. In both senses, and sometimes inseparably, it can be said that discrimination is the essence of culture. Which means that 'barbarities' of the 'civilized' present can never be rationalized as merely the remnants of a superstitious or less enlightened past.

Only critical theory and history conjoined can begin to reveal the tenacious yet mobile forms of discrimination, sexual and otherwise, which organize cultures. In trying to understand these discriminations I have been led back further into history than I thought necessary when this project began. Through that history I have also been led to a fuller recognition of the suffering which attends not only the discrimination and unsuccessful resistance to it, but also successful resistance to it. Trying to bear witness to that suffering—a kind of historical empathy infused with a sense of loss and helplessness inseparable from the simple fact of being alive in the present—requires at the very least that we refuse the temptation simply to write the past according to our current theoretical predilections.

Theory has helped us to see how (for instance) the cultural can be freed from the tyranny of the natural; gender from biology; how social change has occurred, and how it can change again; how to reveal and defend (without fetishizing) cultural difference; how to make visible the 'political unconscious' of our culture. But if theory can show such things, it is because theoretical insights have already been struggled towards by thinkers, writers, activists, and others in specific historical and political struggles where the representative structures of oppression have been massively (if still only ever contingently) in place. More than ever before we need to recover those histories. In certain respects theory enables us to do just that, though not by simply rereading the past through new theoretical lenses; it is also necessary that we use the history recovered to read, question, and modify theory itself. In other words, history reads theory in a way enabled by—which presupposes—theory.

Moving between the early modern and the post/modern, and using history to read theory as well as vice versa, means that theoretical elaboration is interspersed throughout the book, growing from, as well as governing the focus upon, specific issues: the theoretical enterprise emerges from within the historical one.

Centred and Decentred Desires

A case in point is that encounter between Oscar Wilde and André Gide in Algiers, and how it indicates that homosexual dissidence has followed not one but two (contrasting) visions of transgression, one essentialist, the other anti-essentialist. The controversy over essentialism versus anti-essentialism has proliferated in all areas of cultural and gender theory. Perhaps it is now most usefully pursued in relation to those specific histories of dissident cultures which lead to a questioning of some orthodoxies on both sides of the debate and of the simplistic forms in which the binary opposition between essentialism and anti-essentialism is sometimes. For instance, Wilde's transgressive aesthetic suggests that certain aspects of what post/modern theory finds so very contemporary about itself—anti-essentialism especially, and the critique of the depth model of identity and culture[2]—are not so new, having been developed as subversive and defensive strategies in subcultures before more recent manifestations in the intellectual main stream. Further, what for us is a playful post/modern decentring, perhaps dovetailing some of us neatly into the 'needs' of advanced capitalism and leaving the rest necessarily centred around poverty and deprivation, operated very differently in the time of Wilde; in a very real sense, Wilde's own proto-decentring of subjectivity cost him his life. We shall also see, again in relation to Wilde, how deconstructive orthodoxies concerning the limitations of inversion themselves derive from the

---

[2] I call it post/modern because it is under that umbrella that the issue has been debated most acutely. See especially Jameson, 'Postmodernism and Consumer Society', and 'Marxism and Postmodernism'; Eagleton, 'Capitalism, Modernism and Postmodernism'. Of course the repudiation of the depth model already has a 'modern' history anecdotally recorded in, for example, Robbe-Grillet's remark that the essence of modern man was no longer to be found in a hidden soul, but plastered on hoardings, with the consequent necessity of studying the surface of things; or in Andy Warhol's persona: 'The interviewer should just tell me the words he wants me to say and I'll repeat them after him. I'm so empty I can't think of anything to say. I'm not more intelligent than I appear. I'm not really saying anything now. If you want to know all about Andy Warhol, just look at the surface of my films and paintings and me, and there I am. There's nothing behind it' (quoted in Gidal, *Warhol*, 9). It has also been apparent for some while that such disavowals of depth create a charisma inseparable from the depth model being repudiated.

limitations of theory pursued independently of history. In these and other respects Wilde is rehabilitated as a figure of major importance for literary and cultural theory.

Conversely, while some literary theorists deplore essentialism in all its forms, there is ample evidence of its historically progressive function for subordinate cultures. I argue for the importance of André Gide in this respect, a writer largely eclipsed by recent developments in literary and cultural theory. Gide, in seeking to legitimate and affirm homosexuality, conjoins self-authenticity and sexual dissidence, as do three lesbian writers later, both very different from Gide and indeed from each other: Radclyffe Hall, Rita Mae Brown, and Monique Wittig (Chapter 3). These very differences underscore the diverse histories which the concept of essentialism often elides. In a recent study Diana Fuss suggests that essentialism and the theories of identity deriving from it must be neither sanctified nor vilified but simultaneously assumed and questioned (*Essentially Speaking*, 104). In different ways both Wilde and Gide did just that, and lesbian and gay writing has continued to do so. Theirs is also a history which suggests that the essentialist/anti-essentialist opposition is rather less stable than is often supposed in theoretical discourse.

Transgression and its Containment

It remains true nevertheless that the essentialist quest in the name of an authentic self has proved wanting, especially within dominant cultures, and many of its adherents have lost their faith when confronted with the post/modern repudiation of such a self. This is part of a wider crisis addressed in Part 4. As the autonomous self disappears, so the dialectic between law and desire, dominant and deviant, becomes much more complex. 'The crux of our post-modernity', wrote Ihab Hassan in 1982, is 'that fierce dialectic of centers and margins, assimilation and rupture, master codes and idiolects, totalitarianism and terrorism.'[3] Though in terms less apocalyptic, and for rather longer than post/modernism has been fashionable, there have been diverse studies concerned with the complex dialectic between centres and margins, dominant and subordinate cultures, conformity and deviance.[4] From such work there emerges the realization that dissidence may not only be repressed by the dominant (coercively and ideologically), but in a sense actually produced by it,

[3] In the Foreword to the English translation of Mayer's *Outsiders: A Study in Life and Letters*, p. ix.
[4] See e.g. Fanon, *Black Skin, White Masks*; Douglas, *Purity and Danger*; Williams, *Marxism and Literature*; Hall *et al.*, *Policing the Crisis*; Hebdige, *Subculture* (Hebdige's bibliography and suggestions for further reading are also useful); Downes and Rock, *Understanding Deviance*.

hence consolidating the powers which it ostensibly challenges. This gives rise to the subversion/containment debate, one of the most important areas of dispute in contemporary cultural theory.

What becomes apparent from that debate is that the crux of post-modernity is not a straightforward opposition between unchanging, internally undifferentiated versions of the dominant and the subordinate, the central and the marginal, etc. By moving away from the misleading language of entities towards that of social process and representation, there emerge different conceptions of domination and dissidence, these being the subject of much of this book.

Perversion

These different conceptions of domination and dissidence are also what give the concept of perversion increasing importance throughout this study. Part 5 starts with two of the most influential modern accounts of sexual perversion—Freud's and Foucault's. Both accounts, though almost diametrically opposed as explanations, are agreed in discerning perversion to be a culturally central phenomenon. Eventually I develop from perversion, and in particular the fact of its cultural centrality, a specific theory of dissidence. But this is not a theory to be derived from current debates alone, not even one as interesting and important as that between the Freudian and the Foucauldian accounts of the perverse. To develop that theory it proved necessary to return to what might be called the theology rather than the sexology of perversion. So rather than adjudicate between Freud's and Foucault's theories, I seek to retrieve the lost histories of perversion, including the pre-sexological, pre-psychoanalytic scope of the concept. Again, history reads theory but in a way enabled by theory, and thereby includes accounts of:

(1) how the mythology of the two main kinds of pre-sexological pervert, the religious heretic and the wayward woman (Satan and Eve respectively), take us to the heart of some awesome contradictions within Christianity, whereby the original pervert is neither Satan nor Eve but God himself (Chapter 8);

(2) how the theological conceptions of perversion, especially Augustine's theory of the relationship of perversion and privation, are attempts to contain these contradictions (Chapter 9); how, in those attempts, theology (or more precisely theodicy) produces a vision of the perverse which remains active within later 'secular' or 'scientific' accounts of it (e.g. sexology and psychoanalysis);

(3) how the socio-politics of early modern England incorporate and reveal the paranoia, displacements, and disavowals around images of the perverse, especially the perverse as aberrant movement, and especially in relation to gender and sexual difference; Chapter 10 explores perversion and gender in Shakespeare's *Othello*.

In these and other respects the older histories of perversion prove indispensable for understanding what I just now described as the tenacious yet mobile forms of discrimination which organize culture, and, specifically, for perceiving how discrimination is a mercurial process of displacement and condensation, so fluid yet with effects which are brutally material.

Via these histories of perversion I then return to Freud's and Foucault's theories of sexual perversion (Part 6). Regarded in the light of those histories, Freud's theory of sexual perversion is more challenging than many contemporary forms of psychoanalysis allow, including some of a self-consciously rigorous and radical inflection, and for reasons they cannot acknowledge. Chapters 12 and 13 follow the fate of perversion within different strands of psychoanalysis, wherein it is found to destabilize the psychoanalytic project itself. Chapter 14 elucidates Foucault's alternative, materialist account of sexuality. Approached via the earlier history of perversion, and notwithstanding their theoretical divergence, I find a convergence between Freud and Foucault which proves productive for a different history of transgression.

Homosexuality

The diverse histories of perversion, even or especially when not specifically sexual, prove important for a further dimension of this study, namely to see why in our own time the negation of homosexuality has been in direct proportion to its symbolic centrality; its cultural marginality in direct proportion to its cultural significance; why, also, homosexuality is so strangely integral to the selfsame heterosexual cultures which obsessively denounce it, and why history—history rather than human nature—has produced this paradoxical position. In addressing the hostility directed at homosexuality there are those who have been tempted to treat this problem in isolation—socially in the sense of homophobia being regarded as a discrete category of discrimination, psychically in the sense of being an essentially personal—phobic—problem. This is misguided since, to comprehend (for instance) the re-emergence or intensification of homophobia in contemporary Britain and in relation to AIDS especially, we must understand a much longer history wherein homophobia intersects with, for instance, misogyny, xenophobia, and racism. In short the obsession with homosexuality is always about much more than homosexuality (Part 7). I thereby share and strongly endorse the ongoing project of Eve Kosofsky Sedgwick who, through a unique integration of insightful literary analysis and persuasive cultural critique, shows how 'a whole cluster of the most crucial sites for the contestation of meaning in twentieth-century Western culture are ... quite indelibly marked with the historical specificity of homosocial/homosexual definition, notably though not exclusively male, from around the turn of the century.' Those sites include the pairings secrecy/disclosure and private/public. 'Along with and sometimes through these epistemologically changed pairings ... this very specific crisis of definition has then ineffaceably marked other pairings as basic to modern cultural organization.' Among the other pairings which Sedgwick cites and analyses are masculine/feminine, majority/minority, innocence/initiation, natural/artificial, growth/decadence, same/different, sincerity/sentimentality ('Epistemology of the Closet', 43–4).

One manifestation of this is the way that on many levels, and increasingly, contemporary culture is obsessed with representations and images of homosexuality as something at once excessively and obviously *there* yet eluding complete identification. Attitudes expressed towards it—'towards' because even in reasonable discussions of it, it is still usually *elsewhere*—express disavowal, hysteria, paranoia, fear, hatred, vindictiveness, ambivalence, tolerance, and much more.

The signs of this complex scenario are diverse. Consider some of the more obvious. In the case of many major individual artists, intellectuals, and writers, there are increasingly frequent suggestions, and sometimes clear demonstrations, of a significant homosexual element in their lives. The fact of their homosexuality may be less interesting than the reasons why some now feel it to be necessary to demonstrate, and others deny, it. In the case of the philosopher Ludwig Wittgenstein, there have been fierce public controversies over the allegation of his homosexuality (Bartley, *Wittgenstein*, esp. Afterword, 159–97). Reviewers and other cultural commentators usually handle the evidence with liberal nonchalance—not in itself an unwelcome attitude to be sure, but one somewhat belied by the obvious fascination it has for them and their audiences. The discovery in certain artists' work of the homosexual, the homo-erotic, or the homosocial, has in some cases led to far-reaching reinterpretations of it. D. H. Lawrence is one case in point: this one-time prophet of heterosexual liberation is now recognized to have been intensely, ambivalently steeped in homosexual curiosity and desire.[5] The case of Lawrence is also indicative of the way the homosexual question is entering the heart of scholarship: Paul Delany has argued that the new Cambridge edition of *Women in Love* is seriously inadequate in avoiding the major editorial crux of the novel, namely why Lawrence dropped its openly homoerotic 'Prologue'.[6] But the more homosexuality emerges as culturally central, the less sure become the majority as to what, exactly, it is: a sensibility, an abnormality, a sexual act, a clandestine subculture, an overt subculture, the enemy within, the enemy without?

Those cultural theorists who have offered speculative generalizations about homosexuality's apparent centrality have tended to perpetuate earlier confusions. One such is George Steiner, who regards homosexuality as profoundly formative of modernity itself (below, Chapter 20). Another is the influential feminist theorist Luce Irigaray, who has suggested that in effect the fundamental structure of patriarchy is homosexual (below, Chapter 17). Meanwhile, René Girard, famous for an entirely different theory whereby it is now rivalry which is the endemic hidden truth of civilization, has also placed considerable importance on homosexuality: all sexual rivalry, he announces in *Things Hidden since the Foundation of the World*, is 'structurally homosexual' (below, Chapter 17). More recently still, the philosopher Roger Scruton, in the formation of an explicitly reactionary sexual ethics, preoccupies himself with homosexuality, believing it appropriate that homosexuality should arouse a revulsion in accordance with which it should be forbidden. In fact, he believes that such revulsion should be inculcated. I return to Scruton also in Chapter 17; my point here is that the status of homosexuality in his sexual ethic is not as an incidental perversion: as with Steiner, Irigaray, and Girard, homosexuality is theoretically central, being, says Scruton, 'of the first importance at the present time', and leading us, 'when properly considered, to an important insight into morality' (*Dover Beach*, 263).

Such recent centrings of homosexuality persist alongside the older tendency to ignore it, or deliberately write it out of the script. Anthony Wilden, in his brilliantly formidable *System and Structure: Essays in Communication and Exchange*, considers homosexuality in relation to both Montaigne and Freud. In both he finds it only apparently present, the real issue being a deeper alienation. Montaigne's relationship with La Boétie is not 'really' homosexual but bound up with a ' "more real"

---

[5] See Delany, *D. H. Lawrence's Nightmare*; Woods, *Articulate Flesh*; Meyers, *Homosexuality and Literature*; and below, Ch. 17.

[6] In a review of this edition (ed. Farmer *et al.*) in the *London Review of Books*, 3 Sept. 1987.

level of "ontological insecurity"'; Wilden apparently endorses Gregory Bateson's view that Montaigne's homosexuality 'is a metaphor that is not meant' (*System*, 98). Of Freud's theory that repressed homosexuality is a cause of paranoia, Wilden suspects that it is 'no more than a rationalization of the irrationality of personal relationships in the culture at large . . . there are enough real reasons to be paranoid and schizophrenic in western culture, to make it unnecessary to reduce such manifestations of social alienation to fear of homosexuality . . .' (p. 290).

I have chosen this example from Wilden because it is at once revealing and typical of a problem facing the attempt to speak of homosexuality's paradoxical, elusive cultural centrality. It is not that Wilden is simply wrong, and that homosexuality really *is* present in each case and in some easily discernible way. On the contrary, to speak of homosexuality in relation to Montaigne or anyone else in the early modern period is anachronistic (below, Chapter 16). And as for Freud's rooting of paranoia in homosexuality, that too is problematic, at once revealing of the radical insights of his theory, but also of its limitations. The point is rather that in Wilden's contention, and many others which confidently declare either the absence of homosexuality *or* its (repressed) presence, plausible argument proceeds inseparably from questionable disavowal, inheriting the history of homosexuality's paradoxical, incoherent construction. Put another way, the disavowals are now as much a part of the history of homosexuality's actual absence as well as of its presence, overt or repressed.

A more than usually interesting case in point is Klaus Theweleit's two-volume study, *Male Fantasies*. In the second volume Theweleit admits that his earlier refusal (in the first volume) to regard homosexuality as a causal factor in fascist terror (i, esp. pp. 52–63) was motivated by a wish to 'circumvent the guilt that so often characterizes even the most "enlightened" of male responses to this particular complex of issues'. He had in fact then 'considered it more than likely' that 'something akin to a "latent" homosexuality, and an associated "damning up of the drives"' did play its part. It is only when he is able, in the second volume, to be confident that the essential modes of operation of the fascist terror 'can be represented quite adequately without any necessary recourse to the notions of either latent or overt "homosexuality"' (ii. 306–7) that Theweleit feels able to embark on a fascinating exploration of—of what? Not homosexuality exactly, and whatever it is makes it difficult to say exactly what homosexuality is.[7]

---

[7] That difficulty lends plausibility to the reluctance in deconstruction to address homosexuality as more than a category so problematic as not to be worth specifying independently (see especially Robert Young, 'The Same Difference'). But here too plausible argument may be inseparable from questionable disavowal,

It is perhaps as something under erasure, even in its emergence, that homosexuality provides a history remarkably illuminating for the issues of marginality and power upon which contemporary debates, cultural, psychoanalytical, and literary, have been converging. Which is why a recent anti-essentialist critique of gender theory, Judith Butler's *Gender Trouble*, deploys homosexuality to make theoretical trouble for gender, to disarticulate its dominant terms, including those from which homosexuality have been fashioned. Read homosexually (so to speak), heterosexuality is seen to prescribe

normative sexual positions that are intrinsically impossible to embody, and the persistent failure to identify fully and without incoherence with these positions reveals heterosexuality itself not only as a compulsory law, but as an inevitable comedy. Indeed, I would offer this insight into heterosexuality as both a compulsory system and an intrinsic comedy, a constant parody of itself, as an alternative gay/lesbian perspective. (p. 122)

Inevitably then, the term homosexuality has shifting connotations throughout this study. The conception of homosexuality that it works towards is neither an essential identity, as envisaged by Gide for instance, nor exactly the modern constructed identity postulated most notably by Michel Foucault and others.[8] Rather it denotes a cluster of things with more or less specific cultural locations, but with a history which is wider, more diverse, and more complex than the essentialist or even the constructionist view allows. It includes cultures, institutions, beliefs, practices, desires, aspirations, and much else, and changes across all of these. Hence 'homosexual' as I use it is always provisional and context-dependent. More often than not it should appear as here with scare quotes to indicate awareness of those anachronistic assumptions and/or pejorative implications which are of course inseparable from the history of the concept. Instead of scare quotes I resort again to the occasional use of a typographically pretentious '/' as a reminder that the construction of homo/sexuality emerges from a larger discriminatory formation of hetero/sexuality which it continues to be influenced by, but cannot be reduced to; on the contrary, hetero/sexuality is increasingly being problematized by homo/sexuality in its diverse identities, essential, constructed, and otherwise.

and in a way especially revealing of the limitations of an institutionalized deconstruction, given that the homosexual, unlike some other minorities, can often pass within the dominant culture, and to that extent resembles the deconstructive trope itself, at once inside and outside.

[8] A helpful account of the essentialist versus constructionist debate can be found in Fuss, *Essentially Speaking*, esp. 2–6 and ch. 6 *passim*. Other important contributions include Weeks, *Coming Out*, and *Sexuality*; Sedgwick, 'Epistemology of the Closet'; Greenberg, *The Construction of Homosexuality*, 485.

Perverse Dynamics and Transgressive Reinscriptions

Wilde's transgressive aesthetic, along with the lost histories of perversion and, through them, a reconsideration of Freud and Foucault and the paradoxical cultural centrality of homosexuality, facilitate the development for cultural politics of the concept of the perverse dynamic. I suggest that the challenge of the perverse lies less in the once influential psychosexual category of the polymorphous perverse than in the paradoxical perverse or the perverse dynamic. If perversion subverts it is not as a unitary, pre-social libido, or an original plenitude, but as a transgressive agency inseparable from a dynamic intrinsic to social process. Provisionally then, this concept of the perverse dynamic denotes certain instabilities and contradictions within dominant structures which exist by virtue of exactly what those structures simultaneously contain and exclude. The displacements which constitute certain repressive discriminations are partly enabled via a proximity which, though disavowed, remains to enable a perverse return, an undoing, a transformation.

The perverse dynamic signifies that fearful interconnectedness whereby the antithetical inheres within, and is partly produced by, what it opposes. Within metaphysical constructions of the Other what is typically occluded is the significance of the *proximate*—i.e., that which is (1) adjacent and *there-by* related temporally or spatially, or (2) that which is approaching (again either temporally or spatially), hence the verb 'to approach or draw neere' (1623, *OED*), and thus (3) the opposite of *remote* or *ultimate*. As we shall see, the proximate is often constructed as the other, and in a process which facilitates displacement. But the proximate is also what enables a tracking-back of the 'other' into the 'same'. I call this transgressive reinscription, which, also provisionally, may be regarded as the return of the repressed and/or the suppressed and/or the displaced via the proximate. If the perverse dynamic generates internal instabilities within repressive norms, reinscription denotes an anti-essentialist, transgressive agency which might intensify those instabilities, turning them against the norms. It becomes a kind of transgression enabled rather than thwarted by the knowledge that there is no freedom outside history, no freedom within deluded notions of autonomous selfhood. In short, the paradoxical dynamics of perversion in its pre-sexological senses enable an account of dissidence within sexuality which is not—hopefully can never again be—confined *to* sexuality.

In Part 7 the same paradoxical dynamics enable a reconsideration of the homophobia endemic to contemporary society. Homophobia is found to connect with other kinds of discrimination, and marked throughout by an actual or feared return of homosexuality. Chapter 16 focuses on homophobic connections between political dissidence and sexual deviance, and does so through a consideration of 'homo/ sexuality' in early modern England. Chapter 17 explores the homophobic construction of homosexuality in contemporary theories of sexual difference. Writers considered in this section include Luce Irigaray, Julia Kristeva, Roger Scruton, Norman Mailer, and D. H. Lawrence. In both chapters fears of the 'other' are found to involve fears of that which is potentially the 'same as'—not only in the psychic sense that the other is constructed from projected, internal fears, but also in the social sense that the other is often created from, and disavowed as, the proximate. The other is confirmed to be potentially a combination of (1) encountered difference, (2) constructed difference, (3) the object of displacement for fears within/of the 'same'.

As the foregoing reference to the psychic and the social might imply, my analysis of homophobia is written at the point where materialism and psychoanalysis converge with, but also contest, each other. It learns from a range of writers already encountered in the study who situate their own cultural politics within, or derive it from, the tension between theoretically inconsistent perspectives. Those writers include Wilde, Gide, Mieli, Hocquenghem, and finally, in a different but related context, Fanon.

Part 8 explores two cultural instances of transgressive reinscription, the one early modern (cross-dressing), the other post/modern (the putative gay sensibility). Here again, as throughout the study, the possibilities for transgression are seen to be profoundly affected by the cultural construction of subjectivity, and Chapter 18 explores ways in which the early modern and modern forms of subjectivity contrast but also, perhaps unexpectedly, interconnect; the connections between the two are considered with the intention of questioning rather than confirming some prevailing assumptions about each. Thus the early modern instance of transgressive reinscription proves illuminating in relation to its post/modern counterpart. The female transvestite of the earlier period appropriated, inverted, and substituted for, masculinity— in a word, perverted it. This was primarily a question of style rather than sexual orientation. And the elusive, probably non-existent, gay sensibility perverts the categories of the aesthetic and the subjective, restoring both to the cultural and social domains which, in the modern period, they have been assumed to transcend, but which in the early modern period they were always known to be a part of. In relation to Jean Genet, Joe Orton, and others, Wilde's departing remark to Gide—

'never say I'—is now reconsidered in the light of the politics of perversion (the perverse dynamic) to which Wilde's own anti-essentialist aesthetic was such a major contribution.

The last chapter returns to my point of departure, Algiers, but now with Gide there alone, desiring the other of cultural and racial difference. In the provocative convergence of race, colonialism, and homosexuality, I seek a historical perspective on difference itself.

PART 3

Subjectivity, Transgression, and Deviant Desire

3 Becoming Authentic

Essentialist Politics

Chapter 1 contrasted Gide's transgressive ethic with Wilde's transgressive aesthetic; this chapter takes up the subsequent history of the first, the next chapter that of the second.

It would be difficult to overestimate the importance in modern Western culture of transgression in the name of an essential self which is the origin and arbiter of the true, the real (and/or natural), and the moral, categories which correspond to the three main domains of knowledge in Western culture: the epistemological, the ontological, and the ethical. In other words the self is conceived centrally within those domains. Not surprisingly then essentialist conceptions of selfhood have been crucial in liberation movements and social struggles. This is Marshall Berman writing in 1970:

Our society is filled with people who are ardently yearning and consciously striving for authenticity: moral philosophers who are exploring the idea of 'self-realization'; psychiatrists and their patients who are working to develop and strengthen 'ego identity'; artists and writers who gave the word 'authenticity' the cultural force it has today . . . all bent on creating works and living lives in which their deepest, truest selves will somehow be expressed . . . Countless anonymous men and women all over . . . are fighting, desperately and against all odds, simply to preserve, to feel, to be themselves. (*The Politics of Authenticity*, 325)

Compare this with Gide writing nearly fifty years earlier on 26 December 1921 (*Journals*, ii. 282):

The borrowed truths are the ones to which one clings most tenaciously, and all the more so since they remain foreign to our intimate self. It takes much more precaution to deliver one's own message, much more boldness and prudence, than to sign up with and add one's voice to an already existing party . . . I believed that it is above all to oneself that it is important to remain faithful. (Cf. *Journals* ii. 341–2)

It is this convergence of a subjective integrity with its ethical and epistemological counterparts which gives Gide the courage of his convictions. When Edmund Gosse wrote to him in 1927, asking why Gide had to be so explicit about his homosexuality in *If It Die*, Gide replied:

I wrote this book to 'create a precedent', to set an example of candor, to enlighten some persons, hearten others, and compel public opinion to reckon with something of which it is oblivious or pretends to be, to the immense impairment of psychology, morality, art—and society.

I wrote this book because I had rather be hated than be beloved for what I am not. (Gide, *Correspondence with Gosse*, 191)

Later, in a public debate in 1935, Gide made a similar affirmation but now with a more explicit political edge:

Enthusiastically and almost systematically I became the advocate of whatever voice society seeks to stifle (oppressed peoples or races, human instincts), of whatever has hitherto been prevented from or incapable of speech, of anything to which the world has been, either intentionally or unintentionally, deaf. This is probably what leads me to attribute to certain instincts of man an importance that I should be quite ready to recognize as excessive, if I were not too often the only one to listen to their voice.

Justin O'Brien's comment on this attitude is pertinent: 'at the height then, of his communist fervor, Gide saw his championing of the homosexual as parallel to his advocacy of other social issues'. O'Brien also observes, probably correctly, that during the period of Gide's writing career no one else played a greater part in legitimizing homosexuality as a subject in literature (O'Brien, *André Gide*, 283). Gide's conviction of the naturalness of homosexuality leads him to a courageous defence of it, and a refusal to tolerate social discrimination and repression. Further, as he remarks in that letter to Fernandez (above, Chapter 1), it is his insight into sexual discrimination which gives him an understanding of, and a commitment to, resisting other kinds. His homosexuality not only made him sympathetic to the plight of others, it also enabled him to see the connections between sexual and other kinds of repression. We might note too that the qualification in the passage above, to the effect that he might be seen as having attached an excessive importance to the subject (though in fact he did not), is not an apology, but a clearly discerned consequence of his position: in so far as homosexuality is natural it does not need special pleading; it is the contingent fact of social discrimination which necessitates not apology but a clear demand of rights, an insistence on being heard.

Gide's Critics

In summary it is fair to say that Gide's sexual nonconformity was a source of and stimulus to radical insight. One response to this was the intense hostility already noted. Another was to ignore it. A third response has been to recognize but downplay it, as does Enid Starkie: '[Gide] has told us much about his homosexuality, but *I have never felt personally* that this problem is as serious as he thought himself, or would have us believe; not as serious as it need have been if his emotional experience had been different at a critical stage in his development' (*André Gide*, 7). My added emphasis to this passage is meant only to highlight, in the very talk of the personal, an absence of precisely that 'personal' empathy which animated Gide's politics; that Starkie unwillingly displays that lack in a discussion of exactly that which in Gide helped inspire it is revealing but not untypical. It is sometimes tempting to overlook such remarks as merely the prejudice of an earlier age, especially when found in otherwise intelligent studies like Starkie's. If I resist this it is not so much out of a wish to reproach, but because such remarks can be especially revealing of the persistence of residual but still active conceptions of sexuality. What is suggested in this case is the way an older view of homosexuality as a behaviour survives within the newer account of it as an identity. Undoubtedly there is truth in the view which says that the homosexual *comes into being*, is given an identity, in the eighteenth and nineteenth centuries. In its primary, pejorative form, this identity is understood as a pathology of one's innermost being (Chapter 14 below). But the idea of homosexuality as an alienated behaviour, or at least something separable from the person, is in part a mutation of the older idea of deviant sexual practices *as* activity rather than identity. It is perhaps most blatantly apparent in Oliver Bernard's remark about Rimbaud: 'I do not think that his homosexuality matters nearly as much as what sort of person he was' (Rimbaud, *Collected Poems*, ed. Bernard, p. xxx). The person is retrieved from his sexuality.

Though in a very different way, Paul Claudel's attack on Gide also unites old and new views of homosexuality, and via the category of perversion. Later I shall show how the modern sense of sexual perversion as an identity displaces, yet still carries the trace of, a long and complex theological history wherein perversion signifies erring and error. In Claudel's criticism the sexual and the theological senses are clearly run together. According to Claudel, Gide's homosexuality perverted his creativity and his inner self. In a letter of 1926 Claudel tells Gide that 'in the most fundamental sense of the word' he has '*gone astray*'. Years earlier, in 1914, he had written to Gide reproaching him for the explicitly homoerotic passage in his novel *Les Caves du Vatican*. Claudel was appalled, telling Gide that 'if sexual attraction does not lead to its natural conclusion—that is to say, reproduction—it is irregular and evil'. And to be proud of his deviation involves 'not only perversion of the senses, but perversion of judgment and conscience as well'. Gide's transgression is especially reprehensible given that it is a vice which is 'spreading wider and wider'. Claudel also tells Gide that he must excise the passage, adding: 'I tell you again: *you will be lost.* You will lose all position, you will become an outcast among other outcasts, rejected by humanity.' He also (with some reason) reproaches Gide for asking him (Claudel) not to let his (Gide's) wife suspect the truth, while writing a novel which will declare the truth to all of Paris (*Correspondence Claudel/Gide*, 205, 206).

Just as his homosexuality was destroying Gide the person from within, so, thought Claudel, it perverted his art from within. This is Claudel writing to Jacques Rivière about *Les Caves du Vatican*:

That book is really sinister; every sentiment in it seems to have been blighted. It has no shape, insignificant events are brought to the foreground and assume a morbid importance, there are stories without any end to them, and the incidents are strung together, or rather follow upon one another, with the absurdity, the languor, and sometimes the obscenity of a nightmare. (pp. 230, 218)

Because Claudel sees Gide's homosexuality as having perverted both his self and his art, he could not accept Gide's aspiration to behave with integrity in relation to his sexuality. Indeed he regarded Gide's refusal to conceal his homosexuality as itself a perversity. Many years later in an interview he insisted that, 'from the artistic and intellectual point of view Gide is nothing . . . he offers an appalling example of cowardice and weakness'. He also adamantly refused the interviewer's suggestion that Gide's openness about his homosexuality was an act of sincerity and integrity. On the contrary, insisted Claudel, Gide's putative integrity was a sham; he added: 'mirrors fascinate Gide. His *Journal* is just a long series of poses in front of himself. . . . His *Journal* is, from that point of view, a monument of insincerity' (*Correspondence Claudel/Gide*, 234–5).

There is an irony here rather revealing of the tortuous twists in the struggle to represent homosexuality and its relation to subjectivity, nature, and sincerity. Whereas, as we shall see below, Gide could not accept the way Wilde aspired to make his own homosexual desire inseparable from a *repudiation* of the depth model of identity, so Claudel could not accept Gide's aspiration to make his sexuality inseparable from an *affirmation* of the depth model. Underneath his apparent insincerity, said Gide, Wilde was *really sincere* (below, Chapter 5); underneath Gide's apparent sincerity, says Claudel, Gide is *really insincere*, only posing. Like Wilde.

Jean Delay, in his biography of Gide's youth, also disparages the writer's homosexuality, but with a much more explicit appeal to the conservative psychoanalysis I discuss below (Part 5). His study is revealing in two ways. First, he gives an entire chapter to the subject (entitled 'Medical Advice'). Second, the scrupulous distance which Delay as biographer elsewhere adopts to Gide here breaks down. He suggests that Gide's belief that his homosexuality was the corner-stone of his personality was 'fallacious' and that, had he not met Wilde, while there is no reason to think he would not have become homosexual, nevertheless he would probably not have adopted 'the attitude of the arrogant pederast, determined to assert his anomaly as a norm' (*André Gide*, 437). In Delay's view Gide's sexuality remained 'infantile', arrested at a stage between narcissism and heterosexuality. Delay adds: 'This . . . finds confirmation in the basic narcissism of the huge majority of pederasts: "Proceeding as from narcissism, they seek their own image in young people"' (pp. 429–30, 426; the quotation is from Freud's *Three Essays on the Theory of Sexuality*). In short Gide had a 'homosexuality neurosis . . . susceptible of medical treatment, at least today' (p. 441).

In invoking against Gide different versions of the very essentialism he was trying to appropriate, the attacks of Claudel and Delay indicate how difficult was that particular task of appropriation. Even so, the refashioning of essentialism was continued by Gide and others, and was eventually to comprise a crucial dimension of sexual liberation. As such, the long tortuous history of this attempt to disentangle a radical essentialism from its conservative counterparts becomes an especially illuminating instance of cultural struggle more generally.

Nature: (Mis)appropriation and Inversion

In contemporary literary and cultural theory, essentialism is frequently denounced, though often from a theoretical position which is itself ahistorical or even anti-historical, and, to that extent, as Diana Fuss shows in *Essentially Speaking*, sometimes informed by the very essentialism it despises. It is true that personal authenticity has operated as a subcategory of the real, the natural, and the true, categories second only to the divine as principles of identity formation and, correspondingly, of the repressive exclusion of both difference and sameness (identity being, as we shall see, rooted in demarcations between the actually different *and* between the same or the proximate). They are principles which establish from above the subordinate's (natural) inferiority in the established (true) order of (real) identities. That much being so, it is understandable that Guy Hocquenghem, writing in 1972, should say: 'When Gide in *Corydon* attempts to construct a homosexuality which is biologically based, by means of a comparison with other species, he is simply walking foolishly into the trap, which consists of a need to base the form of desire on nature' (*Homosexual Desire*, 48).

In fact, or rather in history, not so foolishly. In Frantz Fanon's *Black Skin, White Masks* (1952) there is a moving chapter describing his thwarted attempts to forge, over and against the racist stereotypes of the black, a sustaining, essential, sense of himself, his history, his culture, and his race. This included his attempting, 'on the level of ideas and intellectual activity, to reclaim my negritude'—only to be utterly devastated and disempowered by the following representation, by Jean-Paul Sartre, of negritude as merely a minor term in the dialectic of human becoming:

In fact, negritude appears as the minor term of a dialectical progression: The theoretical and practical assertion of the supremacy of the white man is its thesis; the position of negritude as an antithetical value is the moment of negativity. But this negative moment is insufficient by itself, and the Negroes who employ it know this very well; they know that it is intended to prepare the synthesis or realization of the human in a society without races. Thus negritude is the root of its own destruction, it is a transition and not a conclusion, a means and not an ultimate end. (Sartre, quoted in *Black Skin, White Masks*, 133)

It is instructive to read again this chapter by Fanon, living as we do in an intellectual climate in which certain advocates of deconstruction, anti-Hegelian though they may be, echo Sartre's account of negritude in their view of the futility of inverting binaries (below, Chapter 4); a climate in which, more generally, the basis of agency and praxis have been so effectively dismantled; in which desire itself has been powerfully 'rewritten' as the effect of domination rather than a source of a resistance to it; or, where desire is still seen as a source of resistance, only because of the way it shatters rather than liberates the self.[1]

Likewise it is useful to recall how Gide's 'naturalizing' or essentializing of desire, as with Fanon's attempt to envision the essence of negritude, has produced a coherent sense of self not so much to escape politics, but as the enabling basis of an oppositional politics. Moreover, as we have seen in relation to Gide and will do again in relation to *The Well of Loneliness*, it is sometimes the appropriation of nature that is the most disturbing to the dominant: to claim to be (in certain respects) the same may be to reveal the limits of nature in an especially damaging

---

[1] As argued by Bersani in *The Freudian Body*, discussed below, Ch. 13.

way—to show for instance how assumptions about natural superiority remain, and *must* remain while heterosexuality is (as usual) still constructed over and against homosexuality. So none of this is to advocate the necessity for an essentialist politics for the here and now. What I am proposing is that we do justice to its histories, avoiding at all costs a 'theoreticist' writing-off of them; second, that we recognize in them the ways essentialism has signified differentially for subordinated as distinct from dominant groups; and third that we recognize how much is to be learned from the histories of essentialism about the social dynamics of both subordination and domination.

Ironically, this is especially important in relation to those groups, including sexual minorities, who have been most the victims of 'nature'. The subordinate know that, while theoretical critique is indispensable for their cultural struggles, the academic deconstruction of dominant ideologies tends not to change them very much—at least not very quickly, speed being, for the subordinate, of the 'essence': sometimes a matter of life and death, always a matter of survival and liberty. So they have preferred other kinds of strategies, including those I have so far associated with Gide: the appropriation of dominant ideologies. We can see the same processes at work in writing subsequent to Gide's. I here address several only of a much larger group of texts from this century, some of which have been contentious and notorious, and all of which are now recognized as significant instances of homosexual representation. I do not regard these texts as deriving from a unified 'gay' sensibility, nor do I see them as comprising a unique genre; rather, they are loosely connected through shared representations of oppression, including self-oppression, desire, consciousness, conflict, misery, and, occasionally, liberation.

Considering such novels in the light of the current preoccupation with marginality, I am struck by how, repeatedly, they focus the recurring dilemmas of the marginal, and especially the dilemma which I have already outlined in relation to Wilde and Gide: which is the right strategy—to engage in a radical critique of the dominant and thereby risk political annihilation (or at least permanent exclusion), or to legitimate oneself in its terms, with all the compromises (and all without a guarantee) which that entails? Different as these strategies are, each is profoundly involved with representation. Later chapters will take up and develop the Wildean strategy; here I explore further the appropriations of nature by and for sexual deviance as instanced so far in Gide, and also briefly consider the kinds of resistance with which such appropriations have had to contend.

A Crime against God and Nature

I remarked earlier the historical shift in the conceptualizing of 'homo-sexuality' from a behaviour to an identity. In the nineteenth century a major and specifically 'scientific' branch of this development comes to construct homosexuality as primarily a congenital abnormality rather than, as before, a sinful and evil practice. Once again, it is important to see how the older conception remained active within the newer. Of numerous available examples of this, I explore one relevant to my other concerns, and in a writer who appears again in this connection in Chapter 17.

In an article first published in 1954, Norman Mailer criticized his earlier tendency as a novelist to assume an intrinsic relation between homosexuality and evil. Hitherto, he says, this association had seemed both 'perfectly natural and *symbolically* just'. But now he perceives it as possibly stemming from fears of his own latent homosexuality. In a later reprinting of the article he adds a note explaining that he wrote it because 'fear of homosexuality as a subject was stifling my creative reflexes'; he speaks also of 'the endless twists of habit and defeat which are latent homosexuality for so many of us'. He realizes that to understand 'the ills of the homosexual . . . one had to dig—deep into the complex and often foul pots of thought where sex and society live in their murderous dialectic' (*Advertisements*, 200, 203, 199).

Given the date, and the place (USA) this confessional retraction is rather remarkable. But like most confessions, it partly pre-empts a more disturbing analysis. What are we to make of the continuing ambivalence and often overt hostility towards homosexuality that resurfaces in Mailer's subsequent writings? Certainly there is more to be said about Mailer and homosexuality; Herschel Parker discusses how initially in *An American Dream* Mailer explores homosexuality and the psychology of masculinity, but suppresses it in revisions.[2] But that fears of latent homosexuality is only part of the story, part of that suppression, is evidenced by Mailer's subsequent view that anyone who has succeeded in repressing his homosexuality has earned the right not be called homosexual.[3] An analysis of homosexuality in Mailer's writing would reveal much more than his own personally problematic relation to it; as we shall see, in Mailer's sexual ethic, as in his culture more generally, homosexuality is found to be implicated in an entire socio-political

---

[2] In *Flawed Texts* (esp. 187–212).
[3] Cited in Altman's *Homosexual Oppression and Liberation*, which contains some brief but acute remarks on Mailer; see esp. pp. 59, 88–92, 176–8; on Mailer's admiration for the way D. H. Lawrence overcame *his* homosexuality, see Ch. 17 below.

conception of gender (below, Chapter 17). Adopting the right attitude, liberal or otherwise, even to the point of confessing one's own possible latent homosexuality, is just one of the more endearing intellectual evasions afforded by good faith.

Precisely because of its indispensability to prevailing organizations of gender and society, there persists the use of homosexuality as a symbol of evil and/or the quintessentially unnatural. Writing in 1977, Jeffrey Meyers comments that 'The great strength of Conrad's underrated novel [*Victory*] is his use of the homosexual theme to portray Heyst's emotional sterility and denial of life' (*Homosexuality and Literature*, 89). This critical estimate is not surprising in one who sees the presence of homosexuality in art as primarily a sexual problem of the artist, one 'sublimated and transcended' in his or her work. Relatedly, Meyers argues (with others) that the virtue of the homosexual novel is its use of 'a language of reticence and evasion, obliqueness and indirection'. As it became possible to speak more openly of homosexuality, this led, he believes, to a harmful explicitness with the result that 'the emancipation of the homosexual has led, paradoxically, to the decline of his art'. As examples of this decline he cites the work of Genet, Burroughs, Rechy, and others (pp. 1 and 3).

This reductive position invites several objections, and one in particular *vis-à-vis* the concerns of this chapter. In a way similar to Mailer's confessional retraction, it individualizes and so evades the issue it addresses. Just as good faith confesses a kind of truthfulness which obscures other kinds of truth more or less unrelated to individual integrity, so the view of the homosexual artist sublimating his desire into great art misses the importance, not least for art, of the socio-political histories of homosexuality. To focus on the psychic dynamic is not necessarily wrong; its drawbacks are mainly a consequence of the assumptions of psychology as a discipline, and of its typical and often crass simplifications as evidenced by Meyers and numerous others. The most revealing analysis is arguably at the point of interconnection of the psychic and the social. At such points we find homosexuality in a relationship with heterosexuality which is not only social (i.e. the homosexual as demonized other, symbol of evil, etc.) nor only psychic (the repressed/sublimating homosexual, etc.) but marked by a proximity in which the social and the psychic are conjoined and in a way which transforms each as conventionally understood. This is the subject of Chapters 4 onwards; as a preliminary instance consider how, in his study of *Dracula*, Christopher Craft detects 'a displacement typical both of this text and the gender-anxious culture from which it arose', whereby 'an implicitly homoerotic desire achieves representation as a monstrous heterosexuality, as a demonic inversion of normal gender relations'. Craft sees here an erotic ambivalence, a 'contrary need both to liberate and constrain a desire' which, in its insistent mobility, threatens to overwhelm gender distinctions. Craft reads *Dracula* as a characteristic if hyperbolic instance of Victorian anxiety over the potential fluidity of gender roles ('Kiss Me . . .', 110–12, 117). The homoerotic is explored within and through heterosexuality, and at the cost of extreme instability. Often the stereotype of the homosexual as evil/unnatural is obsessively adhered to precisely in order to fend off such instability, though rarely securely: 'Every effort to isolate, explain, reduce the contaminated homosexual simply helps to place him at the centre of waking dreams' (Hocquenghem, *Homosexual Desire*, 38).

From Inversion to Authenticity: The Well of Loneliness

Nowhere has the stereotype been more violently invoked than when the homosexual has sought a return to nature. Marguerite Radclyffe Hall's *The Well of Loneliness* (1928) has often been taken as an especially abject instance of such a return. Through a 'masculine' lesbian central character, Stephen, it sought a limited legitimacy for homosexuality by naturalizing it. This was more or less in accord with those contemporary 'scientific' theories transferring homosexuality from the realm of crime and evil into that of medicine. In these theories (now known as the medical model) homosexuality becomes a kind of aberration in nature, significantly called congenital inversion: abnormal yet natural nevertheless. In one sense this appears a dubious improvement, merely replacing evil with abjection.

Yet viewed historically, as a stage in a social process rather than a static representation, it involved rather more. *The Well*, as Jeffrey Weeks and Sonja Ruehl have argued,[4] helped initiate a reverse discourse in Foucault's sense: lesbians were able to identify themselves, often for the first time, albeit in the very language of their oppression. Not immediately but eventually, they created a language, a consciousness which was to develop and change, most crucially perhaps, to change from (as here) a plea for inclusion, to a radical critique of the ideologies effecting exclusion.

In novels like *The Well*, the process of authenticating the inauthentic works by merging, displacing, and replacing negative representations

---

[4] Weeks, *Sex, Politics and Society*, 115–17; *Coming Out*, ch. 9; Ruehl, 'Inverts and Experts'. On the longer history in which the novel played such an important part, see Weeks, *Coming Out*, parts 1 and 2. On Foucault's conception of reverse discourse, see below, Ch. 14.

with more positive ones appropriated from the dominant and transformed in the process. What it is possible to take in this way is
determined by the historical conjuncture and the various and never
predictable outcomes of the specific struggles for representation, as they
occur. In Radclyffe Hall's case she not only appropriated the 'authority'
of the medical model currently shifting homosexuality from the realm
of evil to that of nature, but also brilliantly merged it with more positive
identifications also usurped from the dominant culture.

As Jean Radford observes, Hall draws on contemporary biological
and psychological discourses to contest the religious view of homosexuality as a sinful abomination, but also appropriates religious
discourse in the theme of martyrdom:

By giving her heroine the name of the first Christian martyr, by having her cast
out of Eden (Morton), by linking Stephen's war wound with 'the mark of Cain'—
even her experience of Parisian nightlife is imaged in a Dantean journey through
Hell . . . Hall leads us inexorably to the final scene: the closure device where, like
Christ, Stephen is crucified for her kind. ('An Inverted Romance', 106–7)

Stephen also makes 'the ultimate emotional sacrifice: the renunciation
of the Beloved Mary'. Radford concludes that *The Well* has elements of
religious parable, case history, the social protest novel, and heterosexual
romance fiction; romance and realism, rather than being oppositional
modes, are inextricably intertwined (p. 108).

By conjoining in Stephen the (religious) martyr and the (romantic)
outsider, Hall did something of immense significance: each identity
offers, and reinforces in the other, images of a superior sensibility and
integrity being persecuted by the ordinary and the normal: 'the intuition
of those who stand midway between the sexes, is so ruthless, so
poignant, so accurate, so deadly, as to be in the nature of an added
scourge', declares the narrator. Stephen is described as loving 'far more
deeply' than the normal, but this is a virtue inseparable from 'an endless
capacity for suffering' and an excruciating loneliness of spirit. Stephen
thinks: 'wherever there is absolute stillness and peace in this world, I
shall always stand just outside it' (pp. 100, 173, 125).

In what many readers see as a deep abjection in the representation,
there is, equally, something blasphemous. Stephen the invert is nothing
less than a blend of Cain and Christ, simultaneously transgressing God's
law and sacrificing herself to save an ignorant, philistine humanity. She
is presented as loving and serving more ardently than others and with a
moral sense superior to theirs. This, in the novel, is at once compensa-
tion for her inversion (abjection?) and an aspect of its superiority
(arrogance?). It also marks a significant stage in the slow and fiercely

resisted twentieth-century decline of 'normality'. Bizarre as it may now seem, many subsequent developments in sexual liberation and radical sexual politics can be traced back to the kind of appropriations made by Hall, even those developments which would have appalled her, for example the idea of sexual deviance as potentially revolutionary, subverting the corrupt and oppressive centre from the deviant margins.

Of course, such transgressive appropriations are, from another perspective, conservative and even reactionary alignments. If the abnormal, socially dislocated individual lays claim to being more authentic than the normal, such authenticity is rooted nevertheless in the selfsame categories, spiritual and moral, which make her abnormal to begin with; Stephen is seen by others as 'a true genius in chains, in the chains of the flesh, a fine spirit subject to physical bondage' (p. 225), and by herself as 'hideously maimed and ugly—God's cruel; He let us get flawed in the making' (p. 243). The conservative character of such categories becomes explicit in the novel's endorsement of class privilege and patriotism, both defended according to 'the immutable law of service' (p. 339); and in its blind acceptance of the division between masculine and feminine as also an immutable law, this time of nature. The consequence of this is that lesbianism has to be signified in images of sterility and, moreover, the narrative voice seems unaware of the extent to which it is class rather than nature that constructs the particular notion of masculinity which is being used. As Ruehl nicely remarks, 'what [Stephen] grows up to be is a "perfect gentleman"' ('Inverts and Expert', 25).

But Stephen is also something quite different from the perfect gentleman, namely the 'mannish lesbian'. On this still intensely controversial identity Esther Newton has persuasively defended Hall by emphasizing that aspect of her sexual politics which her detractors have often overlooked (or not wanted to face): 'of those who condemn Hall for assuming the sexologists' model of lesbianism I ask, just how was Hall to make the woman-loving New Woman a sexual being? . . . there was no developed female sexual discourse; there were only male discourses—pornographic, literary and medical—about female sexuality. To become avowedly sexual, the New Woman had to enter the male world, either as a heterosexual on male terms (a flapper) or as—or with—a lesbian in male body drag (a butch).' Newton recalls that during the trial of *The Well* Hall was furiously angry with her own defence lawyer for playing down the sexual dimension of the book's lesbian relationships.[5]

---

[5] Esther Newton, 'The Mythic Mannish Lesbian', 22–3. On the trial itself see Baker, *Our Three Selves*, esp. part 4, 1928–34. For different interpretations of *The Well*, see Rule, *Lesbian Images*, 50–61; Faderman, *Surpassing the Love of Men*, esp. 316–23; Stimpson, 'Zero Degree Deviance'.

If *The Well* is caught in this dilemma, authenticating both the dominant and the subordinate, and unable to acknowledge fully the extent to which the former negates even as it enables the latter, and, more specifically, seeking legitimacy for its deviant hero/ine in the categories of the very order denying her legitimacy, we should perhaps see this not so much as a failure, but an aspect of the contradictions intrinsic to the homosexual subculture at that time, and maybe intrinsic to any excluded group opting for a revisionist rather than a revolutionary politics.

And the fact remains that *The Well* initiated a reverse discourse amid intense controversy: it was declared obscene and banned. Amid antagonism fuelled by a homophobic attack on the book in the *Sunday Express* (by the editor), the British publisher withdrew it. Reprinted in Paris and imported from there, copies were seized and eventually burned after the distributors were successfully prosecuted. This suggests a paradox: at certain historical conjunctures certain kinds of nonconformity may be more transgressive in opting not for extreme lawlessness but for a strategy of inclusion. To be half successful is to lay claim to sharing with the dominant (though never equally) a language, culture, and identity: to participate in is also to contaminate the dominant's authenticity and to counter its discriminatory function. If *The Well* was an abject apology for lesbianism it was also an audacious one, taking over for the female sexual deviant an identity deeply religious and ethical, and this only a few years after the Commons had approved a clause to bring lesbianism under the scope of the criminal law (it was rejected by the Lords) with, presumably, many of the powerful agreeing with Ernest Wild's assertion in the House that lesbianism was a vice which 'debauches young girls, and ... produces neurasthenia and insanity' (quoted from Weeks, *Coming Out*, 106).

Raymond Williams usefully reminds us of the distinction between cultural initiatives which are alternative and those which are oppositional.[6] Gay subcultures have, at different times, been seen as one or the other, or conceivably both. There are those who believe it is possible in principle for gay culture to be integrated into the dominant culture, or at least find acceptance by it. But there are others who argue that, because the prevailing order in some sense requires the denigration of homosexuality, such integration is not possible. The work of those like Dennis Altman rather confirms the second view. Altman regards the repression of homosexuality as 'essential in the formation of male

---

[6] See 'Base and Superstructure in Marxist Cultural Theory', in *Problems in Materialism and Culture*, esp. 40–5; in practice the distinction is often difficult to maintain, as Williams shows in *Marxism and Literature*, esp. 114, 124–7.

bonding, itself the psychological basis for authority, and male dominance, in virtually all existing societies'; he sees its repression as
especially formative in male institutions like the military—hence the
hostility to and anxiety about overt homosexuality in such institutions
(*Homosexualization*, 61). If this is correct, gay culture is only likely to
be accepted if and when a society undergoes fundamental change. In
the interim it remains, almost of necessity, oppositional, contributing to
a critique aiming for that change.

The reception of *The Well* confirms Williams's sense of the complicated connections between the oppositional and the alternative. Subcultures which seek an alternative coexistence within or alongside
dominant cultures may be perceived as equally or even more dangerous
than overtly oppositional ones. Deviant identifications with the dominant paradoxically prove as threatening to it (the dominant) as more
overtly oppositional identifications. Often the subordinate incorporates,
in the act of appropriation, more than it knows of the ruling order, and
often to its cost. But by the same token it may confront that order with
what it is ill equipped to confront in *the form of* its other. Such has
been the case with the subordinate's appropriation of essentialism. The
history of such identifications and incorporations will also assist in a
questioning of the concept of the other, especially its widespread and
often vague use in cultural and theory (below, Chapters 17 and 21):
specifically, it suggests how a terror of the other may be premissed on a
terror of the proximate; not only does the excluded remain adjacent,
but the adjacent becomes threatening in a way that the excluded never
quite does. And we should remember that appropriation is never mere
duplication; almost invariably it involves challenge and transformation—perhaps directly, perhaps by contributing to the grounds for it.

Rubyfruit Jungle: *The Authentic as Oppositional*

Rita Mae Brown's *Rubyfruit Jungle* (1973) is perhaps the second-best
known lesbian novel, *The Well* being the first. In so many ways it seems
an answer to, even a repudiation of, that earlier novel, and, as such,
both a measure of and a polemical contribution to the lesbian-feminist
consciousness of the early seventies. *Rubyfruit* is an acute, picaresque
critique of heterosexual power and hypocrisy. Memorably affirmative
in its representation of lesbianism, it has the yet further advantage of
often being hilariously funny. To carry all this to a wide audience,
without apology, is the achievement which marks it off most clearly
from *The Well*, and marks too the complex changes of the intervening

forty-five years, especially of the decade immediately preceding its publication.

There's an especially funny section in the novel where the lesbian heroine, Molly, gets caught up in the erotic fantasies of a predominantly heterosexual couple. Each partner has cross-gender fantasies: the woman, Polina, imagines she is a well endowed man being admired as such in a men's toilet, while the man, Paul, fantasizes about being a woman in a ladies' room, admired for her 'voluptuous breasts' (p. 206). This complex, fetishistic scenario gets too much for Molly who, with relief, moves on to a 'straightforward' lesbian relationship with Alice, Polina's daughter, 'who hadn't one sexual quirk in her mind'. Possessed of an uncomplicated sensuality and contrasted in this respect with her mother's 'warped Victorian mentality', Alice is celebrated: 'she was there, all there with no hang-ups, no stories to tell, *just herself. And I was just me*' (p. 210; my emphasis).

The reverse discourse has come full circle; the tables have well and truly turned: half ironically, half seriously, the perverts—those possessed of sexual quirks and a warped mentality such that they can 'get off' only on perverse fantasy—have become heterosexually identified. In the case of Paul, the unwholesomeness of his sexuality is apparently compounded by his physical repulsiveness (this is reverse discourse with a vengeance). By contrast the lesbianism is essentially uncomplicated, free of hang-ups. Molly and Alice are (authentically) just themselves; in short, natural; it is the straights who are well screwed up.

We can see then that even this radical critique of the dominant depends for its representation of lesbianism on the strategy of appropriation (of integrity and authenticity) developed in *The Well*, a novel whose view of lesbianism it rejects so conclusively. Additionally there is in *Rubyfruit*, as in *The Well*, the vital appropriation for lesbianism of yet other conventional images of superiority and authenticity, both literary and extra-literary. Thus Molly is 'a combination of Tom Jones and a crusader for justice. She is in all ways outstanding—a straight A student, a fine athlete, an effective leader, and absolutely beautiful' (Faderman, *Surpassing the Love of Men*, 406–7). Additionally she is the tough outsider, coming from a rural background and repeatedly betrayed by those belonging to more sophisticated urban cultures. Eventually she arrives in New York where she not only survives such betrayals, but succeeds with her integrity intact. Indeed her resilience and sheer incorruptibility in the face of exploitation, discrimination, and poverty are saint-like, again echoing *The Well*.

Natural Exclusions

In 1918 Gide enters in his Journal this shameless affirmation—one might say promotion—of homosexual desire:

Had Socrates and Plato not loved young men, what a pity for Greece, what a pity for the whole world!

Had Socrates and Plato not loved young men and aimed to please them, each one of us would be a little less sensible.

He goes on to distinguish between the pederast, sodomite, and invert. The first is 'the man who . . . falls in love with young boys'; the second is 'the man whose desire is addressed to mature men'; the third, 'the man who, in the comedy of love, assumes the role of a woman and desires to be possessed'.

Speaking of his own kind of homosexuality, pederasty, Gide adds that double affirmation which was to become so important to subsequent movements for gay liberation: 'it is not enough for me to say that it is natural; I maintain that it is good'. But on the very same page we find a harsh judgement of the 'invert':

As to the inverts, whom I have hardly frequented at all, it has always seemed to me that they alone deserved the reproach of moral or intellectual deformation and were subject to some of the accusations that are commonly addressed to all homosexuals. (*Journals*, ii. 246–7)[7]

Gide's naturalizing of his own homosexual desire was accompanied by, and for him perhaps required, this internal differentiation—one which separates off those whom he cannot conceive as natural, and displaces onto them some at least of the social stigma of homosexuality. Displacement is internal to subcultures and not only what occurs between them and dominant cultures; Frantz Fanon suggests that the subordinate do this to each other because it is done to them by the dominant (*Black Skin, White Masks*, 102–3; using a concept from *The Politics and Poetics of Transgression* by Peter Stallybrass and Allon White, this might be called 'displaced abjection' (19, 53)).

There is a further factor: to appropriate prevailing ideas of identity as naturalness, and of authenticity as integrity, is also, necessarily, to incorporate other, differential notions of self. Identity becomes both intrinsic and relational: essentially this and definitely not that. Something similar occurs in *Rubyfruit* when Molly first encounters a butch/

---

[7] Gide harks back to this distinction in his posthumous work, *So Be It*, not to abandon it, but to remark that others thought it foolish and discriminatory (pp. 164–5). See also Sinfield, *Literature, Politics and Culture*, 64–5.

femme lesbian bar: 'That's the craziest dumbass thing I ever heard tell of. What's the point of being a lesbian if a woman is going to look and act like an *imitation man*? Hell, if I want a man, I'll get *the real thing*, not one of these chippies' (p. 147, my emphasis). Here the charge of inauthenticity extends to one's own kind, or rather (as with Gide) precisely distinguishes associated others as not properly of one's kind. The cover of the 1978 Corgi edition of the novel exclaims in huge type 'Being different isn't really so different!' Unless of course one remains excluded—i.e. different.

Holy Sinners and Lonely Bars

Like Gide's journal entry of more than fifty years before, *Rubyfruit*'s break into confident self-affirmation involves an internal discrimination that marks off as other a dimension of homosexual culture with its own complicated social history of suffering, survival, and self-affirmation. Across the intervening fifty years, that history surfaces in a number of different novels, especially as a deeply ambivalent encounter with the homosexual underworld. Towards the end of *The Well* Stephen and Mary discover 'the garish and tragic night life of Paris' inhabited by the invert. One bar especially Stephen never forgot for as long as she lived— 'that merciless, drug-dealing, death-dealing haunt to which flocked the battered remnants of men whom their fellow-men had at last stamped under; who, despised of the world, must despise themselves beyond all hope, it seemed, of salvation. There they sat . . . timid yet defiant—and their eyes, Stephen never forgot their eyes, those haunted, tormented eyes of the invert' (pp. 424, 434).

She is repulsed, filled with 'deep depression and disgust'. But the encounter also evokes a compassion born of her own suffering; repudiation and identification co-exist. This deeply conflicted, ambivalent encounter with the homosexual ghetto figures over and again in novels as diverse as *The Well* and *Rubyfruit*, and as different again as Gore Vidal's *The City and the Pillar*, James Baldwin's *Giovanni's Room*, Angus Wilson's *Hemlock and After*, and John Rechy's *Rushes*. Typically the negative side of that ambivalence figures as a shuddering reaction against the transvestite or the camp queen: 'Brockett babbled away, and as he did so his voice took on the effeminate timbre that Stephen always hated and dreaded: "Oh, my dear!" he exclaimed with a high little laugh . . . And his soft, white hands grew restless making their foolish gestures' (*The Well*, 274). The culture of camp is abhorrent not just to the narrative voice of *The Well* but to those of other novels also, even some of the more radical. Camp becomes the quintessential expression of an alienated, superficial inauthenticity.

At one level such encounters serve to siphon off the alienation of the writer/protagonist; authenticity is constituted negatively as that which is left after a projection onto the 'inauthentic' of all the misery, alienation, and sometimes self-hatred which leaves its trace even on the most 'liberated' psyche. In effect, such encounters project and construct an inauthentic other against whom the authentic self is defined. But something more emerges from that ambivalence: some of these alienated others (though rarely the outrageous transvestites or the camp queens) are allowed an understanding unique to, and inseparable from, their social alienation. In that same bar which so deeply disgusts and depresses Stephen, she is engaged in discussion by Adolphe Blanc, 'that gentle and learned Jew', who speaks with and urges a wisdom and compassion that is once again Christlike. He tells her that only the truly exceptional and courageous invert can correct the ignorant persecution of all inverts by those who are normal; that no suffering is ever in vain 'because all things work toward ultimate good; there is no real wastage and no destruction' (p. 437). The holy sinner emerges from the ghetto, and tragic insight—'man learns wisdom through suffering'—becomes the province of the deviant.

In James Baldwin's *Giovanni's Room*, the alienated are again invested with insight, becoming spiritually authentic in and through their sexual inauthenticity. But again, only in relation to internal discriminations. It is in the same kind of bar encountered by Stephen in *The Well*, and also in Paris, that the central character David, struggling against his homosexual desires, encounters *les folles* 'screaming like parrots'. He cannot believe they ever had sex with anyone since 'a man who wanted a woman would certainly have rather had a real one and a man who wanted a man would certainly not want one of *them*' (p. 24). Later, someone comes towards him from the shadows: 'the flat hips moved with a dead, horrifying lasciviousness. . . . the eyelids gleamed with mascara, the mouth raged with lipstick' (p. 33). David, still desperately locked within the norms of sexual difference which are tearing him apart, confronts a parodic inversion of those norms; the chances of a queen making out in such circumstances are pretty remote. David tells 'him' to go to hell; predictably, 'he' replies that it is David who will 'burn in a very hot fire'.

On another occasion in the same bar Jacques, an ageing, lonely, and bitter homosexual, speaks to David with a wisdom resembling Blanc's in *The Well*. But the message is different, no longer one of stoical renunciation and faith in creation. Whereas in *The Well* alienation is contained within the selfsame martyring perspective which in part produces it, here there is a sense that deviant desire might be fulfilled. What is required now is not the courage of renunciation and endurance in the face of an impossible stigmatized desire, but the courage to break free of social hatred internalized as guilt: Jacques insists that David's growing love for Giovanni, ephemeral though it will inevitably be, *can* work: 'you can make your time together anything but dirty, you can give each other something that will make both of you better—forever— if you will *not* be ashamed, if you will only *not* play it safe' (p. 46). In the event David cannot break free; both he and Jacques betray Giovanni, who dies as a consequence.[8]

The tragic subjects of these novels, even as they fail to survive the destructiveness of their society and their own desires, instance or inhabit a paradoxical, brief integrity of the kind which has disappeared from the world. But if they are holy sinners, they are never simply so; integrity and redemption are discovered alongside and even within the distress and deformation consequent upon social persecution and its internalization as failure, guilt, and self-hatred. In these novels and much other writing, homosexuality animates this tragic vision, even or especially when homosexuality is never mentioned. The plays of Tennessee Williams are a more obvious case in point, those of Terence Rattigan one of the less obvious.[9] Hence the significance through contrast of a novel like Manuel Puig's *Kiss of the Spider Woman*, where the very 'ordinariness' of homosexuality circumvents not only the obvious 'medical' terms of its oppression, but also the more complex religious, romantic, and literary terms of both oppression and 'authentic' liberation; homosexuality is decentred, socialized in such a way as to be released from meaning in the sense of being rendered precisely *unremarkable as such*, yet, simultaneously, rendered profoundly significant in other terms. In the bar scenes of *Giovanni's Room*, in the voice of Jacques and others, this recognition of homoerotic desire as at once liberating, intensely significant yet intrinsically unremarkable exists partially, ambivalently.

In the sixties and even more in the seventies and eighties, the homosexual underworld becomes the 'gay scene'—exciting, commercially vibrant, and exploitative; an object of voyeuristic interest for non-gay culture and the source of stylistic innovation, some of which

---

[8] This was akin to Baldwin's own experience of the New York homosexual underworld at the age of 19, as recollected in his 1985 article, 'Here be Dragons', in *The Price of the Ticket*, esp. 681–3.

[9] On Rattigan see Sinfield, *Literature, Politics and Culture in Post-war Britain*, 301, and 'Who's for Rattigan?', 44–6.

eventually migrated into the latter via the commercial channels connecting them. Novels like *The Well* and *Giovanni's Room* give us the old underworld, those like Holleran's *Dancer from the Dance* and Larry Kramer's *Faggots* the new scene. In the shadows of the new scene, often epitomized by those standing there in its literal shadows, a part of it yet removed, were those with histories reaching back into the old underworld.[10]

In the bar scenes of the lesbian and gay novel we also witness the hesitant, conflicted, ambivalent history of essentialism appropriated. To consider that history in relation to *The Well* and *Rubyfruit* is to be reminded of its importance in lesbian culture, and its survival into current lesbian theory. But here crucial distinctions emerge.

Monique Wittig

Diana Fuss has recently remarked a reluctance in lesbian theory to relinquish an identity politics based on essence. She rightly insists that this does not make lesbian theory unsophisticated or reactionary by comparison with its gay male counterpart, where anti-essentialist theory has been widely endorsed; rather, 'lesbians . . . simply may have more to lose by failing to subscribe to an essentialist philosophy' (*Essentially Speaking*, 98–9). My own consideration of lesbian essentialism has occurred in a chapter beginning with Gide's essentialism not in order to subsume it to his, but as a reminder that this tradition has also been crucial in gay as well as lesbian culture, and progressively so in both.

Just as important, the history of the lesbian appropriation of essentialism shows it to be more diverse, complex, and challenging than its critics allow. In fact, it is a history which shows how misleading the umbrella concept of essentialism tends to be: once again, history reads theory. Consider the case of the lesbian theorist Monique Wittig. If, as Fuss points out, Wittig adheres to an essentialist theory of lesbian identity, it is nevertheless inflected and transformed by an uncompromising materialism. That much is epitomized in Wittig's provocative contention that the lesbian is not a woman.

Crucially, Wittig does not seek to legitimate the lesbian via prevailing norms; for example she does not want to naturalize her, or represent her as *essentially the same as* other women, or the same as the subjects of heterosexuality. Rather, Wittig theorizes the lesbian as outside, and in opposition to, those norms. She insists that the category of sex and

---

[10] Significant recent accounts of these earlier cultures, biographical, autobiographical, historical, and imaginative, include Edmund White's *States of Desire*, Lorde's *Zami*, Bartlett's *Who Was That Man*, and Nestle's *A Restricted Country*.

its derivatives—e.g. gender, sexual difference, 'woman' and 'man'—have no natural or biological reality. They are all ideological constructs, effects of an oppressive discourse of heterosexuality. To entertain them in any form is to ratify them. Thus for Wittig there can be no such thing as a specifically feminine writing. To believe there is effectively naturalizes the fact of women's subordination and 'amounts to saying that women do not belong to history, and that writing is not a material production' ('The Point of View', 63). One can and should 'refuse to be a woman' and seek energetically to destroy all the associated categories of sex. Rebellion is all about finding social oppositions within so-called natural differences and abolishing these differences in the very act of making them understood ('The Category of Sex', 64).

So the lesbian stands outside the norms of sex: those norms literally have no place for her: 'women belong to men. Thus a lesbian *has* to be something else, a not-woman, a not-man, a product of society, not a product of nature, for there is no nature in society' ('One is Not Born a Woman', 49). For Wittig this means 'it would be incorrect to say that lesbians associate, make love, live with women, for "woman" has meaning only in heterosexual systems of thought and heterosexual economic systems. Lesbians are not women' ('The Straight Mind', 438). By the same token 'lesbianism provides for the moment the only social form in which we can live freely' ('One is Not Born a Woman', 49).

On the one hand Wittig deplores the universality and essentialism of metaphysics, especially 'the fixed discourse of eternal essences' which legitimates heterosexual tyranny, and, relatedly, the ahistorical, totalizing interpretations of psychoanalysis ('The Straight Mind', 435, 437-8). On the other hand she undertakes a humanist appropriation of both essence and universal. Criticizing Marxism for its refusal to attribute subjectivity to the individuals of oppressed groups, she advocates a new, materialist account of subjectivity: 'since no individual can be reduced to his/her oppression we are confronted with the historical necessity of constituting ourselves as the individual subjects of our history as well'. This 'new personal and subjective definition for all humankind' can only be found beyond the categories of sex and indeed presupposes their destruction (pp. 51-3). For Wittig, 'when one says *I* and, in so doing, reappropriates language as a whole . . . then . . . there occurs the supreme act of subjectivity', itself the most precious thing for a human being; in saying 'I' one becomes 'an absolute subject . . . ungendered, universal, whole' ('The Mark of Gender', 6).

It is customary for her critics to invoke at this point the charge of essentialism. They less often follow through Wittig's appropriation of essence and universal in the specific field which most concerns her, namely writing. It is here that she makes a very important point about subcultural intervention. In 'The Mark of Gender' she carefully prefaces a discussion of her own creative writing with a most revealing summary of a famous contention of Marx and Engels to the effect that 'each new class that fights for power must, if only to reach its goal, represent its interests as the common interest of all the members of a society or, to express things at the level of ideas, that this class must give the form of universality to its thoughts'. The writer has a crucial part to play here since, to destroy the categories of sex and to restore an 'undivided I' requires nothing less than a radical transformation of language as a whole ('The Mark', 9, 7). This transformation, particularly the establishing of a lesbian subject as an absolute I, is the aim of Wittig's *The Lesbian Body*. In this she is inspired by Proust who, in *Remembrance of Things Past*, 'made "homosexual" the axis of categorization from which to universalize' ('The Point of View', 65). She contends that a text by a minority writer only works if it succeeds in 'making the minority point of view universal'; Proust's text does that, as do the much less well known but no less important works of Djuna Barnes; the work of these two writers transforms 'the textual reality of our time' (p. 66).

There is something rather wonderful about Wittig's quite precise, yet perversely extravagant, appropriation of the universal: one is not born a woman but becomes one; one may therefore choose not to be/become a woman; indeed the lesbian is always already not a woman, she is outside a system of 'natural' sexual difference which produces woman and which can and must be abolished. If this is essentialist it is an essentialism which abjures 'nature' and so tends precisely not to work in terms of the 'natural exclusions' remarked above: 'The minority subject is not self-centred as is the straight subject. Its extension into space could be described as being like Pascal's circle, whose center is everywhere and whose circumference is nowhere' ('The Point of View', 65). In an early essay she remarks that the dismantling of sexual difference means there are no longer two sexes, but not one either: there would be as many sexes as there are individuals ('Paradigm', 119). As Roland Barthes observed in his advocacy of a similar idea, what is imagined here is not homosexuality but homosexualities whose very diversity would baffle the binary logic of sexual difference (*Roland Barthes*, 69).

Artful Politics

It is clear that novels like *The Well* and *Rubyfruit* are not passive reflections of 'the real', whatever or whoever's that is, but artful interventions within culture. Of course the same goes for most other novels, even or especially those whose status as 'high culture' obscures the fact. Less apparent perhaps is the way such novels, and indeed literature much more generally, have played a considerable part in the long and continuing struggle for the legitimacy of homosexuality. Widely read novels like these two have reflected social changes but also intervened as agents of change; literature has helped to form some of the identifications appropriated for the reverse discourse of homosexuality. But, arguably, it can only do that when it makes the bid for universality of which Wittig speaks. Hence the importance, though also the danger, for minority writers of the attempt to appropriate dominant categories. One consequence of *not* making that attempt is that their work is disregarded, or regarded only as special pleading on their part. Wittig writes perceptively of how the minority text then becomes a committed text with a social theme which attracts attention to a social problem. As such the text is 'diverted from its primary aim, which is to change the textual reality within which it is inscribed'; it is prevented from carrying out exactly the 'political action' of which it is most capable ('The Point of View', 65).

This defence of the aesthetic is not a repudiation of the political dimensions of literature, but rather of the aesthetic/political opposition which conventionally defines literature. The importance of challenging that opposition is confirmed by the fact that the aesthetic as conventionally understood—art as the non-political—can be equally inimical to Wittig's objective. Homosexuality is accepted but only as the vehicle for something else more worthy because universal. Thus a few sanctioned homosexual novels have always been said to snatch aesthetic merit from the ugliness of their subject. And these became the terms used to sell those novels to as wide an audience as possible, in paperback, in the 1960s and 1970s. Their promotional blurb makes the point. A 1977 New English Library paperback of Mary Renault's *The Charioteer* gives a recommendation (by way of an apology) from *The Observer* in which a somewhat down-market version of the form/content distinction is deployed as a strategy to reach the widest possible market: 'most books on this subject arouse only pity; here there is something more: the separate parts flow together to a taut climax, and at last the book is a novel and not just a novel about homosexuals.'

So Wittig's task is a difficult one for sure. But its urgency is underscored by the fact that existing literature has already stacked the odds against her: modern fiction especially has not only perpetuated negative images of the homosexual, but actively participated in their creation. Lillian Faderman's *Surpassing the Love of Men* is revealing of how nineteenth- and twentieth-century novels produce—often in the face of competing contemporary empirical evidence—the image of the lesbian as predatory, craving of power, and the tormentor and seducer of the innocent (*Surpassing*, especially parts 2 and 3).

Wittig is also right in this: whether homosexuality is demonized, excused, or affirmed, the issue has always been far more than a question of positive or negative images. What is suggested in *The Well* has been manifested over and again more recently at all levels of culture and confirmed by historians of sexuality—namely, that aspects of Western culture itself are condensed in the modern homosexual identity. Partly (though not only) because of that the converse is also true: the recent history of Western culture has been and continues to be extensively influenced by the cultures of homosexuality, and not least because the homosexual identity is discursively condensed within its heterosexual counterpart. But this is to anticipate the project; for now I would only contend that the literature which represents homosexuality is always political. And by that I mean, at the very least, that it is a medium of competing representations which have complicated histories with the potential profoundly to affect people's lives. I do not mean only that reading and writing literature can contribute to the growth of the individual (though it may, and crucially so); it affects those whom it represents in diverse other ways. In the case of homosexuals it has affected their freedom, who or what they are, or are allowed to be, even the question of whether they survive or die, metaphorically, spiritually, and literally. So it is strange that this insistence on the profoundly political aspects of literature so often meets with the reproach that such a view diminishes literature's importance. To me the reverse is true.[11]

It is the political aspects of *The Well* which make it so controversial still. Faderman cites one response to the book—'I had found a copy . . . in the library, and for the first time in my life, I felt a certain shame about my feelings towards women' (p. 323)—and Weeks another: 'When . . . I read [*The Well*] it fell upon me like a revelation. I identified with every line. I wept floods of tears over it and it confirmed my belief in my homosexuality' (cited in *Coming Out*, 101, and *Sex, Politics and*

---

[11] In the year that I finished this book (1990) several letters in the *London Review of Books* attacked cultural materialism, a critical perspective with which I am associated, in just these terms. My only reply is this book, and an appeal to Leo Bersani's recent study, *The Culture of Redemption*, which contests the assumptions about art shared by the writers of these letters.

Society, 117). Such responses, and especially the divergence between them, indicate that, behind the cheerful (though painfully ambiguous) reassurance offered to us by the blurb for *Rubyfruit*—'Being different isn't really so different!'—lies the history of an uncompleted struggle and some fundamental philosophical and political questions. Perhaps this blurb even encourages us to believe that as we emerge from the dark ages into enlightenment we can forget history. Not so. First the ambiguity: does it mean that 'really' we are all different, or all the same? If the same, is this a liberation or a colonization? And who still remains excluded by sameness, or indeed by our current fetishizing of difference? Just how different is the culture which reduces difference to sameness from that which outlaws difference? Finally, is it possible that we fear sameness as much as we fear difference? These are questions taken up in subsequent chapters.

4 Wilde's Transgressive Aesthetic and Contemporary Cultural Politics

The Politics of Inversion

Wilde's transgressive aesthetic relates to contemporary theoretical debates in at least three respects: first, the dispute about whether the inversion of binary opposites subverts, or, on the contrary, reinforces the order which those binaries uphold; second, the political importance—or irrelevance—of decentring the subject; third, post-modernism and one of its more controversial features: the so-called disappearance of the depth model, especially the model of a deep human subjectivity, and the cultural and political ramifications of this. Since the three issues closely relate to each other, I shall take them together.

It is said that Wildean inversion disturbs nothing; by merely reversing the terms of the binary, inversion remains within its limiting framework: an inverted world can only be righted, not changed. Moreover, the argument might continue, Wilde's paradoxes are superficial in the pejorative sense of being inconsequential, of making no difference. There are two responses to this, one theoretical, the other historical. I shall take the theoretical first, since it is necessarily both a general question about deconstruction, and a specific question about the binary and its inversion.

It is an achievement of deconstruction to show the limitations of binary logic in theory and its often pernicious effects in practice; to show how binaries, far from being eternal necessities of cultural organization, or essential, unavoidable attributes of human thought, are unstable constructs whose antithetical terms presuppose, and can therefore be used against, each other. Meaning becomes an effect of difference and deferral. Because its terms are vulnerable to inversion and its structure (via inversion) to displacement, the continued existence of the binary is never guaranteed; it has to be maintained, often in and through struggles over representation. In particular, the terms of the dominant/subordinate binary never denote homogeneous static blocs; the dominant is only ever the more powerful and (possibly) repressive side of a shifting relationship or series of relationships which interconnect, often asymmetrically. Thus any individual typically occupies diverse subject positions, some of which may be dominant, some subordinate.[1] All this is crucial for a study like this one, concerned as it is with several of the binaries which powerfully organize our cultures: natural/unnatural, masculine/feminine, hetero/homosexual; with what hold them in place socially, and what is necessarily disavowed in their political effectiveness—with, in other words, what enables them to endure and yet also renders them unstable.

But we should not deceive ourselves into thinking that to deconstruct these binaries somehow neutralizes their effect in history and/or the here and now. That is an instance of how the indispensability of theory can be deflected into a 'theoreticist' evasion of what it might most effectively challenge. Binaries remain fundamental to, and violently active within, social organization and discursive practices,[2] more so than we usually realize as we live and suffer them daily. But how, then, are they challenged?

Derrida has insisted that metaphysics can only be contested from within, by disrupting its structures and redirecting its force against itself. He defines the binary opposition as a 'violent hierarchy' (*Positions*, 41) where one of the two terms forcefully governs the other, and insists that a crucial stage in the deconstruction of binaries involves their inversion, an overturning, which brings low what was high. In effect inversion of the binary is a necessary stage in its displacement:

I strongly and repeatedly insist on the necessity of the phase of reversal, which people have perhaps too swiftly attempted to discredit . . . To neglect this phase of reversal is to forget that the structure of the opposition is one of conflict and subordination and thus to pass too swiftly, without gaining any purchase against the former opposition, to a *neutralization* which *in practice* leaves things in their former state and deprives one of any way of *intervening effectively*.[3]

Wilde's inversions, operating to subvert a deeply conservative authenticity and the deep subjectivity on which it is premised, were overturnings in Derrida's sense.

Someone famous once said that people make their own history but not in conditions of their own choosing. I think Derrida is saying something similar when he adds that the political effect of failing to

[1] Sedgwick gives a persuasive theoretical formulation of this perspective, and readings to substantiate it, in 'Across Gender', esp. 53–61.

[2] I use 'discursive practice' to indicate the inseparability of cultural formations and the languages used within them; specifically, to denote the interrelationship of (1) representation of the social, (2) interpretation of the social, and (3) praxis within the social.

[3] *Positions*, 41–2, quoted from Culler's translation in *On Deconstruction*, 165–6, which includes a crucial passage in Derrida's original—the first sentence of this quotation—left out of the Alan Bass translation. See also Derrida, *Grammatology*, pp. lxxvi–lxxviii, and Terdiman, *Discourse/Counter Discourse*, esp. introduction.

invert the binary opposition, of trying simply to jump beyond it into a world free of it, is simply to leave the binary intact in the only world we have. Despite this emphasis in Derrida, some of his adherents still want to make that jump, insisting that the inversion of a binary achieves nothing, and opting instead for its ahistorical, conceptual deconstruction. Thus in his account of sexual difference and homosexuality, Robert Young declares that the reversal of a binary 'only remains within its terms and does not challenge it—in fact it only perpetuates it' ('The Same Difference', especially p. 87).

Of course, inversion is only a stage in a process of resistance whose effects can never be guaranteed and perhaps not even predicted. (In)subordinate inversions, if at all successful, provoke reaction. The result is a cultural struggle between unevenly matched contenders, a struggle in which the dominant powers, which transgressive inversion fiercely disturbs, now react equally fiercely against it. But the case of Wilde suggests why, as a strategy of cultural struggle, binary inversion so often provokes such reaction. In actual historical instances, the inversion is not just the necessary precondition for the binary's subsequent displacement, but often already constitutes a displacement, if not directly of the binary itself, then certainly of the moral and political norms which cluster dependently around its dominant pole and in part constitute it. Because in any historical instance the binary holds in place more than it actually designates, its inversion typically has effects beyond itself: inversion may for instance give impetus to cultures denigrated by its subordinate term, and simultaneously throw into disarray the cultures officially sanctioned by its dominant term. Robert Young's article, even as it clearly indicates the importance of Derrida's concept of *différance* for issues of gender, is also an instance of the limitations of the deconstructive trope followed through in abstraction and independently of any historical reference. The limitation is especially marked here, where the most informative work on inversion as a strategy of sexual transgression has been historically grounded in the early modern period.[4]

Reconsidering inversion in the light of this history is also to restore to it dimensions absent from its sexological and psychoanalytic uses. Kunzle, for instance, discussing the iconography of the world-turned-upside-down broadsheets, offers a conclusion which registers the complex potential of inversion and is thereby nicely suggestive for understanding Wilde: 'Revolution appears disarmed by playfulness, the

---

[4] I have in mind especially Kunzle, 'World Turned Upside Down'; Hill, *The World Turned Upside Down*; Davis, 'Women on Top'; Stallybrass and White, *The Politics and Poetics of Transgression*; and Clark, 'Inversion, Misrule and the Meaning of Witchcraft'.

playful bears the seed of revolution. "Pure" formal fantasy and subversive desire, far from being mutually exclusive, are two sides of the same coin' ('World Turned Upside Down', 89).

Notoriously, some of Wilde's contemporaries were not disarmed by his playfulness. In the first of the three trials involving Wilde in 1895, he was cross-examined on his *Phrases and Philosophies* (cited above, Chapter 1), the implication of opposing counsel being that its elegant binary inversions, along with *Dorian Gray*, were 'calculated to subvert morality and encourage unnatural vice' (Hyde, *Oscar Wilde*, 271). There is a sense in which evidence cannot get more material than this, and it remains so whatever our retrospective judgement about the crassness of the thinking behind such a view. Observe also how quickly the spurious distinction I offered a moment ago between the theoretical and the historical responses has already broken down: the theoretical issue has already become a historical one, and in a way which I welcome given the objective of this study to argue for, and exemplify, a cross-reading between theory and history.

One of the many reasons why people were terrified by Wilde was because of a perceived connection between his aesthetic transgression and his sexual transgression. 'Inversion' was being used increasingly to define a specific kind of deviant sexuality inseparable from a deviant personality. As an aspect of this development Foucault has described the change I have had occasion to remark already, namely the way the homosexual had become a species of being whereas before sodomy had been an aberration of behaviour (*History*, 43; see also Chapter 14 below). In fact, the transition he describes was more complicated than he allows, occurring over a greater period of time, and even then (and still now) with cultural and class distinctions. But it is true that, by the time of Wilde, homosexuality could be regarded as rooted in a person's identity and as pathologically pervading all aspects of his being. As such the expression of homosexuality might be regarded as the more *intentionally* insidious and subversive. Hence in part the animosity and hysteria directed at Wilde during and after his trial. He was attacked by the press (in the words of one editorial) for subverting the 'wholesome, manly simple ideals of English life'. Moreover his 'abominable vices . . . were the natural outcome of his diseased intellectual condition'. Sexual perversion is inseparable from intellectual and moral corruption. No wonder the same editorial also imagined Wilde as the leader of a subculture in London, comprised of like-minded, but younger men (Hyde, *Trials*, 12).

This feared cross-over between discursive and sexual perversion, politics and pathology, has sanctioned terrible brutalities against the homosexual; at the same time, at least in this period, it was also becoming the medium for what, following Foucault, might be called a reverse or counter-discourse (*History*, 101, and below, Chapter 14), giving rise to what I explored in Wilde in Chapter 1—a transgressive aesthetic working through a politics of inversion/perversion (again crossing over and between the different senses of these words).

We begin to see then why Wilde was hated with such an intensity, even though he rarely advocated in his published writings any explicitly immoral practice. What kept those 'wholesome, manly simple ideals of English life' in place were traditional and conservative ideas of what constituted human nature and human subjectivity, and it was these that Wilde attacked: not so much conventional morality itself as the ideological anchor points for that morality, namely notions of identity as subjective depth which manifest themselves in these newspaper reports as wholesomeness, right reason, seriousness, etc., and whose criteria appear in the Y column above (Chapter 1). Here, generally, as with Gide more specifically, Wilde's transgressive aesthetic subverted the dominant categories of subjectivity which kept desire in subjection, subverted the essentialist categories of identity which kept morality in place. And even though there may now be a temptation to patronize and indeed dismiss both the Victorians' wholesome, manly, simple ideals of English life and Wilde's inversion of them, the fact remains that, in successively reconstituted forms, those ideals, together with the subject positions which instantiate them, came to form the moral and ethical base of English Studies in our own century and indeed remain culturally central today.

Wilde and English Studies

I am thinking here not just of the organicist ideology so characteristic of an earlier phase of English Studies, one which led, for example, to the celebration of Shakespeare's alleged 'national culture, rooted in the soil and appealing to a multi-class audience', but more specifically of what Chris Baldick in his useful study goes on to call its more enduring 'subjective correlative', namely, the 'maintenance of *the doctrine of psychic wholeness in and through literature as an analogue for a projected harmony and order in society*' (Baldick, *Social Mission*, 213–18, my emphasis).

For I. A. Richards all human problems (continues Baldick) become problems of mental health with art as the cure, and literary criticism becomes 'a question of attaining the right state of mind to judge other minds, according to their degree of immaturity, inhibition, or perversion'. Richards advocates sincerity as 'the quality we most insistently require in poetry', and also 'the quality we most need as critics' (Richards, quoted from Baldick, *Social Mission*, 215). As a conception of both art and criticism, this is the reverse of Wilde's. Similarly with the Leavises, for whom an equally imperative concept was the related one of 'maturity', and one unhappy consequence of which was their promotion of the 'fecund' D. H. Lawrence against the 'perverse' W. H. Auden. As Baldick goes on to observe, 'this line of critics is not only judicial in tone but positively inquisitorial, indulging in a kind of perversion-hunting' which is itself rooted in 'a simple model of [pre- or anti-Freudian] normality and mental consistency' (Baldick, *Social Mission*, 217).

A more sophisticated development of this line of thought persists today. It addresses sexual deviation rather more directly, finding in its putative inadequacy the origin of a debilitating failure of aesthetic vision. As such this criticism bears out Michel Foucault's argument that there has emerged in recent times a belief in profound connections between sex and truth. This belief has two particular manifestations: first, that sexual deviation is thought to be a deviation from the truth; this is a truth embodied in, and really only accessible to, normality, with the result that, even if sexual deviants are to be tolerated, 'there is still something like an "error" involved in what they do . . . a manner of acting that is not adequate to reality'. Its second manifestation is the conviction that 'it is in the area of sex that we must search for the most secret and profound truths about the individual' (*Herculine Barbin*, pp. x–xi).

Many instances of this belief might be cited from evidently dated literary criticism. Consider instead a couple of more recent examples. Jan B. Gordon brings the full weight of a 'phenomenological' perspective to bear on Wilde, finding that

The homosexual in jail . . . is the ultimate reduction of the self-contained, reflex image. And *De Profundis* is the confession of an individual no longer capable of distinguishing self from false self, where all subjects have become objects. Oscar Wilde's condition, in brief, is the one art form where parody, gossip, the epigram, failed development manifested in the denial of growth, and the dehumanization that is part of the pornographic experience all conspire in an utterance that is the pretence of a failed autobiography. ('Decadent Spaces', 53)

In another essay in the same volume, on Swinburne's 'circle of desire', Chris Snodgrass concludes that 'incest—with its correlate, homosexuality—is, of course, the paramount sexual symbol for "loss of difference"'

(p. 82).[5] Such criticism, even where it does not explicitly endorse it, relates to the critical perspective which sought to build an entire world view on the doctrine of psychic wholeness, personal maturity, a firm grasp of the actual, and, where appropriate, a defence of hetero/sexual difference against the undifferentiation of sexual perversion. It is a perspective subjected to fairly relentless critiques in recent years. In particular, its belief in the ontological, epistemological, and ethical primacy of subjective integration, and in the profound connections between sex and truth, have been attacked by one or more of the major movements within contemporary critical theory.

And yet Wilde's challenge to this critical/ethical vision is still largely excluded from consideration; worse, he is still subjected to the judgement of that older vision in its updated yet hardly more discerning mode, as in the examples above. That 'theory' has not rediscovered Wilde is strange, given that we have passed beyond that heady and in many ways justified moment when it seemed that only Continental theory had the necessary force to displace the complacencies of our own tradition. It is also ironic, because even when looking so intently to the Continent, we failed to notice that Wilde was, and remains, a very significant figure there (Pfister, *Oscar Wilde*). And not only there: while the *Spectator* (February 1891) thought 'The Soul of Man under Socialism' was a joke in bad taste, the essay soon became extremely successful in Russia, appearing in many successive editions across the next twenty years. Perhaps, then, there exists or has existed a kind of 'muscular theory', one which shares with the critical movements it has displaced a significant blindness with regard to Wilde and what he represented. If so this almost certainly has something to do with the persistence of an earlier attempt to rid literature and English Studies of a perceived 'feminized' identity.[6] It may also be because, rather than in spite of, the legendary status of Wilde. Whatever, one aim of this book is to argue that Wilde needs to be rescued from some of his admirers and radically rethought by some at least of his critics.

Decentred Subjectivity and the Post-modern

Recent critics of post-modernism, including Fredric Jameson, Ihab Hassan, Dan Latimer, and Terry Eagleton,[7] have written intriguingly on

---

[5] On the significant body of work representing homosexuality as the loss of differentiation, see below, Ch. 17.

[6] See Sinfield, *Literature, Politics and Culture in Post-War Britain*, ch. 5, esp. 63–4, 77–8.

[7] Jameson, 'Postmodernism and Consumer Society', and 'Postmodernism, or the Cultural Logic of Late Capitalism'; Hassan, 'Pluralism in Postmodern Perspective'; Latimer, 'Jameson and Postmodernism'; Eagleton, 'Capitalism, Modernism and Postmodernism'.

one of its defining criteria: the disappearance of the depth model. Eagleton offers an important and provocative critique of post-modernism: 'confidently post-metaphysical [it] has outlived all that fantasy of interiority, that pathological itch to scratch surfaces for concealed depths'. With the post-modern there is no longer any subject to be alienated and nothing to be alienated from, 'authenticity having been less rejected than merely forgotten'. The subject of post-modern culture is 'a dispersed, decentred network of libidinal attachments, emptied of ethical substance and psychical interiority, the ephemeral function of this or that act of consumption, media experience, sexual relationship, trend or fashion'. Modernism, by contrast, is (or was) still preoccupied with the experience of alienation, with metaphysical depth and/or the psychic fragmentation and social wretchedness consequent upon the realization that there is no metaphysical depth or (this being its spiritual instantiation) authentic unified subject. As such, modernism is 'embarrassingly enmortgaged to the very bourgeois humanism it otherwise seeks to subvert'; it is 'a deviation still enthralled to a norm, parasitic on what it sets out to deconstruct'. But, concludes Eagleton, the subject of late capitalism is actually neither the 'self regulating synthetic agent posited by classical humanist ideology, nor merely a decentred network of desire [as posited by post-modernism] but a contradictory amalgam of the two'. And if in one respect the decentred, dispersed subject of post-modernism is suspiciously convenient to our own phase of late capitalism, it follows that those post-structuralist theorists who stake all on the assumption that the unified subject is still integral to contemporary bourgeois ideology, and that it is always a politically radical act to decentre and deconstruct that subject, need to think again (Eagleton, 'Capitalism, Modernism and Postmodernism', 143, 132, 145, 143–5).

Eagleton's argument can be endorsed with yet further important distinctions. First, even though the unified subject was indeed an integral part of an earlier phase of bourgeois ideology, the instance of Gide and the tradition he represents must indicate that it was never even then exclusively in the service of dominant ideologies. Indeed, to the extent that Gide's essentialist legitimation of homosexual desire was primarily an affirmation of his own nature as pederast or paedophile, some critics might usefully rethink their own assumption that essentialism is fundamentally and always a conservative philosophy. In Gide we find essentialism in the service of a radical sexual nonconformity which was and remains largely outlawed by conventional and dominant sexual ideologies, be they bourgeois or socialist. Also, it needs only a glance at the complex and often contradictory histories of sexual liberation movements in our own time to see that they have sometimes (and necessarily) embraced a radical essentialism with regard to their own identity (as does Eagleton's contradictory subject of late capitalism), while simultaneously offering an equally radical critique of the essentializing sexual ideologies responsible for their oppression.

This is important: the implication of Eagleton's argument is not just that we need to make our theories of subjectivity a little more sophisticated, but rather that we need to be more historical in our practice of theory. Only then can we see the dialectial complexities of social process and social struggle. How, for example, the very centrality of an essentialist concept to dominant ideology (e.g. 'the natural'), has made an appropriation of it for a subordinate culture seem indispensable in that culture's struggle for legitimacy; roughly speaking, this corresponds to Gide's position as I am representing it here. Conversely we also see how other subordinate cultures and voices seek not to appropriate dominant concepts and values so much as to sabotage, invert, and displace them. This is something we can see in Wilde. Today the Wildean strategy has re-emerged albeit in a changed form, while the Gidean politics of selfhood have suffered something of an eclipse. That is all the more reason to engage with the histories of both.

Anti-essentialist Politics

The decentred subject of post-modernism contrasts vividly with Berman's summary of the modern individual in quest of authenticity (above, Chapter 2). But whether this post-modern subject is subversive of, alternative to, or indeed actually produced by, late capitalism, is an intriguing and important area of debate. What is certain though is that there are those today who are advancing as criteria of the post-modern what Wilde was using to scandalize his contemporaries in the 1890s. And those contemporaries exacted a heavy price: in a very real sense, Wilde's exploration of decentred desire, and the transgressive aesthetic which emerged from it, cost him his life. In 1898, complaining of his inability to write, Wilde tells Robert Ross, 'Something is killed in me ... Of course my first year in prison destroyed me body and soul. It could not have been otherwise' (*Letters*, 760).[8]

At the very least the case of Wilde will lead us to rethink the antecedents of the modern and the post-modern. Wilde prefigures elements of each while remaining importantly different from—and not just obviously prior to—both. If his transgressive aesthetic anticipates

---

[8] Wilde is also recorded as having said that he died in prison (*Letters*, 493 n. 2).

post-modernism to the extent that it suggests a culture of the surface, the decentred and the different, it also anticipates modernism in being not just hostile to, but intently concerned with, its opposite: depth and exclusive integration as fundamental criteria of identity. Yet unlike some versions of the post-modern, Wilde's transgressive aesthetic includes an acute political awareness and often an uncompromising political commitment;[9] and in contrast to modernism, his critique of the depth model is accompanied not by *Angst* but something utterly different and reminiscent of Barthes's *jouissance*, or what Borges has perceptively called Wilde's 'negligent glee . . . the fundamental spirit of his work [being] joy' (Ellmann (ed.), *Oscar Wilde: Critical Essays*, 174). Gide spoke of Wilde similarly, identifying him with the sculptor in one of Wilde's own parables, smashing the statue of Grief he had previously made in order to make from it that of Joy (*Oscar Wilde*, 56).

[9] Woodcock, in his biography of Wilde, writes interestingly of Wilde's political involvements, including his refusal to support racial prejudices or anti-Semitism and his relation to the Chicago anarchists of 1886 (see Woodcock, *The Paradox of Oscar Wilde*, esp. 138, 148–9).

5 Re-encounters

Never Use 'I'

After his release from prison, Wilde met Gide again, once at Berneval, where Wilde went to stay, and then twice more in Paris. On the first of the Paris meetings Gide was apparently embarrassed to be seen in Wilde's presence. Wilde insisted on paying for the drinks and then told Gide that he was impoverished. Of the second meeting, Gide later wrote, 'the last time I saw Wilde, he seemed deeply miserable, sad, impotent and hopeless' (*Oscar Wilde*, 45). A few days after this last meeting Wilde wrote to Gide asking for 200 francs (Ellmann, 'Corydon and Ménalque', 84).

So the last time they spoke together at any length seems to have been at the Berneval meeting in June 1897. Gide found Wilde quieter, 'no longer the lyrical madman of Algeria'. As Gide was leaving, Wilde said: 'promise me: from now on don't ever write *I* any more.' Gide wrote: 'as I appeared not quite to understand him, he went on, "In art, don't you see, there is no *first* person"' (*Oscar Wilde*, 40).

Gide's accounts of his meetings with Wilde have been regarded with suspicion: it has been said that he exaggerated the extent of Wilde's decline in France after his release from prison; also that Gide never fully acknowledged his artistic indebtedness to Wilde (below, Chapter 7). Gide, though, always insisted on the accuracy of his accounts; he felt that he knew Wilde better than others because he understood Wilde's homosexuality and the difference it made; Wilde confided intimately only in those who shared his tastes and 'no matter how devoted some of his friends may have been, it was only after they turned their backs that Wilde began to live' (*So Be It*, 27). This remark epitomizes one merit of Gide's accounts: in them, for the most part, he claimed to have understood Wilde better than did others because he understood something about, and shared, Wilde's sexual difference, and so was a recipient of Wilde's confidence.

He did not claim, as did some of those others, that he knew Wilde better than Wilde knew himself. Why did others make this latter claim? And why was it so tempting for even the scrupulous Gide to come close to making it when, thirty years later, he returns in his *Journals* to that enigmatic parting remark of Wilde's? If the hysterical and punitive attitudes of Wilde's persecutors were one kind of reaction to his anti-essentialism, we can discern here other less punitive, though not necessarily less disturbed reactions. Retrospective decisions about the 'real' Wilde are revealing of the way essentialist conceptions of sexuality and subjectivity have reinforced ethical notions of sincerity and psychic depth in the formation of modern individuality and modern literature, in a way powerful enough to make of Wilde a legend while effacing what was most challenging about him.

The Truth of Wilde's 'I'

In his *Journals* (1 October 1927) Gide remarks that it was because Wilde had determined 'to make of falsehood a work of art' that he said ' "Never use *I*". The *I* belongs to the very face, and Wilde's art had something of the mask about it ... But ... the informed reader could raise the mask and glimpse, under it, the true visage (which Wilde had such good reason to hide.' On the one hand Gide is here again making a perceptive point about the relationship between Wilde's art and his homosexuality; he rejects the idea that Wilde's sexuality was dictated by his aestheticism—

that he merely carried over into his habits his love of the artificial. I believe quite on the contrary that this affected aestheticism was for him merely an ingenious cloak to hide, while half-revealing, what he could not let be seen openly ... Here, as almost always, and often even without the artist's knowing it, it is the secret of the depths of his flesh that prompts, inspires, and decides.

But Gide cannot approve of, and nor, I think, does he ever quite understand, Wilde's transgressive aesthetic, seeing in it either, as here, a strategy of concealment or a limiting abandonment of depth for surface, sincerity for artifice. Earlier, in 1913 he remarks the 'trappings with which Wilde liked to cover his thought and which still seem to me rather artificial' (*Journals*, 29 June); in *If It Die* he describes Wilde as one who 'covered over his sincerest feelings with a cloak of affectation'. But, adds Gide, the character Wilde played 'was his own; the role itself ... was a sincere one' (p. 274). And later: 'with me ... Wilde had now thrown aside his mask. It was the man himself I saw at last' (p. 276). In the 1927 Journal entry he also sees Wilde's strategy as essentially deficient, involving 'falsehood'; 'affected aestheticism'; 'surface witticisms, sparkling like false jewels'; and 'artistic hypocrisy'. He compares Wilde with Proust, 'that great master of dissimulation', and both of them with himself: 'As for me, I have always preferred frankness'.

Yet only sixteen months later (*Journals*, 10 February 1929) Gide, recalling Wilde, reflects on the extraordinary extent to which apparently authentic feeling and thoughts are in fact culturally engendered. He agrees with Wilde's assertion that life imitates art, and he quotes 'La Rochefoucauld's wonderful maxim: "There are people who would never have been in love if they had never heard of love"', finding it 'applicable to many other sentiments; perhaps to all'. But here too Gide can be seen resisting or at least re-forming the radical implications of Wilde's transgressive aesthetic; his assumption remains that there is an authentic realm deeper than or prior to the social; his point here seems to be that it is extremely difficult to attain and then sustain. That is why, thinks Gide, the vast majority of people are content with conventional sentiment; indeed, he adds, 'not everyone can be sincere'.

Gide's rewriting of Wilde is not so much an evasion as a consequence of the differences between their philosophies of identity and desire and (inseparably) of their differences as writers. At the end of part I of *If It Die* Gide adds a note on Roger Martin du Gard's complaint of the book that it did not say enough. Gide answers that he had tried to say everything, and that what he aims at 'above all is to be natural'. He adds: 'No doubt there is in me some intellectual need that inclines me to simplify everything to excess for the sake of tracing my lines with great purity . . . what hampers me most is having to represent states that are really one confused blend of simultaneous happenings as though they were successive . . . everything in me is conflicting and contradictory. Memoirs are never more than half sincere, however great one's desire for the truth' (p. 232). So Gide is no crude essentialist—he seeks to be faithful to the conflict and contradictions of experience; but what makes it possible to be thus faithful, and what gives such fidelity its significance, as well as generating a certain style—that simplification in pursuit of purity—is belief in sincerity and naturalness of self, and especially of the self that others castigate as unnatural.

Those less sympathetic to Wilde are even more critical of his refusal of depth. According to George Woodcock, 'the main thesis of [Frank] Harris's *Life of Wilde* is that Wilde was a weak, effeminate character of no great moral strength or intellectual profundity, and generally inferior to his robust and deep-thinking biographer'. Note how this passage is totally governed by the surface/depth binary which Wilde persistently inverted and displaced. On one thing at least Woodcock agrees with Harris: to be of importance one just has to be on the depth-side of that opposition; that is the precondition of having moral strength, of being intellectually profound, capable of 'deep thinking'. So, in his own biography of Wilde, Woodcock retrieves his subject for the depth model of subjectivity: 'I believe that Wilde was in fact a more earnest man than he or others believed, and that he was sincere in almost everything he did' (Woodcock, *The Paradox of Oscar Wilde*, 174, 179).

Woodcock, and to some extent Gide, anxiously sought to recentre Wilde in terms of the depth model Wilde repudiated but to which they subscribed; for their own peace of mind (or maybe we should say for their own well-being) they had to discover the hidden truth of Wilde's first person, of that 'I' of which in art he said one should not speak. Alternatively, those like Harris saw Wilde's subjectivity as a flawed inferior to their own; they insisted that he was as subjectively self-centred as them, only deficiently so; his cultivated artificiality was a rationalization of the homosexual's 'deep' inadequacy, his inability to be authentic (i.e. heterosexual). Maybe there is here a kind of revenge for the insecurity generated by Wilde's subversion of the depth model of identity, a revenge which is also a self-justification or, more precisely a self-substantiation: Wilde is recast as the same-yet-flawed; far from subverting authenticity, his was a case of failed authenticity. In effect, and crucially for this attitude, Wilde has to be seen as inwardly *disqualified*.

In both cases—Wilde as *really* sincere (Gide, Woodcock) or Wilde as *really* inadequate (Harris)—he is re-presented in terms of the conventional identities—ethical, psychological, and sexual—which he challenged. His critics, sympathetic and otherwise, could not accept that Wilde's aesthetic was not so much a self-concealment as an attempted liberation from 'self'—and what was at issue here was less his actual self, than selfhood as culturally and oppressively conceived. It is as if they had to reinstate or reinscribe a counterpart of themselves in the provocative, threatening absence which was Wilde's decentred self; as if their own identity could not be stable until they had filled that space with something substantial that would reflect themselves back to themselves. Their counter-repudiation, of Wilde's repudiation of stable identity, had to be in relation to, and in terms of, Wilde himself; he had to be repositioned, reimagined, resubstantiated.

It is not an exaggeration then to say that they reposition Wilde as a subject of, and within, the metaphysic which he displaced. So might he have been said to 'ask for it'? Perhaps: Ellmann's description of Wilde's American tour—'more or less successful confrontations in which his flagrant and unconventional charm was pitted against conventional maleness and resultant suspicion' (*Oscar Wilde*, 174)—might also describe the confrontation between Wilde and other of his contemporaries and many of his readers. Let's push the question harder: should we speak of Wilde as a victim? If I doubt the usefulness of this, it is mainly because this is an observation often made with a complacent assumption that his victimization was the error of a Victorian hypocrisy long since abandoned. It is a familiar political move: the benighted past as scapegoat. If only to question that complacency, we might consider Wilde as several kinds of victim, not only of Victorian hypocrisy but, posthumously, of a much progressed but still repressive resistance which might be called heterosexual humanism. It is a resistance which relates to a tension within humanism itself which, in its strong form, harbours a potential contradiction by conceiving people at once as unique individuals and as instances of a universal human nature: irreducibly different (unique individual) and yet ultimately the same (universally human). And whereas a radical humanism might allow difference in the name of the same—since 'we're all ultimately human'—a reactionary humanism often polices difference in the name of the same—'they are not quite, not yet human'.

PART 4

Transgression and its Containment

6 *The Politics of Containment*

Humanist transgression in the name of an essential self has proved wanting, and its adherents have lost their faith. This is part of a wider crisis: with the post/modern repudiation of the very existence of the essential self, there are those who have become sceptical about the possibilities of effective transgression, and pessimistic about the possibilities of radical change. Most worryingly perhaps, the belief in an autonomous self, that experiential focus apparently necessary for successful opposition to a repressive social order, seems to be unfounded; in those haunting words of Michel Foucault, 'there is no single locus of great Refusal, no soul of revolt, source of all rebellions, or pure law of the revolutionary' (*History*, 95–6).

For the radical humanist especially, the post/modern repudiation of the unified subject seems to disempower the marginal, robbing it of that independence and autonomy which was the assumed precondition of its possessing any subversive agency of its own, or at least any independent cultural identity. The disappearance of the independent experiential *locus* for opposition further suggests that repression infiltrates and constructs consciousness itself: where we once thought there was an essential self, a liberating, uncontaminated otherness/difference constituting the soul of revolt, we find instead only the power which it promised to liberate us from. Even worse, it seems as if the existing social order might actively forestall resistance because somehow preceding and informing it: subversion and transgression are not merely defeated by law, but actually produced by law in a complex process of (re)legitimation.

From such anxious perceptions there emerges the so-called subversion/containment problematic wherein repressive laws are seen not only to defeat us coercively—that much was always obvious—but to inhabit us in ways which ensure our defeat prior to, in ways other than, direct force. Resistance from the margins seems doomed to replicate internally the strategies, structures, and even the values of the dominant.

Unless, that is, resistance is otherwise, and derives in part from the inevitable incompleteness and surplus of control itself? If so perhaps we should think of resistance not in terms of an originating identity, but a reactive agency? Such thoughts lead us to the practice of transgressive reinscription. But consideration of that practice must wait upon a fuller account of the containment argument, and then, in Part 5, the lost histories of perversion.

Versions of Containment

The arguments for containment come in diverse forms. One of its most important developments has been in relation to the early modern period; another is in recent analysis of colonialist discourse.[1] Some of these precede or have developed adjacently to the post/modern critique of the subject (and usefully enlarge its scope), since containment theories have always recognized that identity is an effect of the social domains which subversion and transgression would contest.

First there is the anthropological version which sees allegedly transgressive practices like carnival as not at all disturbing of dominant values but rather their guarantor—a licensed release of social tension, a kind of safety-valve effect which, far from undermining the existing order, actually contributes to its survival.

Second are the psychological versions to the effect that (1) true faith paradoxically lies in honest doubt; (2) it is the sacrilegious who, most knowing the true value of the sacred, are thereby most beholden unto it, *even as* they seek to destroy it; (3) there is nothing so bourgeois as the desire to scandalize the bourgeoisie. A further version of this argument is Richard Sennett's theory of 'disobedient dependence'. Transgression, says Sennett, is perhaps the most forceful element in disobedient dependence, since it involves a defiance based on dependence, a rebellion not against authority but within it: 'the transgressor disobeys but authority relates the terms'. As such this rebellion 'has very little to do with genuine independence or autonomy'; moreover, 'the world into which a person has entered through the desire to transgress is seldom . . . a real world of its own, a true alternative which blots out tha past' (*Authority*, 33–4).[2]

Third is the theoretical version (already discussed above, Chapter 4) which says that to invert a binary opposition (e.g. masculine/feminine)

---

[1] See Greenblatt, *Renaissance Self-Fashioning*, esp. ch. 5; id., 'Invisible Bullets'; Mullaney, *The Place of the Stage*; Dollimore, *Political Shakespeare*, ch. 1, and the introduction to *Radical Tragedy* (2nd edn.); Sinfield, 'Power and Ideology: An Outline Theory and Sidney's *Arcadia*'. On recent work on colonial discourse, see Benita Parry's 'Problems in Current Theories of Colonial Discourse', which addresses the writing of Frantz Fanon, Gayatri Spivak, Homi Bhabha, Abdul JanMohamed, and others. The subversion/containment debate is an additionally significant instance of the development described in Ch. 2 whereby theory reads history and vice versa: a theoretical framework enables a historical enquiry which eventually shows the need to modify the theoretical framework.

[2] Cf. Freud, who in a discussion of transference remarks that 'defiance signifies dependence as much as obedience does, though with a "minus" instead of a "plus" sign before it'. (Freud, *Introductory Lectures on Psychoanalysis*, i. 495).

is to remain within rather than overthrow its oppressive structure. This might be the critique, in theoretical guise, of the 'mannish lesbian'.

A fourth category of containment is developed most persuasively by Michel Foucault in relation to sexuality, but can be formulated more generally to include the other three. I outline it in relation to Foucault in Chapter 14, but will briefly rehearse it here. We have become used to thinking of sexuality as an anarchic and hence potentially subversive energy which conservatives want to control, radicals want to liberate. However, Foucault sees it in terms of socially created identities and desires which enable rather than hinder the operations of power within the realm of the psychosexual. In short, sexuality, far from being an energy which 'power' is afraid of, is actually a discursive construct which power works through.

Containment theory is sometimes seen as having little to do with materialist critique, and is sometimes conveniently disavowed, often by gestural materialists, as a kind of bourgeois intellectual bad faith. But Raymond Williams for one knew otherwise; in 1977, before most current debates were underway, he gave this astute summary of the crucial issue:

The major theoretical problem . . . is to distinguish between alternative and oppositional initiatives and contributions which are made within or against a specific hegemony (which then sets certain limits to them or which can succeed in neutralizing, changing or actually incorporating them) and other kinds of initiative and contribution which are irreducible to the terms of the original . . . hegemony, and are in that sense independent. It can be persuasively argued that all or nearly all initiatives and contributions, even when they take on manifestly alternative or oppositional forms, are in practice tied to the hegemonic: that the dominant culture, so to say, at once produces and limits its own forms of counter-culture. *There is more evidence for this view . . . than we usually admit.* (*Marxism and Literature*, 114, my emphasis.)

Williams rightly insists, nevertheless, that significant breaks with the dominant *have* occurred, and will of course continue to do so. But such breaks can neither be adequately recognized nor developed if the realities and complexity of containment are disavowed. To that end his account is indebted to but also departs from a European Marxist tradition of cultural critique,[3] one which has recognized the complexity and indirect effectiveness of domination, and is acutely aware of the fact that human potentialities have not only been savagely repressed, but also abandoned and repudiated by their former adherents and those with most to gain from them. Some of the most effective Marxist

---

[3] It is described in Anderson's *Considerations on Western Marxism*.

cultural critique this century has attended to the reasons for the failure of potential to be realized in circumstances which should have enabled it. An obvious instance concerns the way that, after the First World War, when conditions seemed right for the development of socialism, fascism won out instead.

Moreover, far from opting for the facile optimism dictated by party dogma, writers as diverse as Walter Benjamin, Antonio Gramsci, Theodor Adorno, Herbert Marcuse, and Louis Althusser have felt it necessary to describe the complexity, the flexible resilience of power structures, and their psychic internalization. These writers have been without illusion—even pessimistic—about the short- or medium-term possibilities of progressive change, and it is not surprising that today there are those living in the societies of advanced capitalism who find a continuing relevance in their work. Specifically, some of the current debates around subversion and containment, and the reactionary or repressive dimensions of high culture, are benefiting from renewed attention to that work. It is in such a spirit that I approach it here: though on balance more critical than accepting of containment theory, I believe it is too often caricatured and disavowed by those unwilling to face its challenge.

Objections

For example, there are those who construe containment theory as saying that resistance is *only ever* an effect of power. This simplistic version of the theory, deriving more from its critics than its advocates, represents power as 'seamless and all pervasive' and resistance, where it exists at all, as 'ultimately self-deceived' (Belsey, 'Towards Cultural History', 164). Resistance is supposed to be self-deceived because it was only ever the ruse of the power which created it—a manufactured threat whose 'suppression' is a strategy of control by the power which produced it. Actually, even this version of containment theory might offer more space for resistance than its advocates sometimes, and its critics usually, allow, since the very activity of producing the threat requires giving it a visibility and identity, both of which, even though initially a charade, may then or subsequently be occupied or appropriated by oppositional forces. Always, though, at a certain cost, and the more so to those implicated in the earlier stages of this process.

Further, when containment theorists are reproached for representing the prevailing structures and mechanisms of power as so unified and omnipotent that resistance appears impossible, the implication is that resistance is never impossible. Perhaps not, but the fact of possibility says little about the likelihood of success. Just as containment theorists should not judge a priori that all subversion is contained, so its opponents cannot decide a priori that all power structures are subvertible; each instance, if it can be decided at all, can only be done so historically.

My own objections to containment theory are as follows:

1. Sometimes it involves a conceptual confusion: subversion, and even more transgression, necessarily *presuppose* the law, but they do not thereby necessarily *ratify* the law. A logical presupposition is elided with a contingent one. It is tempting to imagine that the converse is also true—that containment necessarily presupposes subversion. But this does not in fact follow; we should say rather that containment is always susceptible (in principle, not a priori) to subversion by the selfsame challenge it has either incorporated, imagined, or actually produced (via containment).

2. Containment theory often presupposes an agency of change too subjective and a criterion of success too total. Thus subversion or transgression are implicitly judged by impossible criteria: complete transformation of the social (i.e. revolution), or total personal liberation within, or escape from it (i.e. redemption). Their impossibility is partly guaranteed by the fact that the agency involved in both subversion and transgression is usually assumed to be a local or limited one, and often explicitly subjective or voluntarist. Recall that Sennett tells us that in disobedient dependence the transgressor fails to achieve 'genuine independence or autonomy', a 'real world' of his or her own or a 'true alternative' to that being resisted. But what could such a utopian—not to say idealist—vision of freedom be, in actual political practice, remembering that the transgressor typically emerges from a position of marginality, subordination, and repression—i.e. *relative* powerlessness? What for example, to recall our earlier discussion, could it have been for Hall and other lesbians in 1928?

So although containment theory is not obviously essentialist, and in some respects is just the opposite in that it partly emerges from a perceived failure of essentialist radicalism, and the associated realization that the essential unified self is an illusion, it remains a theory nevertheless generated by, and in the space of, an essential absence of the subject. Hence the unwillingness of some of its advocates to concede that any particular episode of containment may be a stage in a larger process of change in which an apparent 'personal' failure becomes a stage in a longer term success. In idealist culture individual failure or loss is always a kind of absolute failure or loss. But, by the same token, to accuse containment theory of being fatalistic, negative, and even cynical[4] may be to miss the point, since, some at least of those persuaded by it subscribe to a residual (philosophical) idealism that has lost its faith but not its criteria.

3. This brings me to a third objection, one which relates to each of the others, but is independently identified here because most important for my purposes: the containment theorist, like the radical humanist, overlooks the part played by contradiction and dislocation in the mutually reactive process of transgression and its control. The best way to elucidate contradiction and dislocation is through an account of what they both presuppose, and are in turn presupposed by, namely ideology.

Ideology, Dislocation, Contradiction

> It seems we have no other test of truth and reason than the example and pattern of the opinions and customs of the country we live in. *There* is always the perfect religion, the perfect government, the perfect and accomplished manner in all things. (Montaigne, 'Of Cannibals', *Essays*, ed. Frame, 152)

Ideology typically fixes meaning, naturalizing or eternalizing its prevailing forms by putting them beyond question, and thereby also effacing the contradictions and conflicts of the social domain.[5] Materialist cultural critique aims to contest ideology in this sense, and via several strategies. First, by restoring meanings to their histories, it tries to show how meaning is powerfully controlled; Marx's formulation of how ruling classes also rule ideas remains a valid point of departure. At the same time this critique shows the historical contingency of meaning but in a way which does not then imply the arbitrariness of meaning, if by that is meant that it can be simply, subjectively, or unilaterally altered. On the contrary, to recognize that meanings are historically grounded and partly or largely (but never entirely) controlled by powerful interests

---

[4] Ryan, *Shakespeare*, 8, and Lentricchia, *Ariel and the Police*, 99.

[5] To use ideology in this specific and limited sense does not assume the non-ideological to be a value-free scientific discourse. On the contrary, I adhere to this limited sense of the concept in order to indicate that a materialist criticism is always finally *also* an ethical perspective. So my usage precisely differs from that which would describe as ideological *any* system of values. Thus Sumner in *Reading Ideologies* defines ideology as 'the basic or simple elements (the ideas, images, impressions, notions etc) of any form of social consciousness' (20). To designate thus any affirmation of value to be as ideological as (e.g.) a position which seeks to naturalize or universalize its own authority is to rob the concept of ideology of its capacity to distinguish between these crucially different positions. Thus the view that homosexuals are naturally inferior to heterosexuals is (in my sense) ideological; the view that homosexuals are equal with heterosexuals, and deserving of equal rights in law is not, resting rather on an openly admitted ethical commitment to equality (from which the practice of a materialist/political criticism arises). For a philosophical defence of the limited notion of ideology adopted here see Bhaskar, *Scientific Realism and Human Emancipation*, ch. 2. Bhaskar sees as mistaken the development in Marxism which uses the concept of ideology 'positively' to express 'the values or world view of a particular social class (group or sometimes milieu)'. Bhaskar also rejects the extension of the concept 'to embrace the entire cultural sphere, understood as more or less mystificatory' (p. 242).

is also, usually, to show them incapable of easy alterations. Even so, there is rarely a ruling bloc which controls meaning uncontested. As well as being contested by other classes or groups, it will typically also be contested from within: conflict between ruling fractions is an important factor in change, and in the destabilization of ideology.

So the critique of ideology identifies the contingency of the social (it could always be otherwise), and its potential instability (ruling groups doubtly contested from without and within), but does not underestimate the difficulty of change (existing social arrangements are powerfully invested and are not easily made otherwise). The apparent need for propaganda bears out the first and second propositions, the brute force which both supplements propaganda and takes over when it fails, often successfully, bears out the third.

In highlighting the contingency of the social, the critique of ideology may also intensify its internal instabilities, doing so in part by disarticulating or disaligning existing ideological configurations. To borrow a now obsolete seventeenth-century word, the dislocation which the critique aims for is not so much an incoherence as a *dis*coherence—an incongruity verging on a meaningful contradiction.[6] In the process of being made to discohere, meanings are returned to circulation, thereby becoming the more vulnerable to appropriation, transformation, and reincorporation in new configurations. Such in part are the processes whereby the social is unmade and remade, disarticulated and rearticulated.

The critique whose objective is discoherence further seeks to reveal and maybe reactivate the contradictions which are effaced by ideology as an aspect of the control of meaning. I am using the term contradiction in its materialist sense to denote the way a social process develops according to an inner logic which simultaneously, or subsequently, helps effect its negation. Mass communication provides a commonplace example in the censorship which becomes, via the controversy it provokes, the publicist for what it seeks to repress.

Contradictions are manifested in and through representation, infecting its most elementary categories. An instance of this is the way binarism, that most static of structures, produces internal instabilities in and through the very categories it deploys *in order* to clarify, divide, and stabilize the world. Thus the opposition us/them produces the anomaly of the internal dissident. As we have seen with Wilde, and will do again in the discussion of Renaissance cross-dressing (Chapter 19),

---

[6] The *OED* cites Hooker from 1600: 'An opinion of discoherence . . . between the justice of God and the state of men in this world.'

binarism affords the opportunity for transgression *in and of its own terms*; transgression is in part enabled by the very logic which would prevent it.

At a much wider level I draw on three classic paradigms of contradiction deriving from Hegel, Marx, and Freud; each paradigm has changed human history in the course of analysing it: Hegel's theory of the master/slave dialectic, Marx's theory of the fundamental contradiction between the forces and relations of production, and the Freudian proposition that the repressed returns via the mode of its repression. Each paradigm is different from the other two and, arguably, incompatible with them. However, with regard to subversion and transgression they have something in common.

In a revolutionary conjuncture contradictions may contribute to the disintegration of an existing order though only (usually) through terrible suffering, victimization, and struggle. That has to be said. In a non-revolutionary conjuncture contradictions render social process the site of contest, struggle, and change. And, again, suffering, victimization, and struggle. The contradictions which surface in times of crisis are especially revealing: they tell us that no matter how successful authority may be in its repressive strategies, there remains something potentially uncontrollable not only in authority's objects but in its enterprise, its rationale, and even its origin. In short: change, contest, and struggle are in part made possible by contradiction. But also suffering, victimization, and struggle.

Transgressive Knowledge

The surfacing of contradictions is enabled by and contributes to transgressive or dissident knowledge. I propose this as a category additional to those of resistance and subversion and one which might modify the way we use them. The suspicious thing about the concepts of subversion and resistance, at least as they are sometimes used in critical theory, is that they tend always to turn up where we want to find them, and never where we do not—i.e. in relation to ourselves.[7] Also, the very search for subversion sometimes presupposes a view of history as in perpetual crisis, so inherently unstable that the least resistance has instant revolutionary potential. In fact, we should never expect transgression or subversion miraculously to change the social order. If transgression subverts, it is less in terms of immediate undermining or immediate gains, than in terms of the dangerous knowledge

---

[7] In Greenblatt's famous adaptation of Kafka, 'There is subversion, no end of subversion, only not for us' ('Invisible Bullets', 46).

it brings with it, or produces, or which is produced *in and by* its containment in the cultural sphere. This is the transgression that this study explores: the kind which seizes upon and exploits contradictions and which, as a political act, inspires recognition first, that the injustices of the existing social order are not inevitable—that they are, in other words, contingent and not eternal; second, that injustice is only overcome by a radical transformation of the conditions that produce and sustain it; third, that all such transformations are at the cost of destructive struggle.

Thus in the case of Elizabethan and Jacobean drama (one of the principal areas to which containment theory has been applied), my own view is that it contributes not a vision of political freedom, but a searching knowledge of political domination. That knowledge is often incomplete, sometimes confused yet always dangerous. But one simply cannot slide from the dangerous knowledge to political vision, or instantly produce the second from the first. This knowledge *was* challenging: working culturally, it subverted, interrogated, and disarticulated dominant ideologies, helping to precipitate them into discoherence and crisis. But history tells us time and again that from such crisis there may emerge not freedom but brutal repression. And such repression emerges not because the subversive was only ever contained—a ruse of power to consolidate itself—but because the challenge really *was* subversive.

The dangerous knowledge produced by and in relation to transgression must include awareness of that always present, always potentially tragic dialectic between authority and resistance whereby instability becomes a force of repression much more than a force of liberation; dominant social formations can and do reconstitute themselves around the selfsame contradictions that destabilize them, and change can also thereby become an impetus for reaction.

Theories of containment become somewhat more persuasive when we recognize that, like resistance, it too may work dialectically—through, for instance, the displacement of social crisis, generated within and by the dominant, onto the subordinate. Displacement often involves the demonizing of relatively powerless minorities, although it may be misleading to isolate this process from others. In abstraction there are at least three ways whereby the dominant identifies the subordinate (or the deviant) as threatening 'other'. The first is paranoid: the threat is imagined only; in actuality the subordinate is relatively powerless and unthreatening. The second is subversive: the threat is actually or potentially dangerous. The third involves the displacement of crisis and anxiety etc. onto the deviant. In practice some of these will typically coexist, e.g. the first with the third, or the second with the third.

The process of displacement/demonizing can never be assured of success, because it is usually a consequence of some kind of instability in the dominant (perhaps the consequence of another, effective, challenge—the second above), and because here too the demonized must be given a voice, one which can be subsequently inhabited or appropriated subversively (the second is thereby fashioned out of the third). But what stacks the odds in favour of displacement succeeding is the brute fact of the minority's relative powerlessness and probable disrepute. Also of course the struggle is usually in and for representation, especially of *how* instability is represented, and those who control the means of representation have more than a head start. The power of domination is also the power to fashion, apparently rationally but usually violently, the more 'truthful' narrative.

None of this should surprise us; and to point it out is not fatalistic. Indeed it takes us back to the possibilities of resistance as already outlined: since power is dependent upon (though not reducible to) control of representation, to destabilize representation *is* potentially subversive. but this kind of resistance, like any other kind, rarely, if ever, instantly disempowers controlling interests; often it provokes them into reaction; and what then follows is by definition a contest between unequally matched contenders. Established power structures often prove resilient even, or specially, when destabilized. It is *de rigueur* for critics of containment theory to insist that there are always spaces and contradictions for resistance. So there are, but in saying so we would do well to remember the costs of subversion. It is too easy to appropriate the resistance of others for optimistic theoretical narratives of our own, while leaving behind the fuller histories that would complicate those narratives.

In summary then, we have to reckon not only with conflict and contradictions, but with the disavowals and displacements by which they may be reconstituted as, and in, new forces of repression. Tyranny endlessly provokes social disruption within those it subordinates, intentionally or not. That disruption is often marked by a potentially explosive combination of dangerous knowledge, political discontent, and legitimate claim. Equally certain however is that tyranny relegitimates itself in the eyes of some or many precisely by suppressing the discontent it provokes. It deploys its 'superior' forces in the name of law and order; in other words it is a suppression working simultaneously in terms of brute force and intense ideological work at the level of representation. At the same time or separately, tyranny typically displaces crises generated within the dominant (for example between competing factions) onto the subordinate, whose control and extra-repression again serves to relegitimate and sometimes reintegrate the dominant. It is these aspects of the subversion/containment dialectic which seem to me to require analysis; the next chapter considers them in the context of some specific histories. The first two indicate the significance of the histories of sexual dissidence to the subversion/containment dialectic, while the third suggests a connection (via Genet) between this and other kinds of dissidence.

7 Tragedy and Containment

Progress into Reaction

The history of homosexual liberation in Germany is revealing of that fearful dialectic whereby a responsibly progressive development feeds its reactionary counterpart, partially as a consequence of initially gaining ground against it. As Richard Plant observes, the German homosexual rights movement enjoyed its greatest influence 'at precisely the moment that the larger society whose prejudices it sought to change began to spin out of control', and the attacks on Magnus Hirschfeld, its leader, anticipated what was to follow once Hitler consolidated his rule (*Pink Triangle*, 22, 28). The relative success of an enlightened politics enabled its enemies, in a changed conjuncture, to gain ground by representing this progress as something else: decline, degeneration, corruption, anarchy. Such representations then served as purchase points for a reaction against the 'enemies' within and their counterparts without.

Hirschfeld was one of those in the late nineteenth and early twentieth centuries conducting a 'scientific' study of homosexuality, and arguing against its association with evil. As we have seen, it has become a commonplace of the history of sexuality that such work was part of a crucial shift from seeing homosexuality as evil to seeing it as a 'sickness' or congenital abnormality, or, in Hirschfeld's opinion, a third sex. While allaying some prejudices, the third sex thesis fuelled others:

Only after the Nazis had turned his lifework into ashes did [Hirschfeld] concede that, on the one hand, he had failed to prove that homosexuals were characterized by distinct and measurable biological and physiological qualities and that, on the other hand, he had unwittingly deepened popular prejudices by endowing male homosexuals with feminine characteristics. This had only served to confirm the prevailing assumption that because homosexuals were 'not really men', they were therefore inferior. (Plant, *Pink Triangle*, 34)

Hirschfeld had helped to make homosexuals into an identifiable minority—i.e. differentiated in virtue of their identity. The Nazis were not slow to exploit this (pp. 18–19, 30, 33–4). Hirschfeld's motto was 'justice through knowledge'. In practice his work was exploited to fuel the exact opposite of justice.

However, even if his theory, or indeed any other, were correct, this would not *necessarily* have prevented the consequence just described. Even the opposite view, namely that the homosexual identity is not given biologically, but socially constructed, is open to repressive deployment. Progressively, the constructionist argument is aimed against an older persecutory view that homosexuality is wicked and unnatural (against God and nature). But it can also be appropriated by the opponents of homosexual freedom if interpreted as evidence for a policy of sexual correction: if the homosexual has been socially 'made', he or she can be 'unmade'.

As we have seen, Freud moved in a different direction to Hirschfeld, emphasizing not so much the homosexual as different from, but rather as similar to, the heterosexual. He also refused to see homosexuality as an illness, let alone an evil, and several times insisted that many homosexuals are people of high cultural achievement making a valuable social contribution, who are quite conventional in every other aspect of their lives. But this move, like the difference theory of Hirschfeld, could also intensify rather than allay anxieties: the deviant is made uncomfortably like, indistinguishable from, and even, in individual cases, apparently better than ourselves.

Both views—homosexual as other/homosexual in invisible proximity—can be utilized in what Plant calls the 'homosexualizing of the enemy' (*Pink Triangle*, 15). He is referring to the propagandist representation, by their enemies, of Nazis and/or fascists as homosexual. This move typically has as its corollary the association of homosexuality with internal enemies. The Nazis' own deployment of this strategy is chillingly representative. Plant's summary of the reaction to Hirschfeld's attempts at reform in 1898 includes most of the main elements which the Nazis were later to exploit:

homosexuality corrupts a nation; it breaks the moral fiber of the citizens; it is un-Germanic; it is connected with dangerously corrosive left-wing and Jewish elements (this from the right), or it is typical of the dissolute aristocracy and high bourgeoisie (this from the left). Above all, the spread of homosexual behavior would lead to Germany's decline, just as it had always spearheaded the ruin of great empires. Such arguments, recycled . . . would later reappear in numerous Nazi directives. (p. 33)

Altman writing in 1982 supplies a useful larger retrospective: 'in this century totalitarian governments of both the right and the left have been excessively homophobic: in Nazi Germany homosexuals were sent to concentration camps; in Russia and China their existence is denied . . . in Argentina and Chile the present military governments have unleashed extremely crude antigay persecution; in Iran the fundamentalist regime of Khomeini has ordered homosexuals stoned to death' (*Homo-sexualization*, 109). Since Altman wrote this there has occurred, both in the United States and in Britain, a resurgence of homophobia, associated especially but not only with AIDS; even before AIDS a right wing backlash against homosexuality was apparent (see Altman, especially ch. 4, 'The Movement and its Enemies').

Given the mobile, unstable resilience across time of the prejudice, paranoia, and hatred which comprises the homophobia[1] described by Plant and Altman, and the way it is endlessly exploited and displaced into other kinds of antagonism, it is all the more necessary to remember the periods in which it has been successfully resisted or at least allayed. John Lauritsen and David Thorstad point out in their informative study of *The Early Homosexual Rights Movement*, that the Bolshevik government in Russia repudiated all laws against homosexual acts *per se* in December 1917. They quote (p. 64) Dr Grigorii Batkis who in *The Sexual Revolution in Russia* (1923) wrote that Soviet legislation '*declares the absolute non-interference of the state and society into sexual matters, so long as nobody is injured and no one's interests are encroached upon*' (emphasis original). Homosexuality and sodomy were to be treated the same as 'so called "natural" intercourse'. But, as in Germany, the progressive view was overridden or displaced in the process whereby the enemy is homosexualized: not only Stalinists, but others on the left were to develop a mythology in which homosexuality was seen as either the product of bourgeois decadence or fascist perversion. This produced the terrible irony, and a supreme instance of the recasting of victim as aggressor: when homosexuals were being murdered by the fascists, it could be said: 'eradicate the homosexual and fascism will disappear'.[2] The fascists reciprocated by branding any departure from their own ideologies of purity as 'sexual Bolshevism' (Lauritsen and Thorstad, *Homosexual Rights*, 64, 68).

No less important than the containment which involves the demonizing of minority groups, and the turning of progress into reaction, is the containment which destroys difference through a coerced conformity masquerading as voluntary submission. I address this in the next two sections, each of which involves prison writing.

---

[1] This term is elucidated in Ch. 16 below.

[2] Gorky's alleged description of a German slogan, cited by Reich, *The Sexual Revolution*, 210. Vindictive representations of AIDS similarly convey homosexuals, one group most affected by AIDS, as also wanting 'nothing more intensely than to see it spread unchecked. In other words, those being killed are killers' (Bersani, 'Is the Rectum a Grave', 211; cf. Watney, *Policing Desire*, 82).

The Art of Expiation: Wilde in Prison

Experience of suffering in the present may turn us towards the past, maybe to discover something forgotten which contributed towards our suffering, or because every present defeat has a history of other past defeats. But it is exactly then, when the past is potentially most informative in relation to a present vulnerability, that our relation to it runs the risk of becoming most conservative: we find in the past an explanation of the present which is also a comforting deception. Often it comes in the form of 'tradition', wherein we rediscover the eternal verities, and fatalistically accept the recurrence of the past as the only kind of future, possibly the best kind of future.

Tradition thereby becomes a rationalization of a painfully inadequate present, and maybe even of defeat in the present. The repressions inherent in the very notion of tradition must be recognized and confronted.

Oscar Wilde's *De Profundis*, written in prison, involves a conscious renunciation of his transgressive aesthetic and a reaffirmation of tradition as focused in the depth model of identity. This is a work which registers many things, not least Wilde's courage and his despair during imprisonment. It also shows how he responded to the unendurable by investing suffering with meaning, and this within a confessional narrative whose aim is a deepened self-awareness: 'I could not bear [my sufferings] to be without meaning. Now I find hidden somewhere away in my nature something that tells me that nothing in the whole world is meaningless . . . that something . . . is Humility.' Such knowledge and such humility are achieved through deep renunciation; in effect Wilde repositions himself as the authentic, sincere subject which hitherto he had subverted: 'the supreme vice is shallowness', he says in this work, and he says it more than once. And later: 'The moment of repentance is the moment of initiation' (Wilde, *Letters*, 467, 425, 487).

This may be seen as that suffering into truth, that redemptive knowledge pointing to the transcendent realization of self beyond the social, so cherished within idealist culture. Those who see *De Profundis* as Wilde's most mature work, and equate maturity with renunciation and expiation, often interpret it thus. It can be regarded differently, as a containment, a tragic defeat of the kind which only ideological coercion, reinforced by overt brutality, can effect. Atonement, expiation, and renunciation—along with their 'natural' medium, confession—are experienced as voluntary and self-confirming but they are in truth massively coerced through incarceration and suffering. They involve a response to suffering which has profoundly religious antecedents: Wilde survives by rescuing an imaginary spiritual autonomy from a situation which affords no actual autonomy. What Wilde says here of the law is true also of his new relationship to the culture he had hitherto transgressed: 'I found myself . . . constrained to appeal to the very things against which I had always protested' (*Letters*, 492–3).

I mentioned earlier Wilde's remark in 1898 that 'something is killed in me'; prison had, he said, destroyed him body and soul. Commenting on *De Profundis*, Gide remarked that 'Society knows quite well how to go about it when it wants to dispose of a man, and knows means subtler than death . . . For two years Wilde had suffered too much and too passively. His will had been broken . . . Nothing remained in his shattered life but the mournful musty odour of what he had once been' (*Oscar Wilde*, 42).

Ellmann believed that Gide never acknowledged the full extent of his debt to Wilde, and remarked also Gide's tendency to belittle Wilde as a writer.[3] It has also been suggested that Gide exaggerated the extent of Wilde's deterioration as a result of his prison experience (Gide, *Oscar Wilde*, 45). Harsh as it is, and for whatever motives, Gide's critique of *De Profundis* is to the point. He sees it as 'the sobbing of a wounded man', and Wilde's affirmation of humility as a rationalization of the only retreat left to him. And it is a retreat covered over 'with all the sophistries he can muster'. In short, '*humility* was only a pompous name that he gave to his impotence' (*Oscar Wilde*, 50–3). But there is more to Wilde's prison experience than Gide allowed. For one thing Wilde's new-found humility was, as he told Gide later, inseparable from a pity for others which also kept him from killing himself. Both the humility and the pity were a continuation of Wilde's long-standing attraction towards the figure of Christ, most obviously in his view of Christ as the supreme artist.

But in prison the conception had changed. Some of Wilde's earlier remarks about Christ suggested what might just have been the most daring of all transgressive reinscriptions—an oppositional Christ for our own time who would blast the pieties of the conservatively religious into kingdom come and rescue Christ from his adherents.[4] Wilde used to tell several wonderfully heretical parables; Gide and W. B. Yeats, among others, recorded them. Yeats recollects Wilde telling him one day that he had been inventing a Christian heresy:

---

[3] Ellmann, *Oscar Wilde: Critical Essays*, 4; see also Ellmann's 'Corydon and Ménalque', 84–5, 90, and *passim*, and his 1987 biography, *Oscar Wilde*, 336–41.

[4] Interestingly Gide, shortly after his encounter with Wilde in Algiers, contemplated something similar—a book called *Christianisme contre le Christ*.

he told a detailed story, in the style of some early Father, of how Christ recovered after the Crucifixion, and escaping from the tomb, lived on for many years, the one man upon earth who knew the falsehood of Christianity. Once Saint Paul visited his town and he alone in the carpenters' quarter did not go to hear him preach. Henceforth the other carpenters noticed that, for some unknown reason, he kept his hands covered. (*Autobiographies*, 136–7)

What *De Profundis* offers is no such transgressive appropriation but a tame accommodation of self to Christian humility or, as Gide described it, an enforced retreat into it. Gide also said that it was the only retreat left to Wilde. This raises a profound question about the nature of tradition.

In *Discipline and Punish*, a book which he describes as a 'correlative history of the modern soul', Foucault speaks of a crucial change taking place in Western culture towards punishment:

The expiation that once rained down upon the body must be replaced by a punishment that acts in depth on the heart, the thoughts, the will, the inclinations. Mably formulated the principle once and for all: 'Punishment, if I may put it, should strike the soul rather than the body' . . . A new character came on the scene, masked. It was the end of a certain kind of tragedy: comedy began, with shadow play, faceless voices, impalpable entities. (pp. 23, 16–17)

The distinction between physical coercion and 'punishment which acts in depth upon the heart' is an important one, and might seem especially applicable to Wilde as I am interpreting his imprisonment: an incarceration which coerces the subject into expiation. But in Wilde's case it is not so much that incarceration is supplemented with some more insidious targeting of his soul by penal authority—clearly, and amusingly, access to the prison chaplain and the Bible did not count as such;[5] rather, Wilde brings with him the cultural history which will facilitate his spiritual expiation, and he calls it Art. There is no actual penal targeting of *his* soul; it, or rather *the* soul, has already been massively targeted in the aesthetic and cultural traditions in which Wilde is steeped.

Foucault distinguishes between the soul of Christian theology, 'born in sin and subject to punishment', and the modern soul, 'born rather out of methods of punishment, supervision and constraint', creating a subject who is

---

[5] Wilde's encounters with prison chaplains make dismal, farcical reading. One chaplain suggested that Wilde ended up in prison because he had omitted to conduct morning prayers in his household; another, suspecting Wilde of masturbation, wrote to the authorities that 'perverse sexual practices are again getting the mastery over him'; to a third Wilde complained that he could not see the sky from his cell window. The chaplain replied that his mind should not 'dwell on the clouds, but on Him who is above the clouds'. Wilde called him a damned fool and threw him out of the cell (Ellmann, *Oscar Wilde*, 454, 464, 466–7).

already in himself the effect of a subjection much more profound than himself.
A 'soul' inhabits him and brings him to existence, which is itself a factor in the
mastery that power exercises over the body. The soul is the effect and
instrument of a political anatomy; the soul is the prison of the body.
(pp. 29–30, my emphasis).

I have suggested elsewhere how Foucault's 'modern soul' is already
anticipated in the early modern period, and in relation to Christianity.[6]
The case of Wilde further suggests how art, especially in so far as it
derives from that history, is also a constitutive element in the production
of a soul that is the prison of the body, producing its adherent as, in
Foucault's terms, an 'effect of a subjection much more profound than
himself'.

My account of Wilde's renunciation of his transgressive aesthetic is
not reproachful, and not only because I cannot even conceive of a
reproach which, given Wilde's prison experience, would not be crass. I
am concerned rather with the ways that art itself, like religion, is source
of both liberation and containment, of both Wilde's transgressive
aesthetic and its renunciation. Wilde's imprisonment painfully exemplifies the proposition of Frankfurt School theorists like Theodor Adorno,
as paraphrased by Martin Jay in an allusion to Marx which rightly
connects religion and art: Jay refers to 'the inherently ambiguous nature
of high-culture', at once 'a false consolation for real suffering and an
embattled refuge of the utopian hopes for overcoming that very misery'
('Hierarchy and the Humanities', 133). It leads me to speculate that,
had Wilde escaped incarceration and turned his transgressive aesthetic
on Christianity, and created his oppositional Christ, it might just have
been not the supreme instance of containment, not a fatal 'essentialist'
complicity, but his most radical work.

Soledad Brother

Also writing from prison, but some seventy years later and in an utterly
different context, George Jackson described powerfully the ways that
the desperate efforts to survive a violently exploitative society lead the
exploited into collaborative submission; the price of survival may be a
kind of death:

There are millions of blacks of my father's generation now living. They are all
products of a totally depressed environment. All of the males have lived all of
their lives in a terrible quandary; none were able to grasp that a morbid

---

[6] *Radical Tragedy*, pp. xlvi–xlviii.

economic deprivation, an outrageous and enormous abrasion, formed the basis of their character. (*Soledad Brother*, 210)

Other blacks 'embrace capitalism, the most unnatural and outstanding example of man against himself that history can offer' (pp. 206, 249). Jackson speaks too of the mother who tried to make a coward of him because she wanted him to survive, and did so by discouraging his violence, or by turning it inward (p. 249); of the father who had saved his body but at a terrible cost: 'no one can come through his ordeal without suffering the penalty of psychosis' (pp. 210–11). On one occasion when his father visited him in prison Jackson tried to force him to question the 'mental barricades' he had thrown up to protect himself; Jackson wanted to hurl his father 'through Fanon's revolutionary catharsis'. His father replied:

'Yes, but what can we do? There's too many of the bastards'. His eyes shaded over and his mind went into a total regression, a relapse back through time, space, pain, neglect, a thousand dreams deferred, broken promises, forgotten ambitions, back through the hundreds of renewed hopes shattered to a time when he was young, roaming the Louisiana countryside for something to eat. (pp. 211, 213)

An aspect of Jackson's militancy was an intransigent opposition to collaboration, the more exemplary for being based on a sensitive understanding of what drives people to it. His own opposition was hard won, retained in the face of terrible suffering, and eventually cost him his life; he was killed in prison the year after this was written. But his articulation of that intransigence, his translation of it into what Jean Genet, in his introduction to *Soledad Brother*, describes as 'both a weapon of liberation and a love poem' (p. 17) was an act of transgression *within* containment, and inseparable from the tragedy of containment. This was triply the case: first (economically so) in his recognition that 'we are a subsidiary subculture, a depressed area within the parent monstrosity' (p. 214). Second (culturally so) in his observation that it was his years in prison 'with the time and opportunity . . . for research and thought that motivated a desire to remold my character. I think that if I had been on the street from age eighteen to twenty-four, I would probably be a dope fiend or a small-stakes gambler, or a hump in the ground' (p. 203). Third (creatively so) in that his writing became a kind of transgressive reinscription, as Jean Genet, one of its most notorious practitioners, recognized in his introduction to Jackson's prison letters:

the prisoner must use the very language, the words, the syntax of his enemy, whereas he craves a separate language belonging only to his people. . . . It is perhaps a new source of anguish for the black man to realize that if he writes a masterpiece, it is his enemy's language ... which is enriched. ... He has then only one recourse: to accept this language but to corrupt it so skilfully that the white men are caught in his trap. To accept it in all its richness ... and to suffuse it with all his obsessions and all his hatred of the white man. That is a task. (*Soledad Brother*, 22)

PART 5

Perversion's Lost Histories

8 *Towards the Paradoxical Perverse and the Perverse Dynamic*

> What the paradox was to me in the sphere of thought, perversity became to me in the sphere of passion. (Oscar Wilde, *De Profundis*)
>
> [Paradox] is an extension of the normal language of poetry, not a perversion of it. (Cleanth Brooks, *The Well Wrought Urn*)

Introduction

To explore the history of perversion is to see how culture is not only formed, but consolidated, destabilized, and reformed. It is a violent history: perversion is a concept that takes us to the heart of a fierce dialectic between domination and deviation, law and desire, transgression and conformity; a dialectic working through repression, demonizing, displacement, and struggle.

This is not a history of perversion as understood in the modern discourses of sexology and psychoanalysis; however, I show how the pre-sexual history of the concept inheres in modern beliefs about sexual perversion, and with the objective of replacing the pathological concept with a political one. Perversion was (and remains) a concept bound up with insurrection. More generally, and in the light of that history, I want to recover perversion as not only a culturally central phenomenon, but a category from which two concepts emerge that are crucial for insurrectionary critique: the perverse dynamic and transgressive reinscription.

Such an account of perversion is glaringly absent where one might most expect to find it: in, for example, those contemporary forms of psychoanalysis which claim a radical or at least a progressive politics, or in literary and cultural theory. It is also absent, though here predictably so, in literary criticism. So far as most critics are concerned, the crucial part played by perversion in literature is either unperceived, ignored, or disavowed (seen to be not seen), or recognized just sufficiently to make its overcoming one criterion of great literature. Thus my two opening epigraphs: the first voices one of my main themes— the connection between perversity and paradox (the paradoxical perverse); the second is a disavowal of that connection. It should come as no surprise that the first was made by a literary theorist largely ignored by twentieth-century literary critics, the second by one of the more influential such critics.

What is perversion? It is a concept involving:

(1) an erring, straying, deviation, or being diverted from
(2) a path, destiny, or objective which is
(3) understood as natural or right—usually right because natural (with the natural possibly having a yet higher legitimation in divine law).

But why should the prima-facie innocent activity of divergence or departure be so abhorrent? Why, for example, in this, the first *OED* definition of 'perverse', is there the rapid slippage from divergence to evil: 'turned away from the right way or from what is right or good; perverted, wicked'? (This slippage is very old: compare a typical dictionary definition of the Latin *perversus*: 'turned the wrong way, not right'.) Why, relatedly, should a departure from something also be construed as a contradiction or subversion of it? Even the apparently more neutral notion of 'wandering' can be charged with a terrifying negativity, and its representation includes a long and violent history; in our own time it has been most violently active in the way the Christian legend of the forever wandering Jew was reactivated in Nazi anti-Semitism, figuring notoriously in the film *Der ewige Jude* (1940), which, in the words of the film's commentary, compares 'the Jewish wanderings through history' with 'the mass migrations of an equally restless animal, the rat' (cited from Welch, *Propaganda*, 295).

We do not find the explicitly sexual sense of perversion in the *OED* until its 1933 Supplement, and then only cautiously.[1] However, it is the sexual sense of the word that predominates now and, before recovering the history of the concept, I want to consider two important but opposed accounts of sexual perversion, those of Freud and Foucault respectively. Opposed as they are, both nevertheless identify perversion as culturally central.

---

[1] Even in the 1933 Supplement the 'pervert' is defined in a non-sexually specific way as 'one whose instincts have been perverted', although the single citation from a 1906 issue of the *Journal of Abnormal Psychology* makes the sexual sense clear, and normatively so, with reference to 'the most abandoned sexual perverts'. By the time of the 1982 Supplement the psychoanalytic and normative emphases are paramount.

Of the earlier definitions of perversion, one especially is related to the later sexological/psychoanalytic senses; this is the medical meaning which defined perversion as 'one of the four modifications of function in disease' (1842). In the nineteenth century, as Arnold Davidson observes, the sexual instinct was conceptualized primarily in terms of reproductive function, with the perversions being understood as a deviation from or a disregard of that function. Ironically, it was Freud who did most to undermine the functional account of the sexual instinct, with the consequence that, strictly speaking, the concept of perversion no longer made sense (Davidson, 'How to Do the History of Psychoanalysis', esp. 259–77).

The Perverse Centre: Freud versus Foucault

Writing at the beginning of this century, Freud argued that there is actually a sense in which perversion might be pre-cultural or *before* civilization: the infant begins life in a state of polymorphous perversity, and, to the extent that unsublimated perversion is incompatible with civilization, it might even be said to be *beyond* civilization if and when the conflict between the two is resolved in the favour of the former. But Freud also identified perversion as being, or remaining, at the very centre of civilization. Polymorphous perversity is fundamentally incompatible with the demands of civilization and, most importantly, incompatible with sexual difference—itself a central principle of social organization. So in growing to adulthood, and thereby becoming positioned within sexual difference—masculine or feminine, with each of these governed by a prescriptive heterosexuality—perverse desire is not eliminated but transformed, via repression and sublimation, into other kinds of energy which civilization then draws upon—indeed depends upon.

In their sublimated form especially, the sexual instincts place 'extraordinarily large amounts of force at the disposal of civilized activity', and this because they are able to exchange their original aims (sexual) for other ones (social) without their intensity being diminished (viii. 84; xii. 39, 41[2]). The clear implication is that civilization actually depends upon what is usually thought to be incompatible with it (perversion), a proposition which has been strangely shunned inside psychoanalysis and even more outside it. At its worst psychoanalysis has pathologized and even demonized the pervert, especially as incarnated as the homosexual, in ways exhaustively summarized in Kenneth Lewes's recent study.[3] Indeed, it is ironically revealing that this idea of perversion as integral to culture is today associated not so much with Freud's most influential psychoanalytic successors, but with one of their most influential critics, Michel Foucault.

For Foucault also, perversion is endemic to modern society, though not in the Freudian sublimated form, and not because of a process of desublimation or some other kind of breakdown in the mechanisms of repression. It is one of the main arguments of Foucault's *History of*

---

[2] As elsewhere, and unless otherwise indicated all quotations from Freud are from the volumes comprising *The Pelican Freud Library*.

[3] *The Psychoanalytic Theory of Male Homosexuality*; those Lewes cites include Edmund Bergler, 'the most important analytic theorist of homosexuality in the 1950s' (p. 15) who wrote: 'I have no bias against homosexuality ... [but] homosexuals are essentially disagreeable people ... [displaying] a mixture of superciliousness, false aggression, and whimpering ... subservient when confronted with a stronger person, merciless when in power, unscrupulous about trampling on a weaker person' (cited ibid. 15).

Sexuality that perversion is not repressed at all; rather, our culture actively produces it. We are living through what he calls, in a chapter heading, the 'perverse implantation'. Perversion is the product and the vehicle of power, a construction which enables it to gain a purchase within the realm of the psychosexual: authority legitimates itself by fastening upon discursively constructed, sexually perverse identities of its own making.

So Freud's and Foucault's respective theories of perversion are quite different, and, in important senses, opposed. In the one case (Freud) society requires both the repression of perversion, and the reconstitution of its energy in a sublimated form; in the other (Foucault) perversion is not so much a repressed, transformed, and redeployed energy as a construct enabling social organization and control. Nevertheless, Freud and Foucault share a conviction that perversion is not only central to culture, but indispensably so given culture's present organization. It is to make this point about its centrality, and this point alone, that I have cited these two writers at the outset, and not because my project requires that I begin by adjudicating between them. (I return to both in Part 6 below.) In fact I want to proceed by going backwards to early modern England, and do so because I do not think we can adequately assess either the psychoanalytic theory of perversion, or its Foucauldian critique, until we have recovered the complex and revealing history of perversion in some of it pre-Freudian meanings, including its non-sexual meanings. I also go back to early modern England because, far from wanting to psychoanalyse it, I want to use that period, first, to help historicize psychoanalysis, second, to displace a pathological notion of the perverse with a political one, and third, to assist in a larger project of using psychoanalysis against its own most conservative advocates.

The Wiser, the Waywarder

> In the extreme, life is what is capable of error . . . error is at the root of what makes human thought and its history.[4]

I asked earlier why an erring/deviation from something should be construed as a contradiction or subversion of it. One answer might be that straying is the original (if unintended) act of demystification, one which reveals the coercive 'nature' of the prescribed path, the straight and narrow. The path we thought we were on naturally, or by choice, we are in fact on by arrangement, and in straying we discover alternative ways to alternative futures; we might also discover that what kept us to

---

[4] Michel Foucault, intro. to Canguilhem, *The Normal and the Pathological*, 22.

the straight and narrow was its mystified status as the 'natural or right' way (*OED*)—in a word, destiny. Further, if and when authority forces us back into line it becomes apparent that power rather than nature regulates the order of things; in the 'fact' of a natural destiny is discerned a process of subordination. And subordination becomes social subjection precisely because the norms of nature and destiny are internalized subjectively, as an identity as well as a future. At those moments when coercion reveals destiny as subjection, authoritarianism produces the conditions for its own delegitimation (which it typically seeks to counter with further repression), and erring may become a kind of knowledge: 'The wiser, the waywarder', observes Rosalind in *As You Like It* (IV. i. 143); 'then are we in order when we are most out of order', declares Cade in 2 *Henry VI* (IV. ii. 184–5). This is the knowledge of transgressive reinscription.

The error of perversion is never exactly innocent, since the truth it discovers is against nature, a fall into knowledge incompatible with innocence. In 1968 there were those who said: pull up the paving stones and find the beach beneath. But some years before Roland Barthes had said: scratch nature and find history beneath (*Mythologies*, 101). Barthes also said (in different words): pervert nature, and discover liberating differences. That was, and remains, a utopian dream: in reality, pervert nature, if only by straying, and those in charge will pull you in. Even so, straying may produce a glimpse of difference, one which remains with the stray, even as he or she is coerced back to the straight and narrow. And if so, this is not a dream based on the recovery of nature, the beach beneath the stones, but a 'seeing through' nature. After such knowledge there can be little forgiveness and even less innocence. And yet, paradoxically, it is another facet of the perverse that its connection with prelapsarian innocence is never entirely eradicated. Shakespeare's Caliban is the monster with a residual innocence, exemplifying a transgressive knowledge or utopian vision of a world which gives delight *and does not hurt*.

Perhaps this is why, prior to Freud, who recovered and insisted on the innocence of perversion, the dominant definitions of the perverse eradicate any suggestion of innocence. A nineteenth-century edition of Webster's dictionary, distinguishing the 'froward' from the perverse, quotes Crabb: '*perversity* lies deeper; taking root in the heart, it assumes the shape of malignity; a *perverse* temper is really wicked; it likes or dislikes by the rule of contradiction to another's will.' That this account of the perverse is omitted from later editions of this dictionary is just one indication of the way the concept has narrowed in meaning. I return to this in the discussion of Freud, invoking Crabb's definition here because it strikingly accords with the identity attributed to Caliban, by Miranda and Prospero, in *The Tempest*. It also shows how, before the later development identified by Foucault, whereby the pervert becomes a type of person defined by their sexuality, he or she could be a personality type of a different kind, possibly thought of in terms of aberrant sexuality, but more importantly one disposed to evil in terms of perversity contradiction; this again is how Caliban appears in *The Tempest*. We might see also, in this reference to contradiction, a precursor of something else which occurs more dramatically in the later period, and especially in relation to the emergence of the sexual meanings of perversion: contradiction telescoped into, contained within, subjectivity. Extravagant as the claim may seem, this definition of perversion anticipates the dialectic principle of contradiction. This is something else I shall return to.

Nature, Perversion, and Slaves

> A nature can never be made to change; what has been once formed in it cannot be reformed by any sort of change. Change does not involve the nature itself; it necessarily modifies, but does not transform the structure. (Clement of Alexandria, *Christ the Educator*, 165)

In Shakespeare's *Henry V*, Henry's power is said to be rooted in nature—blood, lineage, and breeding: 'The blood and courage that renownèd them | Runs in your veins' (I. ii. 118–19). But it is a power also deriving ultimately from God's law as it is encoded in nature and, by extension, society: France belongs to him 'by gift of heaven, | By law of nature and of nations' (II. iv. 79–80). Conversely, the French king's power is construed in terms of 'borrowed glories', 'custom' and 'mettle . . . bred out' (II. iv. 79, 83; III. v. 29). Through this theory of a descending legitimation of law, from the divine through the natural into the social, responsibility for aggression is displaced onto its victims. Thus war and chauvinism find their rationale, injustice its justification. In the early modern period nature, especially in the form of natural law, performed this crucial bridging function between the divine and the social not only with respect to affairs of state, but the family and class structure. And then, as we will see in the next chapter, doubly so across state, family, and class in terms of gender relations.

Perversion and deviation characterized those who contradicted nature. The fallen, says Milton, 'pervert pure nature's healthful rules | To loathsome sickness' (*Paradise Lost*, XI. 523–4). Put another way, the binary opposition between nature and the unnatural is literally what makes perversion and deviation conceivable, both as demonized categories, and as forms of cultural resistance. But we need also to remember that it takes diverse, historically specific, and variously unstable forms. Francis Bacon writing in 1622 nicely illustrates the connections between nature, power, hierarchy, perversion, and resistance as then conceived: 'for these cases, of women to govern men, sons the fathers, slaves freemen, are . . . total violations and perversions of the laws of nature and nations' ('Advertisement', 33–4). Binary opposites, as Derrida has argued and Bacon here exemplifies, are violent hierarchies. The natural/unnatural opposition has been one of the most fundamental of all binaries, and one of the most violent of all hierarchies. Note how, in the Bacon passage above, the violence of the hierarchy is displaced, through the concepts of violation and perversion, onto its subordinate terms or subjects: sons, women, and slaves.

In *The Tempest* Act 1 scene ii, Caliban is summoned, but only in order to be denounced, and to have his enslavement justified, in a virulent speech by Miranda (which I shall quote shortly). Caliban replies with that memorable counter-accusation: 'You taught me language, and my profit on't | Is, I know how to curse' (362–3). A colonialist view of the play, taking its cue from Miranda, might reason that Caliban uses their language to curse because his is a nature not only incapable of nurture but, worse still, a nature that perverts nature; a nature that corrupts civilized language, even attempting (final obscenity) to rape the woman who taught it to him, and who is daughter of his master. An anti-colonialist viewpoint might argue the reverse: Caliban curses because his 'good nature' has been perverted by the corrupt language of an alien, invading culture.

There is a third possibility: Caliban curses as an effect of language itself. That is, he curses not because language is the transparent medium which allows him to express, and us to see, his essentially perverted nature; nor because a corrupted language perverts his essentially good nature; rather he curses in terms of a language which constructs him as potentially that kind of subject even as he learns it. In this sense he possesses no essential nature, perverted or true, but an identity partly formed in and by language—in this case the language of the colonizer. It is within and by that language that he is made or made able—created/coerced—to curse. The recognition of language as in this way constitutive of identity is quite clearly there, not only in Caliban's haunting reply to Miranda, but in her denunciation of him:

> I pitied thee,
> Took pains to make thee speak, taught thee each hour

> One thing or other. When thou didst not, savage,
> Know thine own meaning, but wouldst gabble like
> A thing most brutish, I endowed thy purposes
> With words that made them known.

(I. ii. 352–7)

Perhaps the most important thing about this passage is that of which it (or Miranda) is completely unaware: the possibility that Caliban already had a language. A different language, the language of the colonial subject, is perceived only as brutish gabbling. This blindness is a crucial factor in the imposition of the dominant language. From that language is fashioned the subordinate, unnatural identity which facilitates the process of domination and enslavement: though Caliban could learn, says Miranda, his nature would not take 'any print of goodness', having that in it which good natures could not abide to be with. Therefore he was 'Deservedly confined into this rock' (351–60). Miranda's language is saturated with the ideology of nature, as indeed are her most elementary perceptions and first encounters; that is why the language of the other is marked by a non-sense characteristic of the brute. The same ideology of nature facilitates the slippage in Miranda's speech from individual to race (Kermode glosses race as 'hereditary nature appertaining to the species'); it is Caliban's unnatural birth and 'vile race' (357), unredeemable and in absolute contrast to 'good natures', which condemn him to subjection.

Caliban disagrees of course: he reckons it is Prospero's need for a slave which has led to the present situation. But even without Caliban's testimony, we already have evidence enough from Prospero's account of his own deposition to doubt the colonialist's appeal to nature. We learn from it that civilized natures have also been 'unnaturally' disruptive. This is a commonplace of the drama. But Prospero's account of civilized disruption also suggests something else, less obvious and rather revealing: it is the inconsistency, contradiction even, in the appeal to nature. Prospero becomes preoccupied with study and it is just this activity—in one sense the quintessentially civilized pursuit—which awakens in his brother, Antonio, a culturally destructive and immoral (i.e. unnatural) ambition, and in strangely inverse proportions:

>   my trust
> Like a good parent, did beget of him
> A falsehood in its contrary as great
> As my trust was.

(I. ii. 93–6)

Initially Antonio is described as parasitic upon Prospero's good nature—'The ivy which had hid my princely trunk, | And sucked my verdure out on't' (86–7)—but this is not quite adequate to the paradox; Propero is closer to it when he describes his own investment in civilization as awakening 'in my false brother | . . . an evil nature' (92–3). So trust has begotten falsehood and the good natured begotten the evil natured. Miranda naturalizes the paradox ('Good wombs have borne bad sons'—1. ii. 119), but the play denaturalizes it, showing how the civilizing process not only fails to subdue disorder, but actively produces it: in addition to Antonio's earlier usurpation of Prospero's power, there is Antonio's and Sebastian's attempt on Alonso's life; then Stephano's and Trinculo's attempt, aided by Caliban, to get the island from Prospero, who of course got it from Caliban. As the paradox is politicized so we are led to a political question: why, given that civilization endlessly produces it own disruption, is it the unnatural Caliban whose attempted rape makes him unredeemable, incapable of nurture? Without at all wanting to minimize the hatefulness of attempted rape, we must ask by what criteria it is made the unredeemable crime of the savage, as if it were not primarily the recurrent crime of the civilized, especially in the role of colonizer. Just as the language of this play discloses the incipient terms of racism, so its representation of nature involves the racist construction of the colonial subject, and one of the primary displacements of colonial violence: the Jacobeans could not foresee the sexually violent history of colonization, but to know that rape was most often the crime of the dominant, of the master, they hardly needed to.

The Tempest suggests how binaries can be destabilized when individuals or groups whose authority is ideologically sanctioned by the dominant term (in this case nature) fight among themselves. Such conflict threatens to reproduce the binary *within* the dominant term: that which distinguished the rulers from others—from, for example, those who are naturally inferior and ruled (necessarily ruled because inferior)—is now used to distinguish rulers from each other in the struggle for ascendancy, which is also a struggle for legitimacy. But there also occurs a struggle for relegitimacy. In this connection we see that the perverse, unredeemable nature created for Caliban within language is more than a strategy for justifying his enslavement along lines I have just suggested; we can also discern in it a displacement of disorder from within the dominant onto the subordinate, achieved via a mapping of the natural/unnatural binary onto the dominant/subordinate hierarchy. Displacement figures significantly in the construction of the unnatural and the perverse. It also points to dangerous instability within the dominant culture, one for which the subordinate is made to pay over and over again, but which also marks the limits of the dominant's powers, and the possibility of its overthrow.

Critics usually miss the point. In a recent study with the promising title *Shakespeare, Politics and the State*, Robin Headlam Wells, discussing *The Tempest*, concludes: 'Shakespeare . . . had enough of the realist in him to recognise, like Machiavelli, that in an imperfect world where men like Antonio and Sebastian exist, there is an overwhelming need for powerful government' (p. 33). To which we might reply, not a little hysterically, *but Antonio and Sebastian are the government*. The latter is brother to the king of Naples, the former the usurping duke of Milan, brother to Prospero. And both are would-be murderers of the king of Naples, in order to advance themselves within the governing élite. To distinguish my notion of politics from Wells's, and in the service of a more adequate concept of Shakespeare's 'realism', as well as anticipating what follows, I formulate here a process intrinsic to domination and social order: an irruption within the dominant destabilizes the binary oppositions legitimating that order. The binary is then in part restabilized through renewed control of those signified by its inferior term, who are typically identified as inverting, perverting, or deviating from the prevailing order, and in the process have displaced onto them responsibility for the disruption occurring elsewhere. This is neatly anticipated in the opening scene of *The Tempest* where the royals not only curse and blame the lower orders for the impending storm—and recall it is 'really' caused by Prospero, one of them—but, in so doing, impede the latter's attempts to save the ship. There is quite a lot of history in that brief opening scene.

The theatre of early modern England provides numerous further instances of how disruption emerges from within the dominant or natural term of the binary—that is, from the very side which defines itself as the agency for excluding, and guaranteeing against, disruption. Consider the kind/unkind opposition as it recurs throughout Jacobean drama, often obsessively. The meanings of both words tend to be complex yet precise, especially in the ways they signify social and psychic instability. Thus unkindness is the perversion of kind, yet just as obviously it springs from kind; the unnatural springs from the natural, hence the then proverbial 'the nearer in kin the less in kindness'. And the *accusation* of unkindness, itself construed as unnatural deviation, is often a terrified disavowal of just that fact: 'his own unkindness | . . . turned her to foreign casualties' (*King Lear*, IV. iii. 43–5). And what, after all, is the source of conflict in the English history which Shakespeare dramatizes but these massive, internecine struggles between kind: not just members of the same state or class, but the very same family? No wonder that these three areas—state, class, and family—are what nature is endlessly called upon to underwrite ideologically. Such is the recurring and challenging insight of this drama: deviation and perversion are what the dominant defines itself against, yet simultaneously deviation and perversion emerge from within, are produced by and displaced from, the dominant. There occurs a 'splitting of the true'.

Recovering Nature

Literary critics of Shakespeare have sometimes celebrated the official Renaissance ideology of nature and even conceived it as applicable to our own time. More often, though, they have nostalgically rehearsed it as a lost ideal. Q. D. Leavis would seem to regard it as a lost ideal capable of recovery when she observes that in past ages

generations of country folk ... had a real social life ... a way of living that obeyed the natural rhythms and furnished them with genuine ... interests—country arts, traditional crafts and games and singing, not substitute or kill-time interests like listening to the radio and gramophone, looking through newspapers and magazines, watching films and commercial football, and the activities connected with motorcars and bicycles. (*Fiction and the Reading Public*, 209)

I do not take Leavis as representative of modern literary critics on nature, nor do I believe that her view of either the earlier or the modern period requires refutation; on the contrary it is the (now) unrepresentative aspects of Leavis's view which make it revealing of something more fundamental and, though in different forms, still prevalent: the way such descriptions tap the legitimating dimension of nature. For Leavis nature figures as that which informs a social existence which is at once integrated, unified, healthy, authentic, and meaningful, a 'real social life' with '*genuine* interests'. Who could ask for more?

Even those who would completely reject Leavis's benign view of nature *vis-à-vis* culture, seeing instead a deep antagonism between nature and culture, have still deployed the concept of nature in a way which legitimates particular cultural formations as inevitable or right. Writers as different and as far removed across history as Hobbes and Freud had one thing in common: the belief that culture involved a necessary control or repression of nature. As Freud puts it, 'the principal task of civilisation, its actual *raison d'être*, is to defend us against nature' (xii. 194). But for many within civilization something like the reverse is true: it is a matter of life and liberty that they be protected, or protect themselves, against civilization's normative deployment of nature, not just in its negative form (Hobbes, Freud) but its positive counterpart (Leavis). Ideologically speaking a benign nature can be as repressive as a hostile one.

Both forms prove notoriously difficult to dismantle. As we shall see, although Freud did much to deconstruct the ideology of nature, it survives within psychoanalysis and perniciously so, especially within its conservative forms, and with some sanction from Freud's own writing. This is just one measure of the tenacity of nature, something we should bear in mind when congratulating ourselves on how easily we see 'through' nature in Leavis, Hobbes, Freud, or whoever.

There is another reason, perhaps the most important of all, for reconsidering nature's history. We live in a time when our very survival would seem to require a return to nature, or at least to ecological awareness. Perry Anderson has predicted that in forthcoming decades the major challenge to Marxism as a critical theory will come from some form of naturalism. His account of the way that in Anglo-American cultures the emphasis on biological determinants of culture and human nature have traditionally been associated with the Right is much to the point: 'the nature in question is invariably at once aggressive and conservative, individualist yet inertial—a standing warning against radical experiment or revolutionary change' (*In the Tracks of Historical Materialism*, 81). Nature works as an ideological restriction on social choice. The Left has traditionally fought such ideas. But recently writers of either socialist or left-liberal persuasion have argued again for another kind of human nature—what Anderson calls a 'protective' rather than a 'restrictive' type. In the work of Noam Chomsky and Barrington Moore it involves the idea of 'natural autonomy or creativity in human beings'. Within Marxism Sebastiano Timpanaro has written about the biological limits of human life. Such notions have a rapidly increasing significance for ecological movements. For Anderson the new naturalism provokes a difficult question about the relation of nature, so conceived, to history. A similar question recurs over and again in sexual politics: what is the relation of biology to gender? In short, 'the relation between nature and history brings us to the long overdue moment of socialist morality. Marxism will not complete its vocation as a critical theory unless and until it can adequately meet it' (pp. 82–4). One would hope that such reconsiderations will include awareness of the way that Marxists, even when contesting conservative ideas of nature, have continued to condone conservative norms created by them, especially in the realm of sexuality.

If, in the process of 'recovering' nature, Marxism or any other political movement ignores the violence and ideological complexity of nature as a cultural concept, it will only recover a nature imbued with those ideologies which have helped provoke present crises. In short there is a danger that much reactionary thought will return on the backs of nature and of those who rightly recognize ecological politics as of the utmost urgency. Of course there are obvious and fundamental distinctions which can help prevent that—between human nature and the nature that is destroyed by human culture; between the ecological and the ideological conceptions of nature. But, as we shall see next, they are distinctions which the concept itself traditionally slides across and between.

Natural Contradictions

> Those people are wild, just as we call wild the fruits that Nature has produced by herself and in her normal course; whereas really it is those we have changed artificially and led astray from the common order, that we should rather call wild. (Montaigne, 'Of Cannibals', *Essays*, ed. Frame)

What can never be entirely eliminated from the concept of nature, because they remain ideologically necessary in certain contexts, are complexities verging on contradictions: nature as a state of pre-social innocence, and nature as a state of destructive bestiality; nature as essentially productive, abundant, fecund, even anarchic, and nature as that in the name of which repression, control, and discrimination occur. Because of such contradictions nature can be used to endorse that which it is ideologically required to repress. Thus Moll, the 'monstrous' and 'unnatural' transvestite heroine of *The Roaring Girl* (by Middleton and Dekker), is described as 'a creature . . . nature hath brought forth to mock the sex of woman' (1. ii. 125–34).

A further and related complexity marks the relationship of culture to nature. Culture is construed both as the (binary) opposite of nature, yet also 'rooted' in nature in the sense that it operates according to, or reflects, natural law; it is at once the antithesis of nature and its natural consequence. Montaigne nicely exploits this in the passage quoted at the start of this section. Redeploying the nature/culture distinction to defend those usually excluded from its domain, and vice versa, he neither exactly inverts the binary nor deconstructs it, but, on the basis on its inherent inconsistency (nature as both the antithesis of culture and its ratification) reverses the conventional position of those groups governed by it.

Such complexities accrue to nature as a necessary or inevitable consequence of its ideological configurations. As such they may be functional. But a functional complexity can become, or be ushered into, a disarticulating contradiction. Even then the situation is never one of simple breakdown. As we saw in Part 3, dominant ideologies may contain contradiction by incorporating it. But incorporation may also render control potentially precarious: enforced inclusion contains the ever-present possibility of violent eruption. Perversion reactivates these contradictions, by revealing the coerciveness of the normal, the arbitrariness of nature, the way both the normal and the natural can maintain regimes of truth only through a demonizing and disavowal, not just of the different but also of the same or the proximate; by revealing also how the celebration of a natural plenitude so easily becomes the fear of difference(s) and, in the face of enough difference(s), the fear of undifferentiation.

Deviation

The pervert deviates from 'the straight and narrow' or the 'straight and true'; even such trite commonplaces as these bear the trace of Western metaphysics, especially its crucial linking via metaphor, of the epistemological with the linear or teleological. If metaphysics survives anywhere it is here, in ordinary language. Its influence may be especially strong in the language of those who, like the robust literary critic, take pride in common sense, thinking of themselves as confidently beyond metaphysics. One of Derrida's contributions is to have shown the pervasiveness of metaphysical categories even or especially within the supposedly non-metaphysical. To understand the continuing influence of such categories, an influence which stems from their residual status—often remaining unrecognized because residual—it is helpful to return to the time of their explicit dominance, and to gain access by 'going through' the trite commonplaces in which they survive more or less unrecognized.

Somewhat over-schematically (and so provisionally) Western metaphysics can be represented in terms of three interrelated tenets: teleological development, essence, and universal, the last two being the source of essential and absolute truth respectively. One good reason for recovering the linguistic histories of perversion is because they have often constituted a transgression of normative and prescriptive teleologies, and the regimes of essential and absolute truth which those teleologies underwrite. Such transgression was especially feared in early modern England, an age obsessed with disordered and disordering movement—from planetary irregularity to social mobility, from the vagrant and masterless man roaming the state, to the womb which supposedly wandered within the body of the 'hysterical' woman. All such phenomena contradicted the principles of metaphysical fixity as formulated in those three main categories—essence, universal, and teleology—three categories which between them have profoundly 'fixed' the social order in Western culture. The charge of perversity was at once a demonizing and a disavowal of an aberrant movement that was seen to threaten the very basis of civilization; this is why time and again metaphysical fixity—fixed origin, nature, identity, development, and destiny—is invoked in the condemnation of such movement.

It is difficult to 'read' the culture of early modern Englsnd until we have understood the extent to which it was pervaded by these fears of aberrant movement, especially (to recall that *OED* definition) a perverse turning away from what is right or good. Such movement signalled all that threatened the desire for or fantasy of a future governed by organized, linear, controlled, and henceforth predictable movement, and for that reason alone aberrant movement was utterly evil and endlessly fascinating. That this was not the concern of the orthodox only can be seen from the briefest consideration of desire and power in any one of a number of Jacobean dramas. In Shakespeare's *Antony and Cleopatra*, Cleopatra's turning away from battle and Antony's following of her are self-destructive, literal deviations that change the course of history. Psychically, as the perverse movement of desire itself, they are refigured as Antony's 'most unnoble swerving' (III. xi. 50); his losing of his way forever and fleeing of himself (III. xi. 4–7); his adoring of his error/erring as he struts to his confusion (III. xiii. 114–15); his casting of Cleopatra as 'Tripple-turn'd whore' (IV. xii. 13); her casting of him as 'the greatest soldier of the world, | . . . turned the greatest liar' (I. iii. 38–9).

Rulers were especially susceptible to the fears of aberrant movement, and in diverse ways. One concerned language itself. As Patricia Parker points out, it is strange for a modern reader, used to believing in the profound separation of poetics and politics, to discover the connections made by Elizabethan rhetoricians between linguistic ambiguity and political insurrection. When Puttenham in his *Arte of English Poesie* refers to the way that, through ambiguous speech and prophecy 'many insurrections and rebellions have been stirred up in this Realme' (p. 260), it is as if evil is not only the opposite of good but perilously adjacent to it; evil inheres not only in the antithetical, but also in the adjacent, the alternative, and perhaps even the same. As Parker shows, other writers make similar connections between the proper discipline of words and social regulation, including Thomas Wilson in *The Rule of Reason* (1551). What is implied in this preoccupation is 'the possibility of an unsettling lack of control over language, as if the very instrument of civil order . . . were open to radical inversion, in the sense of a treachery potential within language itself, or in the subversive uses to which it could be put' (Parker, *Literary Fat Ladies*, 101; see also Barry Taylor, *Vagrant Writing*).

Fear of aberrant movement finds its counterpart in the affirmation of stasis as a metaphysical ideal. Human endeavour, governed by mundane laws of change, decay, and deviation, is ever thwarted in its aspiration, ever haunted by its loss of an absolute which can only be regained in transcendence, the move through death to eternal rest, to an ultimate unity inseparable from a full stasis, 'when no more *Change* shall be' and 'all shall rest eternally' (Spenser, *The Faerie Queene*, VII. ii). This metaphysical vision has its political uses, especially when aiding the process of subjection by encouraging renunciation of the material world and conceiving present suffering as the result of providence or fate, rather than contingent historical circumstance. We might call this the fatalist metaphysic because ultimately it sees movement as at once the stuff of life and what drives life to death. It also tends, with Augustine, to see evil as essentially aberrant movement (below, Chapter 9), and desire as a powerful manifestation of this. For Augustine, sexual arousal—literally the 'involuntary' movement of erection—epitomized fallen human nature out of control of itself. Man's first transgression was what brought death into the world; and since it was the movement of desire which led to that transgression, desire itself is intimately bound up with death (*City of God*, XIV. xvi–xvii).

But metaphysics, as a legitimating structure for human society, cannot rest with the perfection of stasis. To a degree it will convert the idea of stasis into notions of order, structure, and law, but these can never adequately organize the productive energies of society. Because movement itself has to receive a degree of metaphysical legitimation, there is always a need for what we might call an activist metaphysic as well as a fatalist metaphysic. A case in point is the honeybees speech in Shakespeare's *Henry V*, where human endeavour is not denigrated but harnessed in an imaginary unity quite different from that afforded by stasis: 'So may a thousand actions, once afoot | End in one purpose' (I. ii. 211–12). Unity still structures the endeavour because it is in accord with 'a rule in nature' (I. ii. 188). Here teleology takes over from stasis as the governing principle of the metaphysic. The main point is simply that movement is not only harnessed by a unified objective, but both the movement and the objective are regulated by a preordained design:

> Therefore doth heaven divide
> The state of man in divers functions,
> Setting endeavour in continual motion;
> To which is fixèd, as an aim or butt,
> Obedience.

> (1. ii. 183–7)

That this is spoken by the Archbishop of Canterbury as a religious justification of military invasion is much to the point. But what of the disobedient, the subjects of aberrant movement?

Masterless Men, Wayward Women, and Religious Rebels

In the sixteenth century, population growth and the commercialization of agriculture had helped to produce a redundant population of landless men and women. There was real alarm at the growth in unemployment, poverty, and crime. Vagrancy, A. L. Beier shows, became one of the most pressing social problems of the age; governments were terrified of it, reacted vigorously to suppress it, initiating major new developments in state control in the process. The masterless, without a fixed place, identity, or occupation, were perceived as a threat to the state and to social order. Social and economic dislocation was often refigured as the evil of aberrant movement. Beier remarks that it is difficult for us today to recover the meaning which attached to the masterless; today's equivalents 'might be anarchist, terrorist, or (in some western societies) communist' (*Masterless Men*, pp. xviiii, 3, 6, 12, 48). Supplementing actual legislation was what William Hunt has called 'a culture of discipline'—in effect a wider strategy of social and ideological control conceived in ethical and religious terms (Hunt, *The Puritan Moment*, esp. 58–9, 79).

Even more disturbing in certain respects than the masterless man was the masterless, wandering woman, perversely straying and inviting others to do the same. Writers take up the image of the wandering harlot with 'subtil' heart described in Proverbs 7: 'Now is she without, now in the streets, and lieth in wait at every corner . . . Let not thine heart decline to her ways, go not astray in her paths' (10, 12, 25).[5] Parker shows how the image of the wandering woman is implicated even in texts not specifically about her, and how, within this image, we can read 'anxieties about female sexuality . . . about its relation to

---

[5] 1 Tim. 5: 13–15 speaks of widows who 'learn to be idle, wandering about from house to house . . . speaking things which they ought not. . . . For some are already *turned aside* after Satan'. See further Bassler, 'The Widow's Tale: A Fresh Look at 1 Tim 5: 3–16'.

property, to the threat of the violation of this private place if it were to become a "common" place . . . rather than a particular property'. Privatized female sexuality is made a sign and seal of property itself (Parker, *Literary Fat Ladies*, 105–6).

Margaret Soltan has observed how the 'errant woman' also communicated a narrative of fall and conversion. If she refused conversion and social inclusion, 'her absolute isolation confirmed a separation between mayhem and order; while, if she accepted, her piety certified the process of purification . . . inscribed upon the body of the female vagabond was a foretold linear sequence of conversions back to culture'.[6] Soltan also remarks a later development whereby the errant woman came to be linked to 'the penetration of errancy into the heart of civilisation', especially through a connection with prostitution (pp. 109–10).

Although the 'modern' sexual pervert does not appear in the *OED*, the wayward woman figures prominently as one of the two kinds of pervert who recur in the original dictionary's numerous citations for the perverse and its cognate terms. The other is the religious heretic. At the start of the Christian narrative they went together. As Milton put it in *Paradise Lost*, justifying the ways of God to men, Satan created a perverted kingdom and Eve was his first convert. Or rather his first pervert, since 'He in the serpent . . . perverted Eve' (x. 3). In theological discourse perversion may describe the opposite of conversion, signifying that terrible, unforgivable deviation *from* the true faith to the false. It is this use which suggests the first of two central and related paradoxes of the perverse, and another reason why it is so despised and feared—namely that perversion has its origins in, or exists in an intimate relation with, that which it subverts. In one sense this is the case by definition: to err or stray from the right literally presupposes that one was once in the right place. But it goes deeper than that: in Burton's *Anatomy of Melancholy* (1621) it is not his discussion of what sexologists including Freud would later call the sexual perversions that produces the paradoxical sense of the word (though he does indeed discuss these), but his discussion of what might be thought to be their opposite. Quite near the beginning of the *Anatomy* he declares that it is not our bestial qualities that are potentially the most dangerous, but our civilized ones: 'Reason, art, [and] judgement', properly employed, much avail us, 'but if otherwise perverted, they ruin and confound us' (Partition 1, p. 136).

---

[6] Soltan, 'Night Errantry', 109–10. Soltan also remarks the gender distinctions of errancy: whereas female errancy typically involved a turning away or downward movement from innocence to corruption, male erring (as in knight-errant) might imply virtue, initiative, and courage. She connects this gender difference with the linguistic history of the concept: the Old French *errer* meaning to rove or wander, especially in search of adventure, and the identically spelled *errer* meaning to stray from what is right (p. 110).

The Paradoxical Perverse, Dialectic, and Rhetoric

> Every emission of speech is always, up to a certain point, under an
> inner necessity to err. (Lacan, *Seminar*, ii)

Doubtless we could nevertheless 'explain' Burton's contention in Freudian terms: the terrible transition from the quintessentially civilized to its
opposite is an undoing of civilization through desublimation. But even
if that were true, it might be less interesting than something else revealed
by this pre-sexological use of the concept: the shattering effect of
perversion is somehow related to the fact that its 'error' originates
internally to just those things it threatens.[7]

In the early modern period and throughout Western culture to the
present, this paradox recurs in different forms and in different contexts:
the most extreme threat to the true form of something comes not so
much from its absolute opposite or its direct negation, but in the form
of its perversion; somehow the perverse threat is inextricably rooted in
the true and the authentic, while being, in spite of (or rather because of)
that connection, also the utter contradiction of the true and authentic.
This connects with and partly explains another paradox of perversion:
it is very often perceived as at once utterly alien to what it threatens,
and yet, mysteriously inherent within it. Such paradoxes of the perverse,
along with others yet to be identified,[8] constitute what I shall call the
paradoxical perverse, while the perverse dynamic signifies the potential
of those paradoxes to destabilize, to provoke discoherence. Both the
paradoxical perverse and the perverse dynamic are categories with
obvious deconstructive potential—though they manifest not mere unde-
cidability, but a field of cultural representation and social struggle at
once brutally divided and violently implicated. In this respect they are
concepts which connect also with a dialectical perspective.

Dialectic comes from the Greek, where it could refer to the procedure
where an opponent in debate is led into contradiction. Whereas
perversion is a concept typically used to repress and disavow contradiction, the perverse dynamic, like the dialectic, reactivates it but via the

---

[7] It may also be because perversion can imply appropriation, a turning from which is also a taking with/
over; cf. another *OED* entry: 'diversion to an improper use'.

[8] Another paradox: the perversity may be not in the deviation, but the refusal to deviate:

DUKE. Still so cruel?
OLIVIA.   Still so constant, my lord.
DUKE. What, to perverseness? You uncivil lady . . .
                (*Twelfth Night*, V. i. 108–10)

Here the perversity is in adhering to the straight and narrow beyond the call of duty as defined by one's
gender 'superior'; perseverance in the good is so unrelenting that it becomes a perversion of the good—
which then of course begs the question 'whose good?' The subordinate adheres to the conventional ethic in
a way which disarticulates it.

proximate rather than the opponent. Consider Shylock's famous 'Hath not a Jew eyes . . .' speech in Shakespeare's *The Merchant of Venice* (III. i). It is often seen as an affirmation of man's common humanity. But it is also an instance of the perverse dynamic, disclosing not the reassuring static bedrock of common humanity but terrifyingly mobile proximities and interconnections between human diversity. When effaced by, in, and as the discrimination of Jew from Christian, these proximities facilitate the displacement and refiguring of Christian evil as Jewish evil. But these may also become a means of subverting the social order which produces and needs the discrimination: revenge is most effective not outside but inside the law; Shylock pushes the law to its own self-contradicting extreme, undermining the culture he hates with its own law—with, that is, what simultaneously locks him into, and differentiates him from (but only from because within) that culture:

If we are like you in the rest, we will resemble you in that . . . The villainy you teach me I will execute, and it shall go hard but I will better the instruction.

Shylock alerts us to the fact that the dominant does not like to be undone by its (alien) other. But it likes even less to be undone by its (uncanny) deviant. So it construes the latter as the former. Otherness may be rooted in a fear of, a disavowal of, similarity.

Dialectic is also used, again deriving from the Greek, to signify a permanent process of change and transformation. In materialist form this leads to a concern with how social change occurs through struggle, conflict, and interaction; new social formations emerge from the conflicts of the existing ones. One consequence of this is that, eventually, everything becomes what it was not. At the same time dialectical theory might conceptualize the social in terms of a unity. This is definitely not the metaphysical unity of idealism (stasis/harmony/transcendence) but the unity of antagonistic interdependence: groups or classes engaged in struggle are by that same fact violently and inextricably interrelated. The paradoxical perverse and the perverse dynamic disclose important dimensions of both social struggle and antagonistic (social) interdependence. However, the sense of dialectic which they exemplify must be yet further distinguished from two others, the first a facile sense in popular use, the second a more rigorous teleological sense surviving in Marxism. The facile use refers to any kind of conflict which has a vaguely constructive outcome; the more rigorous use is advanced by Roy Edgely: a process of social change is marked by intensified conflict; this leads to 'a moment of revolutionary change . . . that is a change of structure, the destruction of the existing order'; conflict is resolved through 'the victory of one of the sides, of that side, namely, which is needed by the oher but which does not in its turn need that other opposing side' ('Revolution, Reform and Dialectic', 26, 33). As we shall see, the perverse dynamic involves a different conception of the two crucial terms here, change and relationship.

The paradoxical perverse and the perverse dynamic also connect with what might be thought entirely antithetical to dialectics, namely rhetoric. Recently Patricia Parker has shown the relevance for political criticism of rhetorical forms, particularly tropes of reversal, insubordination, and inversion (Parker, *Literary Fat Ladies*, chs. 5 and 6). The use of such tropes, especially their ironic use, can question (for example) gender hierarchies and teleological legitimations of the social order. This also is an effect of the perverse dynamic, and it is worth remarking its similarity to certain rhetorical forms which Parker discusses, especially antimetabole, or as it is called by Puttenham in *The Arte of English Poesie*, 'The Counterexchange'. This identifies the effect produced when, according to one definition, 'two discrepant thoughts are so expressed by transposition that the latter follows from the former, although contradictory of it' (Parker, *Literary Fat Ladies*, 89). As an example in Shakespeare, Parker remarks that the antimetabolic utterances of Falstaff 'leave the trace of a whole unenacted countermovement within the teleology of the history he is cast out by' (p. 94).

Biblical Perversions

A use of perversion in a way which acknowledges its power to subvert internally through an originating, antithetical proximity can be found in a 1954 work of biblical exegesis where the perverse subject is once again female. Commenting on Athaliah's seizing of the throne of Judah in 2 Kings, we are told that 'a sermon might be preached, with her as the supreme example, on the perversion of grand human qualities to ignoble ends'. She was fearless with far-seeing intelligence and yet put these qualities in the service of evil. The text continues: 'We are here reminded that a high degree of intelligence and of native ability uncontrolled by morality is far more dangerous to the social order than ignorance and incapacity'; if this is the result of education, the commentary adds, it were better that such people were not educated in the first place (*The Interpreter's Bible*, iii. 245; compare Dryden as cited in Samuel Johnson's *Dictionary* (1755): 'To so perverse a sex all grace is vain | It gives them courage to offend again').

Predictably, there is significant scriptural precedent for this notion of perversion. In some of its numerous occurrences in the King James version the word is used quite generally, as more or less synonymous

with sin, evil, or wickedness. More specifically it denotes wilful wrong-
ness, the erring/error of men's ways, a transgression which is especially,
rather than ordinarily, indicative of wickedness. Further, it may suggest
a source of disobedience worryingly close to, or even indistinguishable
from, the source of obedience: 'a wicked *man* taketh a gift out of the
bosom to pervert the ways of judgment' (Proverbs 17: 23). In Acts 20:
29–30 the perverse is even more clearly conceived as an inherent form
of evil, a counterpart of external threat ('grievous wolves')—and the
more insidious for being an inner deviation: 'For I know this, that after
my departing shall grievous wolves enter in among you, not sparing the
flock. Also of your own selves shall men arise, speaking perverse things,
to draw away disciples after them.'

Each of these senses gets successively closer to the paradox of
perversion as internal deviation, and hence to its destabilizing dynamic.
They also suggest how the Christian theory of evil is essentially
implicated in perversion. Indeed, the Fall itself is the most dramatic
instance of the perverse dynamic. Or rather it contains the most
dramatic *trace* of that dynamic; in its official form the dynamic is
contained by that other crucial dimension of perversion noted earlier in
relation to Bacon, namely, displacement. John Hick finds in the Fall
narrative what he calls a central pillar of Christian doctrine: our first
parents 'by an inexplicably perverse misuse of their God-given freedom,
fell from grace, and . . . from this fall have proceeded all other evils that
we know' (Hick, *Evil and the God of Love*, 68). Crucially, evil not only
erupts from within a divinely ordained order, but, more telling still,
erupts from within the beings closest to God, those who most fully
participated in his divinity—first the angels, then 'man'—who pervert
their most divine attribute, free will, which then becomes the primary
or, as Augustine asserts, the source of all evil. In short, a negation/
deviation erupts from within that which it negates. Pursuing this
paradox we shall arrive at a point where original sin might be better
described as original perversity. And, as such, it might be viewed not as
the measure of man's depravity, but as the means whereby evil, so
subversively implicated in divinity, is displaced, via Satan, onto the
subordinate term of the God/man binary (man), and then further
displaced onto the subordinate term within the man/woman binary. In
political terms: proximity is a condition of displacement which in turn
marks the same as radically other. But first we need to recover other
nuances of the concept.

Political Perversions

The now obsolete definitions of perversion explicitly indicate its political dimension. For 'pervertible' the OED cites Davenant (1651): 'Armies, if they were not pervertible by Faction, yet are to Commonwealths like Kings Physitians to poor Patients'; and Bryce (1888), who declares that 'new immigrants [are] politically incompetent, and therefore easily pervertible'. Marvell in *Loyall Scott* writes that perversion increases dissensions, Milton in *Doctrine and Discipline of Divorce* of one who will 'divide against himself and pervert his own ends' (*Prose Works*, ii. 290). Milton also speaks of deputies and commissioners being 'perverted' by absolute power to 'injustice and partialitie' (iii. 199).[9] What such uses signify is the whole subverted and displaced by an illegitimate element (faction, immigrant) or attitude ('partialitie') which has become installed as an integral element (armies, deputies, commissioners).

I suggested earlier that there is one sense in which deviation, echoing the innocent sense of wandering, may affirm or at least indicate potential or actual differences which, for whatever reason (and there are several), are intolerable to a prevailing arrangement. But in Davenant's and Milton's usage a fiercer and more significant sense of perversion is suggested. This is where the perverse not only departs from, but actively contradicts the dominant in the act of deviating from it, and does so from within, and in terms of inversion, distortion, transformation, reversal, subversion. Part of the argument which follows is that perversion in this fiercer sense may also reveal potential and actual differences, but now as inherent aspects *of* the dominant or the conventional rather than what it would exclude or define itself against. The paradoxical perverse, activated by the perverse dynamic, reveals the potential for transformations inherent in all social orders as a consequence of their own structure and developmental logic; transformations which dominant factions seek to repress or disavow because contrary to their interests, and which are usually identified as external, or the internal counterparts of what is fundamentally external. So perversion is doubly insurgent—a threat from outside in, and from inside out (the OED offers both meanings for 'insurgent'): hence a surging with/within. The perverse is also precisely insubordinate, a disrupting from a below which is also integral to the above. This connects with a recurring ambiguity: often it remains unclear whether the erring which defines perversion is voluntary or coerced, a wilful straying or a being led

[9] Johnson cites Bacon: 'evil governours or tyrants . . . are often established as lawful potentates; but of some perverseness and defection in the very nation itself' (*Dictionary*).

astray. This ambiguity reflects not just the ever-present anxiety as to human agency (or lack of it), but also derives from the internal/external dimensions of perversion: at once utterly alien to, and yet mysteriously inherent within.

Milton and Perversion

Milton, under the influence of Augustine, provides important instances of the way the paradoxical nature of the perverse endangers the very metaphysic which employs it. He writes that sin is 'not . . . properly an action, for in reality it implies defect . . . For every act is in itself good; it is only its *irregularity, or deviation from the line of right*, which, properly speaking, is evil' (*Prose Works*, xv. 199, my emphasis). As we shall see with Augustine also, the idea of evil as deviation paradoxically implicates it more thoroughly with the good: 'We know good only by means of evil' (xv. 115), while 'that which purifies us is triall, and triall is by what is contrary' (*Prose Works*, ii. 515; cf. 527–8). Indicated here is the potentially punitive and paranoid dimension to the theory, the preoccupation with an evil other who might be invisibly within, and against whom therefore we must be ever vigilant. Certainly the theory offers every encouragement to such paranoia:

Good and evil we know in the field of this World grow up together almost inseparable; and the knowledge of good is so involv'd and interwoven with the knowledge of evill and in so many cunning resemblances hardly to be discern'd. . . . And perhaps this is that doom which *Adam* fell into of knowing good and evill, that is to say of knowing good by evill. (*Prose Works*, ii. 514; cf. *Commonplace Book*, i. 362).

Evil is absolutely and clearly contrary to good, yet in fallen practice barely distinguishable, or only arduously so, or perhaps not at all. Moreover, even if the good *is* made apparent by the contrast, it may, says Milton, simply fail to satisfy (*'non satisfaciunt'*, *Prose Works*, i. 363). But the chances are that it may not even achieve or maintain that contrastive superiority; instead of self-purification through confrontation, there may occur the definitively perverse transformation: 'It is not forgot, [that] the acute and distinct *Arminius* was perverted meerly by the perusing of a namelesse discours writt'n at *Delfi*, which at first he took in hand to confute' (*Prose Works*, ii. 519–20).

Just as trial 'purifies', Arminius seeks to confirm himself, through confrontation, as 'acute and distinct' in judgement, only to be undermined in and through that very act; attempted confutation succumbs to perversion. As Ernest Sirluck notes, 'Milton's own subsequent conversion to Arminianism . . . lends both force and irony here' (*Prose Works*, ii. 520). The context of this reference to Arminius (it is in *Areopagitica*) provides a further irony: Milton's argument here is that those who are most susceptible to subversive literature are not the ignorant but the learned, those very ones who, especially as censors, take it upon themselves to protect the nation from the ignorant, and the ignorant from themselves. Once subverted it is the learned who then seek to convert/pervert the ignorant; it is they who become the 'dispredders both of vice and error' (*Prose Works*, ii. 519–21). Again, perversion discloses subversion to be inherent within those who would police and suppress it.

Subtle conceptual links between error and erring are readily apparent in *Paradise Lost*. Arnold Stein has shown why, in the words of a recent editor, 'error' is 'one of the most resonant key words in the poem'. Stein writes of the brooks' movements at IV. 239 ('With mazy error under pendant shades'): 'Here, before the Fall, the word *error* argues, from its original meaning, for the order in irregularity, for the rightness in wandering . . .' (*Answerable Style*, 66).[10] It is not just the sophisticated linguistic encoding of theological principles which is at stake; the same sophistication points to the instabilities and contradictions of both theology and poem. Thus the ultimate achievement of God's providence is that it brings forth good from evil, whereas the fallen angels will labour to 'pervert that end, | And out of good still to find means of evil'. And if they 'oft-times may succeed', and thereby '*disturb | His inmost counsels from their destined aim*' (my emphasis), it will be because fallen angels know those inmost councils intimately; they were created by them. This also suggests why Satan can pervert 'best things | To worst abuse' (IV. 203–4), and why his perversion of man is more catastrophic than would have been his destruction of man (III. 91–7), and why, in speaking of perversity, Milton has to entertain the most disturbing of all questions for theodicy: 'whose fault' (96) was the Fall? More pointedly still: 'In heavenly spirits could such perverseness dwell?' (VI. 788). In such questions a scandalous, perverse dialectic between good and evil is entertained even in its denial.

Such concepts are also revealing of the poem's attitudes to gender. In Book X Eve's fraudulence and falsity (868, 871) are manifested as 'wandering vanity' (875). Alastair Fowler, perhaps intending to minimize its effect, speaks of this section of *Paradise Lost* as 'mere stock

---

[10] On the general significance of perversion and its cognates in *Paradise Lost*, see Dyson and Lovelock, 'Event Perverse'.

antifeminist lore' (*Paradise Lost*, ed. Fowler, 553). Stock it may be, but it is also virulent, and it is the paradoxical perverse which can both illuminate and undermine it. In that she was formed from his rib, woman's deviation originates internally to man—

> Crooked by nature, bent, as now appears,
> More to the part sinister from me drawn
>
> (x. 885–6)

—she is a 'defect | Of nature' (891–2), which, according to some contemporaries following Aristotle, makes her a defective male (see below, Chapter 17). This derivative status is the basis of women's inferiority, facilitating the displacements of which she is the victim. For example, she is held responsible for the perverse lack attendent upon desire; it is 'Through her perverseness' that man 'never shall find out fit mate', and 'whom he wishes most shall seldom gain' (898, 901). But the same derivative status is also the means for the return of the feminine, not now as the inferior or even the complement of masculinity, but as the insidious cause of its undoing. Observe in *Samson Agonistes* the perverse movement compelled by desire:

> Seeming at first all heavenly under virgin veil,
> Soft, modest, meek, demure,
> Once joined, the contrary she proves, a thorn
> Intestine, far within defensive arms
> A cleaving mischief, in his way to virtue
> Adverse and turbulent; or by her charms
> *Draws him awry* enslaved
> With dotage . . .
>
> (ll. 1035–42, *Poetical Works*, p. 542, my emphasis)

Augustinian Theodicy

> Thou hast rather chosen the weak things of the world to confound the strong, and hast chosen the base things of the world and the things that are contemptible, and things that are not, in order to bring to nought things that are. (Augustine, *Confessions*, trans. Sheed, viii. iv; paraphrasing 1 Cor. 1: 27)

> Nobody wants to be reminded how hard it is to reconcile the undeniable existence of evil . . . with His all-powerfulness or His all-goodness. The Devil would be the best way out as an excuse for God; in that way he would be playing the same part as an agent of economic discharge as the Jew does in the world of the Aryan ideal. (Freud, *Civilization and its Discontents*, xii. 311)

That perversion is a concept which facilitates not just the displacement of evil from God to man, but also man's internalization of evil (in contrast and subsequent to its externalization/displacement by God) is further apparent from another equally disturbing paradox of the perverse, this time one which is inscribed in human nature and which suggests that we are created desiring that which is forbidden us. John Norris exclaims in 1687: 'What strange Perversity is this of Man! When 'twas a Crime to tast th' inlightning Tree He could not then his hand refrain' (*OED*, 'perversity'). What might explain this strange perversity? Augustine provided one answer when he argued that Adam and Eve were already fallen before the definitive transgression in Eden: 'the evil act, the transgression of eating the forbidden fruit, was committed only when those who did it were already evil' (*City of God*, xiv. 13[572]).[11] Here and elsewhere (e.g. xi. 13, 17, 18, and 20) the implication, if not the explicit theology, is that both the angelic revolt in heaven and the human fall in Eden, were predestined.

With the Fall, the flesh began to contend against the spirit 'and with this contention are we all born, *drawing death from our origin*, and bearing nature's corruption, and contention or victory of the first transgression in our members . . . for in [Adam] were we all, since we all were that one man, who, through the woman who was made of himself before sin, fell into sin' (*City of God*, xiii. 13–14, my emphasis). One suspects that this is why, for Augustine, transgressive desire seems almost produced by the law it contravenes; the soul of post-lapsarian man—'delighted with perverse liberty' (*perversum propria delectata*, *City of God*, xiii. 13)—determines to transgress a divine law which he is not merely commanded to obey but which actually constitutes him, such law being 'written in the hearts of men' (*Confessions*, ii. iv).

Dare we surmise from this that divine law not only creates the soul which transgresses that law, but also predestines that transgression by inciting the desire to transgress, the delight of 'perverse liberty'? Certainly Augustine, citing 1 Corinthians 15: 56, recognizes the severe dialectic which lends credence to that proposition: 'the law, which forbids sin, is itself the strength of sin . . . for the prohibition increases the desire to commit the unlawful act, when the love of righteousness is not strong enough to overcome the sinful desire' (*City of God*, xiii. 5[514]). The proviso in the last clause might be said to save the law— except that on Augustine's own account this 'strong enough' love of

---

[11] Unless otherwise stated, quotations from *City of God* are from the Henry Bettensen 1972 translation, edited by Knowles. Page numbers to this edition are given in square brackets. Quotations from the *Confessions* are, unless otherwise stated, from the Sheed translation.

righteousness was not in, or was subsequently written out of, God's original script for the creation.

By tracing back to God this second paradox of the perverse (that man is created desiring that which is forbidden), we in fact trace it back to the first paradox, that perversion originates in that which it subverts, in this case the divine order. A can of worms indeed, but a very old one, as the tortuous history of theodicy shows. It may seem strange that a study of perversion should go so far back into Christian history. But it is here, much further back than Freud, further even than the early modern period, that perversion initially develops its paradoxical power. Kenneth Burke realizes this in his wonderful dramatic re-enactment of a pre-creation exchange between God and Satan:

The Lord [to Satan]: . . . Though made in my image, the Earth People will necessarily incline towards that part of me which you would be, were our realm to be, like theirs, divisible.

Satan: . . . But with these temporal verbalizers, is there to be a *deviant* kind of 'freedom'?

The Lord: You *would* ask that, my lad! I see why I love you so greatly. If *my* negative ever broke loose from me, I'd know where to look for it.

Satan: Milord, I blush!
          (pause.)[12]

Never was a pause more pregnant with desire; indeed, one might say of desire that it was born in that pause.

---

[12] 'Epilogue: Prologue in Heaven', in *The Rhetoric of Religion*, 279–80.

9 Augustine: Perversion and Privation

Augustine has been seen as one of the few great (male) geniuses who changed the direction of civilization, single-handedly in human terms, but providentially from the point of universal history (*Confessions*, trans. Sheed, pp. v–vi). The present study does not share this view of Augustine or his place in history; even so, his influence as a writer who has 'done more than any other . . . after St Paul to shape the structure of orthodox Christian belief' (Hick, *Evil and the God of Love*, 43) cannot be denied. But 'Augustine' occupies no single point in history, providential or secular; rather he exists across time, constituted within and by his own historical moment, and reconstituted since. From the point of view of this study, Augustine was the product of a Christian narrative which he powerfully influenced and within which he has been scripted ever since; the synthesis, development, suppression, and innovation which characterized his own work has been continued with its subsequent transmission. It is in this sense that any account of desire, transgression, and deviation repeatedly encounters Augustine.[1] If my own account seems hostile let me concede at the outset that I have read his writing with the awe consequent upon learning from it something about the world I inhabit now.

Subjectivity and Sin

Augustine regarded sin as intrinsic to human nature and always bound up with perversion, transgression, and death: the perversion of free will leads man to transgress, and it is transgression which brings death into the world (Romans 5: 12; 6: 23). But evil is not a force or entity in its own right, nor was it a part of nature; evil should be understood as privation, a lack of good (*City of God*, xi. 22 [454]). Augustine does not invent the privative theory of evil, but his formulation and development of it remains the most influential, right through to our own time, being even then reworked by philosophers (Heidegger, Sartre) as well

---

[1] I am indebted to Elizabeth A. Clark and Brian Cummings for their advice on an earlier draft of this chapter.

as theologians (Karl Barth, Paul Tillich, Jacques Maritain, and Charles Journet).

Also important is Augustine's contribution to Western subjectivity; Mark Taylor writes in his *Erring: A Postmodern A/theology* that it was Augustine 'who first recognised and defined the principle of subjectivity' (p. 38); I am concerned also with how he bound subjectivity into desire, transgression, the myth of original sin, and an intense preoccupation with death. One reason why Augustine rejected the Manichaean position (on which see below) was that it posited a universe and a self too radically divided. He wanted to insist rather on the unity and wholeness of both. As Neil Forsyth tells us, 'Augustine's theory of sin was, paradoxically, the way in which he learned to understand this wholeness. Like its Manichaean counterpart, this theory had to be a complete explanation both of the individual psychology of the believer and of the cosmos in which he found himself' (*The Old Enemy*, 396). But unity by no means precluded the experience of conflict.

For Augustine the Fall involved a wandering from, a loss of self (Peter Brown, *Augustine*, 168–9). The consequent experience of sinful self-division was acute:

The retribution for disobedience is simply disobedience itself. For man's wretchedness is nothing but his own disobedience to himself, so that because he would not do what he could, he now wills to do what he cannot. (*City of God*, XIV. 15 [575])

Post-lapsarian man is riven with death and desire, the former (death) having entered the world through the latter (desire). How can unity be restored to him? Augustine finds it through a brutally inverted identification with divine omnipotence: whereas God is 'incorruptible, and inviolable and immutable' (*Confessions*, VII. i), man's inverted unity is marked by self-appointed abjection, the internalization of sin, and the sublimation of desire. Henceforth the psychic and ethical cost of this identification with 'unity' would be considerable.

We can see the internalization, the sublimation, and the abjection as sources of the dutiful conforming subject within Christianity. But they also excite something like the opposite of conformity. In the *Confessions* Augustine castigates the arrogant transgressions which preceded his conversion, and one especially, the theft of some overripe pears, apparently unwanted by him or anyone else:

With the basest companions I walked the streets of Babylon ... Our only pleasure in [theft] was that it was forbidden. . . . The malice of the act was base and I loved it—that is to say I loved my own undoing, I loved the evil in *me*— *not the thing for which I did the evil, simply the evil*: my soul was depraved and hurled itself down from security in You into utter destruction, seeking no profit from wickedness but only to be wicked . . . if I took so much as a bite of any one of those [stolen] pears it was the sin that sweetened it. (II. iii–iv, my emphasis.)

Here, as we shall see, there is an intimate connection for Augustine between the non-substantial nature of evil and the pleasure (rather than the gain) of transgression: just as it is not the objective of sin which is evil but the deviation from good, so here it is not the object of theft which pleases but the theft itself. Transgression is a kind of knowledge.

There is an almost 'lyrical' quality about this passage, one which we can trace to Augustine but which is also compounded in the translation. This quality is even more apparent in another translation (Bigg's); a liberty of translation invites us to ponder further how Augustine's conception of the privative theory of evil (non-substantial) emerges from an understanding of the pleasure of transgression:

And I asked what wickedness was, and I found that it was no substance, but a perversity of will, which turns aside from Thee, O God, the supreme substance, to desire the lowest, flinging away its inner treasure and boasting itself an outcast. (VII. xvi, trans. Bigg)[2]

'A perversity of will . . . boasting itself an outcast': here is transgression figured as that paradoxical but powerful conjunction between sin, perversity, and pleasure. That which for Augustine, ties transgression so closely to the nature of evil itself, thus condemning it, is also the source of a pleasure and defiance which will henceforth endlessly unsettle the law which has produced it. Dominant orders establish themselves over and against their 'others'. Augustine's—or should we say Bigg's?— 'outcasts' will identify with those others, even as they (the outcasts) repudiate the order which has created both (the outcasts and the others). Which is to say that outlaws always eventually find themselves alone, bereft even of their others. The outcast that Bigg translates from/into Augustine will figure in what follows, voicing-over some outcast thoughts transcribed into italics more to indicate their awkward positioning than for conclusive emphasis.

Kenneth Burke discerns in the passage describing the theft of the pears a profound connection between perversion and parody, this being

---

[2] The passage in question is obscure, both in Augustine and in the passage from Ecclesiasticus to which he is alluding. Augustine writes: 'Et quaesivi, quid esset iniquitas, et non inveni substantiam, sed a summa substantia, te deo, detortae in infirma voluntatis perversitatem proicientis intima sua et tumescentis foras.' J. G. Pilkington translates: 'a perversion of the will bent aside from Thee . . . and casting out its bowels (Ecclus. 10: 9) and swelling outwardly'; R. S. Pine-Coffin describes the will as being 'bowelled-alive'. The Revised Standard Version of the Ecclesiasticus passage reads: 'How can he who is dust and ashes be proud? for even in life his bowels decay.' This is taken from the Hebrew; it adds a footnote remarking the obscurity of the Greek.

why Augustine regards this apparently minor transgression as his foremost sin: it was, in substance, the complete perversion, or perfect parody, of his religious conversion. First because it was 'a "free" or "gratuitous" crime (*gratuitum facinus*) . . . an act done not for some sheerly utilitarian gain, but out of pure dedication to crime for its own sake'. But this motiveless, non-utilitarian act was also a travesty of the divine since God, for Augustine, was motiveless in *his* creation of the world (to attribute motive to God is to compromise his omnipotence). Further, the theft of the pears 'was sanctioned by a group of like-minded associates, a *consortium peccantium* . . . a perfect parody of the Brotherhood within the Church' (Burke, *Rhetoric of Religion*, 94, 98–9). If perversion and parody profoundly connect, that connection in turn signifies the scandalous proximity of virtue and transgression.

The Manichaean Heresy

Augustine was led to the privative view partly by a wish to refute the Manichaean heresy which threatened the omnipotence of God by giving evil too much being. According to this heresy, evil was coeternal and equal in force with good: Satan was not only fundamentally antagonistic to God, but fundamentally independent of him as well. This put a very different light on creation. The Manichaeans, says Augustine, believed

that God was compelled to the creation of the vast structure of this universe by the utter necessity of repelling the evil which fought against him, that he had to mingle the nature of his creating, which was good, with the evil, which is to be suppressed and overcome, and that this good nature was thus so foully polluted, so savagely taken captive and oppressed that it was only with the greatest toil that he can cleanse it and set it free. And even then he cannot rescue all of it, and the part which cannot be purified from that defilement is to serve as the prison to enclose the Enemy after his overthrow. (*City of God*, XI. 22 [454]; cf. XI. 13 [446])

The branch of religious enquiry devoted to vindicating God's omnipotence in the face of this kind of challenge is known as theodicy. Within theodicy a great deal has been written on the 'problem of evil', or, as it might better be called, contradiction. It arises for any monotheistic religion which insists that God is both perfectly good and unlimited in his power. The philosopher David Hume, paraphrasing Epicurus as cited by Lactantius, formulated the problem like this: 'Is he [God] willing to prevent evil, but not able? Then he is impotent. Is he able but not willing? Then he is malevolent. Is he both able and willing?

whence then is evil?'[3] Both paradoxes of the perverse, especially the second, are manifestations of the problem of evil. Pursued in the context of that problem—to which many have felt there is no satisfactory answer—we shall find that, in the wrong hands, these paradoxes eventually come to pervert the viability of the entire Christian scheme of things. This is one reason why the problem of evil is not only of theological concern; secular philosophy has also addressed it, and not only because some answers to it have become grounds for atheism.

The Manichaean position is a form of dualism, allowing as it does both evil and good to be separate and equally real forces in the universe. Monist views by contrast argue that there is one divine principle manifested as God (or Gods), responsible for both good and evil.[4] Looking again at Augustine's description of Manichaeism just cited, we see how a dualist position, though it makes good and evil separate principles, represents them as inseparable in practice; evil does not simply contest and displace good, but contaminates and 'foully' pollutes it. As we will see, this is crucial, both for dualist and for monist theologies.

In a sense the Manichaeans can be seen as the proximate others of Christianity. Their heresy is one of Augustine's main preoccupations. The fact that he once subscribed to Manichaean belief serves as a preliminary marking of what will become increasingly apparent as we attend to the question of otherness: it keeps turning up within the order or identity which is defined over and apart from it. The *over and apart* of domination becomes the *beneath and within* of otherness. Augustine's theology, I argue, intensifies this tendency. Although it was his intention to clarify it, Augustine leaves the relationship between good and evil notoriously problematic, as the endless arguments within the long history of theodicy testify. It is not my concern to rehearse those arguments, but rather to concentrate on something indispensible to them but which they usually ignore; something crucial for understanding Christianity's contribution to the violent discriminations which constitute our history, namely, the part perversion is made to play in the privative theory of evil.[5] Evil as independent, coexistent difference is

---

[3] *Dialogues concerning Natural Religion*, part x; Lactantius, 'The Wrath of God', in *The Minor Works*, 92–3. I am grateful to Tony Nuttall for this reference.

[4] In the complexities of theology, monism and dualism often coexist or overlap in a state of tension. Augustine's position is monist to the extent that it sees God as omnipotent, the ultimate and single source of goodness and power. But he pulls back from the monist belief that God is responsible for evil, while at the same time insisting that evil is entirely under God's control. He is also monistic in arguing that evil is ultimately a kind of unreality. Augustine can sometimes be found fashioning a monistic theology from a dualistic vision of a world acutely conflicted.

[5] The specificity and complexity of Augustine's use of *perversus* and its cognate terms is sometimes lost in those translations which opt for a very general equivalent like 'wickedness', 'evil', or 'disruption' (see for example Loeb edition 4. 178; 5. 34, 37, 400; 12. 6, 8; 13. 13; 14. 13, 26, 27). Other terms used in

replaced by evil as a turning away from good; *deviation avoids division* (psychic, spiritual, and cosmic)—but only at the cost of another kind or torment, the worse for being internal to unity itself. In a sense perversion becomes the norm for a fallen human nature, to be ceaselessly policed within both self and other.

Perversion and Privation

According to Augustine man is created by God from nothing. His fulfilment lies with God. Life in the post-lapsarian world is an arduous journey back to God, and virtue is largely measured by our refusal to divert or deviate from that path. Evil 'takes its origin . . . from the fact that his [man's] natural being is created from nothing' (*City of God*, XII. 6 [479]; XIV. 13 [572]); evil involves a deviation from God, a regression back towards this original state of non-being. So when man spurns divine subjection, turning from God to himself, it makes him 'less real' than when he adhered to God; 'to abandon God . . . is to come nearer to nothingness' (XIV. 13 [572]); hence the idea of being brought to nothing through sin.

This is the basis of his view of evil as privation, a lack consequent on this perverse falling (XII. 1 [470], XII. 9 [481]) or turning (XII. 6 [477]) away from God,[6] or, more generally, from the higher to the lower, the superior to the inferior: 'When the will leaves the higher and turns to the lower, it becomes bad not because the thing to which it turns is bad, but because the turning is itself perverse [*perversa*]' (XII. 6 [478]); even the act of *doing* evil 'is nothing but to go astray from discipline [*male facere nihil est nisi a disciplinara deviare*]' (*De libero arbitrio*, I. ii. 3.6). To put it another way, the ontological dimension of evil is manifested teleologically: evil is essentially a defect, and its defectiveness lies in a freely chosen act of defection: 'it is the defection in itself that is evil' (*City of God*, XII. 7 [479]; XII. 8 [480]). Moreover, to turn to something 'of a lower degree of reality . . . is contrary to the order of nature' (XII. 8 [480]); being harmful to that order, it is rightly judged unnatural (XI. 17). As for the nature of the evil-doer, this is no more intrinsically evil than that to which he or she turns; indeed, says Augustine in a remarkable passage, 'not even the nature of the Devil himself is evil, in

translation to elucidate the theory of evil as privation include corruption, parasitism, spoiling, vitiation, lack, loss, inversion, malignant inversion, negation. In some recent translations this may be understandably intended to avoid the modern and inappropriate sexological and psychological senses of perversion. Bettenson's translation of *City of God* makes most use of the English perverse/pervert/perversion.

⁶ Compare Augustine's frequent use of the idea of the virtuous person as one who stays on the right path, 'running' straight on, and refusing to be diverted/perverted (Evans, *Augustine on Evil*, 154–60, 164).

so far as it is a nature; *it is perversion that makes it evil [sed perversitas eam malem facit]*' (XIX. 13 [871], my emphasis). Thus 'It is not by nature but by a perversion that the rebellious creation differs from the good, which adheres to God . . . Scripture speaks of "enemies of God"; but these enemies oppose God's sovereignty not by nature but by their perversion' (XII. 1, 3 [472–3]; see also *Confessions*, VII. xvi).

Such are the lengths Augustine goes to in order to eliminate evil from created nature and so exonerate God from the charge either of creating an evil nature as well as a good, or of being opposed by an independent principle of evil. As a result, man is deemed fundamentally perverse, and narcissistically in that the worst kind of defection/perversion involves a turning from God to self, from perseverence in duty to the perverse affirmation of desire, the following of the will's 'own line, and not God's' (XIV. 11 [568]). The cause is pride, 'the start of every kind of sin' (Eccles. 10: 13; *City of God*, XII. 6; XIV. 13):

And what is pride except a longing for a perverse kind of exaltation [*perversae celsitudinis appetitus*]? For it is a perverse kind of exaltation to abandon the basis on which the mind should be firmly fixed, and to become, as it were, based on oneself, and so remain. (XIV. 13 [571])

We begin to see how, in Augustine's scheme, concepts like perversion and deviation bear the full weight of evil. It becomes more apparent if we follow through the worrying consequences of the theory—worrying for Augustine, that is. So, if evil presupposes good this is because it can only exist as the perversion of good (XII. 3 [474]); in effect evil becomes intrinsic to good, not positively, but negatively. It then follows that nothing can be evil except a good:

One in which evil is present is a defective or faulty good; nor can there be any evil where there is no good. From this a strange result emerges. Since every being, insofar as it is a being, is good, when we call a defective being an evil being, we seem to be saying that what is good is evil, and that only what is good can be evil, since every being is good nor could there be an evil thing if the thing itself which is evil were not a being. Nothing, then, can be evil except a good. Although this seems to be an absurd statement, the sequence of our argument forces us to it. (*Enchiridion*, ch. 4, section 13 [p. 378]; cf. *City of God*, XII. 6 [479])

Such are the origins of the perverse dynamic, and it is hardly surprising that Augustine adds (anxiously?), 'yet we must beware lest we bring on ourselves that utterance of the Prophet, where we read: "Woe unto them that call evil good and good evil: that put darkness for light, and light for darkness . . .".'

It is another extraordinary admission: evil can only arise from good;

in a sense good produces evil. At the same time the representation of evil as absolutely other remains necessary; this idea is articulated in Augustine's very conception of the two cities, the one being the city of God, the other the earthly city of sin. One might see the *City of God* as written in an attempt to disavow the implications of Augustine's own theory of evil growing from good, namely that the two cities are really one, or threatening always to merge.

> *Centuries later, as just one aspect of the displacement of religion by sexuality—which was, inevitably, also a process of incorporation, sexuality becoming a surrogate religion—this idea will be echoed, unconsciously I like to think, in Freud's theory of perversion as a narcissistic, libidinal regression from an arduously achieved 'normality'; the displacement of a totality (normal adult sexual identity) by one or more of its parts (the component instincts, these corresponding to an earlier and incomplete phase of sexual development).*

One of Augustine's biographers speaks of 'the fearsome intensity with which he had driven the problem of evil into the heart of Christianity' (Peter Brown, *Augustine*, 397). We see how and why this was so in several specific issues. There is for example Augustine's notorious statement at the beginning of the *Confessions* that even the day-old infant is not free of sin (1. vii). The implications of this were taken up by Julian of Eclanum: towards the end of his life Augustine found himself accused by Julian of doubting the equity of God; of making God directly responsible for the suffering of the innocent—in effect, of holding God 'capable of committing a crime against justice such as is hardly conceivable even among the barbarians' (quoted from Brown, *Augustine*, 392).

That evil remains so inextricably bound up with, some would say indistinguishable from, good, renders the theory permanently unstable. But the same instability could become a kind of strength. The very proximity of evil to good, which makes the distinction between them so precarious, also means that one must necessarily and always seek to distinguish the good from the evil. As Augustine says, one knows evil only through good. From here it is a short step to knowing good by always and vigilantly distinguishing it from evil.[7] Augustine cites

---

[7] Though I concentrate on Augustine, it should be said that he did not invent this way of thinking; he is part of its development within Christianity. Important precursors include Tertullian, who develops the idea of the devil as a corrupter and perverter (*interpolator*) of creation, with the ever-present need to be vigilant against his works, especially as they are manifested in the heretic. In this respect contends J. B. Russell,

1 Corinthians 11: 19: 'Heresies are necessary, to show which of you are in a sound condition' (*City of God*, XVI. 2 [650]). Hayden White sees Augustine as developing this kind of discrimination, focusing on

the sinful, heretical, insane, and damned in order to limn the area of virtue occupied by the pure, the orthodox, the sane, and the elect. Like the Puritans who came after him, Augustine found that one way of establishing the 'meaning' of his own life was to deny meaning to anything radically different from it, except as antitype or negative instance. (*Tropics of Discourse*, 151)

Arguably this simplifies Augustine by neglecting his emphasis on the tortuous internalization of the problem of evil, and by seeing the other as opposite rather than proximate. But it is often under the direct influence of Augustine that this binary identification of good and evil is continued by later writers, for example Aquinas:

Evil cannot be known simply as evil, for its core is hollow, and can be neither recognized nor defined save by the surrounding good ... One opposite is known from the other, as darkness from light. Hence the meaning of evil depends on the meaning of good. (*Philosophical Texts*, ed. Gilby, 163–4)

Beyond both Augustine and Aquinas, reformers like Calvin will make knowledge of one's own salvation inseparable from knowledge of others' damnation: 'Election itself could not stand except as set over against reprobation' (Calvin, quoted in Hick, *Evil and the God of Love*, 132).[8] And for a modern writer on theodicy: 'it might be said, without any paradox in our thought, that *evil proves God's existence*' (Journet, *The Meaning of Evil*, 63).

Going back to Augustine, we see this binary perspective taking another, equally punitive, but now more precarious and unstable form, one which contributes to the terrible power of this theory in the Western tradition. I am referring to the way he squares evil's ultimate or original ontological status, as *nothing*, with actual evil as experienced in the world. Remember that for Augustine nothing in nature is evil, not even Satan. Obviously he had to supplement this account with some theory of the force and perniciousness of evil since, as both John Hick and H. J. McCloskey among many others argue, any theory of evil as non-being simply cannot adequately answer the experienced reality of evil, and the consequent assumption that it is a force or reality in its own

'Tertullian and the other fathers laid the basis for centuries of persecution of Jews, heretics and witches'; heresy becomes the attack on the Christian community *from within* (Russell, *Satan*, 94–6, 98, 106).

[8] In fact Calvin is not only going further than Augustine, but departing from him: Augustine argued both that we cannot know our own salvation, and that the salvation of one person is not dependent upon the damnation of another.

right (Hick, *Evil and the God of Love*, 48; McCloskey, *God and Evil*, 41). Calvin, much preoccupied with the power and pervasiveness of evil—he believed that man had 'perverted the whole order of nature in heaven and earth'—makes a similar point (*Institutes*, ii. 1, 5).

Augustine was aware of the problem. He attempts to solve it with that cluster of concepts signifying perversion, deviation, defection, subversion: *perversus*, *perversitas*, *deviare*, and *defectus*.[9] If, as we have seen, one function of these concepts was to dispense with the ontological being of evil, another is to reintroduce in a surrogate form the 'reality' of evil, not as being *per se*, but as force, agency, or cause, now the more malevolent for its 'unreality'. Here is the beginning of a theory which will feed the violence of our history: 'essentially', perversion becomes the negative agency within, at the heart of, privation. Perversion thus mediates between evil as agency and evil as lack; in bridging this contradiction perversion takes on its own paradoxical nature—which is also the basis of its disturbing power: it is that which is utterly inimical to existence while itself lacking authentic existence, ontological or natural.

Augustine inaugurates a punitive metaphysic which remains influential today, not only inside Christianity—and for theologians occupying conflicting wings of the movement—but outside it too: 'secular' politics is also pervaded by this punitive metaphysic. In the words of Charles Journet, who defends and develops the theory: 'the most radical opposition to which being can be subjected is not contrariety but privation. The paradox of evil is the terrible reality of its privative existence.' Moreover, 'the importance of privation should be judged by the importance of what it destroys; its seriousness increases proportionally as the subject which it erodes is more noble, its needs more sacred and absolute'. For Journet evil is this agonizing paradox, at once non-being and utterly destructive (*The Meaning of Evil*, 47–9, 46). Compare Maritain, for whom the power of privation is only the power of the good it perverts: 'the more powerful this good is, the more powerful evil will be,—not by virtue of itself but by virtue of this good. *That is why no evil is more powerful than that of the fallen angel*' (*St Thomas*, 2, my emphasis). For such theologians, as for Augustine before them, evil cannot be allowed to be a 'positive reality' (Journet, *The Meaning of Evil*, 46, 66) because this would readmit dualism (i.e. the view that evil really does exist, as good exists). Rather, evil is made to 'exist' as 'an *inverted positivity*', a force which is not a force, a 'hollow, but fatal, stigma' whose 'ravages can be limitless, and disastrous, in the order

---

[9] These are related to other concepts in Augustine's theory like *lapsus*, *aversio*, *vitium*, *corruptio*, *negatio*.

both of being and of action' (p. 43). It is a negative agency, a disordered and disordering movement within the good, disrupting both man and the universe. Of the concepts deployed to represent this movement, perversion and deviation remain paramount (see e.g. pp. 45, 53, 166, 176, 199–200, 207–8, 214, 232, 255).

But also from these paradoxes of the perverse is the perverse dynamic born: with that betraying perspective so acute in the sinner turned saint, Augustine recognizes vice as not so much the antithesis of virtue as its perversion, the more dangerous and potentially subversive for being in intimate relation with the good, rather than being an absolute difference or otherness.

> *This threefold implication of evil and good: first, evil as parasitic on good and proportionally so (the greater the good the greater the evil); second, in fallen practice, evil is barely distinguishable from good; third, good is only known through evil. Two kinds of relation between the dominant and the subordinate may arise when their relations are conceived or formed in terms of this threefold proximity. First: those proximities will permanently remind the dominant of its actual instability, all forms of domination being unstable to a varying degree, as well as produce a paranoid fear of impending subversion. So there will be both a justified fear as well as an excess of fear; second, that proximity will become the means enabling displacement and projection, while the justified/paranoid fears will be their motivation: proximity becomes a condition of displacement; which in turn marks the same/proximate as radically other.*

Prescriptive Metaphysics

Augustine's theodicy has been admired as a *tour de force* (Evans, *Augustine on Evil*, p. viii) and criticized as radically incoherent (Hick, *Evil and the God of Love*, 68). It is probably both at once, powerfully persuasive, but with incoherences which have facilitated as well as hindered its influence. The main incoherence, at the heart of the theory, is the idea of evil as being/non-being, negotiated via the concept of perversion. There is another, related, incoherence which involves that slide from deviation to disruption noted earlier: the departure from, being also a contradiction of. As in the main incoherence, perversion plays its part: an intrinsically disordered deviation is also disordering of that from which it departs. Only now we can see that the ascription of perversion is typically supplemented by something else, a prescriptive metaphysic. We can begin to unpack that metaphysic by looking at Augustine's analogies with nature.

The privative theory of evil has been illustrated through an analogy with lameness. Evil is a lack of good as lameness is the lack of ability to walk properly. The analogy assumes that one wants to walk. This is not an unreasonable assumption but nor is it necessarily true. Under the influence of Aristotle and the Stoics, the analogy also assumes that one is not only made in order to walk, but that the divine, natural, and social orders require that one does. It is here that the analogy most clearly breaks down and begs the question. Ironically, in Augustine's theory the prescriptive is parasitic upon the natural, rather as the theory describes evil as parasitic upon the good. Thus the absence of good which defines evil is not simply the absence of *any* good (e.g. as a chair might lack speech, or a slave lack wealth), it is the lack of something which ought to be there 'in the (prescribed) nature of things'. Not only in Augustine but in other writers too, this use of nature conflates a prescriptive ontology—what a thing should be—and a prescriptive purpose—what it should do. Privation is seen to pervert that essential law of a being's existence whereby it remains or becomes what it ought to be, such laws being determined ultimately by God's divine plan and manifested as natural law. And when Augustine defines evil as 'nothing but the corruption of natural measure, form or order [*modus, species, ordo*]' (quoted by Hick, *Evil and the God of Love*, 54) we glimpse the ease with which this metaphysic will be extended from a supposed natural law (and order) to its social counterpart.

Ultimately it is this prescriptive metaphysic, in conjunction with the theory of evil as privation, which allows the slippage between 'departure from' and 'contradiction of'. Their combined force remains with us to this day as a powerful form of discursive control. Hence that first *OED* definition of perverse: 'turned away from the right way or from what is right or good; perverted, wicked'. Required to give an account of Augustine's theology in something less than a sentence, one could do worse than point to this very definition. We might see this as precisely the 'incoherent' force of Augustine's theory as it survives today in ways of thinking which are quite likely unaware of privative theory, and which may even think of themselves as secularist: evil as essential absence becomes a haunting pervasive presence, indistinguishable from, yet with an ever-present potential of perverting and diminishing that which it essentially is not. That this theory has endured may well have something to do with the fact that the crucial association of perversion with evil also preceded Augustine. To forgo the spurious origin is also to understand how structures of thought endure even as we believe they have become obsolete.

Of course in our tradition dualistic conceptions of evil more or less resembling the Manichaean dualism which Augustine denounced remain residually active. Indeed, as already suggested, a Manichaean influence also survives in Augustine's own writing, despite his claims to the contrary.[10] Often a monotheistic and a dualistic conception of evil will be run together, as they are to some extent in Augustine's account of perversion: evil as at once external agency and inner lack—in the conflation of the two, evil becomes utterly alien yet mysteriously inherent. But why the conflation? Peter Brown, with Augustine's *Confessions* in mind, suggests a reason why the Christian became preoccupied with the inward rather than the external threat: 'The Christian's worst enemies could no longer be placed outside him: they were inside, his sins and his doubts; and the climax of a man's life would not [now] be martyrdom, but conversion from the perils of his own past' (*Augustine*, 159). This emphasis on the internalization of evil is important, but we should not forget that evil as traumatic external threat re-emerges with a vengeance: Augustine is led to begin the *City of God* in 410 partly as a response to the sack of Rome, the first time in 800 years that it had been taken by a foreign enemy, and he dies in 430 while his own city is being besieged by the Vandals.

In the Western tradition indebted to Augustine we find evil conceptualized simultaneously as, on the one hand, a foreign force or agency, at once alien, antithetic, and hostile; on the other as an inner deviation, the more insidious for having departed from the true, its point of departure from *within* the true being also its point of contact for the perversion *of* the true. In the conflation of the two, evil becomes at once utterly alien and insidiously inherent.

> *It is a perspective whose complex inheritance will help identify the sexual pervert as a modern incarnation of evil, the more dangerous for having been, before disclosure, indistinguishable from us.*
>
> *Bent on a deviation toward the alien, he or she conversely enables a transmission/admission of the alien into our midst along the lines of his or her departure/deviation. Obscurely, the deviant is always already at one with the alien, even or especially while indistinguishable from us. And thus do we*

---

[10] See for example Clark, 'Vitiated Seeds and Holy Vessels'. Especially interesting is the way Clark shows how Augustine remained haunted by Manichaeism in his account of sexuality and reproduction, and how he was accused of this by his contemporary opponents.

remain ever endangered by invasion/deviation, that doubled
threat requiring endless vigilance, endless discrimination of
the true from the false.

It is part of my larger argument that, with the emergence of the
sexological and psychoanalytic views of perversion, this longer conceptual history is largely lost; or, more precisely, it is telescoped into a
psychosexual narrative, where it remains obscurely yet violently active.[11]
Even to understand that recent history we need to return to Augustine,
seeing how he deploys and develops the concepts of perversion and
deviation, making of them definitive criteria of evil.

Sexual perversion is a modern notion, hardly more than a century
old, and grew from medical discourses which were effectively displacing
religious ones. In keeping with that change, we are told, sexual deviation
comes to be understood as an illness or a congenital abnormality rather
than a sin. However, structures developed within the concept of the
sinfully perverse persist into modern theories of the sexually perverse.
That much has become apparent in the demonizing, punitive response
to the catastrophe of AIDS, but it was always so. Consider for example
the Augustinian echoes in several popular notions of sexual perversion
in our own time: (1) evil, says Augustine, is utterly inimical to true
existence yet itself lacks authentic existence, ontological or natural.
Likewise with the sexual pervert *vis-à-vis* sexual normality. (2) Evil,
says Augustine, is at once utterly alien to the good and the natural and
yet mysteriously inherent within or parasitical upon the good and the
natural. Likewise sexual perversion is utterly alien to true sexuality
(that sexuality which is good and natural) yet mysteriously inherent
within or parasitic upon it, such that this perversion must be rooted out
by the ever vigilant. (3) Evil, says Augustine, has, paradoxically, greater
powers of perversion the greater the goodness and innocence of those
being perverted. Likewise with sexual perversion: this being why,
presumably, in contemporary Britain the young and the military are
thought to be especially at risk. (In that country—and not only there—
homosexuality in the military and for those under 21 is still illegal.)

Displacing Evil

To read Augustine is to encounter the contradictions and tensions of
Christian theodicy at a major point of their development and transmission. We find the concepts of perversion and deviation intensifying

---

[11] Occasionally, as in Claudel's attack on Gide's homosexuality (above, Ch. 3), the theological sense of
perversion remains visible within the sexological one.

those contradictions and tensions, even as they are deployed to contain and resolve them. To requote Journet: 'it might be said, without any paradox in our thought, that, *evil proves God's existence*' (cited above, his italics). 'Without paradox': Journet attempts to use the concept of perversion in a way shorn of the dangerously paradoxical. But it is not difficult to perceive the persisting, paradoxical nature of the perverse and in so doing we find in these later writers the inheritance of Augustine. Most importantly, we find a use of concepts like perversion and deviation in the more or less tortuous theologies whereby evil is displaced from God to man. To the devout this charge of displacement may seem scandalous but it is no more than the clear implication of the history of religion.

In his study of pre-Christian religions Jeffrey Russell has charted the changing conceptions of evil, including the various shifts between and combinations of monism and dualism. Whereas in Western religions, God and the devil have moved into almost absolute opposition, the myths of many earlier societies placed them in close conjunction. What we glimpse in those earlier religions is what Christianity subsequently seeks to disavow. For example God and the devil were said to exist and work together from all eternity; or they were said to be brothers; or God was said to create the devil; or, in an even closer relationship, God was said to beget the devil or produce him from his own essence (*Devil*, 58–9; cf. 98–101). Also of course, in older religions the devil and things related to him (e.g. the underground) were the source of life and fertility as well as death and destruction (*Devil*, 62–4, 172). Russell argues that the most important development in the Hebrew-Christian tradition is the shift from monism, wherein good and evil are seen to coexist within one being, or in an inextricable relationship with each other, to dualism, the extreme separation of good and evil (*Devil*, 250–2). And if the implications of a strong monism were unacceptable (making God directly responsible for evil) so too were those of a full dualism (they diminish the power of God). According to Russell it is this 'unresolved conflict between monotheism and dualism [which] provides the central tension in the history of Christian diabology' (*Satan*, 25).[12]

Perversion and deviation are concepts which facilitated the displacement of evil from God to man during the shift that Russell charts. They continue to bear the marks of the history which is effaced in that very

[12] A significant point in the development of dualism is in the teaching of Zarathustra (shortly before 600 BC), who makes evil a separate and independent force, and Orphism, which sees a dualism between matter and spirit, body and soul (*Devil*, 137–9). Russell offers in passing this generalization on dualism: by insisting upon the struggle of two hostile principles warring for the mind, dualism can provoke a schizophrenic sense of the world as split between the good and the bad, with a strong desire to identify and repress the latter (*Devil*, 100–1). So may it, but so also can the monism of Augustine.

displacement. That is to say, perversion and deviation become lodged at the heart of those contradictions which were to haunt Christianity, and which ultimately sunder faith itself, most notably the beliefs (1) that we are created wicked; (2) that God himself, as the theologian John Hick acknowledges, bears 'the ultimate responsibility for the existence of evil' (Hick, *Evil and the God of Love*, 264); (3) that evil is intrinsic to good.

All three beliefs have the happy consequence of making God rather than Satan the ultimate or original pervert. Such an accusation is anticipated and ingeniously countered by John Donne, who turns it back on itself—'it is the perversest assertion that God gives man temporall things to ensnare him' (*OED*). Here we encounter something else characteristic of the use of perversion as a signifier: like 'nature', it can slide wildly, and it does so because so very much is at stake. Perverse or not, the idea that we are perversely created—that is, created wicked by a perverse God—is a heresy never entirely suppressed in Christianity. It surfaces repeatedly, most memorably perhaps in Fulke Greville's frequently anthologized 'wearisome condition of humanity':

> Borne under one Law, to another, bound:
> Vainely begot, and yet forbidden vanity,
> Created sicke, commanded to be sound:
> What meaneth nature by these diverse Lawes?
>
> ('Chorus Sacerdotum', *Mustapha*)

As we shall see, it is because perversion *contains* contradictions (in the sense of the word outlined above, Chapter 6), that it possesses the power to destabilize the very metaphysic of evil which employs it. We are alerted to as much by two ironies in Augustine's *City of God*. The first concerns the fact that his style is inseparable from the virtue of what he most castigated, deviation:

All his works wander from their main topic, none more than the *City of God* . . . he cannot resist an attractive side-road . . . so that the work sometimes reminds us of one of the disordered masterpieces of the sixteenth or early seventeenth centuries . . . [the reader] may at first be put off by the digressions. (David Knowles, introduction to Henry Bettenson's translation, p. xxxiii)

The second irony is an even more engaging version of the first: rehearsing long before Descartes that most famous proof of subjective being (*cogito ergo sum*), Augustine wrote: 'Si enim fallor sum' (*City of God*, XI. 26 [460]). 'Fallor' has been variously translated as 'am mistaken', 'am deceived', and 'err'. This last, taken from Healey's translation of 1610, may be preferable if only because it picks up something else remarked earlier, the fundamental link between the epistemological and the teleological: in error/to err. Thus Augustine: 'If I err, I am. For he that has no being cannot err, and therefore mine error proves my being.' In other words, Augustine founds his being upon erring movement, that which is the quintessence of the perverse and, as such, necessarily also a movement towards non-being. One in particular of Augustine's own errors was to have certain repercussions. His development of the doctrine of original sin involved a misconstruction of the Greek meaning 'because all have sinned' (Rom. 5: 12) as 'in whom [Adam] all men sinned'. This was to have far-reaching consequences, although it is reductionist to contend, as some do, that the 'entire Western Christian doctrine of original sin was construed squarely on this error' (Hunter *et al.* (eds.), *Milton Encyclopedia*, vii. 177).[13]

Pursuing the paradoxes of the perverse, we have been led to the conclusion that original sin is really original perversion; that God rather than Satan or man (i.e. woman) was the original pervert; that the Fall was a displacement of evil from God to man. But suppose for a moment we let God off the hook, accepting that perversion actually originates with the one-time deputy (Satan), and that Eve was his first convert (or rather pervert). We then arrive at the official line on the Fall of man, as espoused in numerous places, including *Paradise Lost* (e.g. I. 164, III. 92, XII. 547, X. 3). It is a myth of origin which will help legitimate the subjection of women and violence against them for centuries to come. This is the subject of the next chapter.

[13] For a more adequate discussion of this mistranslation, see Kelly, *Early Christian Doctrines*.

10 Othello: *Sexual Difference and Internal Deviation*

The theatre of Elizabethan and Jacobean England provides some especially powerful and intricate enactments of the legitimating power of the natural/unnatural binary, and of its violent breakdown as well as its equally violent enforcement, and the struggles to demystify it as well as those to reconstitute it. Contradictory notions of nature pushed to an extreme, as in *King Lear*, come to threaten the coherence of the concept itself; it splits apart, disintegrates ideologically, succumbing to the very contradictions it was supposed to contain. By contrast, in *Othello* we witness nature ideologically strained to the point of breaking but still holding. Just. It is at this point that the concept may be at once barely coherent and yet most brutally repressive; with the result that, as in *Othello*, the unnatural is foregrounded, violently demonized, and rendered the object of displacement.

Aberrant Movement

Othello explores that anxious preoccupation with perversity as a disordered and disordering movement. Othello is described as the 'erring barbarian' (I. iii. 343), the 'extravagant and wheeling stranger | Of here and everywhere' (I. i. 135–6) Here 'extravagant' condenses deviation, perversion, and vagrancy. For 'extravagance' the *OED* gives as its first entry, 'A going out of the usual path; an excursion, digression. Also, the position or fact of erring *from* (a prescribed path).' The first *OED* entry for 'extravagant' (as an example of which it cites this same passage from *Othello*) defines it as that which 'wanders out of bounds; straying, roaming vagrant'.

It is not only Othello who is described in terms of a tendency towards aberrant movement; had Brabantio lived to see his daughter murdered it would, says Gratiano, have made him 'do a desperate turn, | Yea, curse his better angel from his side | And fall to reprobance' (V. ii. 206–8). Iago vows to 'serve my turn upon [Othello]'; serving one's turn on one's master is precisely not 'truly' to follow him since 'In following him, I follow but myself'. And yet to follow oneself is to be not oneself: 'I am not what I am' (I. i. 42, 59, 66). In one sense the metaphors of truth, linearity, and deviation point simply to duplicity; but also signified is a wilful disarticulation of traditional relations between authority, service, and identity.

Gratiano's description of Brabantio's 'desperate turn', with its echoes of the Fall, shows that destructive deviation may characterize even the most stolid of patriarchs. But Brabantio's turning would resemble his own conception of the way nature is undermined in the case of his daughter: a deviation pressured by the overwhelming terrible external event, a forcing rather than a succumbing. Likewise with the woman when conceived as passive victim. As Cleopatra says of her honour, it 'was not yielded, | But conquered merely' (III. xiii. 61–2). Brabantio thinks of Desdemona as 'A maiden never bold; | Of spirit so still and quiet that her motion | Blushed at herself' (I. iii. 94–6). When Desdemona is imagined as active she becomes perverse, and turning the intrinsic tendency of her will; for her to 'seriously incline' (I. iii. 145) to Othello's tales of mastery over wild and aberrant natures (I. iii. 127 ff.) is strange, but retrospectively less so in one who is supposed to have 'turned to folly, and . . . was a whore' (V. ii. 133).

The opposition of woman as passive/active correlates closely with that of women as madonna/whore. This is not the first time Othello has conceived Desdemona's supposed betrayal in terms of an endless capacity for perverse movement:

> you did wish that I would make her turn.
> Sir, she can turn, and turn, and yet go on,
> And turn again.
>
> (IV. i. 243–5)

This kind of representation of deviant female desire echoes Augustinian privation; its inferiority is marked by a lack which is (perversely and paradoxically) terribly inimical to its masculine superior; Desdemona, in the paranoid masculine imagination, is the lily that festers, the 'weed | Who art so lovely fair, and smell'st so sweet' (IV. ii. 66–7); she harbours an evil inversely proportionate to her apparent goodness:

OTHELLO. Hang her, I do but say what she is: So delicate with her needle, an admirable musician—O, she will sing the savageness out of a bear—Of so high and plenteous wit and invention—
IAGO. She's the worse for all this.
OTHELLO. O, a thousand, thousand times—and then of so gentle a condition!
IAGO. Ay, too gentle. . . .
O, 'tis foul in her.

OTHELLO. With mine officer!
IAGO. That's fouler.

(IV. i. 177–91)

In such perversity female desire repeatedly echoes its original Fall; thus Desdemona is one who fell when she fell in love with what she feared to look on (I. iii. 98).

Twelfth Night offers a similar echo of the Fall, one whose otherwise conventional pun on 'die' becomes even more indicative of the refined version of this culture's misogyny via a further sexual pun on 'flower',[1] and an invocation of the Christian narrative whereby the first transgression (Eve's) brought death into the world. It occurs in an exchange about men's inconstancy which in turn becomes the means of an ironically revealed displacement:

DUKE. . . . however we do praise ourselves,
  Our fancies are more giddy and unfirm,
  More longing, wavering, sooner lost and worn
  Than women's are. . . .
  Then let thy love be younger than thyself,
  Or thy affection cannot hold the bent:
  For women are as roses whose fair flower
  Being once displayed, doth fall that very hour.
VIOLA. And so they are. Alas that they are so:
  To die, even when they to perfection grow!

(II. iv. 32–41)

Strikingly, Orsino here describes the inconstancy of male desire in terms usually reserved for women, and knowingly so, but then implicitly justifies the vagaries of male sexuality in the face of the transience of female beauty and the proneness of women to fall. Viola apparently endorses this, except that she may also be ironically re-turning the insecurity back to its source, growing and dying being a more apt description of male (phallic) sexuality rather than female sexuality.[2]

---

[1] Cf. Shakespeare, *A Lover's Complaint*, ll. 147–8.

[2] Cf. Middleton and Rowley, *A Fair Quarrel*, II. i. 28–30: 'when my judgement tells me she's but woman, | Whose frailty let in death to all mankind | *My valour shrinks at that*' (my emphasis). In Webster's *The Duchess of Malfi* displacement is once again at issue:

CARDINAL.   You fear
  My constancy, because you have approv'd
  Those giddy and wild turnings in yourself.
JULIA. Did you e'er find them?
CARDINAL.   Sooth, generally for women:
  A man might strive to make glass malleable,
  Ere he should make them fixed.   (II. iv. 10–15)

Constancy

The opposite of wayward movement is constancy; to remain rather than to turn. In Act v Othello and Emilia dispute as to whether Desdemona was faithful; Emilia reiterates that she was 'true'; Othello denies it. For a woman to be true is of course to be faithful and, more significantly, to be constant, this being the acquiescence-within-allegiance upon which the relationship fundamentally depends (but not only for women: cf. 1. i. 43–4: 'all masters | Cannot be truly followed'). Is it only the mobility of language, or is it indicative of some deeper *inconstant*, that Desdemona's defection to the 'gross clasps of a lascivious Moor' can be described by her father, *who has already anticipated the event in his dreams*, as 'too *true* an evil'? (1. i. 125, 159, my emphasis).[3] Whatever, Brabantio's dream that his daughter has betrayed him is the dream of the man who fears he cannot control what he possesses. In that, he shares a patriarchal affinity with Othello—whom, in every other respect, he so despises that he dies of grief when his daughter marries him. In this *Othello* vividly reminds us that patriarchal authority simultaneously violently unites and violently divides men in the domestic as well as the military sphere.

Predictably enough, the concept of nature underwrites constancy. But in crisis nature is seen (like its derivative, kindness) either to harbour its opposite, the unnatural, or to collapse into that which it was supposed to guard against. So Lodovico of the wrecked Othello:

> Is this the nature
> Whom passion could not shake? Whose solid virtue
> The shot of accident nor dart of chance
> Could neither graze nor pierce?
>
> (IV. i. 256–9)

If nature powerfully underwrites constancy it is most significantly at those crucial points where constancy has failed. So for Brabantio it is against 'all rules of nature' that Desdemona could desire Othello; 'For nature so preposterously to err', it must have been overwhelmed by witchcraft—'practices of cunning hell' (1. iii. 101, 62, 102), with, perhaps, connotations of sexual aberration. But, as already suggested, this is a view of nature beguiled rather than perverted; even though overwhelmed by witchcraft, the integrity of nature holds, and so therefore does the law of racial and cultural differentiation which has its origin in nature's regulation of culture. Hence Brabantio's repeated

---

[3] See Drakakis's analysis of the political and psychological implications of Brabantio's dream in 'The Engendering of Toads', 76.

appeals to nature even after the 'unnatural' event, the violation of natural law.

Fatal Swerve

When Othello recalls Brabantio's words a crucial and fatal transformation occurs: now nature, in the form of female desire, becomes intrinsically perverse, a 'cunning hell' in its own right:

OTHELLO. And yet, how nature erring from itself—
IAGO. Ay, there's the point: as (to be bold with you)
Not to affect many proposèd matches
Of her own clime, complexion, and degree,
Whereto we see in all things nature tends—
Foh! one may smell, in such, a will most rank,
Foul disproportion, thoughts unnatural.

(III. iii. 229–35)

'Nature erring from itself': the perverse originates internally to, from within, the natural. Here Othello imagines, and Iago exploits, the paradoxical movement of the perverse: a straying *from* which is also a contradiction of; a divergence which is imagined to subvert that from *which* it departs in the instant that it *does* depart. In short, from within that erring movement of the first line, a perverse divergence within nature, there erupts by the last line its opposite, the 'unnatural'. Additionally, misogyny and xenophobia are rampant in the accusation of perversion, and so too is racism:[4] Iago demonizes Desdemona and Othello, she as the one who has degenerate desire, he as the object of that desire. Desire and object conjoin in the multiple meanings of 'will most rank' where 'will' might denote at once volition, sexual desire, and sexual organs,[5] and 'rank' lust, swollen, smelling, corrupt, foul. All this in seven terrifying lines which effectively sign Desdemona's death warrant. It is a passage in which (among others) the natural/unnatural binary is powerfully active. I have tried to represent it diagrammatically in the figure. The central, vertical line represents the binary opposition between the natural and the unnatural; it is in the vertical to signify that the binary is also a violent hierarchy. The erring/aberrant movement is

---

[4] On the alignment of both blackness and femininity with sexual monstrosity, see Newman, ' "And Wash the Ethiop White": Femininity and the Monstrous in *Othello*'. In considering the fusion of misogyny and racism in these lines we should remember that neither is a transhistorical category: the changing nature of patriarchy affects the one, the changing history of slavery and colonization the other. But similarities remain: at the time in question, racism relates to beliefs in cultural and national inferiority, while both misogyny and racism would depend on the general belief that unrestrained sexuality, male and female, is destructive, monstrous, perverse; see especially Loomba, *Gender, Race, Renaissance Drama*.
[5] Cf. Sonnets 134–6.

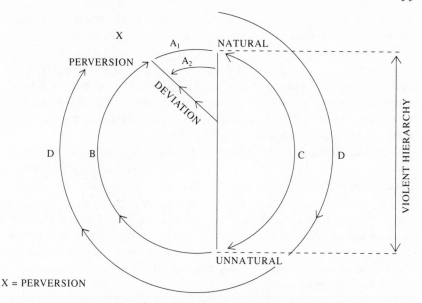

X = PERVERSION

marked as a deviation to the left; this is not arbitrary: psychoanalysis and, more significantly, anthropology confirm an intriguing cultural connection between deviation and left-sidedness. Our language has always confirmed as much: 'sinister', deriving as it does from the Latin for 'left', has, as one of its meanings, 'lying on or towards the left hand' (*Shorter OED*), while the Latin 'sinister' has 'perverse' as one of its meanings (*Cassell's Latin Dictionary*).[6]

The arcs, A_2 to D, represent social and psychic processes inseparable from the operation of the binary, but which it cannot acknowledge in its legitimating function. They are also what makes the perverse dynamic possible (though not in this case). Borrowing from Fredric Jameson, we can call them the political unconscious of the binary. The narrow arc (A_1), running between the natural and the perverse, simply represents the cultural marking or demonizing of difference. It is the identification of a threat which is also a differentiation of it from that which is threatened (the natural). The much wider arc (*B*), running between the unnatural and the perverse, is the field of displacement. That is, it marks the way in which, when the perverse is identified from the position of the natural, there occurs a simultaneous alignment of the perverse and the unnatural: the unnatural is folded up into, thereby

[6] John Donne speaks of 'Modifications, and Temporisings in matter or forme of Religion' as a declining 'towards the left hand'. In the process he reveals another paradox: deviation towards the different involves a move to undifferentiation, a negative inversion of transcendent unity—'to thinke all indifferent, all one' (*Sermons*, vii. 244).

appearing as, the perverse. It is this displacement which helps makes possible the slippage from 'deviation from' to 'contradiction of' noted earlier in the *OED* definition. And what is marked on the other side of the diagram (C) is what really makes the displacement possible: the natural/unnatural binary is only ever a differential relation—that is, a difference which is always also one of intimate though antagonistic interdependence. What is constructed as absolutely other is in fact inextricably related. Hence the double arrow on C.

B and C disclose the operation of A_2: the recognition of the perverse involves a mapping on to the deviation of one part of a split within the natural—nature erring from itself. Just as the unnatural is folded up into the perverse (B), so one part of the split natural is folded down into the perverse. This is marked by A_2. B and A_2 can be imagined as the two hands of a clock, each folding towards the other, and meeting along the axis of the perverse. And we should also remember that this double displacement may be mapped on to either an actual deviation or, as here, an imaginary one.

One might say that when the natural, especially in its guise as the normal (and normative), recognizes the perverse (A_1), it is only ever recognizing itself. But this is not to say that the two are identical, or that one is simply a reflection of the other. In its splitting the natural produces the perverse as a disavowal of itself and a displacement of an opposite (the unnatural) which, because of the binary interdependence of the two (the natural and unnatural), is also an inextricable part of itself. This is represented by that clockwise continuum (D)—from the natural, through the unnatural, to the perverse.[7]

Desdemona allegedly rejects those things to which all things naturally tend. But what is 'nature erring from itself' but bifurcation, the eminently natural process whereby nature reproduces itself? Accordingly in my diagram the perverse deviation might be described as a branching out or an offshoot, and hence Brabantio's/Othello's lines would incorporate the contradiction already remarked: conceptually nature is always enacting or partaking of just that which it is required to repress. But the contradiction is contained, its force reharnessed by the binary it threatened, and which is now restabilized through disavowal and displacement.

[7] A note on this diagram: it aims for a clarity of representation whose effect is to show better the complexity of the processes involved, a complexity which eventually renders inadequate the diagram which made it visible. How, for example, might we map on to it the class antagonism which is an important motivation of the action of the play? The difficulty of doing that is itself illuminating, at least to the extent that it alerts us to the complex and shifting relations between class, racial, and sexual antagonisms.

External Threat/Internal Deviation

It is extraordinary just how much treachery and insurrection Iago manages to displace on to Desdemona in just six lines. How is this possible? *Othello* is partly a play about impending war. Venetian civilization is at stake, at least to the extent that its military has moved to Cyprus to defend the island against the encroaching Turks. As Simon Shepherd observes in his discussion of how the Elizabethans perceived the Turks, they, along with Moors, Tartars, even Persians, constituted the infidel powers which neighboured and threatened European Christendom. He cites the dedication to the work Thomas Newton translated as the *Notable History of Saracens* (1575): 'They were (indeed) at the first very far off from our clime and region, and therefore the less to be feared, but now they are even at our doors and ready to come into our houses' (Shepherd, *Marlowe*, 142). Alvin Kernan has sketched what he sees as the 'symbolic geography' of *Othello*, and the effect it creates of a beleaguered civilization: its outer limits are defined by the Turks—the infidels, the unbelievers—while Othello himself tells of a beyond inhabited by the barbaric and the monstrous. If Venice stands for order, law, and reason, Cyprus is a vulnerable outpost, a garrison town where civilization is to be defended by Othello, 'himself of savage origins and a converted Christian' (*Othello*, ed. Kernan, pp. xxv–xxvii). Richard Marienstras shows how, at this time, England's xenophobia was increasing in spite of, or probably because of, the fact that it was embarking on colonization and expansion: 'in every domain the foreigner was suspect. . . . Every division, every incoherence, constituted a danger' (*New Perspectives*, 103, and chs. 5, 6). The result was a real tension between the anxieties endemic to nationalism, and the ambitions intrinsic to colonialism.

One consequence of tension was a paranoid search for the internal counterparts of external threats. The famous *Homily against Disobedience and Wilful Rebellion* (1571) is obsessed with internal rebellion, the enemy within, weakening the state and rendering it vulnerable to 'all outward enemies that will invade it, to the utter and perpetual captivity, slavery, and destruction of all their countrymen, their children, their friends, their kinsfolk left alive, whom by their wicked rebellion they procure to be delivered into the hands of foreign enemies' (p. 615). In this *Homily* the sin of rebellion encompasses *all* other sins in one (pp. 609, 611–12). Racism clearly played its part here: a royal edict of 1601 expresses discontent 'at the great number of "Negars and blackamoors" which are crept into the realm'; Queen Elizabeth wanted them transported out of the country. The ostensible reason was overpopulation and unemployment among the English, but the representation of black people 'as satanic, sexual creatures, a threat to order and decency, and a danger to white womanhood' was also a factor.[8] Such considerations meant that, for many in early modern England, the implicit confrontation in *Othello* was between civilization and barbarism, and Othello's blackness becomes crucial in just this respect.

According to Iago, Desdemona's 'thoughts unnatural' involve a threefold transgression of 'clime, complexion, and degree'; that is, region, colour, and rank; or, country, race, and class, three of civilization's most jealously policed domains. The same 'nature' (from within which she errs) plays a key ideological role in demarcating the boundaries of these domains, and it does so through the same double process of discrimination/legitimation already encountered. So it is not coincidence that what Desdemona transgresses—country, race, and class— are all three at risk in the war with the Turks. Country, obviously; race in the sense that the enemy is, in the terms of the play, racially and culturally inferior; class, or degree, in the sense that it is the indispensable basis both of the culture being defended and of the military doing the defending; witness Othello's anger at the fight 'on the court and guard of safety'.

Here then is displacement: an external threat recast or 'condensed' as internal deviation. The perverse subject—the desiring woman— becomes, through imagined sexual transgression, a surrogate alien, a surrogate Turk. Perhaps such displacement and condensation, by reproducing internally an imaginary, demonized counterpart of the enemy without, permit a rehearsal of the violence and retribution not as yet unleashed on that enemy? Quite probably, and the way the foreign is reproduced within the domestic is striking. But no entirely functionalist account of this displacement can be adequate to the full extent of its intensity, destructiveness, and paranoia. That is why I have used psychoanalytic terms to describe it. It is also why to understand it we have to explore the vicissitudes of desire as they inform, deform, and reform the psychic and social 'orders'. And why we need to recall that this displacement of the foreign into the domestic is enabled by Othello, a domesticated foreigner. Related to this is the way the internal replication of an external threat is itself replicated in the brawl between Cassio and Roderigo, perceived as being the more threatening for being internal to a beleaguered community and, worse still, taking place 'on the court and guard of safety' and in 'a town of war | Yet wild, [where]

    [8] Jones, *Othello's Countrymen*, esp. 12; Walvin, *Black and White*, esp. 8; Cowhig, 'Blacks in English Renaissance Drama', esp. 4–7, quoted from p. 4; Loomba, *Gender, Race, Renaissance Drama*, esp. 42–5.

the people's hearts [are] brimful of fear' (II. iii. 198, 194–5). The fight risks the *admission* of the alien, not just because the guard is down but because, as a 'barbarous brawl' (154), it is imaged as an internal refiguring of the alien. And the process whereby this external threat reappears as internal disorder is, again, one of *turning*, a perverse deviation into the other: 'Are we turned Turks, and to ourselves do that | Which heaven hath forbid the Ottomites?' (II. iii. 151–2).

The dominant terms of the several binaries in play at this point (reason/passion, order/chaos, Christian/barbarian) are invoked by Othello as supposed guarantors of order; but they are themselves under threat internally (again, the splitting of the dominant term).[9] The most extreme manifestation of this will be Othello's own sexual jealousy. The instability of desire—even or especially desire harnessed within the confines of legitimate heterosexual love—will be shown to harbour the most 'barbarous' passions of all. And so total is the internal subversion effected by desire, that Othello will finally declare that it is he who has turned Turk, the barbarous thus 'turning out' in the 'highest' rather than the 'lowest'. Thus Robert Burton's observation in *The Anatomy*: the civilized, once perverted, does not so much admit the barbaric, as admit to it, discovering it within itself (above, Chapter 8).

Does the fate of Othello confirm, qualify, or discount the charge that this play is racist? Certainly the play enacts a series of displacements of the aberrant and the abhorrent on to the alien. But is it endorsing that process, or re-presenting it for our attention? If the second, then it still remains indeterminate as to whether we, in attending to that process, repudiate or endorse it. Critics and audiences of the play have indisputably done both.

Forget Iago's 'Homosexuality'

The feared internal deviation (Desdemona's perceived identification with the alien) lends urgency to the homosocial alliance[10] between Othello and Iago, whereby masculine honour vows vengeance against both the betraying feminine (Desdemona) and the usurping masculine (Cassio). Within the homosocial perception there is of course a crucial

---

[9] It is simplistic to say that Othello begins as a rational being who then succumbs to passion. Rather Othello submits himself to the negative term of the reason/passion binary after he initially invokes it in the condemnation of others. And the most pernicious element in all this, what effects the subversion of 'reason', is not passion as such, but Iago's sophisticated rationality. As Greenblatt shows, Iago's so-called evil is of the quintessentially civilized kind, the fashioning of self and others (*Renaissance Self-Fashioning*, ch. 6).

[10] 'The male homosocial structure', writes Sedgwick, is that 'whereby men's "heterosexual desire" for women serves as a more or less perfunctory detour on the way to a closer but homophobically proscribed, bonding with another man' ('A Poem is Being Written', 129–30). For a more extensive exploration of the homosocial, see also Sedgwick's *Between Men*).

distinction between female betraying and male usurping: whereas Desdemona's supposed betrayal undoes her, makes her 'foul' and 'false', there is a sense in which Cassio's usurpation makes him, albeit threateningly, more of a man. To be sure he is described as 'loose of soul' (III. iii. 417), but that looseness speaks a certain sexual prowess which becomes the focus for male sexual jealousy. According to Iago, Cassio speaks amorously in his sleep, and (mis)identifies Iago as his lover. So is this the moment when Iago's supposed homosexuality is disclosed via a displacement of it on to Cassio? And if so, does this homosexuality then become the real motive for Iago's otherwise motiveless malignity (rendering it, in other words, the less disturbing because now comprehensible)? Iago's and/or Othello's jealousy may well have a homoerotic component, if only because the homoerotic, like other forms of eroticism, might in principle be anywhere, attached to anyone, and in an indeterminate number of contexts. But we would be mistaken to conclude that 'repressed homosexuality' is the 'real' motivation of the homosocial bond since such a conclusion would obscure much and reveal little. Much more significant for understanding the sexual economy at work here is the way Iago's story, intentionally or not, reveals betrayal/usurpation as the typical *double* focus of masculine sexual jealousy, and a major instability in homosocial bonding. Also significant is the way Iago's story superimposes an excessive usurping masculine desire upon a betraying and unnatural female desire, confirming the culpability of both Cassio and Desdemona, usurper and betrayer, but of course hers more than his.

Cassio has allegedly usurped Othello sexually. And what a terrible ironic coincidence, worse by far than that concerning the handkerchief, that Venice orders Othello home, deputing Cassio to take his place. Here is the most destructive of vicissitudes: the essence of Othello's dignity and power as outsider-turned-insider, namely service to the state (V. ii. 335), now requires him to surrender that power to the one who has (he thinks) already disempowered him sexually. Much agony might be conveyed in some of his least rhetorical, most mundane lines:

> Sir, I obey the mandate
> And will return to Venice. —Hence, avaunt!
>
> > [*Exit Desdemona*
>
> Cassio shall have my place.
>
> (IV. i. 250–2)

Cassio will replace him as governor even as he usurps him as a 'man'. The replacement is legitimate, the usurpation not; but it is because of

that very distinction that in social and psychic terms they are inseparable; such is the power of sexuality but so also the sexuality of power,
and it is why here, as elsewhere in Jacobean drama, the sexually jealous
male paranoically fantasizes his usurping counterpart as strongly as the
(supposedly) faithless woman (see below, Chapter 19). Dwelling on his
ignorance of Desdemona's supposed betrayal, 'her stolen hours of lust',
Othello says, 'I found not Cassio's kisses on her lips' (III. iii. 339, 342).
That he imagines her betrayal 'with mine officer' makes it 'the fouler'—
not only for the reasons just remarked, but also because she has
corrupted the homosocial bond where it *needs* to be strongest (master/
servant) but in practice is often *most* vulnerable. Othello has been made
'nothing of a man' (IV. i. 87) in a way only possible by his homosocial
inferior. So 'she must die, else she'll betray more men' (V. ii. 6). That
resolution, echoing Brabantio's 'Look to her, Moor, if thou hast eyes to
see: | She has deceived her father, and may thee' (I. iii. 288–9), alerts us
again to the primacy and tenacity of the homosocial bond even among
antagonists. It is exploited by Iago, the *actual* betrayer/homosocial
inferior, when he reminds Othello of this very fact: 'She did deceive her
father, marrying you' (III. iii. 208).

There is one further violent and fatal displacement to be observed—
but to whom should we attribute its demonic brilliance, to Iago or to
Shakespeare? Othello reaffirms his own sexuality by sublimating it into
a vow; revenge will be the performance of a displaced but still masterful
virility, anticipated in the vow itself where ritual, rhetoric, and imagery
unite in the effect of controlled urgency and climax, the masterful
orgasm:

> Like to the Pontic Sea,
> Whose icy current and compulsive course
> Ne'er feels retiring ebb but keeps due on
> To the Propontic and the Hellespont,
> Even so my bloody thoughts with violent pace
> Shall ne'er look back, ne'er ebb to humble love,
> Till that a capable and wide revenge
> Swallow them up.

> (III. iii. 454–61)

It is the more urgent and the more controlled for being ritually
underscored—'In the due reverence of a sacred vow | I here engage my
words', and for being deferred: 'Do not rise yet', Iago insists.

Chastity is demonically parodied by Iago as he displaces Desdemona,
evoking in his reciprocal homosocial vow of service the chaste sexuality
of marital fidelity: 'I am your own forever' (480). Is he not also at this

moment a parodic version of that *femme fatale* who undoes the emperor, unmanning even (or especially) in acquiescence? Female beauty has the power to undermine male power, even in the most powerful patriarch of all: 'O, the world hath not a sweeter creature! She might lie by an emperor's side and command him tasks' (IV. i. 174–5). Lying to him while lying beside him; deceitful in acquiescence, disempowering an emperor in the very act of succumbing to him.[11] Again, imagined subversion of the emperor occurs within his innermost sanctuary, and through one who is or should be, especially there, most at his service.

That the homosocial bond is undergoing massive internal manipulations and betrayals is both ironically revealing of the vicissitudes and displacements occurring, and one of their major enabling conditions. If we further recall that the demonized deviant, Desdemona, is no deviant at all, and wonder in passing at what kind of masochistic reparation is at work in Othello's re-enactment of the fatal displacement—identifying himself as surrogate Turk as he kills himself—something terribly revealing emerges: the chaos that comes again when Othello ceases to love is the chaos of displacements which are equally constitutive of, and revealing of, both the social 'order' and the psychic 'order', each inseparable from the other and, in that very connectedness, comprising a dynamic which is neither a chaos nor an order.[12] The social in *Othello* seems at once locked in dislocation and utterly mercurial, a situation perhaps corresponding to the mobility of fantasy and the fixity of power.

Conservative world views work in terms of binaries and by analogy: as ordered government is the antithesis of anarchy, so natural love (heterosexual, patriarchal, etc.) is the opposite of sexual deviation. This structure is given the lie by the perverse dynamic, which indicates that political and sexual ordering is always internally disordered by the deviations it produces and displaces and defines itself against. This is one reason why patriarchy might imagine the greatest threat to it erupting from within that, and those, which it most powerfully controls: the household and women; the foreign erupts within the domestic. Desdemona is mainly confined to the domestic sphere, itself a central point of the patriarchal domain and at the furthest remove from its beleaguered borders—military, political, and economic—and the foreign beyond. So, remarkably, yet in a way all too familiar, the internal deviation which allegedly replicates the external threat is located at the

---

[11] Cf. II. iii. 312–15: 'His soul is so enfettered to her love, | That she may make, unmake, do what she list, | Even as her appetite shall play the god | With his weak function.'

[12] Further displacements are remarked by Marienstras: Iago attributes his own disloyalty to others, and Othello attributes to Desdemona 'the mixture of animality and devilishness that common talk had attributed to himself' (*New Perspectives*, 139, 153).

most protected central region of the patriarchal order, and within one who is, by any substantial criteria, powerless and obedient to the point of abjection.

So we would do well to forget Iago's 'homosexuality'. And to question the 'nobility' it supposedly perverts:

Othello is too simple to be true. The most irritating thing of all is his nobility, which, in his predicament, is nothing more than naivety. When a Black man in the west is portrayed as noble it usually means that he is neutralised. When white people speak so highly of a Black man's nobility they are usually referring to his impotence. It is Othello's neutrality and social impotence that really frightens me. (Ben Okri, 'Leaping Out', 13)

And, third, to repudiate those who invest so heavily in Desdemona's 'virtuous' passivity. That she is actually attempting to live out the prescribed subject position for a woman within sexual difference— chaste, obedient, subordinate, conspicuously faithful—only confirms that because the subordinate is so often the subject of displacement *there is never safety in obedience.* For one thing, to the paranoid, obedience is only ever the mask of duplicity: the obedient woman is always verging on the duplicitous by *virtue* of her silence. Second, a fear that its security can never be total is structured into the social relations of patriarchy, and the (dis)obedient woman is time and again made the agent and vehicle of an ever-feared disruption from within. It is just this fear which Iago and Roderigo play upon when rousing Brabantio at the outset: 'is all your family within? | ... Are your doors locked? ... y're robbed! For shame' (I. i. 85–8). It is a fear which Brabantio knows, and not only in his dreams (though probably there most powerfully); on the one hand Desdemona's transgression is unthinkable because unnatural, a 'treason of the blood'; on the other it is *exactly* what he has anticipated, feared, dreamed of—and tried to prevent: '*How got she out?*' (I. i. 168, my emphasis).

The counterpart of that fear is fascination. Brabantio is fascinated by what he fears. That Desdemona is imagined as the subversive force within should not lead us to overlook that it was Brabantio who actually introduced the 'alien' into his household. He 'loved' (I. iii. 127) Othello, often inviting him as guest. He was the secure senator, fascinated by an exotic stranger so contrasting with the stability of his own existence. And the point when that fascination becomes racist is also exactly where it connects with class:

> The Duke himself,
> Or any of my brothers of the state,
> Cannot but feel this wrong as 'twere their own;

For if such actions may have passage free,
Bondslaves and pagans shall our statesmen be.

(I. ii. 95–9)

Foul as Slander

Othello explores a kind of disorder, instability, and non-rationality which is never 'chaos' as such because it has very specific causes and predictable effects. This is the ordering within chaos and the chaos within order which the binary order/chaos formally disavows even as in practice it exacerbates it.

As we have seen, the diverse instabilities inherent in the beleaguered state, homosocial bonding, homosocial competition, and racist fear, refigure as the inconstancy of woman. It is not only Iago who facilitates this; Roderigo takes for himself the ideal of feminine virginity—'In simple and pure soul I come to you' (I. i. 108)—*even as* he convinces Brabantio of his daughter's disobedience. Female constancy is the paradigm to which other kinds of stability, sexual and political, refer, and upon which they depend, dreadfully and of course impossibly:

EMILIA. For if she be not honest, chaste and true,
There's no man happy; the purest of their wives
Is foul as slander.

(IV. ii. 16–18)

In one sense—certainly for Emilia—this is merely rhetorical: if she is not true no woman is—i.e. of course she is true. But in another sense, one to which the paranoid imagination is terribly susceptible, the supposition confirms what its manifest absurdity was supposed to preclude: all women cannot be true; therefore all women *are* false; therefore she is false. Such is the 'nature' of the inferior (social, racial, or sexual): one instance of deficiency, imagined or actual, confirms the universal deficiency of the entire group. But notice too how sexual betrayal figures in obsessively public terms: foul as slander. Again, the significant others for the cuckolded male are those other men upon whom his honour is socially dependent. And let us remember that Othello *is* dangerously situated; he certainly misidentifies the source of hostility, but not the hostility itself.

The Obscenity of Sacrifice

Truth is never sufficient to allay such an excess of fear—a fear which mirrors itself in the demand for excessive and impossible proof. And because such proof *is* impossible, the demand for it escalates into another even more excessive demand, that for sacrificial reparation: 'I will kill thee, | And love thee after' (v. ii. 178).

Writing on the errant woman, Margaret Soltan observes how the vagrant, wandering woman has figured in narratives of fall and/or conversion (or, as it might more accurately be put, narratives of perversion and/or conversion). For instance, in the Bible, 'womanly vagrancy acts as a recurrent metaphor for Israel's straying from the covenant; the spiritual body, prostituted through promiscuous contact with pagan ways, undergoes mortification and conversion' ('Night Errantry', 109–10).

I find in some critical accounts of Desdemona a half-conscious wish for just such a narrative, except that here a sacrifice of the innocent is imagined to redeem or restore the social order more fully than would have either an actual deviation followed by conversion, or a proof of innocence preventing tragedy. Even as the murder of the innocent is deplored, innocent sacrifice is revered. Such 'tragic catharsis' verges, surely, on the obscene. This is Bradley:

the deed he is bound to do is no murder, but a sacrifice. He is to save Desdemona from herself, not in hate but in honour; in honour but also love . . . terribly painful as this scene is, there is almost nothing here to diminish the admiration and love which heighten pity. (*Shakespearean Tragedy*, 197–8)

Desdemona, the 'eternal womanly' in its most lovely and adorable form, simple and innocent as a child, ardent with the courage and idealism of a saint, radiant with that heavenly purity of heart which men worship the more because nature so rarely permits it to themselves . . . we consent to forgive her for loving a brown man, but find it monstrous that she should love a black one. (pp. 201–2)

She appears passive and defenceless, and can oppose to wrong nothing but the infinite endurance and forgiveness of a love that knows not how to resist or resent. (p. 203)

But there is also an anxiety that she is less than fully passive:

And when we watch her in her suffering and death we are so penetrated [*sic*] by the sense of her heavenly sweetness and self-surrender that we almost forget that she had shown herself quite as exceptional in the active assertion of her own soul and will. (p. 203)

Bradley is not alone in expressing what might be called the masculine erotics of female sacrifice.[13] A more recent, utterly different critic gives voice to a similar vision:

[13] In 'Kiss Me Deadly, or the Des/Desmonized Spectacle', Barbara Hodgdon gives an illuminating account of the way Verdi construes Desdemona in terms of a self-sacrificial passivity, citing a letter from Verdi to his publisher: 'a female who allows herself to be mistreated, slapped, and even strangled, forgives

Othello does not have to kill Desdemona. The play would be more cruel if, in that final and decisive moment he just left her. . . . Othello kills Desdemona in order to save the moral order, to restore love and faith. He kills Desdemona to be able to forgive her, so that the accounts be settled and the world returned to its equilibrium. (Kott, *Shakespeare Our Contemporary*, 98)

Innocent sacrifice will restore the stability both of patriarchal desire and of the social order, thereby momentarily allaying the fear of aberrant movement.

Of the many things at work in the paranoid obsession with female constancy is the fear which settles for nothing less than death. Innocence and submission: the two essential qualities of the sacrificial victim of social crisis, and of the woman in patriarchy, here become one.[14]

Catharsis includes the achievement or perception of a kind of integration. In *Othello* there is never integration. Throughout the play order is a *surface structure*, an arrest of mobility which at the same time intensifies it. Order is not simply the arrangement of the pre-existing, but a structuring of reality which simultaneously produces and represses its opposite, 'disorder'. The social is situated within this dialectic of production and repression, and as such is constituted by extreme tensions between mobility and stasis. The dialectic is at once dynamic and destructive, and manifested among other things as displacements which are not disruptions of order, but major factors in its production and maintenance.

It is via such displacements that ideological formations may not only mask contradictions but, in doing that, also mobilize them. It is also why, when ideology is pushed nearly to incoherence, to the verge of breakdown, those contradictions may be most brutally and effectively mobilized. Such an occurrence is distinct from another wherein ideological legitimation is thrown into such crisis that domination can be sustained only through overt physical force. In practice, however, the two may coexist. 'And yet, how nature, erring from itself . . .': at the moment when the contradictions hitherto contained by the ideological

---

and entreats, she appears to be a stupid thing! But Desdemona is not a woman, she's . . . the type of goodness, of resignation, of sacrifice! They are creatures born for others, unconscious of their own *ego*! Beings that exist in part, and that Shakespeare has poeticized and deified . . . types that have never been encountered, except perhaps in Antigone of the ancient theater.' (Quoted by Hodgdon from *The Verdi Companion*, ed. William Weaver and Martin Chusid (New York: Norton, 1979), 161.) Hodgdon shows how, for Verdi, this sacrificial passivity works to consolidate male subjectivity and perpetuate male artistic practice.

[14] Order is not quite restored until Othello, the agent of this innocent sacrifice, sacrifices himself. Barthelemy points out that at the end of the play Othello becomes both villainous Moor and Justice. His two roles merge (*Black Face Maligned Race*, ch. 5 and esp. p. 159) and cancel each other out.

construct surface and threaten it—when it does indeed become susceptible to disarticulation, most vulnerable to its own force being used
against it—at that very moment Iago reharnesses and reconstitutes that
energy as a force of legitimation/discrimination. At times of crisis there
are always massive pressures for restitution. Iago's success in this respect
depends precisely on an intensification of the wider instabilities within
the state, as well as the social and psychic insecurities of Othello himself.
Let us never lose sight of what occurs in those barely incoherent yet
violently effective displacements worked by and through Iago: the work
of policing boundaries crucial to the maintaining of social domination—
boundaries of country, race, and class—is effaced, dissolved into the
a priori internal regulation of nature.

PART 6

Sexual Perversion:
Pathology to Politics

11 *Freud's Theory of Sexual Perversion*

The process had led to a victory for the faith of piety over the rebelliousness of critical research, and had had the repression of the homosexual attitude as its necessary condition. Lasting disadvantages resulted . . . (Freud, 'Wolf Man')

Conflict

Steven Marcus describes Freud as

one of the last great legatees of the Romantic tradition in European thought. His theories are grounded in the idea of conflict, and this conflict exists in the realm of the normal as much as it does in the pathological. Even his conceptions of integration are touched by it. He sees integration as falling within the larger contexts of conflict and of incompatible needs, contradictory aims, and implacably opposed demands. Such integration as he finds is never complete, rarely adequate, and more often than not unstable. He never envisages the human or the social world as composing now or in the future . . . some harmonious order. (Marcus, *Freud*, 38–9)

Within that broad conflict, we find a more specific one between stasis and mobility. On the one side there is fixation or stasis within psychic disturbance, severe neurosis being seen for example as a state of debilitating deadlock or dislocation or 'a sterile and interminable struggle' (xi. 158). There is too the stasis aimed at by the death wish, the instinct which seeks to dissolve living substance, to bring its units back 'to their primaeval, inorganic state' (xii. 310).

On the other hand there is the radical mobility of desire—what Freud calls, for example, the 'plasticity or free mobility of the libido' (i. 390). Most obviously this concerns sublimation and desublimation, and notoriously, 'the reversal of an instinct into its opposite' (xi. 124). Freud called these various kinds of mobility the vicissitude of the instincts. Vicissitude is one of the most dangerous of Freud's categories. On the one hand it is indispensable for identifying the ways in which psychic and social 'order' is threatened and maintained by extreme psychic and social changes which it can neither control nor acknowledge; as such, vicissitude is the psychoanalytic rearticulation of an earlier preoccupation with perversion as aberrant movement. On the other hand it offers a principle of interpretation with fearful potential for authoritarian misconstruction, whereby something is identified or construed as in actuality its opposite.

Freud's theory of conflict, between a general integration and instability as described by Marcus, and more particularly between fixity and mobility in the realm of desire, may be taken in one or both of two directions: towards the tragic ontology of the human condition, or towards an account of the dynamic of social struggle and change which no narrowly materialist theory can achieve, but which itself remains inadequate and misleading in isolation from a materialist dimension. It is the second option which interests me. I believe it is most radically present in Freud's theory of perversion, and can be recovered in an exploration of the way we find in that theory what I have called the perverse dynamic.

It may be objected that my project is compromised by this inconsistency: I argue that to recover the lost histories of perversion is also to recognize the inadequacies of the sexological and psychoanalytic accounts of desire generally and of perversion specifically; yet, in the process of analysing those histories, I deploy psychoanalytic categories. I concede the inconsistency without regarding it as an insuperable methodological problem. In fact, I welcome the theoretical tension between psychoanalysis and materialism (which is what this inconsistency amounts to), finding in it the impetus to recover the historical and political dimensions which more theoretically self-consistent critiques often gesture towards but rather more rarely engage with, and none more so than psychoanalysis. This is incorporated in this study as a commitment to a cultural analysis generated both *by* the provocative convergences between otherwise incompatible theoretical perspectives, and then *across* their manifest divergences; put another way, the analysis is situated at that point between materialism and psychoanalysis where an overlap is also a gap. Such analysis foregrounds theoretical divergences in the very process of making analytic sense. Again, history is used to read theory as well as vice versa.

Repressive Deployments

In our own century the repressive deployment of psychiatry, and of some forms of psychoanalysis, has been obvious and notorious, and especially with regard to homosexuality.[1] Here too, even within the

---

[1] See especially Lewes's detailed recent history, *The Psychoanalytic Theory of Male Homosexuality*.

most pathological sense of perversion, older theological conceptions survive. As an example I have chosen an essay by Sandor Feldman from a collection called *Perversions: Psychodynamics and Therapy*, edited by Lorand and Balint (and containing an essay on fetishism co-written by Lacan). Feldman writes: 'As a practitioner, I have learned that, essentially homosexuals want to mate with the opposite sex. In therapy my intention is to discover what kind of fear or distress diverted the patient from the straight line and made a devious detour necessary.' All homosexuals, Feldman states confidently, started as heterosexuals. Moreover, 'the main part of the therapy . . . is to emphasize that the patient's original position is a healthy one, given as a precious gift by nature'. The analyst must bear in mind always that

his real goal is to bring the patient to the biologically given heterosexual relationship which is not *created* by the therapy but *liberated* for use. . . . The homosexual will, for a while at least, stubbornly insist that he is a 'born homosexual' . . . that homosexuality remains for him the only route to sexual gratification. This is all untrue. The more convinced the analyst is that an underlying natural personal relationship in sexual and in other ways is present, the more likely will the patient come to the same conclusion as the analyst: that man is born for woman and woman is born for man. (pp. 74–5, 93–4; Feldman's emphasis)

This article is crasser than some, but not untypical in its assumptions. It might be said to exemplify Foucault's view of the way psychoanalytic and other related discourses helped create the category of the homosexual in new mechanisms of social control which include a legitimation of dominant modes of sexuality—i.e. of heterosexual genital intercourse aiming at reproduction within family confines, etc. But I want to add a different point. Feldman couches his narrative of normal psychosexual development in the ordinary-language counterparts of a metaphysical tradition privileging dominant social formations, sexual and otherwise, in terms of essence, nature, *telos*, and universal.[2] He produces an 'essential' hetero/sexuality developing along a teleologically defined path of psychosexual development (this path—Feldman's 'straight line'— being already encoded in the biological origin) to the universally 'natural' goal: heterosexual union. Further, perversion is to nature as deviation/diversion is to the straight line of normality.[3]

---

[2] Writing in 1948, Kinsey and others pointed out that previous so-called 'scientific' classifications of perversions by the pioneer sexologists 'have been nearly identical with theologic classifications and with the moral pronouncements of the English common law of the fifteenth century. This, in turn, as far as sex is concerned, was based on the medieval ecclesiastical law which was only a minor variant of the tenets of ancient Greek and Roman cults, and of the Talmudic law' (Kinsey *et al.*, *Sexual Behavior*, 202; see also Weeks, *Sexuality*, 70).

[3] One way the metaphysic survives in a modern mutation is in the description of the homosexual as

So this theory is not only a crass appropriation of Freud, but a containment of the perverse via a traditional metaphysical schema which helped construct a theology of the perverse and which, as we shall see, Freud rejected. It is worth being clear about this at the outset: Freud had used his account of perversion to subvert theories of sexuality growing from the metaphysical tradition that Feldman reinvokes in his, Freud's, name. In much of his work Freud subverts the traditional metaphysic by retaining and developing the paradoxes and displacements within the semantic field of perversion. In particular, he retains and intensifies the major paradox outlined earlier: the shattering effect of perversion arises from the fact that it is integral to just those things it threatens. Perhaps Freud's most succinct and provocative formulation of this is his assertion that one does not become a pervert, but remains one (viii. 84). His theory reveals, if only at the level of allegory or myth, a crucial dynamic of domination and deviation, insurrection and suppression. So while one of the editors of the book in which Feldman's essay appears claims that all its contributors accept as valid Freud's formulations on the perversions, in fact Feldman's view of them is directly opposed to Freud's in virtually every main respect.

Feldman also reactivates in Freud's name a psychoanalytic moralism which Freud deplored, and which, as Kenneth Lewes shows, has been especially prevalent in the United States. Henry Abelove has charted Freud's disagreement with those American psychoanalysts who resisted Freud's progressive pronouncements on homosexuality, and who 'have tended to view homosexuality with disapproval and have actually wanted to get rid of it altogether' ('Freud, Male Homosexuality, and the Americans', 62). Freud 'knew, despised, and opposed' this moralistic strain, which has dominated psychoanalytic thinking in America, but he never succeeded in overcoming or even mitigating it (p. 62). Abelove quotes a letter from Freud to James Jackson Putnam, an analyst from Harvard who had written to Freud expressing a desire for the analyst to take a stronger moral line with patients. Freud replies: 'Sexual morality as society—and at its most extreme, American society—defines it, seems very despicable to me. I stand for a much freer sexual life' (p. 63). Outside the United States, especially in recent times, the moralism has become muted, but the normative metaphysic which sustains it survives. It informs Elizabeth Moberly's teleological view of gender identity, published in 1983. She writes:

'bent', and the heterosexual as 'straight'; the OED gives as one meaning of 'bent': 'perverted; *spec.* homosexual', and cites a passage from MacInnes's *Absolute Beginners* (1959).

Heterosexuality is the goal of human development, but it implies a heteropsy-chologic personality structure, which is based on the fulfilment of homo-emotional needs and not their abrogation. Homosexuality is not the goal, but it is the means to the goal. . . . The fulfilment of homosexuality is itself the attainment of heterosexuality . . . heterosexual relationships may be stable or unstable . . . but they are not inherently self-limiting as homosexual relation-ships are of their very nature. (*Psychogenesis*, pp. x, 84; for a summary of Moberly's argument see her 'New Perspectives'; see also Segal, 'Interviewed')

All this being said, it remains true that the limitations of the psychoanalytic project itself also facilitate subsequent conservative appropriations of it. In certain respects psychoanalysis actually shares with metaphysics a residual teleology, the idea of a normative sexuality achieved by passing through the sequential stages of a universal psychosexual development. And here above all, to ignore history is to repeat it.[4] But if it is the ahistorical dimension of psychoanalysis which allows the tradition of Western metaphysics to be reinvoked in its name, it is also true that the challenge of the perverse remains inscribed irreducibly within psychoanalysis, as within metaphysics. And there is a real sense in which Freud reactivates that challenge at the theoretical level.

Before elucidating Freud's theory there is one further respect in which we might usefully observe the older conceptions of perversion surviving into their modern sexological counterparts. In a fascinating study Peter Stallybrass and Allon White remark how, in Freud's hysterical patients, 'the broken fragments of carnival, terrifying and disconnected, glide through the[ir] discourse'. Stallybrass and White trace the elimination of carnival and popular festivity from European life from the seven-teenth to the mid-nineteenth century: 'The demonization and the exclusion of the carnivalesque has to be related to the victorious emergence of specifically bourgeois practices and languages which reinflected and incorporated this material within a negative, individual-ist framework.' So carnival did not simply disappear; rather, it under-went 'migrations, concealment, metamorphoses, fragmentations, internalization and neurotic sublimations. . . . In flux, dispersed across new artistic and psychic domains, these carnivalesque fragments formed

---

[4] Normative conceptions of human nature persist even in a radical psychoanalysis. Yiannis Gabriel has argued this in relation to the work of two Freudian radicals, Wilhelm Reich and Erich Fromm. Though differently, each advanced the view that 'human emancipation requires only [!] a revolution in the social base and superstructure and in the psychic superstructure'; it need not touch the all important 'psychic base', the source of an essential goodness and revolutionary potential in human nature. Thus argues Gabriel; both Reich and Fromm posit 'a human core in each individual, which is totally unpolluted by society; human nature is discovered in the profound depths of the individual's soul', itself untouched by society (see *Freud and Society*, 191).

unstable discursive compounds, sometimes disruptive, sometimes thera-
peutic, within the very constitution of bourgeois subjectivity' (*Politics
and Poetics*, 171, 176, 182). Just as the lost histories of perversion
remain active in the psychosexual narrative of desire, so the lost histories
of carnival remain active in bourgeois subjectivity and neurosis. Repression, fragmentation, and return: perhaps this account is already too
psychoanalytic. And yet it remains immensely suggestive, first because
carnival and perversion are connected by a mutual involvement in
inversion, second because of the way it forewarns us that the psychosexual disorder effected by perversion is always more than sexual.

Freud's Theory of the Perversions

The following sketch of Freud's theory, as expounded in *Three Essays
on the Theory of Sexuality*, and further elaborated in later works, has
two main aims. First, I want to explore the way he addresses the
paradoxical dynamic of perversion; in the process I seek to outline,
more generally, a theory more challenging than most contemporary
versions of psychoanalysis allow—even those which have sought to use
Freud in the name of a progressive sexual politics. In fact, since Freud,
we have been faced not only with the crassness of Feldman's version of
perversion but also, within more sophisticated versions of psychoanalysis, with a disregard of Freud's much more challenging account of
perversion.[5] Second, it is part of my longer argument that the perverse
dynamic begins to undermine key aspects of the psychoanalytic project
itself, just as it did within theology earlier.

Freud described homosexuality as the most important perversion of
all (xv. 222) as well as the most repellent in the popular mind (viii. 84),
and as one which, for these reasons (and others), obsessively preoccupies
many cultures, including our own. He also found homosexuality to be
so pervasive in human psychology, and made it so central to psychoanalytic theory, that he became unsure as to whether or not it should be
classified as a perversion.[6] Rather than decide whether or not homosexuality *is* a perversion, I shall show how the concept of the perverse

---

[5] Just one indication of this disregard is the virtual absence of an account of the perversions in the
obligatory summaries of Freud which preface the use of psychoanalysis within literary and cultural theory
(see for example Eagleton's *Literary Theory*). This may be related to the fact that, as Leo Bersani suggests,
the complexity and obscurity of some recent returns to Freud—e.g. Lacan's—have perhaps given an
intellectual respectability to Freud while leaving intact some of the more conservative elements of Freud's
work—e.g. his phallocentrism, the category of neurosis, and a normative notion of psychosexual
development (*The Freudian Body*, 2). As regards the perverse there are exceptions, suggestive rather than
developed, but useful nevertheless. For example, Brooks in 'The Idea of a Psychoanalytic Criticism'
(pp. 7–8) suggests, following Roland Barthes in *S/Z* that 'the work of textuality may ensure that all
literature is, by its very nature, essentially perverse'.

[6] At one stage Freud distinguished the two; later he made the distinction less sharply, and then in

dynamic questions the very perspective which classifies sexual practices as diverse as (say) masturbation and incest as in some sense the same, i.e. perverse.[7] Hence again an insistence that my use of concepts like homosexuality and perversion remain provisional and context-specific. Each has undergone massive changes of meaning, and neither can be taken to refer to a cultural and/or sexual and/or psychic constant. In this and following chapters I shall be following but, increasingly, also questioning the meaning Freud gives to these concepts.

The general importance which Freud attributes to perversion is most apparent in *Three Essays*, first published in 1905. He says: 'the abandonment of the reproductive function is the common feature of all perversions. We actually describe a sexual activity as perverse if it has given up the aim of reproduction and pursues the attainment of pleasure as an aim independent of it' (i. 358). On this account, especially since the arrival of the post-modern, we are presumably all perverts now, actual or aspiring. (One recalls the post-modern anecdote about the foot fetishist who was in love with the foot but had to settle for the whole person.) A more specific definition is clearly required, and Freud provides it: perversions are sexual activities which involve an extension, or transgression, of limit in respect 'either to the part of the body concerned or to the sexual object chosen' (viii. 83). In the first case (the part of the body) perversion would involve a lingering over the intermediate relations to the sexual object—as with the foot fetishist just invoked—relations which 'should normally be traversed rapidly on the path towards the final sexual aim'. That is, reproduction via heterosexual genital intercourse (vii. 62). In the second case (sexual object), it would involve the choosing of an 'inappropriate' object—e.g. someone of the same sex.

In Freud's theory the human infant begins life with a sexual disposition which is polymorphously perverse and innately bisexual. It is a precondition for the successful socializing and gendering of the individual—i.e. for the production of the subject within hetero/sexual difference—that the perversions be renounced, typically through repression and/or sublimation. In this way not only is the appropriate human

---

Introductory Lectures (1915–17) homosexuality was included again in the class of perversions. (See xv. 222, where he declares that homosexuality is the most important of the perversions and so much so that it scarcely deserves the name.) These shifts perhaps reveal both Freud's sense of the significance of homosexuality and his residual sense of the perversions as intrinsically rather than contingently pathological. Lewes suggests that Freud maintained the distinction between homosexuality and perversion (*The Psychoanalytic Theory of Male Homosexuality*, 29–30).

[7] Roger Scruton subdivides perversion into bestiality, necrophilia, paedophilia, sado-masochism, homosexuality, incest, fetishism, masturbation, and chastity (*Sexual Desire*, ch. 10, and below, Ch. 17).

subject produced but so also is civilization reproduced—and doubly so: civilization protects itself against the anarchic nature of the perversions while at the same time tapping them as a source of ordering energy. Repressed and sublimated perversions help to form, and are intrinsic to, normality. They might also be said to be the cement of culture, helping 'to constitute the social instincts' (xi. 437–8); providing 'the energy for a great number of our cultural achievements' (viii. 84; cf. xii. 41). So Freud says of the 'Wolf man' that 'each piece of [his] homosexual libido which was set free [from repression] sought out some application in life and some attachment to the great common concerns of mankind' (ix. 307).

If it is true that one does not become a pervert but remains one (viii. 84), then the real conservative is the pervert (Freud claims that his discoveries have 'quite remarkably increased the number of people who might be regarded as perverts': vii. 86). It is sexual perversion, not sexual 'normality', which is the given in human nature. Indeed, sexual normality, as with ideological formations more generally, is precariously achieved and precariously maintained: the process whereby the perversions are sublimated can never be guaranteed to work; it has to be re-enacted in the case of each individual subject, and is an arduous and conflictual process, a psychosexual development from the polymorphous perverse to normality which is less a process of growth and more one of restriction (vii. 57). Sometimes (again like ideology) it does not work; sometimes it appears to, only to fail at a later date. Civilization, says Freud, remains precarious and 'unstable' (i. 48) as a result. This is especially bad news for those forms of psychosexual identity (e.g. masculinity) which conceive themselves in terms of (psychic) stability, and see it as their function to maintain (social) stability. But even if the process does work, Freud says, it is at the cost of happiness itself; there will always remain a fundamental antagonism between instinctual desire and the demands of civilization (vii. 258–9). If on the one hand sublimated desire produces 'the noblest cultural achievements', they will stem from a renunciation which will forever be the cause of suffering (vii. 259).

Freud also sees an important connection between the repression of the perversions and hostility towards psychoanalysis: 'Society believes that no greater threat to its civilization could arise than if the sexual instincts were to be liberated and returned to their original aims. For this reason society does not wish to be reminded of this precarious portion of its foundations' (i. 48).

What causes the failure of repression and sublimation? For one thing the individual's innate sexual instinct may simply be too strong to submit. This idea suggests the hydraulic theory of sexuality for which Freud has been justly criticized. But he has another account of why it fails. In the article ' "Civilized" Sexual Morality and Modern Nervous Illness' (1908) he makes especially clear a thought which runs through his analysis, namely that there is something counter-effective in the very mechanism of repression, and indeed within the entire civilizing process: instead of transforming perverse desire into civilized achievement, it counter-productively coerces the subject into a perverse or neurotic existence (see e.g. xii. 52); the pain of normality is not just the consequence of a more or less successful renunciation but the effect of a radical contradiction, an extreme dysfunction. This contradiction operates not just between civilization and the instincts, but *within* civilization. I return to this below.

The importance of the perversions in the contradiction between civilization and the instincts is most obviously manifested in the psyche. For example, *all* neurosis is related to the perversions. In all neurotic people, says Freud, 'tendencies to every kind of perversion can be shown to exist as unconscious forces' (vii. 155); their unconscious fantasies show precisely the same content as the recorded actions of perverts (viii. 84). Homosexuality is especially important: 'homosexual impulses are invariably discovered in every single neurotic' (i. 349). Freud insisted that he has never yet come through a single psychoanalysis of a man or a woman 'without having to take into account a very considerable current of homosexuality' (viii. 95). The repression of perverse desire actually generates neurosis; hence Freud's famous assertions that neurosis is the negative of perversions (e.g. at viii. 84).

Certain kinds of paranoia are the expression of desublimated but still repressed homosexual desire. Freud's account of the tortuous process whereby repressed homosexuality comes to be expressed as paranoia can be paraphrased as follows: the proposition 'I (a man) love him' is contradicted by delusions of *persecution* which loudly assert: 'I do not *love* him—I *hate* him'. This proposition then becomes transformed by projection into another: 'he *hates* (persecutes) me, which will justify me in hating him', and ends up as 'I do not *love* him—I *hate* him, because he persecutes me' (ix. 200–1). So paranoia in Freud's analysis is both less delusory and more revealing than its current popular use allows: less delusory in the sense that it is not just a delusion of being persecuted but an active homophobic attempt to persecute; more revealing in that, if Freud is correct, the popular remark 'just because we're paranoid it doesn't mean to say they're not after us' is complicated by the fact that 'us' may well in fact be 'them'.

Unlike some of his followers, Freud precisely does not see perversion as mainly a problem for neurotics. His view of the relationship between the perverted and the normal can be summarized in a threefold form. First, 'some perverse trait or other is seldom absent from the sexual life of normal people' (i. 364); second, rather than an absolute break, there is a continuum between the normal and the perverted (vii. 74); third, we can only understand normal sexuality by understanding its pathological forms (i. 348; cf. vii. 52). Once again, homosexuality is particularly pervasive of this relationship. Indeed, everyone, says Freud, has made a homosexual object choice, if only in their unconscious. In short: 'in addition to their manifest heterosexuality, a very considerable measure of latent or unconscious homosexuality can be detected in all normal people' (ix. 399).[8] All this means that, as regards the differences between manifest homosexuality and heterosexuality, 'their practical significance remains but their theoretical value is greatly diminished' (i. 349)—a formulation which sounds straightforward but becomes less so the more one ponders it, and for reasons suggested by Freud elsewhere: 'from the point of view of psychoanalysis the exclusive sexual interest felt by men for women is also a problem that needs elucidating and is not a self-evident fact based upon an attraction that is ultimately of a chemical nature' (vii. 56–7).

In a footnote added in 1919 to his study of Leonardo, Freud reiterates this argument but with a significant addition: everyone has made a homosexual object choice and 'either still adheres to it in his unconscious or else protects himself against it by vigorous counter-attitudes' (xiv. 191). Such counter-attitudes help constitute what will come to be called homophobia (below, Chapter 16), and relate suggestively to Freud's 1915 account of negation: 'the content of a repressed image or idea can make its way into consciousness, on condition that it is negated. Negation is a way of taking cognizance of what is repressed; indeed it is already a lifting of the repression, though not, of course, an acceptance of what is repressed' (xi. 437–8).

This inextricable involvement of the perverse with the normal partly explains why 'we' experience feelings of hostility towards manifest perversions: 'it is as though no one could forget that they are not only something disgusting but also something monstrous and dangerous—as though people felt them as seductive, and had at bottom to fight down a secret envy of those who were enjoying them' (i. 363). Their very 'multiplicity and strangeness' (i. 346; see also vii. 64) constitutes a

---

[8] Freud reiterates the centrality of homosexuality 'within' heterosexuality in a footnote to *Three Essays* added in 1915: 'libidinal attachments to persons of the same sex play no less a part as factors in normal mental life, and a greater part as a motive force for illness, than do similar attachments to the opposite sex' (vii. 56–7).

threatening excess of difference, leading Freud to compare them with 'the grotesque monsters painted by Breughel for the temptation of St Anthony or to the long procession of vanished gods and believers which Flaubert leads past, before the eyes of his pious penitent [*La Tentation de Saint Antoine*]. Such a medley calls for some kind of arrangement if it is not to confuse our senses' (i. 346, my emphasis).

Freud is unrelenting in finding perversion, especially homosexuality, in those places where it is conventionally thought to be most absent, and where identity is dependent upon that supposed absence (if to be *this* is to be *not that*, then to be discovered to be *that* after all is no longer to be *this*). For example, he sees an inextricable connection between perversion and childhood. It is not only that children are sexual beings but that their sexuality is quintessentially, one might say naturally, perverse (i. 352). All children, says Freud, may well be homosexuals (viii. 268).[9] Conversely, he finds in perversion those qualities conventionally denied to it as part of *its* identity: if children are perverse, it is also the case that there is a quality of childlike innocence about the perversions themselves, there being for Freud a sense in which infanthood is a time of original perverse plenitude, while adult perverse sexuality is understood as 'nothing else than a magnified infantile sexuality split up into its separate impulses' (i. 352). And far from being 'bestial' or 'degenerate' the perversions are intellectual and idealistic:

It is perhaps in connection precisely with the most repulsive perversions that the mental factor must be regarded as playing its largest part in the transformation of the sexual instinct. It is impossible to deny that in their case a piece of mental work has been performed which, in spite of its horrifying result, is the equivalent of an idealization of the instinct. The omnipotence of love is perhaps never more strongly proved than in such of its aberrations as these. *The highest and lowest are always closest to each other in the sphere of sexuality.* (vii. 75, my emphasis)

Similarly, love, far from being that which transcends perversion, may well be that which releases it: 'Being in love . . . has the power to remove repressions and re-instate perversions' (xi. 95). Elsewhere Freud describes the perversions as 'fertile' (i. 391). Might he be deliberately trying to scandalize? Perhaps, especially considering his reference (shortly before a passage just quoted) to those perversions which involve 'licking excrement or . . . intercourse with dead bodies' (vii. 74).

---

[9] Freud also suggests that sublimated homosexuality may play its part in parenthood; he says of Schreber, one of his most famous patients: 'His marriage, which he describes as being in other respects a happy one, brought him no children; and in particular it brought him no son who might have consoled him on the loss of his father and brother and upon whom he might have *drained off* his unsatisfied homosexual affections' (ix. 194, my emphasis).

Moreover this same passage is glossed with the authority of Goethe: 'vom Himmel durch die Welt zur Hölle' (*Faust*, 'Prelude in the Theatre'). Elsewhere Freud finds a similarity between having sex with children and having it with animals, the two being discussed under the same subheading. Generally he is disinclined to spare his readers the details (see e.g. vii. 64–5, 70–3), and his clinical, scientific approach is of a piece with his analysis of disgust at the perversions as 'purely conventional', illogical, and irrational (vii. 64; viii. 83–4). This implies an expectation that we could and should divest ourselves of such prejudice. But this is surely naïve, especially for reasons provided by Freud himself, namely that disgust, shame, and morality are fundamental psychic principles of cultural order (vii. 76, esp. n. 1; vii. 75). Also, of course, he is offering a theory which shows how perversion undermines that order. It occasionally strikes one that Freud really did desire to provoke; that there was a certain perversity in his very procedure, and the claim to clinical detachment is partly a shield from behind which he conducts this at times anarchic provocation (see viii. 32).

That apart, even from this brief account certain implications of Freud's theory are clear. At the very least, a range of central binary oppositions upon which the social order depends (spiritual/carnal, pure/degenerate, normal/abnormal) collapse into relational interdependence—a deep, mutual (if problematic) implication. But even more is at stake: this narrative represents more accurately than most the complex dialectic relations between subordination and insubordination, and its importance in this respect may be increased rather than diminished if we choose to regard it as a mythological or allegorical narrative rather than, as claimed, a scientific account of human psychosexuality. Of course, it may contain elements of both, with their incompatibility contributing not a little to its disturbing implications.

Freud certainly regarded the perversions as potentially highly subversive. Their persistence and ever-threatened re-emergence means not just that individuals remain or become dislocated, but that civilization has failed to secure its own reproduction. When the perversions re-emerge the repressive organization of sexuality which constitutes normality 'falls apart' (vii. 156). In its 'path to perversion . . . the libido has withdrawn from the ego and its laws, and . . . renounced all the education it has acquired under the ego's influence . . . it becomes refractory' (i. 405–6). In its perverse forms the sexual instinct 'goes to astonishing lengths in successfully overcoming the resistances of shame, disgust, horror or pain' (vii. 74). Given that disgust, horror, and shame are crucial internalized cultural restraints, indispensable mechanisms for securing the social order through the psychic order (vii. 64, 76), this is, in Freud's terms, indeed refractory. The same challenge is implicit in his primary definition of perversion as *an extension, or transgression, of limit*, the limit being understood either with respect to the part of the body concerned, or the sexual object chosen (viii. 83); or as a forbidden returning to a stage which civilization and normality demand that we pass through. The perverse returning to this stage means that *the normative goal of a development is subverted by that which it is not, but which it has to pass through in order to be*. In this sense then the perversions are precisely insurrectionary. Interestingly, it is when they become an instance of the (in)subordinate entirely displacing the dominant (for which read heterosexual, reproductive, genital intercourse)—when they oust it completely and take its place in all circumstances (vii. 75)—that Freud is prepared to regard them as pathological.[10] But even then the boundary cannot be clearly drawn, because pleasure and pathology are inseparable:

The feeling of happiness derived from the satisfaction of a wild instinctual impulse untamed by the ego is incomparably more intense than that derived from sating an instinct that has been tamed. The irresistibility of perverse instincts, and perhaps the attraction in general of forbidden things, finds an economic explanation here. (xii. 267)

In statements like this the inversions which characterize Freud's theory become especially apparent: perversion, conventionally imagined as the definitive manifestation of inauthenticity and even degeneracy, becomes here the expression and rediscovery of an original intensity of being; even, perhaps, an original integrity of being.

In summary then, Freud attributes to the perversions an extraordinary disruptive power: they subvert, first, the genital organization of sexuality, thereby sabotaging the whole process of normative psychosexual development (or subjection) upon which civilization depends; and second, sexual difference itself, along with the entire functional aspect

---

[10] The idea that sexual deviation involves a fierce, perverse partiality is quite common. George Steiner invokes it in discussing Genet: 'In Jean Genet there is no such completeness [as in Proust]. On the contrary there is a fierce striving for partiality' (*On Difficulty*, 121–2). It echoes an older, more inclusive criterion of evil. Augustine asserts that pride, the source of all evil, is a turning from the fullness of God to the partiality of the self. But in Freud, unlike Augustine, the partiality of perversion is not necessarily less than the whole, since perversion retains its connection with the polymorphous perverse, the original plenitude of being; also it defies the 'limit' prescribed by culturally ordered sexuality, replacing reproduction with pleasure. Plenitude may remain an ideal, but for many within the Augustinian tradition certain kinds of plenitude—cultural, sexual, and racial diversities, for example—are intolerable. Yet again the hatred and fear of sexual nonconformity relates to other kinds of, and wider, fears—for example, the fear that too much diversity will exhaust our resources, crowd our space, divert us from the effort of a necessary progress, or fragment the discipline and order of the social body. In such fears it becomes especially apparent that the kinds of organization and progress which our culture values seemingly require not only 'rational' forms of control and exclusion, but their paranoid counterparts.

of sexuality, whether it be biological (reproduction) or social (sublimation). Further, perversion 'also subverts many of the binary oppositions upon which the social order rests: it crosses the boundary separating food from excrement (coprophilia); human from animal (bestiality); life from death (necrophilia); adult from child (pederasty); and pleasure from pain (masochism)' (Silverman, 'Masochism and Male Subjectivity', 33). Lastly, perversion affords more pleasure than those forms of organized desire based on its repression (and this apart from the pleasure of transgression itself), and it may be produced by what is conventionally assumed to be at the furthest possible remove from it, that is, being in love.

Crucially, according to Freud, perversion is ineliminable. It remains manifest in three principal ways: an active practice for some; the repressed constituent of neurosis in others; the unstably sublimated basis of civilization itself.

Antagonistic Dependencies

I have set Freud's account of perversion against Feldman's not in order to return to Freud—to recover the authentic voice of psychoanalysis— but to follow further the complex history of perversion, and to stress Freud's own deconstructive assault on normality. Via Freud we can see that the concept of perversion always embodied what has now become a fundamental deconstructive (or post-structuralist/modernist or whatever) proposition: whatever a culture designates as alien, utterly other, and incommensurably different is rarely and perhaps never so. Culture exists in a relationship of difference with the alien, which is also a relationship of fundamental, antagonistic, discursive dependence—most obviously (though not only) in terms of the binary opposition (Derrida's 'violent hierarchy') and its political unconscious. *The absolutely other is inextricably within.* Jonathan Culler has summarized the process with characteristic lucidity: 'Freud begins with a series of hierarchical oppositions: normal/pathological, sanity/insanity . . . conscious/unconscious, life/death'. In each case the first term has been conceived as prior, and the second, situated on the margins of the first, 'an undesirable, dispensable deviation'. Freud shows what is at stake in our desire to repress the second term: 'Understanding of the marginal or deviant term becomes a condition of understanding the supposedly prior term'— hence the revolutionary impact of Freud (Culler, *On Deconstruction*, 160–1).

Culler is approaching Freud from and for the practice of an urbane form of deconstruction, and I suspect that Freud goes farther than he allows.[11] After all, Freud argues not just that civilization understands itself through perversion, but that the latter, via sublimation, remains integral to the former. Using again that pleasurably inappropriate metaphor of growth, we can say that civilization is rooted in perversion. One does not become a pervert but remains one; put differently, every insider was once, and in a crucial sense remains, an outsider; every inlaw remains an outlaw. If, as has been argued, and most persuasively perhaps by Jacqueline Rose, the importance of psychoanalysis lies in its account of how identity is necessarily unstable, then this is never more so than in Freud's account of perversion. At every stage perversion is what problematizes the psychosexual identities upon which our culture depends.

If culture's repeated disavowal of the centrality of perversion is expressed in and through the endless demonizing of the manifest pervert, it is also true that the perverse dynamic both reveals and undermines the double process of disavowal and displacement which demonizing entails. Perversion, in the form of the perverse dynamic, destroys the binary structure of which it is initially an effect. Freud brilliantly identifies these processes in psychic terms, and his categories offer a way of analysing them in social terms; I am thinking especially of his concepts of repression, disavowal, negation, and splitting. One of the most astute accounts is in his article 'On Repression' (1915):

the objects to which men give most preference, their ideals, proceed from the same perceptions and experiences as the objects which they most abhor, and . . . they were originally only distinguished from one another through slight modifications. . . . Indeed . . . it is possible for the original instinctual representative to be split in two, one part undergoing repression, while the remainder, *precisely on account of this intimate connection*, undergoes idealization. (xi. 150, my emphasis)

Also crucial are his accounts of how disavowal always involves a simultaneous acknowledgement of what is being disavowed (xv. 438–40), and of the operation of what he calls reactive reinforcement:

Contrary thoughts are always closely connected with each other and are often paired off in such a way that *the one thought is excessively intensely conscious while its counterpart is repressed and unconscious*. This relation between the two thoughts is an effect of the process of repression. (viii. 89; cf. Stallybrass and White, *Politics and Poetics*, 189–90)

---

[11] Deconstruction may be most illuminating when it sees itself as the practice of deviation and perversion; see Derrida, 'My Chances/Mes Chances', where he embraces deviation as a mythology (in Smith and Kerrigan eds., *Taking Chances*, esp. 6); also his theorizing of the supplement in terms of perversion in *Grammatology*, esp. 144–52.

And, as we have seen already, in his view that negation bears the indelible print of what is negated. Negation facilitates a controlled return of the repressed: the content of a repressed image or idea can make its way into consciousness on condition that it is negated (xi. 437–8).

Such are the processes which produce the perverse and which are in turn destabilized by the perverse dynamic and the paradoxical perverse. The perverse dynamic also reveals displacement as one of the main vehicles of repression, negation, and disavowal, and itself works in terms of displacement. Indeed, it may be that, of all Freud's concepts, displacement is the most appropriable for a cultural politics.[12] Yet Freud's own reluctance to use the concept in this way is indicated in a story which appears in several places in his work:

> There was a blacksmith in a village, who had committed a capital offence. The court decided that the crime must be punished; but as the blacksmith was the only one in the village and was indispensable, and as on the other hand there were three tailors living there, one of *them* was hanged instead. (i. 209; see also vi. 267 and xi. 385–6)

In using this story as a specific example of the way displacement works, Freud describes it as a joke. Without wishing to diminish its humour we might add that it is also a rather acute example of the socio-political working of displacement, as Freud's gloss elsewhere indicates only too well; it shows, he says, how 'punishment must be exacted even if it does not fall upon the guilty' (xi. 386). But here too he seems disinclined to follow this insight through into the socio-political dimension, restricting it to exemplifying an individual psychic mechanism (the way neurotic acts of revenge can be directed against the wrong people).

If Freud's theory of perversion anticipates a fundamental tenet of the post-structural or the post/modern, the pre-Freudian history of perversion manifests the dynamic which both Freud and the post-structuralists identify. And it is in exploring that dynamic in its pre-Freudian history that we see very clearly the limitations of the Freudian model of displacement. Freud discloses the displacement of sexuality into culture, for example, via sublimation. But displacement also *goes the other way*: as we saw in Chapters 8–10 above, and especially in *Othello*, social crisis and conflict are endlessly displaced into sexuality. And this may well be the more important kind of displacement. Certainly it is why today perhaps the most crucial task for a sexual politics—literally a

---

[12] Even one of Freud's most intransigent critics, David E. Stannard, agrees on the importance of his concept of displacement, it being, according to Stannard, one of the few Freudian concepts which has, to any extent, weathered the rigours of empirical investigation (*Shrinking History*, 94 and 107).

matter of life and death for some—is to chart this displacement of the political *into* the sexual (in contrast, for example, to *liberating* the sexual). Recovering and developing the concept of the perverse dynamic is fundamental to that task.

'Civilized' Sexual Morality and Social Critique

Freud's theory also incorporates the second paradox of the perverse outlined in Chapter 8, that we are created with forbidden desire. But such desire in Freud is more natural than unnatural; it is that notorious 'piece of unconquerable nature' (xii. 274). This results in an inversion of the 'tragic ontology': for Greville in his 'Chorus Sacerdotum' (above, Chapter 9) we are created sick and commanded to be sound; for Freud we are created sound and commanded to conform in a way which produces sickness. We can see this most clearly in Freud's article '"Civilized" Sexual Morality and Modern Nervous Illness' (1908), which is also one of the most interesting points at which his account of psychosexuality moves towards social critique, and brings me back to the contradiction within civilization (as distinct from that between civilization and the instincts) mentioned above. I approach this article via a rehearsal of an elementary but important critique of his work.

It has been said of Freud that, whereas he saw the individual as 'internally divided, racked by ambivalence, packed to the ears with contradiction and strife', he nevertheless 'utterly failed to see society in the same light', this being because, 'like most other psychologists who have attempted to generalise their concepts into a social theory . . . he operated with a consensual model of society' (Connell, *Which Way is Up?*, p. 11). Nevertheless, continues Connell (and here he is referring to the argument of R. Osborne's 1937 study, *Freud and Marx*), Freud's theories remain fundamentally dialectical, focusing on contradiction and transcendence, and doing so with concepts which are inherently critical and subversive (pp. 15, 13). To the extent that Freud's theories are dialectical (and it is arguable, depending on which texts are chosen), this is nowhere more so than in his account of perversion. The dynamic of perversity as he outlines it does indeed become contradictory in a dialectic sense, and so marks one of those important breaks in Freud when his theory suddenly has challenging implications for a materialist analysis. However, because the break in question occurs here, in relation to sexual perversion, it is where materialist critics of a conventional disposition least expect, or want, to find it.

In '"Civilized" Sexual Morality' Freud's focus for the failure of repression shifts from the subjective to include the social, in other words, from the instinctive drive that resists repression—the subject's 'unyielding . . . innate constitution' (xii. 39)—to the social forces which inhibit repression. Although only partially so, this goes along with a shift of attention from psychosexual pathology to social dysfunction. Freud argues that 'civilized' sexual morality—that is, the sexual morality imposed by and within modern civilization to secure its survival—results in increased neurosis and deviation. He distinguishes three evolutionary stages of civilization ('kultur'): 'a first one, in which the sexual instinct may be freely exercised without regard to the aims of reproduction; a second, in which all of the sexual instinct is suppressed except what serves the aims of reproduction; and a third, in which only *legitimate* reproduction is allowed as a sexual aim. This third stage is reflected in our present-day "civilized" sexual morality' (xii. 41).

More than any other kind, modern civilization demands high levels of sexual repression, the energy of the sexual instincts being 'displaced' (pp. 39–40) or sublimated into increased or higher cultural activity and development. But there is a limit to the extent to which this can work, and in practice the result is that in avoiding the pressure to sublimate, the individual may turn to perversion and other forms of deviation which run counter to the requirements of civilized sexual morality. Most notably, such deviations undermine marriage, the institution which is central to that morality. Freud presents civilized sexual morality as immensely damaging, not only to the individual, but also to the social order which it is its rationale to protect and perpetuate (see especially pp. 47–8); once again he speaks of desublimated perversions as not merely alternative to civilized sexuality, but actively hostile towards both it and the social order which that sexuality shores up.

Freud also discusses at length the role of sexual repression in causing neurosis. Again, neuroses are described as the negative of the perversions 'because in the neuroses the perverse impulses, after being repressed, manifest themselves from the unconscious part of the mind—because the neuroses contain the same tendencies, though in a state of "repression" as do the positive perversions' (p. 43). On this model neurosis is understood as a failed suppression of perversion, one which is no less injurious both to the individual and to civilization, than perversion in a non- or desublimated form:

I must insist upon the view that neuroses, whatever their extent and wherever they occur, always succeed in frustrating the purposes of civilization, and *in that way actually perform the work of the suppressed mental forces that are hostile to civilization.* (p. 54; my emphasis)

There are further twists in this destructive struggle between desire and morality. Freud asserts that 'the psychical value of sexual satisfaction increases with its frustration' (p. 45). Suppression can be said to have an opposite effect to that intended, intensifying rather than reducing or transforming. He also suggests how that dysfunction occurs at a structural level within society, as well as within the individual subject. He begins his article by citing long extracts from several 'eminent observers' (p. 35) on the connection between increasing nervous illness and increasing pressures within modern civilized life. Freud's own emphasis in his article falls on one principal cause of neurosis, namely the increased pressure to renounce and sublimate desire in the interest of civilization. Predictably, this corresponds to the emphasis in the authorities he cites—with the exception, that is, of the first, W. Erb, who stresses the extent to which modern civilization incites rather than represses desire. This is Erb, as quoted by Freud:

City life is constantly becoming more sophisticated and more restless. The exhausted nerves seek recuperation in increased stimulation and in highly-spiced pleasures, only to become more exhausted than before. Modern literature is predominantly concerned with the most questionable problems which stir up all the passions, and which encourage sensuality and a craving for pleasure, and contempt for every fundamental ethical principle and every ideal. It brings before the reader's mind pathological figures and problems concerned with psychopathic sexuality, and revolutionary and other subjects. (pp. 35–6)

Political assumptions and values are apparent here, and even more so in the fuller extract quoted from Erb by Freud.[13] It is not my concern even to try to disentangle them. The point is rather that Freud incorporates into his argument a view of modern civilization as actively producing that which, according to Freud, it needs to suppress and sublimate for its own survival. This occurs both at the individual level—desire intensified through frustration—and at the social level—desire incited as well as suppressed.

So what occurs in Freud's account is a kind of reversal of the repressive function; an almost opposite effect emerges, and occurs not contingently but necessarily, as a consequence of the developmental logic of civilization whereby it pushes itself always to the point of dysfunction. The result is that what culture 'should' repress it actually begins to produce, and it produces it in the very act of repression. A violent dialectic emerges here between repression and perversion, and it

---

[13] This analysis of the relationship between civilization and perversion also figured in the debate as to whether perversion was hereditary or brought about environmentally. As Sulloway points out in his useful overview of this debate, it was yet one more stage in the endless nature–nurture controversy (Sulloway, *Freud*, ch. 8, 'Freud and the Sexologists', esp. p. 288).

is at this point that Freud elucidates a crucial dimension of the perverse dynamic. It is also at this point that Freud and Foucault might be compared rather than contrasted, not least because ' "Civilized" Sexual Morality' is a fascinating commentary on the authority/subversion/containment process: in Freud's theory culture develops to a point where it begins to produce, instead of sublimating, perversion; it incites what it should conceal, isolates what it should absorb, pressures into an independent existence what it should transform. And where this results in neurosis rather than sublimation, it is effectively destroying the subjectivity it should be fashioning. We might say in such instances that authority does indeed produce its own subversion, and precisely in the effort to contain it.[14]

Surviving Repressions

' "Civilized" Sexual Morality' has about it a deceptive facility. It reads so fluently that one can at first miss the full extent to which Freud is presenting a view of society, as well as subjectivity, as deeply and negatively conflicted. Corresponding to this is a certain ambivalence towards sexual deviation. At first sight Freud's attitude towards deviation is more judgemental in this article than elsewhere. He asserts that auto-erotic, 'substitutive' sexual practices like masturbation 'predispose to the numerous varieties of neuroses and psychoses which are conditional on an involution of sexual life to its infantile form' (p. 51). Here the teleological view of psychosexual development begins to look normative in much more than a descriptive sense. Of masturbation Freud goes on to say that 'in the phantasies that accompany satisfaction the sexual object is raised to a degree of excellence which is not easily found again in reality' (p. 51). Of other, perverse, activities he says they are 'ethically objectionable, for they degrade the relationships of love between two human beings from a serious matter to a convenient game attended by no risk and no spiritual participation' (p. 52).

What is interesting about these last two quotations is that Freud is both speaking for and undermining the perspective of 'civilized' sexual morality. The perverse dynamic has become part of his narrative. Even as the deviations are being condemned, he complicates the judgement by ascribing a form of idealism to the fantasy life of masturbation, and playfulness to interpersonal perversions. Who, after all, could *not* be

---

[14] Without judging the correctness or otherwise of Freud's theory, it can be observed that it did not obviously require this dialectic. Presumably it might be plausibly argued that as civilization consolidates itself, its repressive and sublimating tendencies could be alleviated rather than intensified. In fact, radical Freudians argued something like this.

tempted by the prospect of sexuality liberated from seriousness, risk, and spiritual participation. Freud adds a remark from 'a witty writer' to the effect that 'Copulation is no more than an unsatisfying substitute for masturbation' (p. 51). He covers himself by describing this remark as a cynical, witty inversion of the truth. But in fact it is no more than the implication of his own theory, less an inversion of the truth than a truthful inversion. Irony and ambiguity apart, this article also constitutes a quite direct critique of civilized sexual morality and its sanctioned form, heterosexuality. Freud insists that it is utterly destructive of relationships even, or especially, within marriage, and particularly for women; the intellectual inferiority attributed to women he would trace back to 'the inhibition of thought necessitated by sexual suppression' (pp. 50–1). In the words of John Fletcher, this essay presents a 'picture of heterosexuality as a casualty ward of psychic cripples and walking wounded, of male impotence and female frigidity' ('Psychoanalysis and Gay Theory', 93–4), so much so that Freud himself is led to remark, 'we may well raise the question whether our "civilized" morality is worth the sacrifice' (p. 55). Freud also suggests that whereas men may evade repression via perversion, women are driven to neurosis. At the same time, his explanation of why this is so—namely that they possess a weaker sexual instinct (p. 43) and are less capable of sublimation (p. 47)—reminds us more clearly than anything else in this piece of the limitations in the psychoanalytic theory of sexual difference.

Freud is almost contemptuous of sexual abstinence, which he has often found to produce 'well-behaved weaklings who later become lost in the great mass of people that tends to follow, unwillingly, the leads given by strong individuals' (pp. 48–9). And he evinces barely disguised respect for the person who refuses to conform sexually and thereby 'becomes a "criminal", an "outlaw", in the face of society—unless his social position or his exceptional capacities enable him to impose himself upon it as a great man, a "hero"' (p. 39). Correspondingly there is less sympathy than might be expected for those who 'wish to be more noble-minded than their constitution allows' and so fall victim to neurosis. He adds, wryly, 'they would have been more healthy if it could have been possible for them to be less good' (p. 43). As he put it some years later: 'perverts who can obtain satisfaction do not often have occasion to come for analysis' (x. 184). He also states unequivocally that it is an obvious social injustice that morality should demand of everyone the same conduct of sexual life. The critique of civilized sexual morality lends credence to those who find in Freud's writing a 'deeply-buried libertarianism' (Connell, *Which Way is Up?*, 8–9); remarks elsewhere in Freud support that, including that from 'Wolf Man' which heads this chapter, where it is observed that the suppression of 'the homosexual attitude' leads to the victory of 'the faith of piety over the rebelliousness of critical research'. This is especially pertinent, given that most of what Freud wrote fitted into the latter category, and was often a direct attack on the former. But it is not necessary to insist that Freud was consciously writing a subversive text. He may have been; or his goal may have been a strategic ambiguity reflecting ambivalence. The important point is that, consciously or not, the dynamic he identifies within the subject, and within the social order, finds its way into his own text as a result of what he has 'discovered' about perversion, its repression and sublimation.

12 *Deconstructing Freud*

Other complications, too, may arise but they can easily be fitted into the general scheme. (Freud, 'Dora', viii. 90)

Freud acknowledged that his theory *needed* homosexuality: 'Before I had learnt the importance of the homosexual currents of feeling in psychoneurotics, I was often brought to a standstill in the treatment of my cases or found myself in complete perplexity' (viii. 162). But to what extent did he actually discover these 'homosexual currents' or rather construct something which his theory needed? It might be said that he half discovered, and more than half produced them— if only to register their paradoxical, excessive, and often fraught status in psychoanalytic theory. Whatever, once invoked, 'homosexuality' kept problematizing not only the prevailing categories of psychosexual normality—something which Freud clearly wanted it to do— but also the theory which needed it, and which its discovery initially enabled. The various ways in which it did so, either independently, or as a representative of the perversions, is the subject of this chapter.

Leo Bersani writes: 'as an antidote to the denunciation of psychoanalysis as the most sophisticated modern technique for the definition and control of desire' there has been a movement to deconstruct Freud, one which makes it seem naïve to assume that 'he is saying what, for the most part, he obviously thought he was saying' (Bersani, *The Freudian Body*, 1–2). By typically looking for or provoking an incoherence, a kind of breakdown deeply revealing of something other within, deconstruction enacts that now obsolete early modern sense of *disco*herence (above, Chapter 6) which the perverse dynamic always implied; to that extent, deconstruction is an inherently perverse procedure for which homosexuality is an eminently suitable subject. Before pursuing this intriguing connection between homosexuality, perversion, and deconstruction, there is another kind of problem in Freud, more mundane yet equally important. It concerns the tension between theory and evidence.

Deconstructing Freud (1): Theory versus Evidence

One way homosexuality causes a problem for psychoanalysis is quite straightforwardly: some of the things Freud subsequently discovered via his theory simply did not fit the theory. Here it is necessary to recall Freud's commitment to empirical evidence, no matter how inadequate it might seem. The theory of psychoanalysis was, Freud reminded his readers in 1919, based on observation (x. 192). He also supported the recording and acknowledging of cultural and individual difference; we find him agreeing with Ferenczi that a large number of different conditions have been 'thrown together under the name of homosexuality', and it is perhaps in recognition of diversity that he also approves Ferenczi's use of homoeroticism as a better word than homosexuality (vii. 58). Freud further approves of the displacement of the pathological theory of perversion by the anthropological (vii. 50), and typically invokes a historical perspective when challenging conventional prejudice against homosexuality (e.g. viii. 83–4). Sulloway concludes that Freud was not only in close touch with the anthropological movement of his time, but also an influential participant in it (*Freud*, 318).

But there emerges also in Freud's writing a doubt as to the adequacy of his theory in relation to the cultural diversity revealed by anthropology, and presumably his own experience, clinical and otherwise,[1] and limited as the former may have been. In places his theory cannot adequately account for that diversity, and especially in the case of homosexuality. For example, he speaks of the sexual aim of homosexuals as operating 'in a manner that is not yet quite understood'; similar remarks on homosexuality are scattered throughout his work: 'why some people become homosexual . . . we are frankly not able to explain' (vii. 354); 'psychoanalysis has not yet produced a complete explanation of the origin of inversion, nevertheless . . .' (vii. 56 n. 1910; see also vii. 57 n. 1915; vii. 58–9; vii. 167).

In 1920 Freud refers to 'the various forms of homosexuality, which *incidentally* are manifold' (ix. 376, my emphasis). In fact, such diversity is never incidental, and has only been disregarded in psychoanalysis because so difficult to accommodate to some of its founding, and often transhistorical, categories. Repudiating the stereotypes of the homosexual and the heterosexual Freud remarks, simply, 'Experience . . .

---

[1] The question of Freud's own homosexuality, though relevant, is neither presupposed nor proved in my account. In letters to Ferenczi in 1910 Freud speaks of the overcoming of his own homosexuality, of having succeeded 'where the paranoic fails' (*Complete Letters*, 2–4). See also Moi, 'Representation and Patriarchy: Sexuality and Epistemology in Freud's Dora', esp. 190; Gay, *Freud: A Life for our Time*, 86–7, 274–6.

proves the contrary', adding moments later: 'The *mystery* of homo-sexuality is . . . by no means so simple as is commonly depicted in popular expositions' (ix. 398, my emphasis). This last remark nicely illustrates the different implications of his theory: on the one hand a recognition of the way diversity contradicts the assumptions of preju-dice; on the other an inclination to constitute homosexuality as a mystery and thereby invite yet further misconceptions, now erudite rather than popular. But perhaps this mystery is mainly the problem of homosexuality within and for psychoanalysis.[2]

What emerges in Freud is a tension between a recognition of actual homosexual diversity and a wish to organize it conceptually within a theory of desire which duplicates the problem,[3] and leads him into inconsistency. One such inconsistency is especially apparent. As we have seen, a major implication of his theory is that desublimated, non-repressed perversion involves an undoing of civilization. If neuroses are the negative of the perversions, and the pervert achieves a psychic health at the cost of refusing sublimation, or undergoing a desublimation, then, in a way which echoes the biblical idea that non-procreative sexuality is a waste of seed (casting it among the rocks), the pervert expends unsocialized libido at the expense of the social order. At the very least the active pervert is as 'useless for society' as the neurotic (xii. 43).

Yet, against this, Freud several times makes the empirical observation that practising homosexuals may be especially civilized (see i. 345; vii. 49; viii. 84; x. 208). He also suggests a connection between this fact (being civilized—'social feeling'—x. 208) and a 'new mechanism' (yet another!) in the aetiology of homosexuality, namely that it 'not infrequently proceeds from an early overcoming of rivalry with [other] men' (x. 208). He also speculates on 'the remarkable fact, the explanation of which might carry us far', that 'homosexual love is far more compatible with group ties, even when it takes the shape of uninhibited sexual impulsions' (xii. 176; cf. xi. 96, xi. 377), and observes that 'certain homosexuals' are relatively free of the anal character—that is, a compulsion towards parsimony, orderliness, and obstinacy, 'reaction formations or counter forces' generated by the repression of anal eroticism (vii. 215, 211).

---

[2] Elsewhere Freud speaks of that 'multiplicity of determining factors' which affects a person's 'final sexual attitude' (vii. 57). But is such perception of multiplicity even compatible with speaking of a final sexual attitude? Shouldn't we at least speak of attitudes (plural), none of which is necessarily final? Compare *Civilization and its Discontents*, where Freud begins with an acknowledgement of 'how variegated the human world and its mental life are', and the danger of large generalizations about that world, only to proceed, notoriously, to give one such generalization after another. But if Freud can be easily criticized for frequently generalizing from too little evidence, what makes the criticism plausible is his own admitted reliance on such evidence, and his 'scientific' notion of what a theory should be.

[3] This is especially apparent in Freud's notoriously inadequate analysis of Dora. See e.g. the essays collected in Bernheimer and Kahane eds., *In Dora's Case: Freud–Hysteria–Feminism*.

Freud seems aware of this inconsistency between seeing non-repressed or desublimed perversion as damaging to society, yet actual homosexuals as more than usually socially minded, and makes an attempt to address it, rather feebly, at the end of another essay, 'Some Neurotic Mechanisms in Jealousy, Paranoia and Homosexuality': 'In the homosexuals with marked social interests, it would seem that the detachment of social feeling from object-choice has not been fully carried through' (x. 208). The fact remains that, within the Freudian scheme of things, an active homosexual with strong social involvement is something of a contradiction (cf. Hocquenghem, *Homosexual Desire*, 96). So this was never only a matter of a theory being unable to account for some new evidence; it was also where the theory itself was becoming internally incoherent, where homosexuality begins to disable that which it initially enabled. If, as Laplanche and Pontalis remark, 'the lack of a coherent theory of sublimation remains one of the lacunae in psychoanalytic thought' (*The Language of Psychoanalysis*, 433), it is in part because of the contradiction represented by the active homosexual with strong social involvement—of which, of course, there have been many, even within 'official' history.

Even so, I am concerned not to invoke too quickly the charge of theoretical incoherence, if only to avoid underestimating the extent to which these inconsistencies are related to Freud's rational and, historically speaking, progressive commitment to the empirical. Bersani speaks disparagingly of 'the guardians of the empirical in the American Psychoanalytic Association' and with every reason. In the face of the manifest limitations of the empirical as conceived within such institutions, there has been a tendency to rest everything on theoretical speculation. But theory alone does not rescue the subordinate from the repressive and exploitative representations of the dominant. A rigorous concern for evidence, especially the evidence of cultural specificity and cultural difference, and a commitment to its rational assessment, have always been important factors in dismantling the ideological (mis)representation of the subordinate by the powerful, whether it be in terms of class, sexuality, or race. Subordinate cultures have never been able to afford to dispense with the 'historical real', or 'rationality', even though it is those within such cultures who know, better than most, the dominant ideological bias of concepts such as rationality and realism, and the way that dominant ideologies are typically structured so as to override contradictory evidence.[4]

---

[4] Just one material instance: Bernard Sheehan shows in *Savagism and Civility* how English mythologies of native Indian cultures in Virginia in the early seventeenth century would override evidence to the contrary.

Deconstructing Freud (2): Perversion against the Oedipus Complex

The Oedipus complex has been conspicuously absent from my account so far, especially given its status as the most fundamental principle of psychoanalysis: 'the importance of the Oedipus complex', wrote Freud in 1920, 'has become more and more clearly evident; its recognition has become the shibboleth that distinguishes the adherents of psychoanalysis from its opponents' (vii. 149–50). I am not persuaded by Freud's theory of the complex. Certainly I do not believe that it has universal applicability.[5] Further distrusting the obviously conservative use to which the complex has been put within psychoanalysis, I must remain, in Freud's intransigent terms, an opponent of psychoanalysis rather than its adherent.

What exactly is the Oedipus complex as defined by psychoanalysis? It is not easy to summarize clearly, being a complicated and arguably confused theory; Freud himself never gave a systematic account of it (Laplanche and Pontalis, *The Language of Psychoanalysis*, 283). Essentially it is a theory of how the human being becomes positioned within the existing system of social and sexual difference as a result of a critical and fraught relationship with his or her parents. Laplanche and Pontalis again:

In its so-called *positive* form, the complex appears as in the theory of *Oedipus Rex*: a desire for the death of the rival—the parent of the same sex—and a sexual desire for the parent of the opposite sex. In its *negative* form, we find the reverse picture: love for the parent of the same sex, and jealous hatred for the parent of the opposite sex. In fact, the two versions are to be found in varying degrees in what is known as the *complete* form of the complex. (pp. 282–3)

In the resolution of the complex, elements of the psychic and sexual life of the child which are incompatible with its social/sexual positioning within the polarities of sexual difference are repressed and sublimated, especially its incestuous desires, but also the perversions more generally. In John Fletcher's succinct formulation, the law of the Oedipal polarity commands, in effect: 'you cannot *be* what you desire; you cannot *desire* what you wish to be' ('Psychoanalysis and Gay Theory', 101, 114). The

---

[5] Frantz Fanon repeatedly encountered this problem in his pioneering psychoanalytic consideration of the psychology and psychic effects of racism. Usually Fanon rejected the universalizing claims of the discipline in favour of cultural (rather than sexual or racial) difference, especially *vis-à-vis* the Oedipus complex which, 'like it or not . . . is far from coming into being among the Negroes'. He contends, explicitly against Lacan, that 'it would be relatively easy for me to show that in the French Antilles 97 per cent of the families cannot produce one Oedipal neurosis. This incapacity is one on which we heartily congratulate ourselves (*Black Skin, White Masks*, 151–2; cf. 93).

entire theory is thus built upon a disjunction between desire and identification, itself a key element in two of the most normative principles of psychoanalytic theory, especially since Freud: the idea of the naturalness of heterosexuality, and its achievement through a process of universal, sequential psychosexual development.

It is worth remarking with Juliet Mitchell—not so much in defence of Freud, but to indicate the contradictions in his work—that although it was his 'discovery' of the Oedipus complex which led him to assume a natural heterosexuality, the rest of his work at that time argued against this (Mitchell, introduction to Lacan, *Feminine Sexuality*, 12). As regards the second principle, the sequential model of sexual development, Sulloway observes that Freud did not invent it. Again the objective here is neither to disparage nor to exonerate Freud, but to see better his historical positioning. Contrary to the Freudian legend, argues Sulloway, this crucial idea was established in the sphere of sexual studies by Havelock Ellis and Albert Moll several years before Freud's similar views became well known (*Freud*, 310). Moreover Freud not only 'endorsed a development conception of libido (including sequential stages)' but, above all, 'he rationalized such phenomena within a biological, and Darwinian, conception of sex. . . . Thus, the ideas of Freud, Fleiss, and the sexologists were all part of a major conceptual offshoot of the Darwinian revolution' (p. 318).

Sequential development is fundamental for Freud. Apart from the complex itself, which is something one arrives at and moves through, successfully or otherwise, on the way to a positioning within hetero/ sexual difference, we need only ponder some of Freud's other key concepts to see further the part which the idea of development plays in his work: fixation involves arrested development, regression its reversal. In 1935 he wrote a now famous and much quoted letter to a woman concerned about her son's homosexuality. Among other things he says: 'Homosexuality is assuredly no advantage, but it is nothing to be ashamed of, no vice, no degradation, it cannot be classified as an illness . . .' He goes on to point out (again) that highly respectable individuals including great philosophers and artists have been homosexual. In these respects, as Henry Abelove points out, this letter encapsulates Freud's liberal attitude on the subject. But there is more of this letter, rarely quoted by those who invoke it as evidence of Freud's liberalism. For example: 'we consider [homosexuality] to be a variation of the sexual function produced by a certain arrest of sexual development'; and, as for 'treating' it: 'sometimes we succeed in developing the blighted germs of heterosexual tendencies which are present in every homosexual' (Abelove, 'Freud, Male Homosexuality, and the Americans', 59). With characteristic succinctness, Jeffrey Weeks makes the crucial point: 'A "development" assumes an appropriate end result, and "arrest" an artificial blockage' (Weeks, *Sexuality*, 73).

Perverse Insurrections

In 'A Child is Being Beaten (A Contribution to the Study of the Origin of Sexual Perversions)', published in 1919, Freud wants to propose 'the derivation of perversions from the Oedipus complex' (x. 179). But he is unable to do so confidently, not least because he also sees perversion as struggling with and against the complex, 'forcing [it] into a particular direction, and by compelling it to leave an unusual residue behind' (x. 178). Already perversions are disrupting that from which they derive, that which is invoked to explain them. And things got worse, as we can see from the following summary of the potentially ludicrous position psychoanalysis comes to occupy in its repeated attempts to 'explain' homosexuality as a series of 'unsuccessful' resolutions of the Oedipus complex:

it is still widely believed that a boy turns out to be homosexual when he identifies with his mother and becomes effeminate. . . . Or, by identifying with his mother, he later wants to repeat the joys he experienced with her by choosing boys whom he can treat as his mother treated him. Or without identifying with her at all, his wish to have sex with his mother becomes transformed into a wish to enjoy the kind of sex she enjoys. Or maybe he is really heterosexual after all, but is in love with his mother and wants to stay true to her, so he gives up all other women. Or simply by loving her too much he can have his sexuality prematurely aroused at a time when it has nowhere to go but toward other boys. Or if she is a mean mother, he comes to hate her, ever afterward disliking and distrusting all women. Or whether he loves her or hates her, on discovering she has no penis he develops a 'castration complex' that forces him to turn to other males in a need for sex-with-safety. (Tripp, *The Homosexual Matrix*, 78–9)

If, as I suggested in the previous section, attempts to account for homosexual diversity have pushed psychoanalytic theory into inconsistency and even absurdity, this is most acutely the case in relation to the Oedipus complex. Perversion proves the undoing of the theory which contains it. Of course Tripp's account is an oversimplification, a parody even. Granted, but those complexities within psychoanalysis to which appeal is made to 'save' the complex also contain and perpetuate the incoherence which makes the parody possible. Even *within* psychoanalysis the complexity which might save the complex comes to undermine its normative function. Thus, it has to be conceded that the fully elaborated forms of the Oedipus complex are 'extremely complex and ambiguous. Their mechanisms are not straightforward and unidirectional, and the relevant component forces undergo a bewildering variety of transformations, repressions, and conversions into their opposites.' Worse still from the normative point of view, 'the only way we can continue to maintain that heterosexuality is the natural resolution of the Oedipus complex is *further to complicate its mechanism*' (Lewes, *The Psychoanalytic Theory of Male Homosexuality*, 78, 80, my emphasis). Reading Tripp's summary in the light of this, it is easy to be reminded of the geocentric/Ptolemaic theory of the universe and the way it had to become increasingly complicated to account for ever more complex stellar movement, finally succumbing to inconsistency and facilitating the epistemological break into heliocentric theory. Except that as yet psychoanalysis has encountered no such break.

If, as Lewes shows, homosexuality became, within psychoanalysis, a victim of the normative regime inaugurated by the Oedipus complex, on the subsequent 'perverse' reading of Freud, the Oedipus complex increasingly becomes a casualty of homosexuality. It is only relatively recently that psychoanalytic critics have begun to read Freud in this way, taking up those dimensions of his work which explore the insurrectionary 'nature' of the perversions. Particularly intriguing is the way that, in the formulation remarked earlier, homosexuality becomes a refusal of that polarity at the heart of the Oedipal injunction: 'You cannot *be* what you desire, you cannot *desire* what you wish to be' (Fletcher, 'Psychoanalysis and Gay Theory', 114); in refusing this polarity homosexuality would also appear to be refusing to conform to that fundamental division between desire and identification which is not only at the heart of the Oedipal injunction, but fundamental to our gender system and indeed to our entire culture.

One line of analysis sees the insurrection in the terms of the Oedipal drama: perversion is a refusal or attempted subversion of those organizing principles of culture which are secured psychosexually, principles which include sexual difference, the law of the father, and heterosexuality. This perspective usually assumes that these struggles are contained, or at least can be explained, *by and within* psychoanalysis. However, another line of enquiry finds in the insurrectionary nature of the perversions a challenge not only to the Oedipal law, but to the entire Oedipal drama as a theory: perversion comes to challenge the integrity of the psychoanalytic project itself. The next two sections consider each of these two lines of enquiry.

Creativity

Janine Chasseguet-Smirgel's *Creativity and Perversion* exemplifies the first kind of analysis. Because she accords considerable subversive, but also creative, potential to it, and exceptionally so within the orthodox psychoanalytic tradition, perversion emerges in her analysis as much more than arrested development. At the same time, and in this same preoccupation with creative subversion, we can see especially clearly how psychoanalysis is a translation into more or less exclusive psychosexual terms of enduring Western mythologies: for Chasseguet-Smirgel the pervert is the incarnation of some of the most enduring archetypal rebels and trangressive strategies that the West has known, including some of those designated by the pre-sexological concept of perversion discussed earlier. The pervert is at once creative and destructive, seeking to escape the human condition (p. 12) and to rival God (p. 5) by reducing created order to confusion and/or monstrousness—the hubristic generating the hybrid (pp. 6 ff.); the pervert also parodies and inverts right order (pp. 10–11), turning the world upside-down and inside out. If the Bible offers us the founding categories of civilization—division, separation, distinction, differentiation—the pervert is engaged in a Lucifer-like striving to bring everything back to nought (pp. 3, 4), eroding the differences between the generations as well as those between the sexes (p. 2).[6] Augustine would have understood this.

Through an interesting variation on the deviation metaphor, Chasseguet-Smirgel describes the pervert as one who refuses to travel the long path to sexual maturation via the Oedipus complex, preferring instead 'the short path' (p. 29); or, as she puts it elsewhere, the pervert is one who wants to pass without sitting the exam (p. 34). So Freud is right, she thinks, in describing the pervert as *artful* (pp. 26, 151). One is tempted to add that if the shortest path must, almost invariably if not by definition, be straighter than the longer path, then presumably the pervert is here going straight. Chasseguet-Smirgel also argues that the pervert has a special disposition to be artistic because of a compulsion to idealize (p. 91), although in the case of Oscar Wilde's writing (she thinks), this idealization only thinly masks sadism and anality. In what is quite possibly the nadir of psychoanalytic criticism, and certainly one of its more infelicitous examples, she reads *Dorian Gray* as a novel in which 'We [*sic*] see clearly' that 'anality is not so much changed by the

---

[6] Compare Francis Pasche who, writing in 1964, contended that the fantasies underlying homosexual object choices involve a rebellion against God, a wish 'to correct, to remake, thwart, parody and finally destroy the divine creation, that is to say, the creature of the Father' (cited in Fletcher, 'Psychoanalysis and Gay Theory', 113).

idealization process as it is merely covered with a coating of glittering jewels, like the Happy Prince, or as in the dream of [a patient of Chasseguet-Smirgel's] who conceals the logs or the chocolate under a coating of silver' (p. 98).

In *Creativity and Perversion* the creative-anarchic challenge of the perverse is collapsed or reduced to an exclusively psychosexual subversion—the struggle to displace the 'genital universe of the father' through a regression to the 'anal-sadistic universe of confusion and homogenization' of the pervert (pp. 2, 11). Perversion operates *vis-à-vis* the Oedipus complex, trying to elude its fatal character, rebelling against its universal law, and its correlative, the threat of castration (pp. 82, 151).

Masochism

Kaja Silverman's 'Masochism and Male Subjectivity' also explores the challenge of perversion but with a very different emphasis, combining as she does greater psychoanalytic sophistication with a more searching sexual and cultural politics. But she too argues that 'the concept of perversion is . . . unthinkable apart from the Oedipus complex, since it derives all its meaning and force from its relation to that structuring moment and the premium it places upon genital sexuality' (p. 32). She argues that at certain moments perversion can pose a radical challenge to sexual difference (p. 33). Pointing out that the perversion which has received most attention, namely sadism, is also the one most compatible with conventional heterosexuality, Silverman chooses instead to focus on masochism, and male rather than female masochism. She sees perversion as possessing a double nature, being 'simultaneously a capitulation and a revolt' (p. 32), and characterized by exaggeration: at the heart of masochism for example is a distinct talent for impersonation, mimicry, and masquerade. Her fascinating critique/reading of Freud moves towards the view that the male masochist

acts out in an insistent and exaggerated way the basic conditions of cultural subjectivity, conditions that are normally disavowed; he loudly proclaims that his meaning comes to him from the Other, prostrates himself before the Gaze even as he solicits it, exhibits his castration for all to see, and revels in the sacrificial basis of the social contract. The male masochist magnifies the losses and divisions upon which cultural identity is based, refusing to be sutured or recompensed. In short, he radiates a negativity inimical to the social order.[7] (p. 51)

---

[7] This reading/critique moves beyond Freud to include other more recent writing on perversion, especially Theodor Reik's *Masochism in Sex and Society*, and Gilles Deleuze's *Masochism*.

Masochism is also one focus of Leo Bersani's *The Freudian Body*, a study exemplifying more clearly the second line of analysis mentioned above, whereby the perversions are shown to challenge the psychoanalytic project itself, especially its conservative manifestations. There is one mode of high deconstruction whose severity is all about going nowhere and which concedes as much in, or sometimes as, its rationale. There is another kind, exemplified by Bersani's study, which is equally severe but different in its effect. In forcing a text to stall, or pressing it into discoherence, it discloses new meanings, new potential. Bersani finds that 'the psychoanalytic authenticity of Freud's work *depends upon* a process of theoretical collapse ... [which] is ... a function of its own development'. Further, by exploring those moments in Freud when he 'appears to be resisting the pressures of an argument he does not make, will not make, we may become more aware of the politically radical currents of his thought' (pp. 3 and 2).

Freud's account of perversion is a contributory factor in this collapse. Bersani's analysis of sadism and masochism, which, it should be recalled, Freud described as 'the most common and most significant of all the perversions' (vii. 70), is fascinating. He takes his cue from Jean Laplanche, who detects a movement in Freud's dialectic whereby sex of its very nature perverts the biological:

the *exception*—i.e. the perversion—ends up by *taking the rule along with it*. The exception, which should presuppose the existence of a definite instinct, a preexistent sexual function, with its well defined norms of sexual accomplishment; that exception ends up by undermining and destroying the very notion of a biological norm. The whole of sexuality, or at least the whole of infantile sexuality, ends up by becoming a perversion. (*Life and Death*, 23)

Bersani likewise reads Freud in a way which leads him to find that 'a so-called aberrational "part" of sexuality—masochism—may *be* the "whole"', with the result that there is created 'a kind of geological shifting in the entire classificatory system of psychoanalysis'. There occurs a centring of what was construed as marginal because of rather than in spite of its marginality. 'Could it be', he asks provocatively, that this 'marginal manifestation of sexuality constitutes its elusive "essence"—or, more exactly that it is the condition of sexuality's emergence?' For Bersani 'the marginality of sadomasochism would consist of nothing less than its isolating, even its making visible, the ontological grounds of the sexual' (Bersani, *The Freudian Body*, 89, 37, 41).

This view of perversion as revealing the fundamental nature of all desire was also advanced by Jacques Lacan, one of Freud's most influential successors. In *Seminar* he declares that

In adults, we are aware of the palpable richness of perversion. Perversion, in sum, is the privileged exploration of an existential possibility of human nature—its internal tearing apart, its gap, through which the supra-natural world of the symbolic was able to make its entry. (i. 218)

It is 'the fundamental uncertainty of the perverse relation, the fact that it can find no way of becoming grounded in any satisfying action, [which] makes up one aspect of the drama of homosexuality. But it is also the structure which gives perversion its value' (i. 221). Homosexuality becomes exemplary of the truth of desire itself; alluding to Proust's 'quite stupendous analysis of homosexuality' in *Remembrance of Things Past*, Lacan observes that the homosexual subject

exhausts himself in pursuing the desire of the other, which he will never be able to grasp as his own desire, because his own desire is the desire of the other. It is himself whom he pursues. . . . The intersubjective relation which subtends perverse desire is only sustained by the annihilation either of the desire of the other, or of the desire of the subject . . . in the one as in the other, this relation dissolves the being of the subject. (i. 221–2)

Homosexuality is made exemplary of the tragic ontology of desire, which is condemned to the playing out of something like the Hegelian master/slave dialectic—from which, says Lacan, 'at every stage, I take my bearings' (i. 222). In Lacan's theory the dialectic is less a process than an energized fixation permanently haunted by loss.

But with Lacan we have moved back to the first of the approaches mentioned earlier, one which sees perversion as exemplary of the truth of desire as revealed *by* psychoanalysis; in this seminar at least, the psychoanalytic project is in control of its revelation. For Bersani, by contrast, it is a revelation which subjects to collapse the psychoanalytic project which facilitated it.

It could be argued that this collapse is primarily historical rather than logical, most effectively discrediting not the theory *per se* but those historical developments within psychoanalysis wherein the Oedipus complex has been normatively deployed. If so, the distinction I have proposed, between the perverse challenge as something explicable within psychoanalytic terms as opposed to that which undermines the psychoanalytic project from within, blurs. Granted, theoretical distinctions are always blurred in the history of any theory's diverse appropriations and developments. Further, psychoanalysis undoubtedly has an internal logic whereby it can be endlessly, if always selectively, refashioned into new narratives with more acceptable socio-political implications as these become necessary. Recently this has occurred with the Oedipus complex. Particularly important are contributions by Kaja

Silverman and Kenneth Lewes indicating how the complex can be retheorized in pluralistic and quite startlingly creative ways.[8] Lewes, in contesting the normative account of the complex, and showing how the very idea of 'resolution' begs the crucial question, discerns twelve possible outcomes of it *vis-à-vis* sexual identity and object choice (pp. 82–3). Silverman discerns in the Oedipal scene a potential cast of characters including, for the male homosexual, not only the mother and father, brother and sister, nursemaid, governess, and tutor, but also 'the desiring subject him or herself, now in the guise of the desired object'.[9] She finds within the homosexual configurations of the Oedipus complex a challenge to and subversion of the heterosexual imperative; a scrambling of the narrative sequencing of human sexuality; an eroticizing of the male body in its entirety; a negation of the most fundamental principle of male subjectivity, namely the identification with masculinity, and thereby a challenge to sexual difference itself. In relation to Freud and Proust, Silverman rewrites the Oedipal scene in new configurations of identification and desire.

It could be argued that the susceptibility of psychoanalysis to being so imaginatively rewritten constitutes a limitation rather than a strength in that a theory which offers so little internal resistance to such diverse appropriations loses its force as theory. If so the historical challenge becomes again almost though not quite logical: rewritten thus creatively, the Oedipus complex becomes so multivalent an allegory of desire and its vicissitudes that it loses not only its original normative power but, inseparably from that, its explanatory power.

At the very least we can say that homosexuality remained a problem for Freud. Try as he might he never adequately accounted for it, and this despite the fact that his *Three Essays* suggested that it did not need the kind of explaining which he subsequently strove so hard to give it. Homosexuality returns for Freud as well as for the subjects of his case histories, and his preoccupation with it is symptomatic of just that which he would explain: its troubling centrality to, and disruption of, the normal. The problem is reduplicated with the perversions more generally. Freud used perversion as 'a weapon with which to throw the traditional definition of sexuality into question' (Laplanche and Pontalis, *The Language of Psychoanalysis*, 307), only to find that it remained as a principle of disruption within his own normative theories, and something which could be, and was, turned against them. In psychoanalysis, as in theology before it, perversion, or more exactly the

---

[8] Lewes, *The Psychoanalytic Theory of Male Homosexuality*, 77–94; Silverman, 'A Woman's Soul Enclosed in a Man's Body', forthcoming in *Male Subjectivity in the Margins*.
[9] Here and subsequently cited from MS.

paradoxical perverse, undoes the theory which it initially served. It is at such points, such moments of discoherence, that Freud's rewriting of the perverse dynamic becomes most visible.

One final, ironic, instance of this *vis-à-vis* the Oedipal drama. At the heart of the Oedipus myth as inherited from Greek mythology is a homosexual encounter. That Oedipus kills his father and marries his mother is well known. Less so is the fact that the tragic sequence is initiated because Oedipus' father, Laius, loved a beautiful youth, Chrysippus. Hera, the guardian of marriage, is angered by this and punishes the Thebans for not preventing that love. So the very myth which psychoanalysts appropriate to normalize heterosexuality already has homosexuality inscribed at its centre; that which normatively sanctions heterosexuality is rooted in what it would contain. Mythologically, the perverse dynamic was always already there.

13 From the Polymorphous Perverse to the Perverse Dynamic

Psychoanalysis and the Polymorphous Perverse: Norman O. Brown and Herbert Marcuse

In post-war sexual politics there were those who explored the idea that if we could desublimate the polymorphous perverse, we would not only liberate ourselves from repression, but liberate an energy which might transform the whole social order. It was a powerful idea: the undifferentiated desire of polymorphous perversity, liberated into its *own* truth, freed from repressive constraint, would become an inherently subversive force. So, for example, in his 1959 study *Life against Death*, Norman O. Brown argued that our survival, as individuals and as a species facing the possibility of nuclear destruction, depended on undoing repression: 'we either come to terms with our unconscious instincts and drives— with life and with death—or else we surely die', and not least because 'the dynamic of history is the slow return of the repressed'. We must abolish repression and resurrect the body, becoming 'polymorphous perverse', achieving a 'Dionysian' rather than an 'Apollonian' consciousness—a 'consciousness which does not observe the limit, but overflows; consciousness which *does not negate anymore*' (pp. x, 230, 307–8, his emphasis; see also his ch. 12).

And yet such notions of what might actually comprise a liberated desire, polymorphous or otherwise, were revealingly culture-bound. Notoriously, radical psychoanalysts incorporated into their vision of liberated desire some of the most basic prejudices of the society they wanted to transform with that desire. Thus, even as he spoke of a transhistorical instinctual structure, Wilhelm Reich, the most famous of all sexual radicals, articulated it in terms which presupposed hetero-sexual genital norms.[1] Brown, for his part, is rather unspecific about what Dionysian liberation will amount to; from his general tone it would seem to be tamely and safely mystical. Transgressing limits is to do with a vague notion of inclusiveness rather than active contravention: 'Dionysus reunifies male and female, Self and Other, life and death. . . . Freud saw that in the id there is no negation, only affirmation and

---

[1] See Altman, *Homosexual Oppression*, 75; Weeks, *Sexuality and its Discontents*, 161–70.

eternity' (p. 175). Behind Brown's argument for a radical desublimation of desire is a fairly familiar and conventional metaphysic, one which avoids the disturbing implications of Freud's theory of the perversions even as it appropriates his idea of the polymorphous perverse.

Outside an explicitly homosexual politics, the most oppositional reinterpretation of sexual perversion was probably that of Herbert Marcuse. In *Eros and Civilization* he argued that the perversions are a rebellion against the tyranny which would subordinate sexuality to procreation, and the institutions which would secure such subordination. The perversions, rejecting the performance principle and upholding sexuality as an end in itself, thereby also 'reject the entire enslavement of the pleasure ego by the reality ego' (pp. 49–50). As such they are also a 'symbol' of what has to be suppressed: their free practice endangers not only the orderly reproduction of labour power but 'perhaps even of mankind itself'. They also suggest the ultimate identity of Eros with the death instinct but in a way which, 'loosened beyond the danger point', deviates from the existing destructive and institutionalized forms of that identity (p. 51). Marcuse also transvalued the idea of regression as it figures in perversion, proposing that the reactivation of childhood wishes and attitudes is not necessarily regression in the pejorative sense and may well be the opposite—'proximity to a happiness that has always been the repressed promise of a better future. In one of his most advanced formulations, Freud once defined happiness as the "subsequent fulfillment of a prehistoric wish"' (p. 203).

Psychoanalysis and Homosexual Politics: Guy Hocquenghem and Mario Mieli

The politics of polymorphous perversity were taken up more directly, and confrontationally, for a homosexual politics, especially by Guy Hocquenghem in *Homosexual Desire* (1972) and Mario Mieli in *Homosexuality and Liberation* (1977). It is no part of my project to revalidate an essentialist metaphysic of sexual transgression; but I do want to recover the contribution made towards it by a psychoanalytically informed homosexual politics. That contribution was ignored then, and doubly so later when essentialist radicalism became unfashionable. Had it not been ignored, the eventual contribution of that radicalism might have been different. Moreover, there remains something to be learned now from the different inflexions of homosexual politics at that time.

So, for example, Stephen Frosh, in a book called *The Politics of*

Psychoanalysis, points out in his survey of libertarian Freudianism that it remained fundamentally individualistic (pp. 159–64). But Frosh concentrates almost entirely on hetero/sexual psychoanalytic radicalism, ignoring Mieli who, as we shall see, was both libertarian and collectivist in his vision. Frosh also ignores Hocquenghem who, though libertarian in a more individualistic sense, nevertheless proposed an anti-humanism which produced a quite different conception of desire, and of psychic and social repression, from that found in Brown and Reich, or even Marcuse. Further, whereas Reich could declare that 'beneath' neurosis, 'behind all these dangerous, grotesque, unnatural phantasies and impulses, I found a bit of simple, matter-of-fact, decent nature' (Weeks, *Sexuality and its Discontents*, 162), neither Hocquenghem nor Mieli affirm such a naïve view of the naturalness of desire—not least because the history of 'nature' is in part the history of the putative unnaturalness of homosexuality and hence of its persecution. It is not surprising that Reich's decent bit of nature turns out to be culturally specific, a legitimation of heterosexual genitality. Both Hocquenghem and Mieli could be said to situate themselves within, to write from, the blind spots and evasions of Brown's and Reich's psychoanalytic radicalism. And to the extent that they remain essentialist, it is in ways very different from Reich and Brown. Finally, the differences between Hocquenghem and Mieli, as well as between them and Reich, suggest once more the inadequacy of essentialism as a blanket, universally pejorative category.

Drawing on psychoanalysis to explore the perversity of desire, Hocquenghem and Mieli sought to divert it from its existing co-option to conservative ends. Not without difficulty: as with psychoanalysis's relation to feminism, its relationship to the lesbian and gay movement is fraught. The discrimination perpetuated by psychiatry and psychoanalysis against homosexuals is notorious (above, Chapter 11). For this reason alone, and understandably so, there are those within the lesbian and gay movements who have rejected psychoanalysis in total. Others like Hocquenghem and Mieli (also Dennis Altman and Jeffrey Weeks) have sought to use it in the activity of interrogating it, deploying psychoanalytic categories as well as exposing the repression of homosexuality in the very practice of psychoanalysis itself. While retaining the Freudian insistence on the cultural and psychic centrality of homosexual desire, these writers have transvalued the category of desire and in some cases sought to use it against psychoanalysis, breaking the latter's stranglehold on the psychosexual, and opening it up to a broader socio-political analysis along lines suggested in the previous chapter. So theirs were not simply applications of psychoanalysis, but radical appropriations of it, and a using of it against its own far-reaching heterosexual bias.

Most of these writers argue that, whether or not the Oedipus complex is the corner-stone of psychoanalysis, it is certainly its most fundamental and reprehensible error, and is probably theoretically incoherent as well. But coherent or not, the Oedipus complex is seen to be one of the most important enabling concepts for the repressive and discriminatory use of psychoanalysis. So though in quite different ways, they aspire to liberate desire from the chains of Oedipal theory. Most importantly for my purposes these writers are acutely aware of the perverse dynamic as it survives in the Freudian psychosexual narrative, and much more so than their more obviously influential counterparts in contemporary, psychoanalytically informed, cultural criticism.

In his brilliant polemic *Homosexual Desire*, Guy Hocquenghem argued that 'Freud discovers the libido to be the basis of affective life and immediately enchains it as the Oedipal privatisation of the family. ... At a time when capitalist individualisation is undermining the family by depriving it of its essential social functions, the Oedipus complex represents the internalisation of the family institution.' On the one hand 'Freud asserted the universality of homosexual desire, as a translation of the polymorphous perverse', only then to enclose it 'not geographically but historically, within the Oedipal system' (pp. 60–1, 65).[2] On this reading that system helps ensure the reproduction of the family, of heterosexuality, and hence of a repressive social order. In a manner at once exhilarated and incisive, and unmistakably of the liberationist moment, Hocquenghem turns psychoanalysis inside out, showing how Freud's followers rewrote some of his more challenging insights along reactionary lines; how, for instance, they have projected the paranoia of the homophobe on to the homosexual, making it now a cause of homosexuality rather than a symptom of its repression, hence 'reversing Freud's scheme in the crassest possible way' (p. 47).[3] Psychoanalysis, he says, supports the 'phallocratic' basis of modern society, and the repression through guilt of anal eroticism (p. 114).

Borrowing from but also developing Deleuze and Guattari's attack on psychoanalysis in *Anti-Oedipus*, Hocquenghem cogently if controversially repudiates Freud's attempt to contain homosexuality within the repressive parameters of the Oedipal drama, and argues for the

---

[2] Cf. Weeks: 'psychoanalysis represents both the discovery of the mechanisms of desire, and the means of its recodification and control. Sex is the secret which needed to be both discovered and controlled. Freud's analytic work, as opposed to his theoretical constructions, offer some evidence for this recodification even as the moment of discovery' (*Sexuality and its Discontents*, 144–5).

[3] On Freud's account of paranoia see above, Ch. 11.

subversive power of desire released from Oedipal repression. But is Hocquenghem merely exalting the same thing which for centuries moralists have castigated and warned against, or is he working with a radically different understanding of desire? He is probably doing both, and with the second possibility preventing the first being the inverted platitude it might otherwise be. In a way which is nothing if not provocative, Hocquenghem argues that if 'homosexuality is connected with the anus, and anality with our civilisation' (p. 85), and if the repression of anal libidinal energy is a precondition of capitalist society, becoming, in Freud's words, 'the symbol of everything that is to be repudiated and excluded from life' (vii. 104)—then its liberation offers nothing less than a revolutionary opportunity.

To reinvest the anus collectively and libidinally would involve a proportional weakening of the great phallic signifier, which dominates us constantly both in the small-scale hierarchies of the family, and in the great social hierarchies. The least acceptable desiring operation (precisely because it is the most desublimating one) is that which is directed at the anus. (p. 88)

Homosexuality is not simply what is excluded from the relations of identity and conventional roles, it is their repressed precondition, and this repression produces 'an ascent towards sublimation, the superego and social anxiety'. But the other side of that desire, its unrepressed form, involves a 'descent towards the abyss of non-personalised and uncodified desire'. Herein lies its subversive dimension for Hocquenghem: 'Homosexual desire is neither on the side of death nor on the side of life; it is the killer of civilised egos' (pp. 81, 136). In his vision of deviant desire disintegrating normalized identity, Hocquenghem anticipates those like Leo Bersani who have explored the shattering effect of desire, and the very different work of those like Jacqueline Rose whose deployment of psychoanalysis within a feminist framework stresses the disruptive, precarious dimensions of identity in relation to desire (below, Chapter 17).

Mario Mieli's *Homosexuality and Liberation* is a rather different appropriation/critique of Freud, but for the similar end of a radical homosexual politics. Mieli would retain the idea of the Oedipus complex but insists that it is impossible to make use of it analytically without a complete recasting of the theories that bear on it (p. 51). His own somewhat tortuous and hypothetical version of such a move presents the homosexual as someone who resists some of the multiple repressions which occur with the Oedipal triangle (father, mother, child); who refuses, for example, to renounce identification with the parent of the same sex. This he sees as something potentially positive, rather than, as in most psychoanalytic theory, a negative indication of arrested development.[4]

Homosexuality and Liberation was written out of Mieli's involvement in the Italian and British gay movements in the seventies. Mieli wrote as an unashamed universalist, humanist, and revolutionary, which makes him triply unfashionable today. His universalism is based on belief in a transcultural human bisexuality, an 'infantile polymorphous and "undifferentiated" erotic disposition' which he calls 'trans-sexuality' (p. 25), and which heterosexuality represses. As for his humanism, it is more faithfully exemplified in quotation than definition: 'the homosexual, by liberating himself, sets the heterosexual an example of gay strength and dignity, of a new way of being human, which is no longer based on interpersonal negation, but on mutual understanding, desire and satisfaction' (p. 161). As a revolutionary, Mieli wanted the overthrow of the existing social order, believing this could only be accomplished with and in relation to a radical liberation of desire itself: 'sexuality is hidden at the base of the economy, so that Eros is actually *substructural*'—not merely a secondary issue at the superstructural or cultural level, as the traditional Left has claimed (p. 216). Mieli ends his book optimistically: 'I believe the movement for the liberation of homosexuality is irreversible, in the broader context of human emancipation as a whole. It is up to all of us to make this emancipation a reality' (p. 230).

The universalism and humanism to which Mieli subscribed were also used by other sexual radicals, but Mieli puts them to different and more provocative ends. So, for instance, he contends that in the present state of sexual alienation it is only gay men who can really love women because 'genuine love for the other sex cannot be accompanied by the full desire, auto- and alloerotic, for one's own sex' (p. 45); heterosexuality may be premissed as much on a fear of the same as on an embracing of the different (an issue I return to below, Chapter 17), one consequence of which is that some heterosexual men inflict on women 'a mediocre, neurotic and egoistic desire' (p. 46). Further, the liberation of gay desire can 'break open the closed world of the traditional

---

[4] Others have advanced similar or related rereadings of the Oedipal scenario based on the view that, while the girl's identification with the mother reinforces her gender identity, for the boy 'male gender identity can only be achieved through a process of disidentifying with the mother and forming a counter identification with the father [involving] a *repudiation* of the primary maternal identification' (Fletcher, 'Psychoanalysis and Gay Theory', 106). But, because the male can never successfully eradicate his initial primary identification with the mother, masculinity remains an inherently unstable, defensive structure. Homosexual identification with the mother can then be understood as a refusal, or repairing, of the damaged psychic structure which is masculinity. Oscar Wilde arrived at a similar insight without the ponderous psychoanalytic apparatus, and Fletcher quotes him to good effect: 'All women become like their mothers. That is their tragedy. No man does. That is his' (p. 103).

heterosexual couple, and above all dispel the murky fog of possible betrayals, infidelities and jealousies that weigh upon it, poisoning it day and night' (p. 131). Liberationist homosexuality turns the tables, or rather gets up from the psychoanalytic couch and puts heterosexuality there in its place and offers its services as analyst. Mieli would take the challenge of homosexuality yet further *inside* heterosexuality: 'there is nothing more gay than fucking with a guy who was previously convinced that he didn't feel any sexual attraction for other men, and who then . . . starts to burn with desire in your arms' (p. 68).

But he carries this through into an enquiry as to why the gay man might want to seduce the straight, especially the quintessentially masculine man—*bêtes* as they are called in France—finding here evidence of internalized oppression (p. 161). He also appropriates ideas of the carnivalesque for anal eroticism (pp. 137–45), analyses the fear of homosexuality as revealed in ordinary language (pp. 140–2), argues for the importance of coming out in the workplace (pp. 224–8), and, drawing on Freud's demanding insight that the ego is a precipitate of abandoned object-cathexes whose history it continues to contain, suggests the following relationship between homophobia, masculinity, and misogyny:

The 'normal' male ego . . . is largely determined by a series of abandoned homosexual object-cathexes, these being transformed into narcissistic libido and subsequently directed at heterosexual goals. Onto these heterosexual 'objects' the male projects the 'femininity' he has had to repress. The woman, then, is subject to the male in two ways: the man forces on her both his masculinity (a condensation of alienated homosexual desire) and his own 'femininity'.

As for male bonding, this is the grotesque expression of a 'paralysed and unspoken homosexuality, which can be grasped, in the negative, in the denial of women, whom [males] speak of phallocratically . . . reducing them to a hole, i.e. to something that does not exist. The suppression of homoeroticism is here always bound up with the oppression of women by men. The negated homosexual desire makes its resurgence via the negation of woman' (pp. 34, 127).

In some respects these two books by Hocquenghem and Mieli are classic statements of liberation radicalism, at the heart of which is a provocative inversion epitomized in the very concept of homophobia: 'it's not we who are sick but you'. A range of values are wrestled from the dominant culture for gay liberation and, simultaneously, the dominant is found to harbour negative tendencies of the kind it used to attribute to homosexuality. Further, both books endorse the idea of heterosexuality as based upon the repression of homosexuality, and invest the liberation of the latter with potential for radical social change. Both are also exercises in transgressive reinscription, not only because they turn psychoanalysis against itself, but also because they discover homosexuality at the heart of heterosexual identity, be it in terms of repression, disavowal, or as its negative other. But there are also important differences between the two.

Mieli envisioned a liberation of desire and of the human(ist) subject, essentializing both in the process. In contrast, Hocquenghem sets desire *against* the subject, or more exactly sets homosexual desire against the repressed and repressive 'natural' heterosexual subject of bourgeois culture: the false unity of that subject is shattered by the desire it represses. Also he would use that desire to subvert the very concept of nature which functions as the bedrock of other kinds of sexual radicalism. Yet, if only in the way that he would draw so much potential power from desire, Hocquenghem also is dependent on an essentialist model of the same, even as he repudiates an essentialism of the human subject and of nature. To be drawn to this kind of writing now is, perhaps, because and not in spite of its being of a time which is not ours; both books are situated somewhere before the current repudiation of desire as revolutionary, yet both are also too close, too implicated in the present, to be consigned to the past. Mieli's utopianism is not ours and could not be, and not only because of the catastrophes of recent history. Nevertheless now more than ever we need to bear witness to its affirmation. Borges recognized joy as the fundamental spirit of Wilde's work (above, Chapter 4); joy is something also present in Mieli and, differently, in Hocquenghem; in Mieli it is a humanitarian joy, in Hocquenghem the anarchic joy of anti-humanism.

Authenticity at the Margins: John Rechy's Sexual Outlaw

The sexual radicalism of the post-war period had other sources than psychoanalysis, influential though that was. Others identified sexuality as the source of authentic being and existential integrity, and revalued the sexual deviant as a kind of anti-hero. Homosexuals became potentially revolutionary because marginalized and excluded; according to Marcuse, they were one of the minorities who would help effect the 'Great Refusal'. The dislocation of such deviants, their unsuccessful socialization, gave them an enforced independence from the dominant ideologies of normality and 'nature' which allegedly kept the majority within the system. The work of John Rechy pushes this vision of subversive deviance to a romantic extreme; the homosexual becomes a Romantic Outlaw, the 'archetypal outsider' (*The Sexual Outlaw*, 299). But because of the pressure of political realities which Rechy, as a participant in gay culture, cannot ignore, *The Sexual Outlaw* also interrogates that romanticism from within.

With the reaction against 'promiscuity' outside but also to some extent inside gay culture, Rechy's *The Sexual Outlaw* is now seen by some as embarrassingly *passé*. But it has a history and a significance beyond its immediate context, not least as a dramatization of the tension between, and as an attempt to integrate, two strands of liberation: anarchic desire and political engagement. The book has two subtitles—*A Documentary*, and *A Non-fiction Account, with Commentaries, of Three Days and Nights in the Sexual Underground*. It has two epigraphs: one is from Melville's *Moby-Dick*, on the narcissistic image being 'the ungraspable phantom of life' itself; the other is from Albert Camus's *The Myth of Sisyphus*: 'Living an experience, a particular fate, is accepting it fully . . . it is not a matter of explaining and solving, but of experiencing and describing.' In fact, *The Sexual Outlaw* not only experiences and describes, but also seeks to explain the intense experiences of contradiction in the realm of desire.

The book opens with Jim, its main protagonist, preparing his body for the 'sexhunt' whose arena 'will be streets, parks, alleys, tunnels, garages, movie arcades, bathhouses, beaches . . .' (p. 21); clandestine, outlawed sex in the deserted shadows of public spaces which also become 'battlefields' (p. 28). For it is here that the (male) homosexual confronts and transgresses the repressive sexual laws of his society, experiencing

> The joy of promiscuity.
> And the pain.
> Ecstatic freedom and release.
> Loneliness, desolation.
>
> (p. 285)

The language is familiar: romantic *and* religious. Familiar too is the trope whereby the forbidden scandalously appropriates, aligns with, its antithesis: 'promiscuity, like the priesthood, requires total commitment and sacrifice' (p. 32). Predictably then, ecstasy and *Angst* are not mutually contradictory but mutually reinforcing: 'the outlaw world . . . beautiful yet drenched in recurrent despair' (p. 299). Nor is it surprising that Rechy views the deviant as someone in whom *Angst* and suffering become redemptive. It is an idea quite different from, yet so clearly rooted in, romantic and Christian antecedents. The individual suffers to despair and into truth, and in the process paradoxically becomes authentic: 'In the sex-moments pressurized into high intensity by life-crushing strictures challenged, the sexual outlaw experiences to the utmost the rush of soul, blood, cum through every channel of his being into the physical and psychical discharge of the fully awakened, living, *defiant* body' (p. 300). Although she would probably have been appalled at the language, Radclyffe Hall might have recognized the sentiment.[5]

At the same time, Rechy rages against oppression, and attributes extraordinary political potential to transgressive sexuality:

Promiscuous homosexuals (outlaws with dual identities . . .) are the shock troops of the sexual revolution. The streets are the battleground, the revolution is the sexhunt, a radical statement is made each time a man has sex with another on a street. . . .
Cum instead of blood. Satisfied bodies instead of dead ones. Death versus orgasm. Would they bust everyone? With cum-smeared tanks would they crush all? (pp. 299, 301)

In relation to such passages it is tempting to see Rechy as trapped in romantic/tragic self-glorification inseparable from naïve fantasies of revolutionary omnipotence. And there may indeed be a sense in which *The Sexual Outlaw* signals at once the apotheosis and the demise of the romantic quest for authenticity, the last stage of its restless search ever further outward in search of new marginal extremes of being. As the quest exhausts itself in the one domain, it moves to another temporarily more invigorating because more marginal, yet destined also to become exhausted. Eventually the search must expire altogether at some point so distant from its origins that regeneration becomes impossible. This would make Rechy's radicalism, at least from the vantage point of a severer 1990s sexual politics, highly suspect. The indictment might go thus: *The Sexual Outlaw* is the supreme instance of subversion contained (above, Part 4); it masquerades as a subversive attack upon, and a revolutionary alternative to, a repressive sexual ideology, but in fact is merely a mutation of that ideology experientially perpetuating precisely what is being politically rejected. So what appears to be political commitment is nearer a kind of political bad faith—witness the fact that the outlaw world Rechy celebrates actually perpetuates an alienation between gay people leading to those suicidal lows that even Rechy cannot successfully dissolve into romantic *Angst*.

Except that once more there is a transgressive knowledge which at

---

[5] On the survival of individualistic assumptions within a radical homosexual politics, see especially Shiers, 'Two Steps Forward, One Step Back'.

once grows from and threatens containment. One of the most interesting 'Voice Over' chapters is entitled 'Contradictions, Ambivalences, and Considerations'. Rechy asks: 'What kind of revolution is it that ends when one *looks* old . . . in which some of the revolutionaries must look beautiful?' (p. 285). He remarks how (for him) promiscuity is a kind of vicious circle, an endless evasion of the very questions and conflicts it invokes: 'I resolve the clashing contradictions by joining the sexhunt in the streets' (p. 288). Rechy is also aware of the extent to which the outlaw is created from and by the terms of his oppression:

For centuries homosexuals . . . have been prosecuted and persecuted. The law tells us we're criminals so we've become defiant outlaws. Psychologists demand we be sick and so we've become obsessed with physical beauty. Religion insists we're sinners and so we've become soulful sensualists. The result is the unique, sensual, feeling, elegant sensibility of the sexual outlaw.

Narcissism itself becomes an art-form (pp. 193–4, 196). In these and other ways *The Sexual Outlaw* indicates how the outlaw flourishes in the very society which represses him. As Rechy puts it elsewhere, the pressures of oppression 'produce [the outlaw], create his defiance', and, once created, the defiance is hardened by the same repression (p. 31); the intensity of promiscuous deviant sex derives in part from what denies it and what it challenges (pp. 31, 300). The desire for oppression to be transcended in ecstatic, subjective terms is always thwarted by the re-emergence of the social from inside of desire.

The anthropological analysis of containment (above, Chapter 6) presents deviance as a functional marking of social boundaries; what is forbidden or disturbing is situated spatially just beyond a margin which, in its dividing role, connects as well as separates the prescribed and the proscribed. But this spatial metaphor of the forbidden-just-beyond obscures the more challenging insight of the perverse dynamic whereby the other is internal to the society which marks him or her thus. Rechy is half aware of this when he remarks that his promiscuous homosexual outlaws, the supposed shock troops of the sexual revolution, will 'tomorrow . . . go to offices and athletic fields, classrooms and construction sites' (*Sexual Outlaw*, 299). The perverse dynamic also suggests that the anthropologist's boundary between the lawful and the illicit is not so much a dividing line as the visible manifestation of an overlap. Something like this is true of Rechy's gay cruising grounds—derelict land, parks, parking lots, beaches—all public spaces and places where straight and gay both go without mixing or meeting, and where for the most part one of these groups is unaware of the other's presence. There are revealing occasions when this ceases to be so, as when the 'straight' man goes here for his deviant sex with minimal compromise, or the gay-haters to hurt, maim, and kill (pp. 293–6). The latter thereby exemplify in one of its most brutal manifestations the dominant's 'need' of its deviants, and with a chilling, perverse irony: in the gay culture of Rechy's time, and about which he writes, the gay male appropriates machismo as a sexual style, and the gay-basher finds himself confronted with a parody of himself. Compare Joseph Bristow: 'this butch style (which is one of many gay styles) is pleasurable because it achieves sexual contact by negotiating a cultural form—hardened masculinity—that is predicated upon homophobia. This type of gay identity, there-fore, consciously inhabits a publicly acceptable one which is, in fact, its enemy. It appears that the mocking laughter of parody . . . is at work here. But this mockery of masculinity is also driven by a desire for the symbol it derides' ('Being Gay', 71).

The Sexual Outlaw has its own boundaries and its own kinds of containment. These too reveal more than they permit. Near the end of the book Jim witnesses a scene of sado-masochistic fist-fucking which disgusts him. Earlier Rechy acknowledges the 'beckoning power' of S. & M. but deeply distrusts it. What others see as a playful critique of real violence he sees as all too close to it (pp. 277–80). But in Rechy's novel *Rushes*, published in 1979, two years after *The Sexual Outlaw*, S. & M. is incorporated by being bestowed with that same redemptive potential which had hitherto excluded it. Much of the novel takes place in clubs, arenas for tortured integrity and an agonizing lack of fulfilment amid orgies of liberated desire. The torture and the lack are at once intensified and hesitantly transcended by the desire. Even as Rechy romanticizes suffering, he wants to show how gay culture acts out unromantic truths about desire and human nature which straight culture represses (p. 186).

Relinquishing the Pure Source of the Revolutionary

Times change, and sexualities with them. I return again to that passage in Foucault's *History of Sexuality* where he declares that there is no single *locus* of revolt, no pure source of the revolutionary. The historical importance of a radical, essentialized, transgressive sexuality is that it became the experience/identity for a utopian vision of the future; desire inherited the religious fervour which once repudiated sexual desire as the precondition for its own spiritual transcendence, and that which had been disavowed returned to appropriate the source of the dis-avowal. Sexuality became redemptive, took on the power both to *break away* from the present and to affirm a radically different future. This may now seem misguided, deluded, and deluding. Yet to hear this vision denounced in terms ignorant of its histories is to wonder if such repudiations are not in turn further evidence of a slide back into the conservatism, fatalism, and inertia which that vision sought to overthrow.

Even so, be it reluctantly, with relief, or maybe even with anger at the delusion it fostered, many would now agree that the polymorphous perverse has finally exhausted itself as a pure source of the revolutionary; it remains only as a narrative affirmation of diversity at once nostalgic and utopian, looking simultaneously backwards and forwards. As, perhaps, for Freud, given that the regressiveness of the polymorphous perverse was the occasion for some of his more progressive thoughts. He once wrote that the only success he had had in the 'removal of genital inversion or homosexuality' involved making access to the opposite sex possible for someone who had hitherto been exclusively homosexual, 'thus restoring his *full* bisexuality. . . . One must remember that normal sexuality too depends on a restriction in the choice of object' (ix. 375–6, my italics). In the attempt to remould deviant desire Freud discovers its obstinacy, even or especially in that incompleteness which it shares with normal desire; an incompleteness which, again in the case of both the deviant and the normal, bears their histories. There are many reasons why, in Fredric Jameson's words, history is what hurts, one of them being that it is the past which in part produces this present incompleteness. But it is also an incompleteness which, in raising the possibility of a 'full bisexuality', affirms a future potential beyond the normal, incorporating the latter in the act of displacing it. It is in such ways that the narrative of the polymorphous perverse may, as I say, be at once nostalgic and utopian, as in the remark of Freud's picked up by Marcuse: 'the subsequent fulfilment of a prehistoric wish' (above).

And before finally abandoning it, let us retrieve one further historical trace within the polymorphous perverse. A now obsolete sense of 'diversity' gives, as one of its meanings, 'perversity'. Perversity once involved diversity. Perhaps this corresponds with the close historical links between heresy and sexual deviation; after all, diversity is, in its own way, as dangerous as heresy. To deviate or to be diverted from the straight and narrow might be to encounter diversion as diversity; to divert in that direction was itself to pervert by introducing diversity where there was the one way. Which is why John Donne could warn against 'a Diversion, a Deviation, a Deflection, a Defection from this Rectitude, this Uprightnesse' (Sermon on Ps. 64: 10). It is also in this context that Donne speaks of 'tentations', a now obsolete form of 'temptations' and 'specially expressing experimental trial, as distinct from enticement to evil' (*OED*). In more ways than one, the polymorphous perverse echoes—maybe contains—a history it displaces.[6]

If this connection of the perverse with the diverse was never entirely obliterated by a normative psychoanalysis, nor are we confined to finding its traces only in the radical analyst's over-investment in the polymorphous perverse. It is a connection which survived outside psychoanalysis, and why Gide could write in 1932 of a liberation into sexuality as also a liberation from it: 'those who refuse to understand always imagine that one is looking for (exclusively) satisfactions. No, but rather liberation; the possibility of going beyond, permission on the contrary to think of something else . . . *Corydon*, far from being the evidence of an obsession (as [René] Schwob sees it), is the token of a release. And who can tell the number of those whom that little book has, likewise, *released*?' (*Journals*, 27 Dec. 1932).

---

[6] Compare Weeks on the linguistic connection of diversity/perversity: 'For while all the terms relating to "perversity" suggest a hierarchy of sexual values in which "the perversions" are right at the bottom of the scale, "diversity" hints at a continuum of behaviours in which one element has no more fundamental a value than any other' (Weeks, *Sexuality*, 69). What is fascinating is that in the sexologists who preceded Freud, and even more in his own work, perversity retains a connection with diversity, operating along the lines of Weeks's description of what is implied in the latter. It is true that the classification and explanation of the perversions entailed a reinforcement of the heterosexual norm which they were contrasted with; but the same procedure inevitably enlarged the sphere of the sexual, and here, argues Weeks, 'were the seeds of a modern view of an infinite sexual variety' (p. 71). It is a variety confirmed by fairly recent anthropological study of homosexuality—recent because of the prejudice within anthropology itself against homosexuality as an area of study (Blackwood (ed.), *Anthropology*, pp. ix–xii).

14 *Perversion, Power, and Social Control*

BALDWIN: People invent categories in order to feel safe. White people invented black people to give white people identity.

GIOVANNI. It's insane.

BALDWIN. Straight cats invent faggots so they can sleep with them without becoming faggots themselves.

GIOVANNI. somehow.

BALDWIN. somehow—!

(James Baldwin, *Dialogue*, 88–9)

The Rise of the Deviant

I indicated earlier that the most significant recent theory of perversion derives not from Freud's successors but from one of their most influential critics, Michel Foucault. I shall consider Foucault's account shortly, after a brief look at the deviance theories which relate to and in certain respects anticipate it, theories deriving from anthropology, phenomenology, the sociology of deviance, radical criminology, and Marxist subcultural theory.[1] There are important differences between them, but all such theories rejected earlier conceptions of deviance as something (1) extraneous to the social order, (2) a by-product of it, (3) intrinsic or essential to the deviant subject. The inadequacy of such accounts had been apparent at least since the realization that 'bad' socialization helps produce deviance. From this realization there emerged a certain liberal tolerance: deviants are a victim of circumstance, and, even if not exonerated, to be treated with 'understanding'. A further stage in the cautious rehabilitation of deviance saw their behaviour as a kind of protest against an alienating social order; on this view the deviant, while remaining a victim, also became part hero or anti-hero in an existential quest for the authenticity which society stifled.[2]

---

[1] See e.g. Hall *et al.*, *Policing the Crisis*; Downes and Rock, *Understanding Deviance*; Hebdige, *Subculture*.
[2] See Pearson, *The Deviant Imagination*, esp. 11, 24; and on the homosexual as deviant in post-war literature, see my 'The Challenge of Sexuality'.

In a further development the deviant was, as it were, *written back into* the social order: the very category of deviance came to be regarded as a construction, something created in a process of social ascription. Earlier notions of bad socialization often assumed a malformation of the individual; in this further development there is not necessarily an assumption of an essential individual separable from his or her social identity; to retrace his or her 'creation' is to learn less and less about the deviant subject *per se*, and more and more about him or her as the bearer of a social process, and about the dominant social formations identifying him or her. To simplify somewhat, and make obvious the questionably functionalist basis of much work in this vein, we could say that society needs its deviants in order to reproduce itself.

Robert A. Scott, from within this perspective, says that deviance is so important that 'order itself may be impossible without it' ('Framework' 28). A formative text for this perspective was Kai Erikson's study of New England Puritans which argued for the social necessity of deviance not only because it functions to define the boundaries of a society, but also because those boundaries must be repeatedly confirmed. So, for instance, 'in a figurative sense, at least, morality and immorality meet at the public scaffold, and it is during this meeting that the line between them is drawn' (*Wayward Puritans*, 12). That line is also repeatedly redrawn in a process whose violence is made apparent enough in this example of the scaffold. Scott, who cites the scaffold lines from Erikson observes:

Deviance is a rejuvenating force as well. . . . To contain and control deviance and thereby to master it, is to supply fresh and dramatic proof of the enormous powers that are behind the social order. The visible control of deviance is one of the most effective mechanisms by which a social order can tangibly display its potency. The act of harnessing things that are dangerous helps to revitalize the system by demonstrating to those who live within it just how awesome its powers really are. ('Framework', 28–9)

Is it an attempt at anthropological neutrality giving the wrong impression, or is there indeed here an identification with the social order displaying its potency?

In such theory we find what might be described as a (philosophically) idealist conception of deviance, society being conceived as a totality or organic unity with an integral dynamic structure which needs to be 'revitalized' (Scott's word). Relatedly, the social structure is conceptualized in anthropomorphic and psychic terms, desire for order and terror of chaos being postulated as its most fundamental ordering principles. So, according to Peter L. Berger and Thomas Luckmann,

The legitimation of the institutional order is also faced with the ongoing necessity of keeping chaos at bay. *All* social reality is precarious. *All* societies are constructions in the face of chaos. The constant possibility of anomic terror is actualized whenever the legitimations that obscure the precariousness are threatened or collapse. (*The Social Construction of Reality*, 121; cf. 115–16)

'Order' comes to be described in almost mystifying terms; 'the yearning for rigidity is in us all', says Mary Douglas in her classic study, *Purity and Danger*, adding: 'it is part of our human condition to long for hard lines and clear concepts' (p. 191). What is in danger of being ignored or understated is not just the injustice, exploitation, violence, and struggle in the order/disorder opposition—and in the dominant/deviant relationship in which it is typically manifested—but also the fact that these putative attributes of the social psyche are not the necessary preconditions of social existence *per se*; usually in fact 'order' and 'chaos' are culturally specific ideologies legitimating contingent relations of power. Consequently, when Barbara Babcock describes symbolic social inversions—to which deviance is frequently related—as 'creative negations' (Babcock, *The Reversible World*, 32; cf. 21, 29, 31) we might remark that they may be more desperate than creative—struggles to be free of, or to subvert, forms of violent domination.

In short, the symbolic 'harnessing' of the deviant is rarely creative, regenerative, or benign; it involves a violence open to any authority which wants a witch-hunt/scapegoat—whether for paranoid reasons (it feels threatened but is not); for rational reasons (it feels under threat and really is), or for cynical reasons (a reassertion of social order is always good for business, especially for those in power). At the very least we should recognize that the process being described is usually more destructive than regenerative. And more complex: as we have seen in relation to the pervert, the trouble with the notion of scapegoating is that it signifies a complex social reality in a way which simultaneously forecloses on its analysis. To reiterate: what we call social order is not just a system typically privileging one or more groups or classes at the expense of others; nor just a system that legitimates itself through the demonizing of others, but an almost permanent condition of dislocation stemming directly from its own contradictions or logic. This dislocation (chaos) is typically displaced, ideologically re-presented as an effect of society's enemies, external and internal, protection from whom is the society's rationale (order).

Now from an ethnographic perspective, Hans Peter Duerr has pointed to the creative potential of crossing 'the boundary between wilderness and civilization'. He argues that what he calls the 'archaic mind' was aware of this and, to that extent, 'we moderns are much more ignorant about ourselves and about our limitations than humans were earlier' (*Dreamtime*, 75). In the past 'those who wished to come to know the essence of culture needed to go into the wilderness'; likewise with themselves: 'archaic mentality ... is characterized by a belief that humans can gain a clear *consciousness of themselves* by confronting what a person *is* and *simultaneously* is not. Much more clearly than we moderns, archaic humans recognized themselves in what they were not' (pp. 65, 74). Criticizing a modern opinion that the world view is best 'which enables the organism to reduce uncertainty as much as possible', Duerr comments that it fails to realize that 'what is strange and uncertain may also be stimulating and liberating' (p. 313).

Of course—as Duerr's study elsewhere implies—it is not quite as simple as that. Though probably not in a position to verify his analysis of 'archaic' cultures, there are many who can confirm the experientially liberating potential of strangeness. But again, what has to be added is that modern cultures (and within those cultures particular classes and other groupings) do in fact define themselves in terms of what they are not, often with deeply destructive effects. To that extent 'wilderness' is already a construct of the 'civilized'. Nor should we necessarily romanticize the stranger. Most colonizers begin as such. The kindness of strangers is not always benevolent.

Michel Foucault: The Deviant as Construct

In important respects Foucault's analysis of sexual deviance (broadly conceived) would seem to meet some of these objections, at least to the extent that he discovers not the rejuvenative or insightful potential of deviance, but the insidious, manipulative complexities of power, and the paradoxical relationship of deviants to it. In Foucault's scheme deviants come to occupy a revealing, dangerous double relationship to power, at once culturally marginal yet discursively central. Even as the sexual deviant is banished to the margins of society, he or she remains integral to it, not in spite of but because of that marginality.

Through a sustained but mostly implicit critique of psychoanalysis, Foucault's has become an influential account, at once historical, anti-teleological, and anti-normative. He begins from the fundamental proposition that sexuality is not (as in Freud) a stubborn drive or a natural force which civilization seeks to sublimate, hold in check, or otherwise regulate; it is rather 'a historical construct' which enables the operation of power relations, 'a result and an instrument of power's designs'. The power that controls sexuality does not primarily work through prohibition, law, or taboo, thereby establishing the boundaries of the permissible. Indeed, 'we must . . . abandon the hypothesis that modern industrial societies ushered in an age of increased sexual repression'. On the contrary, we have witnessed 'a visible explosion of unorthodox sexualities' (*History*, 105, 152, 49).

However, Foucault does not deny that prohibition has existed as an aspect of that power; rather, power primarily works by producing, multiplying, dispersing, inciting, and intensifying sexualities. He speaks of power's 'polymorphous techniques', thereby attributing to power what Freud attributed in his scheme to perverse desire; in effect, what Freud saw as the element of the desire which threatened power, Foucault attributes to power itself (*History*, 47, 37, 11). Foucault presents us with a strange dialectic between power and pleasure, or what he would rather call the '*perpetual spirals of power and pleasure*'. He envisages a historical development whereby 'power operated as a mechanism of attraction; it drew out those peculiarities over which it kept watch. Pleasure spread to the power that harried it; power anchored the pleasure it uncovered' (p. 45, his emphasis).

So why did we ever imagine that desire was of necessity repressed? One obvious answer would be the conservative one: we imagined desire to be a dangerous anarchic force which must be suppressed or at least harnessed. But Foucault discerns another rationale, more romantic and radical in aspiration but no less mistaken:

What sustains our eagerness to speak of sex in terms of repression is doubtless this opportunity to speak out against the powers that be, to utter truths and promise bliss, to link together enlightenment, liberation, and manifold pleasures; to pronounce a discourse that combines the fervor of knowledge, the determination to change the laws, and the longing for the garden of earthly delights. (p. 7)

Sexuality becomes a displaced religion: 'the lyricism and religiosity that long accompanied the revolutionary project have, in Western industrial societies, been largely carried over to sex' (p. 8). In particular, the bourgeoisie subordinated its soul to sex by conceiving of sex as that which constituted the soul's most secret and determining part (p. 124). We demand of sex 'that it tell us our truth, or rather, the deeply buried truth of that truth about ourselves which we think we possess in our immediate consciousness' (p. 69); in our culture we have to pass through sex to have access to our own intelligibility and identity (pp. 155–6). The truth and sovereignty which we have assigned to sex have made it worth dying for, but not in the Freudian sense: 'it is in this (strictly historical) sense that sex is indeed imbued with the death instinct' (p. 156).

Foucault conceives the power which invents and works through sexuality as everywhere and active, but elusively so. Sometimes it takes on the attributes of both a dominant formation indistinguishable from its ideological legitimation: 'power is tolerable only on condition that it masks a substantial part of itself' (p. 86). And because of this secrecy which is almost a duplicity, power remains in this argument a kind of agency, one which is ubiquitous and pervasive yet also insidious and unlocatable; everywhere vaguely, nowhere primarily. It is a force which creates, subjects to surveillance, and controls, and yet which lacks identifiable being. It hints of the metaphysical and the conspiratorial— a strange conjunction indeed.

For Foucault the sexual perversions are a key instance of the foregoing theory, especially of how power creates and controls. In the last two centuries we have witnessed 'a multiple implantation of perversions', accelerated in the second half of the nineteenth century by the consolidation of a new 'technology of sex' whose two great innovations were 'the medicine of perversions and the programs of eugenics' (pp. 37, 118). So, for example, although masturbation may have been designated as the evil to be eliminated, in fact it becomes a kind of support to power, made to proliferate rather than disappear; via this kind of support 'power advanced, multiplied its relays and its effects, while its target expanded, subdivided, and branched out, penetrating further into reality at the same pace' (p. 42). Freud saw childhood as a battle between instincts (or drives) and the demands of civilization; Foucault sees it as just one of the domains in which power operates.

With the implantation of perversions goes a new specification of individuals. Here Foucault offers his widely cited, but increasingly disputed, account of the emergence of the homosexual. Whereas sodomy was once a category of forbidden acts, the homosexual now came into being as a type of person:

nothing that went into his total composition was unaffected by his sexuality. It was everywhere present in him: at the root of all his actions because it was their insidious and indefinitely active principle ... the sodomite had been a temporary aberration; the homosexual was now a species. (p. 43)

Arnold Davidson gives support to this argument when he reminds us that perversion as a noun had a conceptually derivative place in moral theology, whereas in nineteenth-century medical discourse it becomes conceptually central. Theologically one was described as a pervert according to one's ethical choices, not one's identity (Davidson, 'Sex and the Emergence of Sexuality', 45–8).

So for Foucault perverts emerge not, as the Freudian might argue, because, 'having tried to erect too rigid or too general a barrier against sexuality, society succeeded only in giving rise to a whole perverse outbreak and a long pathology of the sexual instinct' (p. 47), but because they are required as 'the real product of the encroachment of a type of power on bodies and their pleasures' (p. 48).

In outline Foucault's hypothesis that sexuality and sexual perversion are in a crucial sense *produced* is persuasive, especially if we think of it as supplementing and crucially transforming—rather than dispensing with—the repressive hypothesis. However, different as it is from earlier sociological and anthropological accounts, Foucault's theory remains vulnerable to the charge of functionalism.[3] It is also the case that at first sight there is little possibility in Foucault's account for effective resistance, let alone insurrection. But Foucault does discuss, albeit briefly, the implications of his theory for the forms resistance takes: 'Where there is power, there is resistance, and yet, or rather consequently, this resistance is never in a position of exteriority in relation to power'; there is no single source of opposition but rather a plurality of resistances which are 'inscribed [within power] as an irreducible opposite' (pp. 95–6). This opposition between power and resistance must be understood as a 'complex and unstable process whereby discourse can be both an instrument and an effect of power, but also a hindrance, a stumbling block, a point of resistance and a starting point for an opposite strategy. Discourse transmits and produces power; it reinforces it, but also undermines and exposes it, renders it fragile and makes it possible to thwart it' (p. 101). For example there is no question, says Foucault, that the nineteenth-century discourse on perversity made possible new forms of social control. On the other hand it also made possible what he calls '"reverse" discourse', whereby 'homosexuality began to speak in its own behalf, to demand that its legitimacy or "naturality" be acknowleged, often in the same vocabulary, using the same categories by which it was medically disqualified' (p. 101).

We know that the centre remains vulnerable to marginality because its identity is partly created and partly defined in opposition to (and therefore also *at*) the margins. But the concept of reverse discourse suggests another dialectic sense that the outsider may be said to be always already inside: a return from demonized other to challenging

---

[3] As Weeks has pointed out (*Sex, Politics and Society*, 9). See also Ignatieff, 'State, Civil Society and Total Institutions'.

presence via containment, and one involving a simultaneous, contradictory, yet equally necessary appropriation and negation of those dominant notions of sexual identity and human nature by which it was initially excluded and defined.[4] These are those modes of transgression I traced through Gide, Wilde, Radclyffe Hall, and others, whereby the sexual deviant returns from abjection by appropriating and negotiating, or inverting and displacing, just those terms which relegated him or her to that state in the first place. But as we begin to recover this 'complex and socially significant history of resistance and self-definition which historians have hitherto all too easily ignored',[5] we discover that diverse strategies were involved, and the inadequacy of 'reverse discourse' as a blanket term. Recall how, for example, in relation to the binaries which organize and define the deviant—especially the natural/unnatural binary—this reverse discourse has worked through at least four reverse-discourse strategies (Parts 1 and 3 above):

1. Someone like Gide seeks to partake in the dominant term rather than the inferior one ('we're natural too'); this involves a struggle for inclusion *within* the very concepts which exclude the subordinate, a struggle which is simultaneously an appropriation and transformation *of* those concepts.

2. In Radclyffe Hall's *The Well of Loneliness* the strategy is to transvalue the negative identity through (e.g.) assimilation with other more positive ones, medical, cultural, religious, and literary.

3. In *Rubyfruit Jungle* the effect is to reverse the respective dominant/subordinate locations within the binary ('we're natural/superior; you're unnatural/inferior').

4. A different strategy is to destabilize, subvert, and displace the binary through inversion, or a turning back upon, a transgressive reinscription within, the dominant, to destroy at base the categories responsible for one's exclusion—as in Wilde's transgressive aesthetic.

Foucault's account of sexual deviance contradicts Freud's, especially in Foucault's insistence that perversion is not an innate desire which is socially repressed, but an identity and a category which are socially produced to enable power to gain a purchase within, and through, the

---

[4] Incidentally, literature testifies over and again to the way the outsider returns to the point of his or her social/psychic creation, literally or in fantasy, this being one reason why 'it could fairly be said that the failure to transform, tame, familiarize, or domesticate the ambiguous presence from "the outside" (another territory, another world—or just another house) is one of the permanently generative themes of Western literature' (Tanner, *Adultery*, 26).

[5] Weeks, *Sex, Politics and Society*, 117; see also Weeks's equally important *Coming Out*; Plummer (ed.), *The Making of the Modern Homosexual*; Greenberg, *The Construction of Homosexuality* (who contests Foucault's argument about the historical emergence of homosexuality).

realm of the psychosexual. But the corollary of this—that resistance is always *inside* power, as its irreducible opposite—comes intriguingly close to what my own reading of Freud has suggested, namely a resistance operating according to the perverse dynamic: homosexuality returns in and as a reverse discourse, moving from the margins to the centre, from construction to presence but a presence still in terms of, or working in terms of, the initial construction; incipient, halting, yet finally challenging precisely because 'power' has created, become dependent upon, incorporated it. The perverse dynamic suggests a connection between theories otherwise fundamentally opposed.

Foucault offers an anti-psychoanalytic account of sexuality which restores both sexuality and the perverse dynamic to history. But now, in part because of the emergence of the psychoanalytic perspective, sexuality and the perverse dynamic are inextricably connected. That fact also suggests that the bid for legitimation in terms of an essentialized conception of desire (Gide, Radclyffe Hall) is in important respects misdescribed as *only* essentialist: the return of the homosexual as a categorized, essential identity was also to some extent also the reverse, and perversely so—a de-essentializing insinuation of itself within, and thereby a disturbance of, the order of sexual difference which had created it; an insinuation succinctly expressed in the liberationist slogan 'we are your worst fears and your best dreams'. Thinking history in terms of the perverse dynamic begins to undermine that binary opposition between the essentialist and the anti-essentialist—so strangely persistent within literary and cultural theory, even as the theory criticizes binarism. It also lends support to Diana Fuss's contention that in the last resort 'essentialism underwrites theories of constructionism and . . . constructionism operates as a more sophisticated form of essentialism' (*Essentially Speaking*, 119).

15 *Thinking the Perverse Dynamic*

The Risk Between

In the preceding seven chapters (Parts 5 and 6) I have sought to retrieve and develop the concept of perversion. Starting with the earlier semantic fields of perversion, formal definitions were found to be significant, partly for what they convey directly but also for the cultural dynamic which their use sought to control, repress, and disavow. In attempting to recover *what* is repressed and disavowed—the unacceptable histories of perversion—I have been led beyond formal definitions to a conceptual development which in turn has facilitated historical recovery.

This fourfold procedure—(1) attention to formal definitions, provoking (2) a historical enquiry which in turn leads to (3) a conceptual development facilitating (4) a further historical recovery—I see as a materialist project, albeit one which on the way necessarily risked the encounter with psychoanalysis.

The risk is or should be mutual: Freud was aware of the paradoxical nature of desire, not least because of its fundamental perversity. But psychoanalysis, in discovering that perversity, needs also to address a perverse dynamic inextricably bound into desire but not reducible to it, however defined. To recover the history of perversion is to rethink some of the most basic classificatory categories which have organized and, in a sense produced, sexuality. It is also to disclose the perverse nature of the social; to move from the pathological to the political, from a narrative of psychosexual development to the violent dialectic of social process. And, finally, to recognize that a challenging concept of the perverse lies not any longer in the polymorphous perverse, but in the paradoxical perverse or the perverse dynamic. Perversion subverts not in the recovery of a pre-social libido, or an original plenitude, but as a dynamic intrinsic to social process. And sometimes, but never only, as insurrectionary desires which emerge within the selfsame conformist orders that proscribe them.

Thinking the Perverse Dynamic: Some Propositions.

The perverse dynamic is not an identity, a logic, or an economy, so much as an anti-teleological dialectic producing knowledge in opposition to destiny.

The other may be feared because structured within an economy of the same: the homophobic are disturbed by sameness within, or as a defining feature of, the other, that is, homosexual congress between the *same* gender construed as the endangering *other* of heterosexuality.

This sameness is not the conventional unity of the essential (Individual) or the universal (Man, Human Nature), but an interconnectedness so radical that most societies believing in the Individual, Man, and Human Nature have to disavow it. The corollary of which is that discrimination may operate not in spite of our sameness but because of it; sameness, far from being what (e.g.) the racist or the homophobe simply fails to see—that which, when recognized, will disarm him or her ('can't you see, we're all the same really, the same underneath?')—can become the focus of racism and homophobia. The same can become the incommensurability of the other.

So the perverse dynamic transvalues sameness, abandoning self-identity for the unstably proximate; it discloses not an underlying unity in the name of which social division can be transcended, but a radical interconnectedness which has been and remains the unstable ground of both repression and liberation; the ground from which division and discrimination are both produced and contested.

So we are not all the same. We are differences which radically proximate.

The terms of a binary interrelate, interdepend. But to differing degrees: in one kind of interdependence the one term presupposes the other for its meaning; in another more radical kind of interdependence the absolutely other is somehow integral to the selfsame. In the latter, absence or exclusion simultaneously becomes a presence. This is what the concept of perversion has historically both recognized and disavowed, and what the paradoxical perverse and the perverse dynamic disclose. When the inversion of a binary reveals the proximate it is always more than a mere reversal, more even than the utopian unity of the binary dissolved or displaced. The inversion of a binary produces not merely reversal but proximities where there was difference.

To be against (opposed to) is also to be against (close up, in proximity to) or, in other words, up against.

The perverse dynamic challenges not by collapsing order but through a reordering less tolerable, more disturbing, than chaos. Its difference is never the absolutely unfamiliar, but the reordering of the already known, a disclosure of a radical interconnectedness which *is* the social, but which present cultures can rarely afford to acknowledge and must instead disavow.

The perverse dynamic reidentifies and exploits the inextricable connections between perversity, proximity, paradox, and desire. As did Oscar Wilde: 'what the paradox was to me in the sphere of thought, perversity became to me in the sphere of passion.' But he wrote that from prison, and it was a knowledge for which he paid with his life. So in creating a politics of the perverse we should never forget the cost: death, mutilation, and incarceration have been, and remain, the fate of those who are deemed to have perverted nature.

That cannot be the last proposition: in perverting nature we identify with others, and two especially; the one an erotics of proximity—

[that] nearness so pronounced that it makes all discrimination of identity, and thus all forms of property, impossible. Woman derives pleasure from what is so near that she cannot have it, nor have herself. She herself enters into a ceaseless exchange of herself with the other without any possibility of identifying either (Irigaray, *This Sex*, 31)

—the other a politics of proximity—

The language of critique is effective not because it keeps for ever separate the terms of the master and the slave . . . but to the extent to which it overcomes the given grounds of opposition and opens up a space of 'translation': a place of hybridity, figuratively speaking, where the construction of a political object that is new, *neither the one nor the Other*, properly alienates our political expectations, and changes, as it must, the very forms of our recognition of the 'moment' of politics . . . This must be a sign that history is *happening*—within the windless pages of theory. (Bhabha, 'The Commitment to Theory', 10–11)

PART 7

Beleaguered Norms and Perverse Dynamics

16 *Homophobia (1):*
Sexual/Political Deviance

Part 5 considered two contending theories of perversion and homosexuality, one deriving from psychoanalysis, the other from anthropological, sociological, and historical perspectives, in which Foucault's *History of Sexuality* was both a culmination and a new departure. Henceforth, primarily for convenience of reference (and so provisionally), I shall designate the second account materialist. This post-Freudian, materialist reinterpretation of sexual deviance diverges so considerably from the sexological/psychoanalytic tradition that perversion comes to signify quite differently. This becomes even more so when deviance is regarded in the light of the pre-Freudian, pre-sexological histories of perversion. Two points made before are thereby worth reiterating: first, that the meaning of perversion is crucially context dependent; second that one objective of this book is to restore to the concept dimensions which were obscured within the sexological/psychoanalytic traditions, though remaining inscribed within them, especially in Freud's texts.

The reiteration is necessary partly because conventional sexological and psychoanalytic assumptions prove so difficult to dislodge. In response to my attempts to historicize perversion it has been said: 'OK, we see how you might want to rescue homosexuality from the pejorative category of a perversion, but surely not incest or bestiality?' This response misses the point on several counts. First because a recovery of the histories of perversion precisely disarticulates the sexological and psychoanalytic classifications which would lump together as perversions homosexuality, incest, bestiality, etc. Second, because those histories eventually facilitate a reversal in the object of analysis: at a certain stage it is no longer homosexuality, or the perversions as ordinarily understood, which need explaining, but (among other things) the classification of heterosexuality as the norm with homosexuality as its perverse other, and the splitting, displacements, and paranoia which accompany that division.

It is through the only recently developed concept of homophobia that this reversal proceeds. Indeed, the charge of homophobia is itself a kind of reverse discourse facilitated by the dynamic of perversion itself. As

Ken Plummer observes, whereas once it was the homosexual who was viewed as sick, now it might be the heterosexual who is charged with pathology: 'Whereas once the homosexual was identified by a long series of character traits, it is now possible to identify the traits of the homophobe: authoritarian, cognitively restricted, with gender anxieties' (Plummer, 'Homosexual Categories', 62). Most provocatively, those gender anxieties are found to harbour a repressed homosexuality. As we shall see, the reversal remains inadequate in that it conceives of homophobia in mainly psychosexual terms, and phobic ones at that. However I do not propose that we too quickly problematize the concept out of existence, since some of the questions it begs, even in its inadequate form, are just the sort which need to be asked.[1] The broad sense in which I shall be using homophobia is loosely descriptive of a manifest phenomenon: the hatred, fear, and persecution of, the raging at, homosexuality and homosexuals.

Man-holes

In the UK in 1983 there was a by-election in Bermondsey, London. Its run-up included a homophobic attack on one of the candidates, Peter Tatchell, whose political 'extremism' was regarded as inseparable from his sexual 'deviance'. It was largely mobilized by sections of the press, to a degree then unprecedented, but which heralded the onset of the intensified homophobia which has characterized that country ever since.[2]

Taking only the period in which this book has been written, and limiting the location to the UK, there have been numerous similar press-provoked scandals in which the homosexual has kept turning up where he or she should not, especially at the 'respectable' centre of things: in MI5, the Houses of Parliament, as parliamentary candidate, school-teacher, council employee, prison chaplain, vicar, guard to the Queen Mother, film star, circuit judge, to cite only some (and some whose lives have been destroyed by homophobic media harassment). The same press represents homosexuals as the corrupters of public morals, of children, the family, and even the armed forces; or as deviants conveying

---

[1] Those who regard the concept of homophobia as too psychological to be of use for a socio-political critique might usefully consider Frantz Fanon's suggestive deployment of a comparable concept, negrophobia, as a manifestation of racism (*Black Skin, White Masks*, esp. ch. 5, 'The Negro and Psychopathology'). On the history and the limitations of the concept of homophobia, see Plummer (ed.), *The Making of the Modern Homosexual*, as above, and also chs. 3 and 6; Altman, *The Homosexualization of America*; Sedgwick, *Between Men*; Watney, *Policing Desire*, esp. 44–56; Kitzinger, *The Social Construction of Lesbianism*, esp. 57–62; Pharr, *Homophobia*; Bristow, 'Homophobia/Misogyny'.

[2] On the by-election see Tatchell's *Battle for Bermondsey*, and on the recent history of homophobia in Britain, Watney's *Policing Desire*.

to other aliens (their external counterpart) the state's innermost secrets. As Simon Watney indicates in *Policing Desire*, hysteria over AIDS has fuelled press hate-campaigns, virtually fascist in their vindictiveness. One end result has been an increase in the extent to which gays and lesbians have been subjected to physical violence, including murder and mutilation.[3]

In many instances this homophobia is crude. But it is none the less effective for that, and it would be wrong to see it, as do some liberals, as a superstitious remnant from a blighted past. That contemporary homophobia, even or especially in its crudest forms, is not a residual superstition, can be seen in that initiating attack on Peter Tatchell. It may well have been rooted in a repressed homosexuality according to the psychoanalytic model. Indeed Tatchell, in his book on the events of those months, surveys the hate mail sent to him and concludes as much (*Battle*, 72). More significant though was a displacement into, a condensation within, the homosexual of a whole range of political fears and anxieties made possible by existing and long established represen-tations of homosexuality:

Dear Mr Tatchell

When I lived in Bermondsey, until my family were bombed out while I was fighting to protect my country from outside evils, we had a saying, Bermondsey was a place where men were men and women counted as 'manholes' and members of the 'Middlesex Regiment' would not be tolerated. So why don't you piss off back to where you come from and leave the decent people of that once great borough alone. This country is in enough trouble without the likes of you, and Tariq Ali etc, stirring it up. Anyway what is wrong with that land of sunshine Australia, that you want to leave it, is it because you have to work for your living there? (quoted from Tatchell, *Battle*, 72)

In this letter, masculinity—'when men were men'—is vigilant against 'outside evils', especially racial infiltration and homosexuality, the latter conceived as sexual ambiguity ('Middlesex Regiment'). Each provokes fears of a social decline which in turn evokes imperial decline: 'that once great borough' where men were men, women were 'manholes', and queers were given short shrift.

It is a letter which indicates several things about homophobia, and three in particular. First and most obviously perhaps, it shows how homophobia is often integral to a conventional kind of masculine identity. But already more is going on than first appears. I have already

---

[3] The full extent of that press obsession, in all its self-serving and at times fascist vindictiveness, has for some years been effectively documented by Terry Sanderson in his 'Mediawatch' column in the monthly UK journal *Gay Times*. These columns are probably the most informative record of the extent of press homophobia in the UK in the 1980s.

had several occasions to remark that binary oppositions are, in Derrida's phrase, violent hierarchies. From this letter we can see how the opposition masculine/homosexual is a conflation of two other classic binaries: masculine/feminine; hetero/homosexual. It is often observed that misogyny and homophobia go together. One reason is that this conflation of binaries enables a merging of misogyny and homophobia, each of which then potentially expresses the violence of the other. Second then, homophobia often intersects with other kinds of phobia and hatred: in this case, and rather economically, not only misogyny but also racism and xenophobia. While different kinds of discrimination are not to be conflated, I believe there is something to be learned from homophobia about other kinds. Third, the analysis of homophobia demands both the psychoanalytic and materialist perspectives, not least because, as this letter suggests, it is so obviously and inseparably both a psychic and social phenomenon. I remarked earlier my interest in a cultural critique situated at the points where these two perspectives converge without ever becoming compatible; at the points of overlap which are also gaps. This is nowhere more necessary than in the analysis of homophobia. I believe too that this analysis must proceed historically, which is why I approach it via the now familiar historical detour.

It is customary to frame the history of homosexuality with reference to the essentialist/constructionist debate (homosexuality as essential human given versus homosexuality as socio-historical construct). Important as this is, it tends to ignore other histories. Here I focus on the genealogy of two aspects of discrimination already addressed by this study, namely displacement between the political and the sexual, and the idea of perversion as an inimical absence.

Political and Sexual Subversions

The mythology which, as in the Tatchell affair, connects sexual deviation and political subversion is very old. It is typically inflected by other kinds of fears, especially religious and racial ones. A case in point is those forms of nationalism committed to policing not only actual geographic borders and literal or legally defined aliens, but symbolic and ideological boundaries (both internal and external) between the normal and the abnormal, the healthy and sick, the conforming and the deviant. Himmler launched his attack on homo/sexuals on the basis that they, like the Jews, were involved in a conspiracy to undermine the German race.[4] Such associations of sexual deviance and political threat

---

[4] See Plant, *The Pink Triangle*, esp. ch. 3, and Mosse, *Nationalism and Sexuality*, esp. 168.

have a long history sedimented into our language and culture. The term 'buggery', for example, derives from the religious as well as sexual non-conformity of an eleventh-century Bulgarian sect which practised the Manichaean heresy and refused to propagate the species; the *OED* tells us that it was later applied to other heretics, to whom abominable practices were also ascribed.

Arthur N. Gilbert has written about a particular instance of the way social and political crisis provokes renewed urgency in the policing of sexual deviance. During the Napoleonic wars the number of prosecutions for sodomy increased. To understand why, argues Gilbert, we need to understand the construction of the sodomite, his association at that time with evil, rebellion, and insurrection, and the belief that to tolerate his sin was to court the possibility of divine revenge (as with Sodom and Gomorrah). This mythology found an immediate focus: the sodomite was perceived as an internal deviant who refigured a foreign threat, in this case the threat from the French. Gilbert refers to a dissertation by Richard Allen Soloway which shows contemporary fears of Christianity falling before the atheistical, licentious, and immoral foreigner ('Sexual Deviance and Disaster', 98, 99, 100–1, 110–11). The sodomite becomes a virulent image of this threat, embodying a foreign infection which in turn is linked to social disorder and economic collapse at home. A violent, enduring mythology is activated to make sense of immediate socio-political crisis and fear.

This analysis suggests that if, in periods of intensified conflict, crisis is displaced on to the deviant, the process only succeeds because of the paranoid instabilities at the heart of dominant cultural identites. Further, such displacements of non-sexual fears on to the sexual deviant, be he or she actual, imagined, or constituted in and by the displacement, are made possible because other kinds of transgression—political, religious—are not only loosely associated with the sexual deviant, but 'condensed' in the very definition of deviance. It is a process especially apparent in early modern England, not least because of the differences between its categories of sexual deviance and ours.

At that time sodomy was associated with a whole range of evils, including insurrection and heresy; all such evils could be, and often were, 'imagined' in the form of, or at least in relation to, the sodomite. Recent studies emphasize the different ways homo/sexuality was conceptualized in early modern England—a difference so considerable in fact that 'homosexuality' becomes anachronistic, since at that time there was neither the concept nor, exactly, the identity it signifies.

Briefly, the argument is as follows: the homosexual is a creation of modern discourse, medical, sexological, and psychological, as evidenced by the fact that the word 'homosexual' was coined in 1869: neither it nor the sexual sense of perversion appeared in the OED until its 1933 Supplement. The nearest concepts to it in early modern England were probably sodomy and buggery. As we saw in Chapter 14, Michel Foucault argues that before the nineteenth century the sodomite was someone who performed a certain kind of *act*; no specific *identity* was attributed to, or assumed by, the sodomite. The attribution or assumption of this identity marks the creation of the homosexual.

Alan Bray and Jeffrey Weeks have given historical support to this view, though not without qualification;[5] I remarked in Part 1 some further reservations. Additionally, we should recall that, before the nineteenth century, the meanings of terms like sodomy and buggery might have been even wider than is suggested by Foucault's argument. Sodomy was associated with witches, demons, werewolves, basilisks, foreigners, and (of course) papists; and it apparently signified a wide range of practices including prostitution, under-age sex, coitus interruptus, and female transvestism. Socially, sodomy was repeatedly equated with heresy and political treason; metaphysically, it was conceived as 'sexual confusion in whatever form', a 'force of anarchic disorder set against divine Creation', not a part of the created order but an aspect of its dissolution. As such it potentially functioned as a perverse dynamic— neither a part of created nature, nor a sexuality in its own right, but rather 'a potential for confusion and disorder in one undivided sexuality'.[6]

Imaged in such terms, the sodomite indeed became the supreme instance of the demonized other. But *so* extreme was the sodomite's construction that most of those actually engaging in 'homo/sexuality' did not identify themselves with it; not only did they not have our modern categories, but the prevailing categories were so far removed from how they saw themselves, that apparently the connection was not made. Nor was it made by the authorities—except, apparently, in times of political and social crisis, the eruption of class hatred, religious and political persecution.[7]

Certainly then in early modern England the ways of conceptualizing

---

[5] See esp. Weeks, *Sex, Politics and Society*, 1–11; Bray, *Homosexuality in Renaissance England*; and Greenberg, *The Construction of Homosexuality*. Greenberg, while defending the view that homo/sexuality has been differently defined in different historical periods, contests the extreme 'constructionist' view usually derived from Foucault, namely, the idea that the homo/sexual as a distinct species originated only about 100 years ago (p. 485).

[6] Bray, *Homosexuality in Renaissance England*, 14, 25, 19, 68, 103, 112; Greenberg, *The Construction of Homosexuality*, esp. 20, 275, 279; see also Weeks, *Coming Out*, 11–14, and Goldberg, 'Sodomy and Society'.

[7] Greenberg, *The Construction of Homosexuality*, 298 and 323; Bray, *Homosexuality in Renaissance England*, 71.

sexuality and sexual deviance were fundamentally different from ours, as were the perceived relations between sexuality and subjectivity. That individuals prosecuted for sodomy did not necessarily identify themselves with the demonized sodomite of official discourse also lends credence to Foucault's distinction between sodomy as a kind of behaviour, and homosexuality as a modern identity. But we should not rely too heavily on that distinction. There remain certain continuities which should give us pause.

Laura Levine has pointed to an interesting relationship in early modern England between fears of sodomy and fears of the theatre. She observes that the frequent indictments of theatre for encouraging sodomy are symptomatic of the anti-theatricalists' fear that gender difference is ever under threat of breakdown and, more generally, their fear that 'under the costume there is really nothing there or, alternatively, that what is there is something foreign, something terrifying and essentially other' ('Men in Women's Clothing', 135; see also Chapter 17 below). Such arguments suggest that the perception of the sodomite was already implicated in the constructions of gender and sexual difference, and, through them, of identity, subjectivity, and social ordering more generally, and the anxieties attendant upon all these things.

Moreover, it is not true that prior to the nineteenth century (or eighteenth, depending on when the change was said to occur) sexual deviance was conceptualized only as a form of behaviour. I suggest that in early modern England the sodomite, though not an identity in the modern sense, could and did denote subject positions or types; 'he' precisely *characterized* deviant subject positions as well as denoting the behaviour of individuals.[8] Sodomy was not thought to originate in a pathological subjectivity (the modern pervert); rather, the sexual deviant was the vehicle of a confusion never only sexual, and sexual in a way different from the sexological and psychoanalytic accounts. As such the deviant was the point of entry into civilization for the unnatural, the aberrant, and the abhorrent, the wilderness of disorder which beleaguered all civilization; a disorder in part, but rarely only ever, sexual. And if sodomy signified diverse types of evil, so too might evil itself infiltrate civilization through diverse subject types. Both forms of diversity were subject to either displacement or condensation. Displacement might involve a sliding along the signifying chain which connects the different manifestations of evil and subject types, conflating two or more of them; thus the sexual deviant may also 'be' a witch, an

---

[8] And conversely, as I point out in relation to Gide (above, Ch. 3), the behavioural criterion survives *vis-à-vis* the 'modern' homo/sexual identity.

insurrectionary, or a papist. Condensation might entail the one kind of subject and/or manifestation standing in for the whole domain of evil, incurring responsibility for the whole in the process of being made to signify it. Hence condensation and displacement were, and are still, related ways of *identifying* the deviant. It is in these terms that we find sodomy lurking in the cultural histories of the deviants in early modern England, and in a way which throws light on the persistence today of the connection between political and sexual subversion, and the condensation/displacement of social crisis *into* sexuality.

Wilde: The Pernicious Absence

As we saw with the pre-sexological theories of perversion, condensation and displacement are strangely enabled by the view of perversion as an inimical threatening absence. What is not often recognized is the extent to which this theological sense of perversion as the negative agency at the heart of privation, hence an inverted positivity, survives into the 'modern' sense of perversion/homosexuality as a profoundly inimical, vitiating lack (of normality, of truth).

Increasingly the fate of Oscar Wilde has been analysed in relation to the construction of the modern homosexual along lines suggested by Michel Foucault. Again, this is important and relevant, but so too is this older history. After he had been found guilty of homosexual offences and sentenced to two years' imprisonment with hard labour, the press subjected Oscar Wilde to vicious attack. As we saw in Chapter 4, the London *Evening News* accused him of trying to subvert the 'wholesome, manly, simple ideals of English life', and connected his sexual perversion with intellectual and moral subversion. He possessed, as the *Daily Telegraph* conceded on 27 May 1895, 'considerable intellectual powers'. It advocates 'a reaction towards simpler ideas . . . for fear of national contamination and decay'. Queensberry, in a letter published in the *Star* on 25 April 1895, expresses the connection clearly enough when he describes Wilde as 'a sexual pervert of an utterly diseased mind' (Goodman, *The Oscar Wilde File*, 133–4, 99).

Reading through the press comment on Wilde we find the same fear of cross-over between sexual perversion and intellectual and moral subversion. On the one hand the world of normality and conformity is stridently affirmed. It is variously described as 'health and right reason', the 'wholesome', the 'healthy and unvitiated', and characterized by 'unalterable standards of right and wrong' (Goodman, *The Oscar Wilde File*, 78, 133, 134). By contrast Wilde and his art are described as 'false', 'cheap', 'shallow and specious', 'nerveless and effeminate', marked by an 'unreality' and 'essential emptiness and frivolity' (pp. 75, 78, 133, 134). The oppositions invoked in these descriptions—the substantial versus the insubstantial, depth versus shallowness—are just the ones Wilde inverted and subverted. Here they are reinvoked to discredit Wilde, yet in a way which still acknowledged him as a threat. But why? In the terms of the binaries invoked, and reinstalled right-way-around, he should have been perceived as *only* shallow, specious, ineffectual. Not so: these editorials identify Wilde as very evil. His falsity and hollowness are not just the opposite of the true and the wholesome, but threaten to undermine it. He is not only spurious but also 'diseased', the two being inseparable.

Something informing these descriptions of Wilde and his art is a fear of degeneration as conceived by writers of the time.[9] It was not just that degenerates were thought to be intelligent and gifted; their intelligence manifested one of the most disturbing paradoxes of the perverse: a vitiating regression to the primitive *from within* an advanced cultural sophistication. For these commentators Wilde represents both a cultural 'decay' and a resurrection of 'pagan viciousness' and 'primal errors' (pp. 98, 134). Recall that for Robert Burton in 1621 it was not our bestial qualities that were the most dangerous, but our civilized ones perverted (above, Chapter 8); now, the civilized in perverted form *is also* the primitive and bestial. Here is the *Telegraph* again:

opinions and principles like [Wilde's] have from time to time manifested themselves all down the course of history, generally in over-ripe civilisations wavering on the brink of decay. In the next place they are found side by side with great intellectual brilliance, and ... clothed in glamour which hides the hollowness within. (Goodman, *The Oscar Wilde File*, 134)

Decline, brilliance, hollowness: such things, essentially empty in themselves, nevertheless undermine the nation. Again, sexual perversion echoes attributes of Augustinian privation: evil lacks authentic being itself ('the hollowness within') and because, rather than in spite of, that fact is utterly inimical to true being. What is simultaneously acknowledged and denied is that 'wholesomeness' is not invaded from without so much as corrupted from within. Its own strength is turned against it. Thus while Wilde is merely 'a parasite, an excrescence, an aberration' (p. 78), those allegedly most susceptible to his perversion are quite

---

[9] Writing from prison to the Home Secretary on 2 July 1896, pleading remission, Wilde himself was also to appeal to degeneration theory in explanation of his conduct. Wilde refers to Max Nordau's account in *Degeneration* of 'the intimate connection between madness and the literary and artistic temperament', and implicitly concedes that Nordau, who devotes a chapter to Wilde, was correct in representing him as 'a specially typical example of this fatal flaw' (*Letters*, 401–2).

otherwise: the family in general, young men at university, sometimes even their tutors, boys at public school, maidens, and novelists (p. 133).

This might plausibly be dismissed as 'Victorian stupidity' were it not for the fact that in Britain in 1988 a similar view was actually inscribed in law. Here too the emphasis was on the susceptibility of the 'innocent' to the specious; section 28 of the Local Government Act 1987–8 states that a local authority shall not

(a) intentionally promote homosexuality or publish material with the intention of promoting homosexuality;
(b) promote the teaching in any maintained school of the acceptability of homosexuality as a *pretended family* relationship. (my emphasis)[10]

How could anything so demonstrably inferior to the real thing ever pretend to be it, and with such potential (or feared) success that the parliament of an 'advanced western democracy' must legislate against it? Because still in 1988, under the pressure of social instability and political crises, homosexuality could be regarded as a kind of privation or error, an 'inverted positivity', an inimical, pernicious, inauthenticity always threatening to return from within the true and the authentic.

The Return of Homosexuality

If the trouble with the materialist view of perversion is its tendency to functionalist reduction (above, Chapter 14), the Freudian position faces equally intractable problems, though of a different kind. Considered from a materialist perspective it has at least three damaging limitations: first it tends to construe sexuality in terms of an original pre-social plenitude, an initially unstructured natural energy; second (and consequently) sexuality is conceived in certain of Freud's central texts as a drive with hydraulic characteristics; third, a phenomenon like homophobia, when it is not being blatantly disregarded, is explained too much in terms of the subjective, psychic repressions of its agents. The consequences of this last point can be pernicious, actually encouraging a way of thinking whereby the aggressor in homophobic violence is somehow identified with his or her victim: both are homosexual, the one repressed, the other overt. Or, as it is sometimes switched round in

---

[10] For a fuller analysis of this bill and its significance in contemporary Britain, see Anna Marie Smith, 'A Symptomology of an Authoritarian Discourse'. Though this law might well have something to do with the attempted resuscitation of 'Victorian' morality in Britain in the 1980s, that cannot explain the appearance of proposed legislation in the USA in 1981 with rather similar wording: 'no federal funds may be made available . . . for the purpose of advocating, promoting, or suggesting homosexuality, male or female, as a lifestyle' (from proposed 'Family Protection Act' before the US Congress in 1981, cited in Clarke, 'The Failure to Transform', 197).

homophobic (or just careless) thought: the victim is somehow the same as the aggressor and hence in some vague sense complicit with the aggression.

But it would be wrong to hold psychoanalysis entirely responsible for this slippage. It stems also from the inherent violence of sexual subordination and the (mis)representation which (re)produces it, especially in and through the category of the sexual deviant. We saw in Chapter 7 how the enemy is 'homosexualized', with the result that, even while homosexuals were being imprisoned and murdered by the Nazis, it could be said that to eliminate homosexuality would be to get rid of fascism. A further vicious twist in this kind of representation, again remarked by Richard Plant in *The Pink Triangle*, concerns the way that in the Nazi concentration camps homosexual inmates were held responsible by non-homosexual inmates for crimes committed by homosexual guards: 'homosexual guards, however hostile, were seen by non-gay prisoners as belonging to the homosexual underclass. Thus, homosexual prisoners were often tainted by the crimes of homosexual guards—even though they themselves were often the victims' (pp. 166–7).

A related problem with the psychoanalytic account is the implication that so many different kinds of close relationship between heterosexually identified men, be they complicated or simple, conflicted or supportive, brutally vindictive or discerningly tender, are *really* rooted in repressed homosexuality. This way of thinking has to be one of the blinder alleys that we have been led up by psychoanalysis. Hence the importance of Eve Sedgwick's category of the homosocial: we must insist that there are different kinds of masculine heterosexual alliance that are not necessarily (though may be) homosexual, repressed or overt; but we also need to make this point in a way which does not then privilege this distinction between the sexual and the non-sexual since this is to re-establish the primacy of the sexual, something partly responsible for the original misrepresentation. Having said all that, the Freudian model stands as an indispensable starting-point for identifying a certain kind of homophobia, namely that conjunction of hatred, paranoia, and desire (repressed, ambivalent, or overt) which characterizes some of those same heterosexually identified men in their relationships with lesbian and gay people. Misleading as it often is, the notion of the repressed homosexual does accurately describe some people.

More revealing than their obvious differences are those points of overlap between the materialist and the psychoanalytic accounts. First, both theories suggest an eventual return of homosexuality: in the one (psychoanalytic) it is a psychic return of the repressed from within, in the other (materialist) a social or cultural return from without; either an inner resurgence of desire through the breakdown of psychic repression, or the oppositional approach via the proximate of the demonized other from beyond, from the social margins where he or she has been discovered, constructed, displaced. Either way he or she returns to disturb the heterosexual norm, especially in its masculine form, and does so according to a psychic and/or social dynamic which is intrinsically perverse: deviance emerges from the terms of its exclusion, eventually undermining that of which it was initially an effect, and which depended upon its exclusion. We have already seen how the psychic return of homosexuality is central to Freud's account of neurosis, possibly becoming, in Hocquenghem's phrase, the 'killer of civilised egos' because such egos are rooted in and conditional upon the repression of that same homosexual desire which returns. Meanwhile its social and cultural return has been explored in the literature of Wilde, Gide, and others, as well as in reverse-discourse theory of which the very concept of homophobia is an instance. It is probably the case that we live in a time when the cultural return of homosexuality exacerbates, even intensifies, the psychic return of repressed homosexuality.

This suggests a second and related sense in which the psychoanalytic and the materialist perspectives converge: both suggest that identity—individual and cultural—involves a process of disavowal, exclusion, and negation. In the first it is the negation of desire, in the second, of the culturally defined other of cultural difference. The following remark of Dennis Altman's, even if not strictly correct historically, rightly implies how the negation of desire and the negation of difference are in practice often inseparable: 'the original purpose of the categorization of homosexuals as people apart was to project the homosexuality in everyone onto a defined minority as a way of externalizing forbidden desires and reassuring the majority that homosexuality is something that happens to other people' (*Homosexualization*, 72).

A yet further, intriguingly perverse, aspect of this convergence involves the phenomenon whereby the culturally negated other becomes the focus of the very desire which is being policed within the dominant culture: the other, in the very process of being identified, displaced, and negated, becomes the object of—indeed may actually incite—desire. Such desire for the other may be less the result of a desublimation of repressed desire than a consequence of desire itself being structured by social repression generally: thus the other may be cathected as (an)other beyond repression. Romantics know about this.

Divergence

These two areas of convergence also direct us to the main area of divergence and the reason why, though in actuality inextricably related, the psychic and the cultural return of homosexuality still need to be distinguished. On the Freudian model it is the repression and sublimation of homosexual desire that helps secure identity and social organization. Conversely, on the materialist model it is much more homophobia itself, as an aspect of the construction of homosexuality and independently of the question of the actual subjective repression of desire, which helps secure a coerced identity and social organization; homophobia enforces the heterosexual norm by policing its boundaries: 'Homophobia is only incidentally directed against homosexuals—its more common use is against the 49% of the population which is male . . . The taunt "What are you, a fag?" is used in many ways to encourage certain types of male behaviour and to define the limits of "acceptable" masculinity.'[11]

So, whereas in the psychoanalytic account, homophobia might well signal the precariousness and instability of identity, even of sexual difference itself, in the materialist socio-political account it typically signals the reverse, namely that sexual difference is being secured, homophobia being 'a mechanism for regulating the behaviour of the many by the specific oppression of a few' (Sedgwick, *Between Men*, 88).

Even in the first case, where homophobia is the expression of repressed desire, we should neither overestimate its destabilizing effects, nor regard its homophobic projection as an always ultimately futile effort to avoid the crippling effects of repression and/or neurosis. Indeed, even where homophobia *is* directly connected with a disturbing repression and/or neurosis, the actual psychic dislocation involved may be very effectively *offset* by the political and cultural gains of homphobic displacement. Such displacement *may* be a symptom of a continuously destructive semi-repression, but it may also be an effective way of minimizing within oneself, or a group, disabling complications within identity. Also, even if a subject is never directly or completely 'freed' from repression by its displacement, he or she may be empowered in other ways—for example, by being seen to be homophobic in a homophobic culture. Relatedly, as a means of securing sexual difference, homophobia may also be a displacement of homosocial anger—resentment at coerced identification and the persistent intimidation to conform. If so, then there is a sense in which homophobia may feed itself,

---

[11] G. K. Lehne, quoted in John Marshall, 'Pansies, Perverts and Macho Men', in Plummer (ed.), *The Making of the Modern Homosexual*, 153–4.

securing the framework (sexual difference) which promotes and intensifies its displacement as anger.

So while homophobia may sometimes originate in and, as it circulates socially, reconnect with repressed desire, the latter cannot be homophobia's necessary condition since it often circulates without it, and in a socio-political form which is more rapid, more widespread, more economical, and possibly more destructive. Instead of positing psychically repressed homosexuality as the necessary and/or sufficient cause of homophobia, we might better regard socially proscribed homosexuality as one of homophobia's several interconnected and enabling conditions, none of which is independently either necessary or sufficient. It is often difficult in retrospect, or even contemporaneously for that matter, to discern the part that psychic repression plays in any instance of homophobia. But, for the reason just given, it is hardly imperative that we should.

But even this important distinction between the psychoanalytic and the materialist account is complicated by another equally important convergence: since, in cultural terms, desiring the normal is inseparable from and conditional upon not desiring the abnormal, repression remains central to identity, individual and cultural, even—or indeed especially—for the materialist view of homophobia as a strategy of social control. Initially this appears not to be so, since while the Freudian model posits a repression within the subject, the materialist model posits a repression outside the subject in the form of its other. But the latter still involves psychic repression: the identity of the normal is inseparable from, rooted in, what it is not, what is socially excluded. In principle, of course, whether the repressed constituent of identity is outside or inside the subject makes a difference. But in practice how exactly might that difference be discerned? In both cases the repressed/ excluded remains subjectively/socially central. Or rather, the distinctions between the repressed and the excluded, the subjective and the social, break down, especially when we recall that the other is often constructed via, or in terms of, the proximate. So, for instance, while it may be that specific instances of homophobic panic are provoked by repressed homosexuals (in the Freudian sense), the panic may only 'take' socially, because of the other kind of repression—exclusive identity formation—as it affects a far greater number.

Desire and Disgust

In their remarkable study, Stallybrass and White argue that 'the bourgeois subject continuously defined and re-defined itself through the exclusion of what it marked out as "low"—as dirty, repulsive, noisy, contaminating. Yet that very act of exclusion was constitutive of its identity. The low was internalized under the sign of negation and disgust.' But, they add, '*disgust always bears the imprint of desire.* These low domains, apparently expelled as "Other", return as the object of nostalgia, longing and fascination' (*Politics and Poetics*, 191, my emphasis). Conversely, desire bears the imprint of disgust: even as the low other becomes an object of longing, it is simultaneously that on to which is displaced a self-disgust that inheres at the centre of bourgeois desire, and for that matter other forms of desire. The difference of the other becomes a displaced and intensified facet of the same, the object of desire and disgust. The disgust which inheres in desire is not, as the Freudian analysis might suggest, necessarily generated by or focused upon the repressed constituent of the self; it *may* be, but what I am pointing to here is an additional structural interdependence of desire and disgust. So even when homophobia is not obviously a projection of repressed desire, being more a hostile response to the intolerably different, even then, the homosexual, through condensed association, may be one on whom is projected the repressed disgust inherent in desire.

The convergence I have been exploring does not suggest that we should collapse materialism and psychoanalysis into each other. Rather a theoretical conflict indicates that we need to pluralize the notion of repression, as we need to pluralize that of homophobia, and even that of desire itself. There are different kinds and the differences are crucial, helping to mark the otherwise indistinguishable overlaps in historical actuality, *and* the crucial differences made by historical factors. Let us finally return to that letter written to Peter Tatchell in 1983. Many interrelated fears and phobias are suggested by that image of women as 'manholes'. Anal phobia perhaps, or fear of sexual engulfment, maybe even castration itself. Either way, in this masculine imaginary the vagina signifies a most disturbing absence, a hole which is also privation, deficiency, lack, a negativity which engulfs and vitiates what is full. 'Either way': maybe in this imaginary, or at least in its unconscious, the homosexual is also a vagina. But isn't this 'manhole' also a condensed image which, like the letter generally, fearfully anticipates engulfment in the return of those actual others ('outside evils') whose subordination, persecution, or exclusion has hitherto seemed to guarantee a sexual, racial, and national purity—women, homosexuals, foreigners? I am reminded that with the literal manhole—the actual thing in the street— we can indeed walk all over it. But don't we also know, if only in our dreams, that even as we do so we will one day just as surely fall down it?

Homophobia (2): Theories of Sexual Difference

The criminal classes are so close to us that even the policeman can see them. They are so far away from us that only the poet can understand them. (Wilde, 'Maxims')

The way we see the other is connected to the way we see ourselves. The other is ourselves as the stranger. (Ben Okri discussing *Othello* and race, 'Leaping Out')

'Difference' is a fashionable concept. So too is 'the other', that highly charged embodiment of difference. I propose a distrust of both concepts. Several kinds of difference figure in contemporary cultural theory but two especially: sexual difference (deriving usually though not invariably from psychoanalysis) and cultural difference, with each of these complicated by a third kind of difference which construes meaning and identity in terms of difference or, more exactly, differential relations.[1] I shall call this third kind 'semiotic difference'.

The homosexual is significantly implicated in both sexual and cultural difference, and for two main reasons. First because he or she has been regarded (especially in psychoanalytic theory) as one who fears the difference of the 'other' or opposite sex, and, in flight from it, narcissistically embraces the same sex instead. Difference and heterogeneity are sanctified, homogeneity is distrusted. The eminent Kleinian psychoanalyst, Hanna Segal, has recently declared the adult homosexual structure to be inherently pathological, disturbed, and perverse, and this because of an inbuilt, narcissistic desire for the same: 'homosexuality is of necessity a narcissistic condition, as the name itself betrays. Loving homo—the same as me not hetero—the other, different. . . . Heterosexuality can be more or less narcissistic, it can be very disturbed or not so. In homosexuality it's inbuilt' ('Interviewed', 212). In some instances 'sameness' comes to signify the tyranny of Western patriarchal metaphysics, and homosexuality its practice or, more vaguely, its metaphor. Luce Irigaray speaks of a dominant philosophic logos with a

---

[1] Barrett in 'The Concept of "Difference"' helpfully identifies three contemporary uses: (1) experiential diversity, (2) positional meaning, (3) sexual (difference). My two principal kinds of difference correspond to her first and third, but only partly, since I consider her second kind (which corresponds to my semiotic difference) to be inseparable from (and also what complicates) the first and third.

'power to *reduce all others to the economy of the Same* [and] *eradicate the difference between the sexes*'. It is manifested as a 'dominant phallic economy' which is described as hom(m)osexual (sometimes hom(m)o-sexual) and rooted in singularity—'The *one* of form, of the individual, of the (male) sexual organ, of the proper name, of the proper meaning . . .'—and characterized by censure and repression. Conversely woman's pleasure is 'more diversified, more multiple in its differences'. Metaphorically sameness is associated with perversion in an almost Augustinian sense: 'the artifice of sameness' involves a process of 'turning away, of deviation, and of reduction'. Irigaray goes further, exalting the metaphor of homosexuality as a kind of anti-difference into nothing less than a far-reaching theory of patriarchal society. She contends that 'the exchanges upon which patriarchal societies are based take place exclusively among men' and that 'this means that the *very possibility of a sociocultural order requires homosexuality* as its organizing principle . . . all economic organization is homosexual'. But such homosexuality must in some sense be repressed; overt 'masculine' homosexuality is subversive, says Irigaray, because it openly interprets the law according to which society operates and in so doing threatens it: 'once the penis itself becomes merely a means to pleasure, pleasure among men, *the phallus loses its power*' (*This Sex*, 74, 24–8, 128, 171, 192–3; her emphases).

The second reason why the homosexual is involved with difference is because, contrary to what the foregoing theory implies, she or he has, in historical actuality, embraced both cultural and racial difference. The relationship to these other kinds of difference has, for some homosexuals, constituted a crucial dimension of their culture. Sexually exiled from the repressiveness of the home culture (to which psychoanalytic theory has contributed in no small part with theories like the one just mentioned), homosexuals have searched instead for fulfilment in the realm of the foreign. Not necessarily as a second best: over and again in the culture of homosexuality, differences of race and class are intensely cathected. That this has also occurred in exploitative, sentimental, and/ or racist forms does not diminish its significance; if anything it increases it. Those who move too hastily to denounce homosexuality across race and class as essentially or only exploitative, sentimental, or racist betray their own homophobic ignorance. This crossing constitutes a complex, difficult history, one from which we can learn. I shall argue for the importance of this history for all three kinds of difference—sexual, cultural, and semiotic—as they figure in current theory. Although I concentrate in this chapter on sexual difference and on cultural and racial differences in the last chapter, it is worth remembering that in some contexts they interrelate.

First a by now familiar digression via the early modern, where we find rather different conceptions of sameness and sexual difference.

Turning into a Woman

> Does not lassitude succeed intercourse because of the quantity of seed lost? 'For a man is formed and torn out of a man'. See how much harm is done. A whole man is torn out when the seed is lost in intercourse. (Clement of Alexandria, *Christ the Educator*, 172–3)

In an influential if controversial essay, Thomas Laqueur has proposed that relatively recently in our history there occurred a radical reinterpretation of the female body. An old and enduring model of sexual difference, developed most powerfully and resiliently by Galen in the second century A D, had stressed the homologous nature of male and female reproductive organs; women were said to have the same genitals as men, only inside rather than outside. To be sure there were important differences: the male was more perfectly developed than the female because hotter; but these were differences conceived on a hierarchical, teleological model of sexual development. In the eighteenth century this model gave way to another based on absolute differences of kind:

A biology of hierarchy grounded in a metaphysically prior 'great chain of being' gave way to a biology of incommensurability in which the relationship of men to women, like that of apples to oranges, was not given as one of equality or inequality but rather as a *difference* whose meaning required interpretation and struggle.

Laqueur finds in the political, cultural, and economic transformations of the eighteenth century a context in which 'the articulation of radical differences between the sexes became culturally imperative'. Further, in a world in which science

was increasingly viewed as providing insight into the fundamental truths of creation, in which nature as manifested in the unassailable reality of bones and organs was taken to be the only foundation of the moral order, a biology of incommensurability became the means by which such differences could be authoritatively represented. (Laqueur, 'Orgasm', 24, 35).

In the earlier theory[2] man is separated from woman as different stages in a teleological development. Here is a most revealing instance of the way a difference within the same, teleologically construed, can make a great deal of difference: in effect a difference of degree can be as real as

---

[2] MacClean, in *The Renaissance Notion of Woman*, sketches the longer history of this view going back to Aristotle. See esp. ch. 3. See also Laqueur's *Making Sex*.

a difference of kind but in a different way: the lesser is inferior and thereby inimical in a way the antithetical cannot be, and the same becomes more different than difference itself. But never utterly— i.e. securely—*other*.

Perhaps this helps explain something noted by Laura Levine: in the numerous tracts attacking the Elizabethan and Jacobean theatre and its dress and gender transgressions, there is a fear that men dressing as women will lead to an erosion of masculinity itself. Levine contends that these tracts, even as they confidently sermonize on the fixed nature of identity, especially gender identity as prescribed by God and signified through dress difference, display a deep anxiety that identity is *not* fixed; that, underneath, the self is really nothing at all ('Men in Women's Clothing', 126 and 128). Further, they feared that 'doing' what a woman does (on the stage and in women's clothes) leads to 'being' what a woman is; the most unmanageable anxiety is that there is no essentially masculine self (p. 136), and cross-dressing in women's clothes can lead to a man 'turning into' a woman. Stephen Orgel discerns in the theatre of this time the fear that man's superior development could be reversed— 'that men can turn into—or be turned into—women; or perhaps more exactly, can be turned *back* into woman, losing the strength that enabled the male potential to be realized in the first place.'[3]

Perhaps what is at work here is a fear of the other as same not unlike the fascinated fear of the primitive in the notion of 'going native': a metamorphosis into the radically other which is no more than an all too easily imagined regression into one's own 'primitive' past. So we begin to understand the masculine fear in the early modern period of being effeminized—*not*, as might be the case today, by erotic contact with other men, but by excessive contact with women. This too seems to have involved the fear of regression; in social terms the inferior who stands opposite one in the world, thereby confirming one's superiority, *also stands behind one*. Man regresses into his other (his same), who says: frailty, thy name is man, thy same is woman.

In a bizarre and disavowed way this antiquated pseudo-scientific theory of male and female sexuality might usefully recall something remarked more recently by Gayle Rubin, namely that modern sexual difference theory, far from being an expression of natural differences, actually involves the suppression of natural similarities ('Traffic in Women', 179–80). But it is not my intention to rehabilitate this theory,

---

[3] 'Nobody's Perfect', 14. Orgel remarks also the sense in which children then shared the common gender of childhood, both boys and girls being dressed in skirts until about the age of 7 (pp. 10–11). For other assessments of the Aristotle–Galen sexual metaphysic, see Greenblatt, *Shakespearean Negotiations*, ch. 3, and Parker, *Literary Fat Ladies*, ch. 9.

or to suggest that it is allegorically preferable to current theories of sexual difference. My argument does not even assume that it was a dominant way of thinking in earlier periods. Rather I cite it here as a historical antecedent whose very strangeness alerts us to several facts relevant to what follows: first, and most obviously, that sexual difference is not a biological given so much as a complex ideological history; second, that current theories of sexual difference are of relatively recent origin, and quite probably still haunted by older views, including this one; third, it suggests that 'before' sexual difference the woman was once (and may still be) feared in a way in which the homosexual now is—feared, that is, not so much, or only, because of a radical otherness, as because of an inferior resemblance presupposing a certain proximity; the woman then, as the homosexual in modern psychoanalytic discourse, is marked in terms of lesser or retarded development.

Sexual Difference, Homosexuality, and Psychoanalysis

As Mandy Merck points out at the beginning of an acute and informative summary, in recent times the theory of sexual difference has exerted a profound influence on psychoanalytically inspired cultural analysis ('Difference and its Discontents', 2). Recently the theoretical tide has turned against it. Colin MacCabe puts it thus:

What is really problematic is that psychoanalysis produces a theory of identity [i.e. sexual difference] which does not allow for a genuine heterogeneity and contradiction in our diverse identifications. It does not simply make the claim that one difference is more important than all the others but articulates all further identifications in terms of a primary sexual identification. (*Theoretical Essays*, 10)

If we further remark the way sexual difference is often presented within psychoanalysis as unavoidable and ineluctably fraught with pain, so much so in some cases that it warrants description as a tragic ontology,[4] it becomes tempting to dismiss it as an expression of existential *Angst* suitably dressed in pretentious intellectual rigour and elegant abstraction, and, as such (some might add), the epitome of psychoanalysis itself. In fact, sexual difference theory is informed by, and responsive to, more than that; it intersects with other notions central to the psychoanalytic project. Such notions impart to sexual difference theory its distinctive intellectual and existential charge. I have in mind two

---

[4] Merck, 'Difference and its Discontents', 7; for further criticism of sexual difference theory, see Scott, 'Gender: A Useful Category of Historical Analysis', 1086, and de Lauretis, *Technologies of Gender*, ch. 1.

especially: the first involves what might be called the impossibility of desire, the second the notion of desire and/or identity as involving an ineluctable splitting.

Like other key notions in psychoanalysis, the sense of desire as a quest for an always impossible self-completion in or through the other has a long though often unrecognized history. In this case Kaja Silverman has usefully remarked the importance, for Jacques Lacan's version of this argument, of Aristophanes' conception of the person as an original androgynous whole (in Plato's *Symposium*). The human subject is conceived in terms of an essential, intrinsic lack; it is a fragment of something larger and more primordial, whose existence is dominated by the desire to recover its missing complement (*The Subject of Semiotics*, 152).[5] But the complement remains forever out of reach and desire thereby becomes, for Lacan, a kind of 'derangement', with the subject 'caught in the rails—eternally stretching forth towards the *desire for something else*—of metonymy' (*Écrits*, 167). But the subject is not only split in the sense of needing the other to complete itself; it is also split because its identity is actually informed by the other, by what it is not:

If the unconscious means anything whatsoever, it is that the relation of self and others, inner and outer, cannot be grasped as an *interval between polar and opposites* but rather as an irreducible dislocation of the subject in which the other inhabits the self as its condition of possibility. (Weber, *The Legend of Freud*, 32–3, his emphasis)

For Lacan desire itself becomes a splitting within the subject: 'desire is neither the appetite for satisfaction, nor the demand for love, but the difference resulting from the subtraction of the first from the second, the very phenomenon of their splitting' (Lacan, *Feminine Sexuality*, 81). Recall that Lacan regards homosexuality as a definitive manifestation of this tragic ontology (above, Chapter 12).

As Lacan's invocation of metonymy suggests, such formulations are evidently influenced by the semiotic model, sometimes called the linguistic or, later, the deconstructive, turn to difference. It sees meaning as always fundamentally incomplete because dependent on a potentially infinite relationship to what is different or absent; completion of meaning is always thereby deferred. Hence Jacques Derrida's influential concept of 'différance' (translated in English as at once difference and deferral), a concept enabling us to 'reconsider all the pairs of opposites

---

[5] The myth is actually more complicated than the form in which it is recalled, and of dubious significance as an allegory for sexual difference theory since Aristophanes speaks of there being originally three sexes, not two. When Freud recalls this 'poetic fable' in *Three Essays* he alludes to a twofold division (vii. 46); in *Beyond the Pleasure Principle* he describes it more accurately (xi. 331).

on which philosophy is constructed and on which our discourse lives, not in order to see opposition erase itself but to see what indicates that each of the terms must appear as the *différance* of the other, as the other different and deferred in the economy of the same'. Of 'all the oppositions that furrow Freudian thought' it can be said that 'one is but the other different and deferred, one differing and deferring the other' (*Margins of Philosophy*, 17–18). The potential of this conceptual theory for the psychoanalytic account of desire is nicely remarked by Gayatri Spivak: desire, she says, is a deconstructive structure, one that 'forever differs from (we only desire what is not ourselves) and defers (desire is never fulfilled)' (*Grammatology*, p. lxxviii).[6]

The influence of the semiotic model within psychoanalysis is important but, as we shall see, it is often incorporated into sexual difference theory in a form which manages to exclude what the model is especially sensitive to, namely the way oppositions which constitute meaning are fundamentally binary, yet cannot ultimately be contained in and by binary closure even as, in practice, the binary remains a fundamental principle of social and psychic ordering.

In Juliet Mitchell's account sexual difference becomes the archetypal split, and castration its symbol:

because human subjectivity cannot ultimately exist outside a division into one of two sexes, then it is castration that finally comes to symbolise this split. . . . The trauma captured in splitting is that one isn't there; the same trauma that castration comes to symbolise is that one is incomplete; the trauma that can be lived over and over again in the endless by-ways of life's failures and imperfections. (*Revolution*, 307)

Mitchell adds, 'Bisexuality is a movement across a line, it is *not* androgyny' (p. 308, her emphasis). Perhaps this tenet of psychoanalytic thought derives from the fact that, for Freud, '*bisexuality is the coincidence of two heterosexual desires within a single psyche* . . . within Freud's thesis of primary bisexuality, there is no homosexuality, and only opposites attract' (Butler, *Gender Trouble*, 61, her emphasis). Whatever, Mitchell's remark suggests how, even when recognized as a fact of culture rather than biology, sexual difference remains fairly absolute within psychoanalytic theory. As in the Fall narrative, which it

---

[6] I remark another comparison, though again of the kind which invites not a conflation of the early modern and the modern, but a rethinking of each: 'Men [are] for ever gaping after future things . . . We are never in our selves, but beyond. Feare, desire, and hope, draw us ever towards that which is to come, and remove our sense and consideration from that which is, to amuse us on that which shall be, yea when we shall be no more. *Calamitosus est animus futuri anxius* (SEN. Epi. 98). A minde in suspense what is to come, is in a pittifull case' (Montaigne, *Essays*, trans. Florio, i. 25).

resembles in more ways than one, there seems to be no going back; our original innocence, the wholeness of an original bisexuality, is never retrievable. Sexuality is the Fall into desire as lack. This leads some adherents of psychoanalysis, especially those of a Lacanian disposition, to regard sexual difference—or rather hetero/sexual difference as it should really be called—as both tragic and heroic. Once again the psychoanalytic narrative echoes a theological one. For Judith Butler this renders the Lacanian narrative 'ideologically suspect' in that it remains rooted in 'a romanticization or, indeed, a religious idealization of "failure", humility and limitation before the Law' (*Gender Trouble*, 56). This dimension of Lacan also finds a precedent in Freud: 'the programme of becoming happy, which the pleasure principle imposes on us, cannot be fulfilled; yet we must not—indeed, we cannot—give up our efforts to bring it nearer to fulfilment by some means or other' (xii. 271).

So the related notions of desire as lack, the impossibility of desire, and the desiring subject as ineluctably split have a history in Western thought older than psychoanalysis. As I have argued in previous chapters, reconsidering that history helps us to reconsider psychoanalysis, especially the way it incorporates yet obscures the perverse dynamic. Post-Freudian forms of sexual difference theory are not only largely ignorant of that pre-sexological, pre-psychoanalytic history; they even tend to obscure the significance and scope of Freud's *own* emphasis on the significance of perversion within sexual difference. Thus the Lacanian account of the impossibility of desire often cites the following passage from Freud's 'On the Universal Tendency to Debasement in the Sphere of Love': 'It is my belief that, however strange it may sound, we must reckon with the possibility that something in the nature of the sexual instinct itself is unfavourable to the realization of complete satisfaction' (vii. 258).

But while Lacanian critics frequently invoke this passage, they less often consider Freud's extraordinary and provocative remarks in this same essay as to *why* he thinks desire and satisfaction have become incommensurable. He gives two possible reasons, both of which involve the repression of the perversions. Because of the barrier against incest, the final object of the sexual instinct 'is never any longer the original object but only a surrogate for it. . . . When the original object of a wishful impulse has been lost as a result of repression, it is frequently represented by an endless series of substitute objects none of which, however, brings full satisfaction' (vii. 258). And, of the instinctual components necessarily repressed and sublimated in the service of culture, the coprophilic is one of the most significant, says Freud: 'the excremental is all too intimately and inseparably bound up with the sexual; the position of the genitals—*inter urinas et faeces*—remains the decisive and unchangeable factor' (vii. 258–9). Freud singles out sadistic desires as a further group incompatible with civilization and requiring renunciation. Yet the effect of the repression of such perversions always remains, and '*can be detected in sexual activity in the form of non-satisfaction*', even while their sublimation leads, says Freud once again, 'to the noblest cultural achievements' (vii. 259, my emphasis).

So for Freud the lack inherent in normalized desire, its impossibility of satisfaction, is structured into sexual difference, and is a direct consequence of the repression of perverse desire. And if perversion is, as we have argued (and in Freud's own terms), what potentially subverts sexual difference (Chapter 11), the silence of psychoanalytic advocates of sexual difference theory on this topic is both significant and damaging to their project.

The two interrelated psychoanalytic tenets just outlined suggest a radical instability in both identity and desire. In an article arguing for the importance of psychoanalysis for feminism, Jacqueline Rose cautions against a political appropriation of psychoanalysis which would leave behind some of its most challenging discoveries, especially of the disruptive power of the unconscious *vis-à-vis* identity and sexual difference. Here is Rose's own summary of a position persuasively argued throughout her work:

The unconscious constantly reveals the 'failure' of identity. Because there is no continuity of psychic life, so there is no stability of sexual identity, no position for women (or for men) which is ever simply achieved. Nor does psychoanalysis see such 'failure' as a special-case inability or an individual deviancy from the norm. 'Failure' is not a moment to be regretted in a process of adaption, or development into normality, which ideally takes its course. . . . Instead 'failure' is something endlessly repeated and relived moment by moment throughout our individual histories. . . . Feminism's affinity with psychoanalysis rests above all, I would argue, with this recognition that there is a resistance to identity at the very heart of psychic life. (*Sexuality in the Field of Vision*, 90–1)

But again, what is often left out of such accounts of the unconscious, even as it is invoked as the prime destabilizer, is the importance of the perversions in precisely this respect: Freud insisted that what is operative from within the unconscious, producing this very instability, is repressed perversion.

Crucially, the psychoanalytic rationalization of sexual difference as a tragic split which in turn effects the failure of identity often goes along with an account of the alleged narcissistic limitations and failures of homosexuality. This returns us to the association of homosexuality with sameness remarked at the outset. As we saw there, Segal and Irigaray have recently elaborated this view, but its origins are clearly in Freud whose early case-studies, as Mitchell observes, originate the idea that 'the homosexual was choosing not another of the same sex, but himself in the guise of another' (*Psychoanalysis and Feminism*, 34; see e.g. Freud, ix. 198).

Irigaray's work is nuanced in ways often ignored not only by her critics but by those who appropriate it, especially those who consider her to have demonstrated that homosexuality represents the true nature of patriarchy; who believes that, as a sexual practice between the same, homosexuality becomes indicative of patriarchy's fundamental refusal or fear of difference. As Jane Gallop puts it:

Irigaray has discovered that phallic sexual theory, male sexual science, is homosexual, a sexuality of sames, of identities, excluding otherness. Hetero-sexuality, once it is exposed as an exchange of women between men, reveals itself as a mediated form of homosexuality. All penetration . . . is thought according to the model of anal penetration. The dry anus suffers pain; the penetrated is a humiliated man.

In short, Irigaray had allegedly discovered 'the homosexual closed circuit . . . which underlies our supposed heterosexual culture' (Gallop, *Feminism and Psychoanalysis*, 84–5). One path of enquiry leads Gallop to repudiate this 'homosexual economy' and speculate thus: 'I wish to speak of radical heterosexuality, a true openness and love for the *heteros*, the other, an intercourse between two modalities. . . . And any relation between members of the same sex which allowed their differ-ence, did not assimilate both to one fantasy, would be heterosexual.' But Gallop had doubts, or rather confesses an ambivalence: 'But we cannot be sure that this radical notion of "heterosexuality" is not just an alibi for the comforting norm' (pp. 127–8). More recently Gallop has remarked her suspicion of the wish to deny sexual difference because it 'might be but another mode of denying women', adding: 'I distrust male homosexuals because they choose men over women just as do our social and political institutions, but they too share in the struggle against bipolar gender constraints, against the compulsory choice of masculine or feminine' (*Thinking through the Body*, 113).

It is a testimony to the pervasiveness and tenacity of the homophobic tendencies of the psychoanalytic tradition that, despite the acute aware-ness on the part of feminists appropriating both Freud and Lacan that the writing of both contains anti-feminist tendencies, its homophobic dimensions are sometimes actively perpetuated in feminist accounts of sexual difference theory.[7] This is acutely ironic in the light of Kenneth Lewes's recent argument to the effect that the psychoanalytic bias against male homosexuals derives from an initial gynaecophobic stance in psychoanalysis whereby 'the fear and denigration of women which hover at the perimeter of analytic discourse become displaced onto the theory of male homosexuality'. Lewes contends that, whereas these gynaecophobic tendencies were from the start challenged by women analysts, the same could not occur in relation to the homophobia of the discipline since homosexuals were systematically excluded from it, with the result that 'the psychoanalytic discourse on homosexuality has been and still is formulated by non-homosexuals about homosexuals' (*The Psychoanalytic Theory of Male Homosexuality*, 21, 237–8). At the same time, and as we have already seen, 'homophobia' is an inadequate term to describe all this since what is at issue is not personal phobia so much as the recurrence in mutated form of structures integral to cultural identity and social formation. That much is apparent from one further and final instance of the negative construction of homosexuality within a psychoanalytically informed account of sexual difference. I refer to Julia Kristeva's somewhat obscure remarks about 'the role that the pervert, with his invincible belief in the maternal phallus and *his obstinate refusal to recognise the existence of the other sex*, has been able to play in anti-semitism and the totalitarian movements that embrace it'. Who exactly Kristeva means becomes even less clear as she adds: 'Let us recall the fascist or social-fascist homosexual community (and all homosexual communities for whom there is no "other race"), and the fact that it is inevitably flanked by a community of viragos who have forgotten the war of the sexes and identify with the paternal Word or its serpent.' Problematic as sexual difference may be, there is no alternative: we must, continues Kristeva, 'go on waging the war between the two races without respite, without a perverse denial of the abyss that marks sexual difference or a disillusioned mortification of the

---

[7] Of course there are other reasons for the tension between homosexuality and feminism, but they too sometimes involve the status of homosexuality as a perversion (conventionally understood). Bronski disputes with those feminists who argue that 'where there is any attempt to separate the sexual experience from the total person, that first act of objectification is perversion' (Bronski, *Culture-Clash*, 164, quoting from Barry, *Female Sexual Slavery*, 226).

Jane Gallop, in an interesting discussion of perversion in relation to Roland Barthes and homosexuality, considers its problematic status in feminism. She points out that large sectors of the feminist movement stand in 'violent opposition to perversion which is understood to be male. The pervert—child molester, rapist, porno fan, fetishist, voyeur, exhibitionist, sadist, masochist, etc.—is seen as a symptom of an aggressive, male sexuality that is inherently perverted and a primary enemy of feminism.' Set against male perversions is a feminist vision of 'an egalitarian relation of tenderness and caring where each partner is considered as a "whole person" rather than as an object of sexual fantasy' (*Thinking through the Body*, 107). Both Owens, 'Outlaws', and Bristow, 'Homophobia/Misogyny', have important things to say about this tension.

division'.[8] In her fuller and discerning reading of Kristeva, Judith Butler finds that lesbianism comes off pretty badly too; by implication Kristeva's theory 'designates female homosexuality as a culturally unintelligible practice, inherently psychotic'. What Butler says of this account—namely that it 'tells us more about the fantasies that a fearful heterosexual culture produces to defend against its own homosexual possibilities, than about lesbian experience itself' (*Gender Trouble*, 86–7)—might also be said more generally of the way homosexuality is conceptualized in sexual difference theory.

But if, as I have suggested, the structures of identity formation at work here are fundamental to our existing cultural forms, they cannot be considered as stemming only from the psychoanalytic tradition. The concepts of difference and otherness, and the belief that sexual deviance leads to undifferentiation, have a philosophical and theological history, both of which antecede and influence psychoanalysis.

Otherness Philosophically Speaking: Roger Scruton

It is from an avowedly philosophical perspective that Roger Scruton announces 'the major structural feature of perversion' to be 'the habit of finding a sexual release that avoids or abolishes the *other*, obliterating his embodiment with the obscene perception of his body'; as such, believes Scruton, it is narcissistic and often solipsistic (*Sexual Desire*, 289, 343).

Scruton seeks to build an explicitly conservative sexual ethic on the Hegelian proposition that 'the final end of every rational being is the building of the self—of a recognisable personal entity, which flourishes according to its own autonomous nature' (p. 299). This involves the recognition of the other as an end in himself (p. 301). In gender terms this means that it is 'precisely when most compelled to see yourself *as* a woman or *as* a man, [that] you are confronted with the mystery of the other [sex] who faces you from across an impassable moral divide' (p. 306). In this confrontation across the divide of gender one is compelled to put one's whole being at risk (p. 307). Desire directed

---

[8] *Kristeva Reader*, 145, my emphasis. While the editor of this volume, in introducing the selection which includes the above quotations, warns us that the publication by Kristeva from which they are taken has been criticized for being 'ethnocentric', she makes no mention of its homophobia. See also Owens, 'Outlaws', who takes issue with 'a number of feminist writers [who] have informed us that philosophy, fascism, even capitalism itself, are basically homoerotic formations' (p. 223). Once again this is the victim as agent argument remarked in earlier chapters; compare Joseph Bristow's succinct formulation *vis-à-vis* Irigaray and others: 'Such an argument gives the impression that gay men are the culprits of the sexual inequalities—between homosexual and heterosexual, man and woman—we have to struggle against. The glaring contradiction— that homosexual desire creates the oppression of homosexuality—appears over and again in sociology, literary theory and varieties of feminist criticism' ('Homophobia/Misogyny', 64).

across sexual difference, towards the other gender, elicits not its simulacrum (as in homosexuality) but its complement: 'Male desire evokes the loyalty which neutralises its vagrant impulses; female desire evokes the conquering urge which overcomes its hesitations' (p. 309).

Homosexuality is included as a perversion because it is denied this 'fundamental experience' of otherness-across-gender. The homosexual 'knows intimately in himself the generality that he finds in the other': 'in the homosexual act I remain locked within my body, narcissistically contemplating in the other an excitement that is the mirror of my own' (pp. 307, 310). In normal or right sexuality, argues Scruton, we not only give recognition to the other's person in and through our desire for him or her, we also accord them accountability and care in the process.

Among many possible objections, I shall note in passing just three, chosen because each indicates limitations which Scruton shares with other advocates of sexual difference theory. It is ironic that by privileging sexual difference Scruton shows himself the victim of precisely the modern intensification of sexuality which in other ways he might regard as contributing to a legitimation of the perversions he repudiates. This is further apparent from the way he makes broad social and ethical dimensions of human relations (accountability and care) the *necessary* condition for normal or right sexuality. In fact, there is no reason why (e.g.) homosexuals should not afford accountability and care to their partners, in the course of either a long relationship or a very short one. But accountability and care no more have to be the absolute precondition, the ever-present animating ethic, of sexual relations, homosexual or otherwise, than they do of any other kind except in the obvious sense that care of some kind is the precondition of almost any shared social activity. That such care may well characterize those activities which Scruton declares cannot possess it is suggested by Andrew Lumsden's appropriately *passing* remark on the casual, anonymous sexual encounter: 'for now I can only generalize: as I've known it, men are never so peaceful, so unviolent (physically and emotionally), so graceful with each other (no matter how "crude" the act) as they are—as we are— when content to take each other without the addition of names, or beds, or flats, or even of any clear impression of one-another's looks' (*Gay News*, 235 (Mar. 1982), 17).

Second, simply in what Scruton classifies as perversions—masturbation, bestiality, necrophilia, paedophilia, sado-masochism, homosexuality, incest, fetishism—he shows himself to have accepted uncritically the sexological/Freudian classification of perversions as developed in the nineteenth century.[9] Again he is taking over precisely the 'modern' definitions and oppositions, between the normal and pathological, the natural and unnatural, etc., which have been shown to be both confused and ideological in the narrow sense.

Third, Scruton reanimates the deep self as the defining principle of a normal sexuality. His argument deploys the old jargon of authenticity, now combined with the jargon of otherness; despite his Hegelian framework, Scruton deploys this jargon as an exalted metaphor which does little more than bestow a spurious profundity on a normative sexual politics which is at heart timid, conservative, and deeply ignorant.

Mailer on Lawrence and Sexual Difference, or: The 'Full Rigours of the Fuck'

The feminized male has always been suspect, be he the advocate of unisex, androgyny, or, now, the play of the post-modern.[10] Why so? One reason might be that androgyny typically envisages a unity ostensibly beyond sexual difference, but in fact inseparable from it; androgyny especially has too often been a genderless transcendent which leaves sexual difference in place.[11] But conversely, as I have already remarked, when Juliet Mitchell insists that 'bisexuality is a movement across a line, it is *not* androgyny', she also leaves too much of sexual difference in place. Both the androgynous evasion of sexual difference, and the psychoanalytic insistence on it, disavow the homo-erotic knowledge of its *other side(s)* and the perverse dynamic which so radically implicates masculine and feminine not only within each other but, much more disturbingly, with what each excludes. This knowledge lurks around the feminized male, which is one reason why he tends to be rendered either safely fashionable, or denigrated.

Freud thought 'the essentially repressed element is always what is feminine. What men essentially repress is the paederastic element'

---

[9] Although Scruton's frame of reference is thoroughly philosophical, and despite the fact that he roundly attacks the psychoanalytic perspective on sexuality (see esp. ch. 7), his own defence of sexual difference owes more to that perspective than he admits.

[10] See Moore, 'Getting a Bit of the Other'.

[11] In *Men and Feminism in Modern Literature* Declan Kiberd finds it 'unfortunate that [Oscar Wilde's] theatrical performance of homosexuality should have obscured his far more revolutionary teaching on the androgyny of the full person' (p. 27). At least, for Kiberd, Wilde is granted to be on the right lines, and the 'full person' is something beyond hetero/sexual difference. Even so, the validation of androgyny tends to be an evasion rather than an incorporation of difference. This is even more clearly so in George Steiner's preference for Proust's inclusiveness over Genet's fierce partiality: 'Where our imagination moves deepest it strives beyond sexuality, which is, inevitably, division, to an erotic whole' ('Eros and Idiom', 121).

(Mitchell, *Revolution*, 304).[12] It all depends of course on what is meant by 'the feminine'. Surely this of all concepts, and especially in the context of the homoerotic, must not be essentialized. Because they are so pervasive, and because their subordinate terms remain so powerfully denigrated, the erotics of active/passive should not be identified as coextensive with masculine/feminine, and should not be thought identical across the hetero/homosexual divide. However, the association between homosexuality and femininity is not necessarily insulting to either; on the contrary, as Kaja Silverman shows, there are ways in which it might be just the reverse, especially when we contest the stereotypes of both. This is what Silverman does, finding femininity centrally within male homosexuality, but in the process insisting that 'we have barely begun to understand the full complexity of "femininity", whether we locate that signifier at the site of woman, or at that of the homosexual man'.[13] Undoubtedly the perception of the homosexual as feminized remains strangely disturbing—the supreme symbol, in the eyes of those like Norman Mailer, of a range of deep failures including the demise of masculinity, the abdication of masculine power, the desire for self-destruction, and, beyond that, the loss of difference.

Exploring heterosexist fears of homoerotic passivity, Leo Bersani remarks some similarities between the contemporary representation of homosexuals in relation to AIDS, and the nineteenth-century representation of prostitutes in relation to venereal disease. Both kinds of representation betray fears and fantasies about sexual passivity and sexual promiscuity: women then, and gay men now, are imagined to engage in a passive promiscuity which is really an unquenchable appetite for destruction; AIDS has 'reinforced the heterosexual association of anal sex with a self-annihilation originally and primarily identified with the fantasmatic mystery of an insatiable, unstoppable female sexuality'. Bersani discerns in such associations the possibility of a seductive yet intolerable (i.e. unconscious) image of the male 'unable to refuse the suicidal ecstasy of being a woman'. He further remarks how, even in cultures which do not regard sexual relations between men as unnatural or sinful, male sexual 'passivity' may be associated with inferiority, inadequacy, and even pathology. Summarizing Foucault's account in volume ii of *The History of Sexuality* of how in ancient Greece homosexual passivity was regarded with suspicion, even though

---

[12] Freud once remarked that the point at which he felt most ineffectual as an analyst was in trying to persuade a woman to abandon her wish for a penis, 'or when . . . seeking to convince a man that a passive attitude to men does not always signify castration and that it is indispensable in many relationships in life' ('Analysis Terminable and Interminable', 252).

[13] 'A Woman's Soul Enclosed in a Man's Body', in *Male Subjectivity at the Margins*, forthcoming; cited here from MS.

homosexuality as such was accepted and even glorified, Bersani concludes: '*To be penetrated is to abdicate power*' ('Is the Rectum a Grave?', 222, 211–12, his emphasis).

For all its brilliant rhetoric and endearingly dishonest struggle to regain a masculine integrity, Norman Mailer's defence of D. H. Lawrence in *The Prisoner of Sex* conveys finally a certain desperation in the face of apprehensions similar to those which Bersani explores. But this desperation is not to be stereotyped; it is not so much the result of being a man, not even of being a 'real' man, but rather of being psychically and sexually locked into the fantasies and fears of sexual difference. I shall be turning to Lawrence shortly; here it is Mailer's account of him which is intriguing. For Mailer, Lawrence's greatness lies in part in his heroic struggle against his destiny, which was to be homosexual: 'he had become a man by an act of will, he was bone and blood of the classic family stuff out of which homosexuals are made, he had lifted himself out of his natural destiny which was probably to have the sexual life of a woman' (p. 154). To repeat, the association between homosexuality and the sexual life of a woman is not necessarily insulting to either; it is only that Mailer's denigrating version of it forewarns of the crassness of the version of sexual difference which constitutes both the origin and horizon of his vision, and once again indicates an intense apprehensiveness in the face of imagined male passivity, and the way it is often conceived in terms of a denigrated and denigrating femininity at once utterly alien to yet strangely inherent within the male.

Mailer apparently concurs with the belief he attributes to Lawrence, that 'men and women can survive only if they reach the depths of their own sex down within themselves' (p. 147). Androgyny, or what he calls the 'liberal supposition' that it is good for men and women to become more and more alike, creates in Mailer an aversion, 'a species of aesthetic nausea' (pp. 134–5). Relatedly, for him, the evils of our times are indicated in the way that, allegedly, the polymorphous perverse has come to prevail over procreation, contraception over conception, and the anus over the vagina—'as if the mark of a civilization dying should be a mountainous sense of excitement for the hole which presides over waste' (p. 162). Also definitive of that decline is the loss of sexual difference as epitomized in—no surprise—homosexuality:

Where a man can become more male and a woman more female by coming together in the full rigors of the fuck . . . homosexuals, it can be suggested, tend to pass their qualities over to one another, for there is no womb to mirror and return what is most forceful or attractive in each of them. So the male gets more womanly and the queer absorbs the masculinity of the other. (pp. 171–2; cf. p. 162)

Whereas prior to 1954 the male homosexual was for Mailer a rather facile symbol of evil (above, Chapter 3), now he epitomizes a more insidious and actual kind of evil: the undoing of otherness, and a drive towards undifferentiation echoing biblical 'confusion'.

The Masculine Dilemma: Wanting to Be What the Other Is

In *The Masculine Dilemma* (1980), subtitled 'A Psychology of Masculinity', Gregory Rochlin offers a different version of the homosexual male, but one which is once again in the service of defending an updated heterosexual masculinity, and its primacy within a sexual difference metaphysic. Drawing on psychoanalysis, Rochlin 'rewrites' masculinity in a way which makes a virtue of what was hitherto thought of as, or experienced as, a defect: its much remarked insecurity. His argument is as follows: a man's masculinity is indeed insecure; it is an endless trial, a 'precariously held, endlessly tested, unstable condition' (p. 91). In this it is almost tragic: 'the unique vulnerability to failed expectations is the fatal flaw in the masculine ego . . . the testing of masculinity knows no bounds . . . to prove oneself remains a lifelong necessity. . . . It gives rise to many of man's anxieties and failures as well as to his often extraordinary achievements' (pp. x, xi). The critique of masculinity which says, 'for all your confidence you as man are insecure and afraid', is not repudiated but incorporated; man's insecurity is embraced as an enhancing vulnerability. Rochlin appropriates for masculinity, albeit in a form so highly selective it might hardly be recognized, that sense of the inherent instability of identity which Lacanians and others have taken from psychoanalysis for feminism.[14]

Rochlin 'feminizes' masculinity to just the degree required to rehabilitate it as the dominant term in the masculine/feminine binary, and he does this through the by now familiar move of positing homosexuality as the inadequate yet threatening third term. Masculinity can be problematized, even feminized, so long as homosexuality remains as its defining other. So, for Rochlin, the homosexual is a sexual coward who will not risk the competitiveness of male rivalry. He quotes approvingly an anonymous 'youth' who believes that gay men have given up the battle between men: 'they've submitted to men. . . . They can't meet the

[14] Rochlin even tries to recuperate for masculinity a crude version of the psychoanalytic argument about desire being built on loss and lack. In his final chapter, titled 'Many Desires', he comments that men are especially prone to experiencing desire as a kind of loss (he seems to be talking of impotence, literally and metaphorically) and concludes by complaining of Freud's famous question about woman—what does she want?—that a similar question was not framed for men. But, he adds, 'Should we put it to him, his reply is predictable. *Evermore!*' (pp. 288–9).

standards of manhood. That takes incredibly high performance, competitiveness, winning all. Being "gay" gets you out of the competition of manhood' (pp. 84–5). So the confession of vulnerability does not involve a more thoughtful relationship to homosexuality; rather the reverse. In fact Rochlin's theory of heterosexual masculinity remains dependent on a precise and hostile positioning of the homosexual *vis-à-vis* the heterosexual male. Once again, the male homosexual is someone who refuses to risk himself in relation to the other, but now the risk is not in relation to the opposite sex (as in Scruton and Mailer), but to the same sex as rival. In this account homosexuals are essentially failed men, and the arbiters of what it takes to be a successful male are of course not women but other males.[15]

It might be said that Rochlin is not to be taken seriously, being merely a popularizing psychologist. From my point of view that is exactly why he should be taken seriously, and not only because of his apparent prestige.[16] However, if necessary, his argument can easily be traced back to Freud. In 'The Psychogenesis of a Case of Homosexuality in a Woman' Freud announces a newly discovered 'cause' of homosexuality, what he calls 'retiring in favour of someone else'. The idea is that the person turns homosexual as a way of avoiding competition, conflict, or tension with a significant other. Freud cites one young man in relation to his father and another in relation to his twin, as well as the main case, a young woman in relation to her mother: 'If, then, the girl became homosexual and left men to her mother (in other words "retired in favour of" her mother), she would hitherto remove something which had hitherto been partly responsible for her mother's dislike' (ix. 385; cf. Tripp, *Homosexual Matrix*, 78–9, cited above, Chapter 12).

Perhaps the manifest intrinsic confusions which surface in each of the foregoing theories are enough to write them off, and to show how the same/different metaphysic is nothing more than a potently confused, highly discriminating mixed metaphor. But there is more to be discovered by thinking their confusions and discriminations to the surface, and to that end I consider one further 'explanation' of homosexuality along similar lines. This one is cited in the text of a discussion printed in Girard's *Things Hidden* and, though not by him, is offered in support of his general thesis that culture is organized in terms of mimesis and desire. It is a thesis which includes the proposition that all sexual rivalry

---

[15] Not surprisingly Rochlin accepts the idea of homosexuality as caused by the lack of a proper separation from the mother (pp. 6, 85).

[16] Most ominously perhaps his presidency of an 'Institute for Continuing Education in Child Psychiatry' (dust jacket).

is 'structurally homosexual'. We are told the story of a man (unidentified, so for convenience I shall refer to him as *X*) who, though 'exclusively heterosexual' had become interested in another younger man on the occasion of finding himself in a triangular relationship with him and his (i.e. the younger man's) fiancée at a dinner party. When the younger man eventually left his fiancée for *X*, the latter completely lost interest in him. The older man explains why: 'Take my word for it—homosexuality is wanting to be what the other is' (p. 337). Apparently, for the 'exclusively heterosexual' *X*, homosexuality is not a submitting to another man but a competition with, a displacing of, him. 'I want to be in your place' collapses temporarily into 'I want you'; identification merges with desire, which is then a desire to be/displace the male as other. But only temporarily: once he has displaced the other *vis-à-vis* the desired object, he loses interest.

So here is a contrast: whereas for Rochlin homosexuality is an opting out of masculine competition, for *X* it is a direct expression of it; or, more exactly, homosexual desire is inseparable from and dependent upon mimetic rivalry between males. But there are revealing similarities between the two explanations, quite apart from the fact that in both cases the 'authority' on homosexuality is an avowed heterosexual male, and one cited anonymously at that. More significantly, in each case what is primary is the male–male rivalry. Homosexuality is invoked to 'explain' or ratify (rather than question) aspects of the male homosocial relationship. The sexuality of Rochlin's youth is clearly governed—one might say overdetermined—by his relation to other males. And when *X* says homosexuality is wanting to be what the other is, the other is now not the other (opposite) sex, but the same sex, and *X*, as avowed heterosexual, has described his desire to displace the male. To consider the rationale of such explanations is to suspect that, rather than homosexuality being a fear of the other (sex), heterosexual masculinity involves at least intense anxieties about, and probably fears of, the same (sex), and constructs/explains homosexuality in terms which project, disavow, and legitimate those anxieties. This fear of the same, or of the proximity of the same, or of the threat of the same, structures the violence not only of the homosocial, but of sexual difference itself.

Kinds of Hating

I have outlined a handful of sexual difference theories wherein homosexuality is associated with, or is seen to be expressive of: (1) the true, negative, nature of patriarchy, (2) a negation of what is truly vital and creative in (heterosexual) desire, (3) anti-Semitism, totalitarianism, and fascism, (4) an obliteration of the autonomy of the other, (5) anal negativity, solipsism, and sterility and de-creation, (6) the undifferentiation of a dying culture, (7) a cowardly refusal of homosocial rivalry, (8) the definitive expression of homosocial rivalry.

These accounts derive from diverse current perspectives which should not be conflated—psychoanalysis, philosophy, and what might be called the metaphysical vision of the cultural critic and creative writer. But this very diversity renders their shared tendency to demonize homosexuality as a fear of difference, or, more actively, as a drive towards undifferentiation and de-creation, the more remarkable. And in all of them homosexuality echoes Augustinian privation—the more pernicious for being deeply, inherently inadequate, a kind of non-being and inauthenticity: an inimical absence which provokes paranoia and on to which is projected the fear of difference inherent within sexual difference.

D. H. Lawrence and the Metaphysics of Sexual Difference

> All neurotics, and many others besides, take exception to the fact that '*inter urinas et faeces nascimur* [we are born between urine and faeces]'. (Freud, xii. 296)

Once again, via a somewhat backward chronology, I have left Lawrence's account of sexual difference until last. This increasingly disregarded and often despised writer proves rather revealing of how the perverse dynamic disrupts theories of sexual difference like those just examined.

In three respects at least D. H. Lawrence's attitude to homosexuality was typical: first, he seems to have been able to accept it only in an idealized and spiritual form; as Paul Delany puts it, he wanted not a lover but a spiritual brother.[17] Second, in his writing he tends to present actual homosexuals (e.g. Loerke in *Women in Love*) as decadent others who draw off that which for Lawrence complicates the ideal homoerotic brotherhood. Third, his anxieties about homosexuality were conjoined with class antagonism. His well-known hostility to the Bloomsbury group included a homophobic preoccupation with the sexuality of some of its members; in a letter to Bertrand Russell on 12 February 1915 he said: 'The ordinary Englishman of the educated class goes to a woman now to masterbate [*sic*] himself. Because he is not going for discovery or new connection or progression, but only to repeat upon himself a

---

[17] *D. H. Lawrence's Nightmare*, esp. 53, 88–9, 224, 289, 313.

known reaction. When this condition arrives, there is always Sodomy' (*Letters*, 285).[18] Again, homosexuality is thought of as a narcissistic repudiation of sexual difference. From his study of Lawrence at that time, Paul Delany concludes that the writer had 'strong homosexual impulses which he felt morally bound to repress' (*Nightmare*, 50). The same letter also indicates how certain heterosexual anxieties structured in and by sexual difference are projected by Lawrence on to the homosexual, a move which his critics sometimes follow in trying to save him from the taint of homosexual desire. Eugene Goodheart, for instance, describes Birkin as suffering from a homosexual fear of women. This is quoted and endorsed by Meyers (*Homosexuality and Literature*, 148), who goes on to describe Lawrence's *Aaron's Rod* as possessing many components of 'a homosexual novel' including 'an intense hatred and fear of women, who are characterised in two male gatherings as threatening, frightening and repulsive', and 'a symbolically castrated hero who is afraid to let himself go in heterosexual love and runs away from his three women' (p. 154).[19] Once more a misogyny produced internally to and largely by hetero/sexual difference is projected on to homosexuality.

But there is more to be said about Lawrence; much more than was usually said in the days when he was celebrated as a prophet of straight liberation, and more than is often said when he is castigated from the vantage point of contemporary sexual politics.

Lawrence audaciously sexualizes Western metaphysics. His theories are well enough known for me to sketch them only briefly. The emphasis falls repeatedly on the individual, the self which is a law unto itself. Essentially, 'the soul wishes to keep clean and whole. The soul's deepest will is to preserve its own integrity, against the mind and the whole mass of disintegrating forces' (*Studies in Classic American Literature*, 185).

Lawrence also celebrates the 'other', but often as a foil for the integrity of self; affirmation of one's own pure self is presented as the precondition for recognizing the other. Especially the other of sexual difference. Lawrence placed enormous emphasis on the duality of, and opposition between, the male and female principles: 'except in infinity, everything of life is male or female, distinct' (*Phoenix*, 443). In this broad sense, sexual difference was the fundamental principle of his

[18] Cf. Lawrence's 'The Noble Englishman' (*Complete Poems*, i. 446–7): '. . . Ronald, you know, is like most Englishmen, | by instinct he's a sodomist | but he's frightened to know it | so he takes it out on women.'

[19] Compare Declan Kiberd who says that Lawrence's repeated denunciations of homosexuality were not 'so strident as to warrant the suspicion that he was protesting too much', and that Gerald and Birkin in *Women in Love* flirt with homosexuality only very mildly and then only because they have temporary difficulties with women (*Men and Feminism*, 138, 151).

entire metaphysic, the terms in which its main absolutes, selfhood and wholeness, were realized. If 'the final aim of every living thing, creature, or being is the full achievement of itself' (*Phoenix*, 403) it can only do this through another—typically the other of sexual difference. Ideally the theory encompasses the desire for both an integrity of self, and an integration with another. But for Lawrence the two conflict and in ways which echo the psychoanalytic account of desire:

> Why were we crucified into sex?
> Why were we not left rounded off, and finished in ourselves,
> As we began,
> As he certainly began, so perfectly alone? . . .
>
> The Cross,
> The Wheel on which our silence first is broken,
> Sex, which breaks up our integrity, our single inviolability, our deep silence,
> Tearing a cry from us. . . .
>
> That which is whole, torn asunder,
> That which is in part, finding its whole again throughout the universe.[20]

One resolution to the problem was for the other to submit to the one, the woman to the man, the weaker man to the stronger man. For Lawrence submission to the integrity/mastery of another is an erotically charged solution to a primary metaphysical conflict which was always more than sexual. The intensity of this erotic charge is only slightly less remarkable than its investment, a kind of reverse sublimation whereby neurosis is fantasized sexually as a potent purity inviting submission: 'What do I care if he kills people? His flame is young and clean' (*The Plumed Serpent*, 410). But precisely because purity is invested with such a tremendous erotic charge, fears of 'impurity' remained insistent and corrosive, and in a perversely dynamic proximity disavowed along lines suggested by Freud's remarks at the beginning of this section, and in a passage from 'Repression' (1915) worth citing again in this context:

the objects to which men give most preference, their ideals, proceed from the same perceptions and experiences as the objects which they most abhor, and . . . they were originally only distinguished from one another through slight modifications . . . Indeed . . . it is possible for the original instinctual *representative* to be split in two, one part undergoing repression, while the remainder, *precisely on account of this intimate connection*, undergoes idealization (xi. 150, my emphasis).

---

[20] 'Tortoise Shout', *Complete Poems*, i. 363–7.

In his essay 'Pornography and Obscenity' Lawrence invokes this idealization/abhorrence distinction between the sex functions and the excrementory functions:

[they] work so close together, yet they are, so to speak, utterly different in direction. Sex is a creative flow, the excrementory flow is towards dissolution, de-creation. . . . In the really healthy human being the distinction between the two is instant, our profoundest instincts are perhaps our instincts of opposition between the two flows.

But in the degraded human being the deep instincts have gone dead, and the two flows become identical. (pp. 313–14)

As harmful as a mixing of the flows is masturbation. Producing shame, anger, and futility, it is masturbation which, for Lawrence, constitutes the most pernicious evasion of otherness, becoming 'perhaps the deepest and most dangerous cancer of our civilization', and 'certainly the most dangerous sexual vice that a society can be afflicted with, in the long run' ('Pornography', 317).

Masturbation symbolizes a wider social malaise rooted in solipsistic self-regard. In a review essay written two years before 'Pornography and Obscenity', Lawrence attacks the way we have (allegedly) come to think of ourselves in modern civilization. He finds the masses obsessed by an abysmal social insanity, an aspect of which is the tendency of the individual to see himself as 'a little absolute unto himself'. Whereas 'the true self, in sex, would seek a *meeting*, would seek to meet the other', this being the 'true flow', sexuality today is merely greedy, blind, self-seeking, and 'therefore, since the thing sought is the same, the self, the mode of seeking is not very important. Heterosexual, homosexual, narcissistic, normal, or incest, it is all the same thing. . . . Every man, every woman just seeks his own self, her own self, in the sexual experience.' Such self-regard is the wider evil which masturbation epitomizes. The solution is for people to get back into touch, to 'utterly break the present great picture of a normal humanity . . . and fall again into true relatedness' ('Review', 470–2).

In 'Pornography and Obscenity' Lawrence does not precisely equate homosexuality with the twin evils of masturbation and the excremental flow. In fact, he allows that 'even in homosexual intercourse' there is a 'give and take' quite absent from the real evil, masturbation. But elsewhere, as in Lawrence's attacks on the Bloomsbury group, homosexuality becomes symptomatic of cultural malaise rather as does masturbation here. In particular it is seen to share masturbation's refusal of the other in favour of the self. And via a now explicit association with anality, especially sodomy, homosexuality becomes a paradigm of sterility and solipsism, while heterosexuality is regarded as the way back to a dynamic, creative encounter with the other: in the woman the man embraces 'all that is not himself' and from that embrace 'comes every new action' (quoted in Delany, *Nightmare*, 79). Here is a valorization of the different/same binary similar to that already encountered in Gallop, Scruton, Mailer, and others. In Lawrence's essays it goes along with that familiar stance of hard-earned adjustment whereby sickness is always someone else's problem—the masses, the modern world, women, homosexuals, whoever. In his introduction to the privately printed edition of *Pansies*, for instance, Lawrence castigates Swift for his 'gnashing insanity', his 'insolent and sickly squeamish mind', at the thought that 'Celia shits'. Lawrence feels like going back and saying to her 'It's all right, don't take any notice of that mental lunatic' (p. 304), thereby offering a new inflection of the erotic triangle: intervening between Swift and Celia, Lawrence displaces his own anal neurosis on to Swift while offering his healthy ideal self to Celia—or rather he seeks to become his ideal self *in her eyes*. At such moments the narcissistic dimension of relating to otherness becomes apparent. But for its full significance, and a rather more liberating version of it, we might recall Wilde's wonderful anecdote about Narcissus and the river as related by Gide:

When Narcissus died, the flowers of the field asked the river for some drops of water to weep for him. 'Oh!' answered the river, 'if all my drops of water were tears, I should not have enough to weep for Narcissus myself. I loved him!' 'Oh!' replied the flowers of the field, 'how could you not have loved Narcissus? He was beautiful'. 'Was he beautiful?' said the river. 'And who could know better than you? Each day, leaning over your bank, he beheld his beauty in your water . . .'
Wilde paused for a moment . . .
'If I loved him', replied the river, 'it was because, when he leaned over my water, I saw the reflection of my waters in his eyes.' (*Oscar Wilde*, 2)

Lawrence's masquerade of adjustment involves a projection of his own fears, anxieties, and neurosis which, in the Swift/Celia case, is especially revealing because in the same breath he consciously repudiates the scapegoating process which partly comprises that projection (pp. 303–4). But Lawrence dramatizes something else: if, within the construction of homosexuality as a fear or refusal of otherness, there may be a projection by the male heterosexual on to the homosexual of his fear of *the woman as other*, there may also be a disavowal of the heterosexual's fear of *the homosexual as the same*—that is, a fear of those gender proximities and interconnections, including Lawrence's opposed energy 'flows', whose feared mutual implication compromises not only the ideology of sexual difference, but the cultural formations which it underwrites. It is in this complicated sense that misogyny and homophobia once more interconnect, and otherness may be said to inhere within the same.

Lawrence remained too preoccupied with what in his adjusted mind he projected, disavowed, or consciously repudiated; homosexuality especially remained too fascinating for either his strenuous vision of psychic adjustment or his banal view of sexual difference as unity in opposition to remain unharassed by it. In a letter to Henry Savage on 2 December 1913 he writes: 'I should like to know why nearly every man that approaches greatness tends to homosexuality, whether he admits it or not' (*Letters*, 115). This fascination with, and obvious susceptibility to, homosexual desire occasionally contributes to some brilliantly perverse writing wherein the idealization/abhorrence splitting described by Freud is reversed, and a metaphysic of absolute difference is desublimated into the cathected, dialectic proximity of the perverse dynamic.

The obvious way of approaching those moments in which this occurs is via Lawrence's astonishing description of intense, concealed homosexual desire in the suppressed prologue to *Women in Love*:

it was for men that he felt the hot, flushing, roused attraction which a man is supposed to feel for the other sex . . . the male physique had a fascination for him, and for the female physique he felt only a fondness . . .

In the street it was the men who roused him by their flesh and their manly, vigorous movement . . .

He love his friend, the beauty of whose manly limbs made him tremble with pleasure. He wanted to caress him.

And then in his soul would succeed a sort of despair, because this passion for a man had recurred in him. It was a deep misery to him. And it would seem as if he had always loved men, always and only loved men. And this was the greatest suffering to him.

This was the one and only secret he kept to himself, this secret of his passionate and sudden, spasmodic affinity for men he saw. He kept this secret even from himself. He knew what he felt, but he always kept the knowledge at bay. (*Phoenix II*, 103–4, 107)

Lawrence also remained fascinated by anality, and in *Women in Love* (ch. 23, 'Excurse') there is that celebration of the potency of heterosexual anal intercouse where desire would, at the very least, seem to confuse his distinction between anality and sexuality proper:

It was a dark flood of electric passion she released from him, drew into herself. She had established . . . a new current of passional electric energy. . . . It was a perfect passing away for both of them, and at the same time the most intolerable accession into being, the marvellous fullness of immediate gratification, over-whelming, outflooding from the source of the deepest life-force, the darkest, deepest, strangest life-source of the human body, at the back and base of the loins. (pp. 353–4)

Meyers finds 'The equation of the anus with the life source . . . an obscene and outrageous idea' (*Homosexuality and Literature*, 148) and concludes that Birkin is using Ursula as a homosexual substitute—this being even more perverse than homosexuality proper because (accord-ing to Clifford Allen in a book ominously titled *Homosexuality: Its Nature, Causation and Treatment*) the anus in homosexual love sym-bolizes the vagina and 'anal intercourse is only unconscious incestuous behaviour' (p. 50, quoted by Meyers, *Homosexuality and Literature*, 178). In so far as I understand the logic here, heterosexual sodomy is surrogate homosexuality and homosexual sodomy is surrogate hetero-sexuality—or rather surrogate heterosexual incestuous genital inter-course. Perhaps such interpretations are intriguing not so much because of their rather desperate commitment to the metaphysical primacy of heterosexual genital intercourse—that is merely banal—but because they reveal the tortured cultural and psychic logic which that commit-ment entails.

The anal intercourse in chapter 16 of *Lady Chatterley's Lover*, though once ignored,[21] has become even more notorious than that in *Women in Love*:

Though a little frightened, she let him have his way, and the reckless, shameless sensuality shook her to her foundations . . . It was not really love. . . . It was sensuality sharp and searing as fire, burning the soul to tinder.

Burning out the shames, the deepest, oldest shames, in the most secret places. It cost her an effort to let him have his way and his will of her. She had to be a passive, consenting thing, like a slave, a physical slave. . . . She would have thought a woman would have died of shame. Instead of which the shame died. . . . There was nothing left to disguise or be ashamed of. . . . But it took some getting at, the core of the physical jungle, the dark and deepest recess of organic shame. The phallos alone could explore it. And how he had pressed it on her! (pp. 258–9)

Should such passages lead us to say that Lawrence was a heterosexual sodomite or 'repressed homosexual'? Neither: let us say rather that what is most significant about such passages is the way so much is

---

[21] It is ironic that at the Chatterley trial the prosecution made no mention of the sodomy episode; if it had it might have won the case. Nor, of course, did those defending Lawrence mention it; they spoke of him as profoundly, even religiously virtuous on the question of desire and sexuality. See Rolph (ed.), *The Trial of Lady Chatterley*, and Dollimore, 'The Challenge of Sexuality'.

fantasized from the position of the woman (including anal ecstasy and, elsewhere, Lawrence's almost as notorious worship of the phallus), and in a voice which is at once *blindingly heterosexist and desperately homoerotic*. At such moments he may be *most* culpable *vis-à-vis* a responsible sexual politics (lesbian, gay, and feminist), but most revealing about the 'nature' of sexual desire. Further, if Lawrence's celebration of heterosexuality is dependent upon a repression of, a disavowal of, and a displacement on to, homosexuality, such passages are animated by a homoerotic desire *consciously and artistically sublimated into heterosexuality*. By sublimation I mean here not the conversion of sexuality *per se* into a higher, non-sexual aim, but the displacement of one kind of sexuality into another—or, more exactly (and this is the sense in which I still subscribe to Freud's notion), the contamination of a higher (i.e. socially approved) sexuality by a lower (i.e. proscribed) one. And such displacement and contamination are made possible by that radical interconnectedness between the two which the lower knows and the higher disavows. In short, Lawrence finds ecstasy not in heterosexuality *per se* but its radical perversion, and he does so by reactivating the perverse dynamic at the heart of desire. We might say that the narrator is being fucked by the same in the position of the other—a formulation intentionally ambiguous as to who exactly is in the position of the other, since it is both: the narrator is in the position of the woman being fucked by the other of woman (man).[22]

[22] Although I am using perversion in a very different sense, it is not unrelated to Lawrence's creative engagement with those specific sexual fantasies of which Gregory Woods has written engagingly: 'Although Lawrence characteristically sees the female genitals as a ripe, bursting fruit, to be sucked dry, they are at their most succulent, when overflowing with semen from the withdrawn phallus. Man masturbates over woman's open vagina, from which cup he then drinks his own semen. Cunnilingus is Lawrence's oblique image of fellatio' (*Articulate Flesh*, 131).

PART 8

*Transgressive Reinscriptions,
Early Modern and
Post-modern*

18 *Subjectivity and Transgression*

Part 1 explored how, in the post/modern period, issues of transgression and subjectivity are inextricably bound together. The same is true of the earlier period, but with important differences which are often disregarded. In English studies especially the modern and the early modern have been erroneously conflated. In particular, essentialist conceptions of the self which took effective hold only in the Enlightenment, then to be subsequently developed within (for instance) Romanticism and modernism, have been retrospectively read into the early modern period.[1]

Nosce Teipsum

Consider that great imperative of this period, *nosce teipsum*, know thyself. Today, for critical theories as different as Marxism and post/modernism, know thy discursive formations:

In acquiring one's conception of the world one always belongs to a particular grouping which is that of all the social elements which share the same mode of thinking and acting. . . . The starting-point of critical elaboration is the consciousness of what one really is, and is 'knowing thyself' as a product of the historical process to date which has deposited in you an infinity of traces, without leaving an inventory. (Gramsci, *Cultural Writings*, 423)

But surely for the early moderns also: terminology apart, did not *nosce teipsum* only ever mean something like that? Is that not why Montaigne could say 'the more I frequent and know myselfe . . . the less I understand myselfe'; why also he discovers that 'I have nothing to say entirely, simply, and with soliditie of my selfe without confusion, disorder, blending, mingling . . .' (*Essays*, trans. Florio, iii. 282, ii. 12)?

Though generally appropriated by humanist criticism as a recognizable origin of itself, *nosce teipsum* may nevertheless have something

---

[1] Anne Ferry usefully reminds us that although we typically read Hamlet as possessing what we would call an 'inner life' or 'real self', in fact 'almost none of the terms now used to describe Hamlet as a figure displaying a distinctively modern consciousness existed in the sixteenth-century. Our ways of describing internal experience would have been as unfamiliar to Shakespeare as to Wyatt and his contemporaries' (*The 'Inward' Language*, 29–30). For considerations of gender in the intervening period, and from perspectives relevant for my project, see Castle, *Masquerade and Civilization* 'Nussbaum and Brown' (eds.), *The New Eighteenth Century*; Maccubin (ed.), *'Tis Nature's Fault*; and Rousseau and Porter (eds.), *Sexual Underworlds of the Enlightenment*.

crucial in common with the formulations of post-structuralism. Of the few central beliefs uniting the various post-structuralisms (and connecting them with post/modernism) this is one of the most important: human identity is to be seen as constituted as well as constitutive; constituted (not determined) by, for example, the pre-existing structures of language and ideology, and by the material conditions of human existence. Thus is the subject decentred, and subjectivity revealed as a kind of subjection—not the antithesis of social process but its focus.

In the early modern period also the individual was seen as constituted by and in relation to—even the effect of—a pre-existing order. To know oneself was to know that order. Consider Richard Hooker's declaration: 'God hath his influence into the very essence of all things, without which influence of Deity supporting them their utter annihilation could not choose but follow' (*Laws*, ii. 226). Or the commonplace with which Sir John Davies begins his *Nosce Teipsum*: God wrote the law directly into the hearts of our first parents. Hooker concurs: the law of Reason, the universal law of mankind, is 'imprinted' in men's souls and 'written in their hearts' (i. 166, 228). The biblical source is Jeremiah: 'saith the Lord, I will put my law [Torah] in their inward parts, and write it in their hearts' (31: 33). Heart [leb] here signifies the seat of thought, not emotion, so is more akin to 'mind'; hence, to labour the analogy somewhat, law is written into identity and consciousness rather than heart in the modern sense. When Montaigne and Bacon stress the determining power of social custom they are developing the same idea of an order prior to and determining of consciousness, though now of course with the crucial difference that it is a non-teleological order, historical rather than divine, material rather than metaphysical.[2]

Obviously there are far-reaching differences between early modern metaphysics and post-structuralism. For one thing the early modern view of identity as constituted (metaphysically) was also, and quite explicitly, a powerful metaphysic of social integration. In other words, to be metaphysically identified was simultaneously to be socially positioned—the subject in relation to the prince, the woman in relation to the man, and so on. Metaphysics here underpins a discursive formation of the subject, of subjection. This link between subjectivity and subjection, which for the (political) post/modernist has to be disclosed before it can be disarticulated, is, by comparison, both assumed and manifestly endorsed in the Renaissance. Another difference: within Renaissance metaphysics a constituted identity might nevertheless be essentially fixed

---

[2] For further analysis of custom in this respect, see my *Radical Tragedy*, esp. 9–19.

(e.g. the soul as divine creation) in a way the post/modernist would probably reject (identity is not only constructed but contingently so).

The Cogito: Augustine, Descartes, and Lacan

> Would Hamlet have felt the delicious fascination of suicide if he hadn't had an audience, and lines to speak? (Jean Genet, *Prisoner of Love*)

The Cartesian *cogito*—*cogito ergo sum* (I think therefore I am)— conventionally if somewhat simplistically marks a major point in the emergence of Western individualism. More exactly, it is seen to mark a point in a process of transition from the idea of self as metaphysically constituted to the idea of self as an individuated, autonomous essence; self-consciousness rather than divine or natural law becomes constitutive of subjective identity. As we saw in Chapter 9, Augustine gives a memorable earlier version of the Cartesian *cogito*: 'Si enim fallor sum'— if I am deceived, then I exist. In contrast to Descartes's emphasis on a self-constituting autonomy born of certitude, Augustine's formulation registered man's uncertainty, and that inseparably from dependency upon a prior ordering of selfhood.

As part of his project of recasting psychoanalysis in post-structuralist terms, Jacques Lacan has rewritten the Cartesian *cogito* in a way that might be seen as approximating more to Augustine's formulation than Descartes's: 'I think where I am not, therefore I am where I do not think'.[3] Augustine might have grasped the point of this formulation quickly enough, if only because of what he and Lacan share in common: a sense of identity as constituted rather than constitutive, an effect of the pre-existing. Augustine would also have understood Lacan's invocation of Rimbaud: 'Je est un autre' (I is (an)other). Of course, and again, the differences are considerable; after all, the unconscious, that which in psychoanalysis undermines conscious autonomy, and in relation to which Lacan rewrites the *cogito*, is a modern discovery. A massive step forward from Descartes then, but also perhaps a step back to Augustine. After all, if we were to ask which was the more metaphysical, divine law or the psychoanalytic unconscious, some might reply, 'the unconscious, though not by much'. Whatever, I do not find it surprising that Lacan admired Augustine, and credits him with

---

[3] In context: 'What is needed is more than these words with which, for a brief moment I disconcerted my audience: I think where I am not, therefore I am where I do not think. Words that render sensible to an ear properly attuned with what elusive ambiguity the ring of meaning flees from our grasp along the verbal thread. What one ought to say is: I am not wherever I am the plaything of my thought; I think of what I am where I do not think to think' (*Écrits*, 166).

foreshadowing psychoanalysis (*Écrits*, 20). In discussing a different though related issue, Lacan observes that 'the latest developments in modern thought on language' are only a rediscovery of what was already known to Augustine, who 'orients his entire dialectic around these three poles, error, mistake, ambiguity of speech'. This is especially significant given that, according to Lacan, 'Every emission of speech is always, up to a certain point, *under an inner necessity to err*' (*Seminar*, ii. 249, 260, 264; my emphasis). Or, as Augustine might have put it, language is, of its (fallen) nature, always potentially perverse.

For sure then, the post/modern, in dismantling and displacing some of the ideological formations of the Enlightenment, Romanticism, and modernism, finds itself in a paradoxical but illuminating relationship with the early modern. One way of putting this would be to say that with the deconstruction of these intervening cultural developments, we can see the early modern clearly once again. This is emphatically not the claim I am making here. For one thing, those intervening formulations have been profoundly determining of our own culture and consciousness, and their influence cannot be erased; even deconstructed, they continue to exert an influence. It is not just that there survive undeconstructed residues of, say, Romanticism and modernism, or that the constructed forms echo still within the deconstructed (although they clearly do survive in these ways); it is also that they exert an influence *in and as* their newly deconstructed state. The recent past informs the post/modern, even or especially as the latter is changing our understanding of that past.

I would say rather that, both despite and because of the obvious and considerable differences, post/modernism is helping us to understand again what the early modern period already knew but in a quite different form: identity is *essentially* informed by what it is not. It also helps us to see that if (as was apparent in the early seventeenth century) identity is clearly constituted by the structures of power, of position, allegiance, and service, then any disturbance within, or of, identity could be as dangerous to that order as to the individual subject. Hooker, in a now famous passage, asked: 'see we not plainly that obedience of creatures unto the law of nature is the stay of the whole world?' (*Laws*, i. 157). Equally plainly, in this view disobedience is literally world-shattering; to transgress or deviate from the law of nature, to 'fail, or swerve' (i. 185) from one's allotted course, is a perversion which brings ruin not only to the transgressive agent, but to every other dependent entity. The metaphysical construction of subjectivity is at once an admission and production of its disruptive potential, a disruption in and of the very terms of its construction. It also suggests, paradoxically, that the less autonomous individuality is thought to be, the more it might be marked by a potentially subversive agency. But this is to anticipate the argument; for the moment I want only to observe that a conception of the self as socially and/or metaphysically constituted produces one idea of transgression, and that of the self as ideally (if not actually) unified and autonomous, quite another.

19 Early Modern: Cross-Dressing in Early Modern England

In *Surpassing the Love of Men* Lillian Faderman records two separate cases of women in France in the sixteenth century who were punished for using transvestite disguise and deploying dildos in their lesbian relations.[1] From one, modern, point of view, these women's transgression is suspect. I am not referring to the conservative perspective which condemns sexual deviance *per se*, but to another viewpoint, one which might actually endorse deviance in principle, at least if it were seen as a quest for authentic selfhood of the kind explored in Chapter 3. But here, precisely, is the problem; even (or especially) from this radical perspective, the women's behaviour is seen as inauthentic, not truly transgressive: in their use of men's clothing and the dildo they were trying to imitate precisely that masculine order which they should have been escaping or at least repudiating. In short, their transgression was motivated by false consciousness. That at any rate is how those who are viewed as their modern day counterparts are regarded by the heroine of *Rubyfruit Jungle* (above, Chapter 3); and the anonymous interviewee cited by Esther Newton: 'I hate games! I hate role playing! It's so ludicrous that certain lesbians, who despise men, become the exact replicas of them!' ('The Mythic Mannish Lesbian', 7).

But the question remains: why were those two Frenchwomen in the sixteenth century found so threatening? One of them was sentenced to be burned alive, and the other hanged, punishments dictated, apparently, not by their sexuality as such but their transvestism and use of the dildo—at once, I want to suggest, appropriations of masculinity, inversions of it, and substitutions for it.

I have already explored in relation to Gide and others the kind of rebellion whose test they retrospectively failed, namely, transgression as a quest for authenticity: underpinning and endorsing the philosophy of individualism, it suggests that in defying a repressive social order we can dis-cover (and so be *true* to) our *real* selves. For convenience of reference I shall call this idea of transgression humanist.

---

[1] Faderman, *Surpassing the Love of Men*, 51; the cases, occurring in 1535 and 1580, are recorded by Henri Estienne in *Apologie pour Herodote* (1566) and Montaigne in *Journal de voyage*; see also Crompton, 'The Myth of Lesbian Impunity', 17. Drawing from it different implications, Stephen Greenblatt begins his essay 'Fiction and Friction' with the episode recorded by Montaigne (*Shakespearean Negotiations*, 66).

As I have tried to show, the significance for our culture of humanist transgression, this escape from repression into the affirmation of one's true self can hardly be overestimated. But its prevalence has led us to misconceive both the significance and practice of transgression in the earlier modern period, and also in some of our own contemporary subcultures. What intrigues me about that earlier period, especially its drama, is a mode of transgression which finds expression through the inversion[2] and perversion of just those pre-existing categories and structures which its humanist counterpart seeks to transcend, to be liberated from; a mode of transgression which seeks not an escape from existing structures but rather a subversive reinscription within them, and in the process their dislocation or displacement. I call this 'transgressive reinscription', a concept elaborated shortly in relation to the transvestite. Other examples in the Renaissance include the malcontent who haunts the very power structure which has alienated him, seeking reinscription within it but at the same time demystifying it, operating within and subverting it at the same time; the revengers whose actions constitute an even more violent bid for reinscription within the very society which has alienated and dispossessed them; the assertive women, the 'women on top' described by Natalie Zemon Davis who simultaneously appropriate, exploit, and undermine masculine discourse.

Humanist transgression in the name of authenticity has never been able to comprehend this other kind of transgression, that peformed in the name of inversion, perversion, and reinscription.

Transgressive Mimesis: Faustus and Vagabonds

Stephen Greenblatt draws upon several of the containment arguments outlined above (Chapter 6) in his pioneering study *Renaissance Self-Fashioning*. In this immensely rewarding contribution to Renaissance studies, he argues that Marlowe's heroes remain, in effect, contained. Essentially, they remain embedded in what they oppose: 'they simply reverse the paradigms and embrace what the society brands as evil. In so doing, they imagine themselves set in diametrical opposition to their society where in fact they have unwittingly accepted its crucial structural elements.' In *Faustus* for instance 'the blasphemy pays homage to the power it insults' (pp. 209, 212). Greenblatt has in mind here that extraordinary moment when Faustus seals his pact with the devil by

---

[2] Anthropological and historical studies of inversion in the Renaissance have stressed both its ubiquity and its cultural significance. But precisely what and how it signified, and whether it disrupted or ratified the dominant forms being inverted, depended crucially on context and cannot be decided independently of it. See Ch. 4 n. 4 above.

uttering Christ's dying words on the cross: 'consummatum est'. Faustus wilfully ends himself; he sells his soul to the devil. Creation recoils; his blood congeals. Via the expression of a perverse masochism, with its disturbing mix of abjection and arrogance, this act, in one sense the supreme antithesis of everything Christ died for—he died after all to save us all—is identified as Christlike.

Is not this transgression contained, the unintended reverence paid by the sacrilegious to the sacred? Or is it rather a transgressive reinscription, a demonic perversion of the sacred? What else, after all, was Christ in his death but the keenest image of abjection and arrogance, the epitome of that transgressive masochism which has played such an important part in making and unmaking our culture, not least in the figure of the martyr, and which figures over and again in the cultural depictions of the crucifix? Via the dynamic of the perverse, Faustus violates Christianity in the name and image of Christ; assimilating Christ to his opposite he discloses that opposite within Christ. Similarly, as I have argued elsewhere,[3] this play collapses God into his antithesis, those contemporary secular tyrants who were legitimating their injustice in the name and image of God. What we witness here is something resembling the Freudian proposition that the repressed returns via the very images, structures, and mechanisms of repression itself: the words which consummate the renewal of man, his salvation, these words return to signify the opposite of salvation which is damnation, and they signify also the desire which only damnation can acknowledge and which salvation must repress.[4]

Consider another, quite different instance of transgressive reinscription. The late Gāmini Salgādo once described the vagabonds of the Elizabethan low-life pamphlets as follows:

Seen through the disapproving eyes of respectable citizens they were nothing but a disorderly and disorganized rabble, dropouts from the social ladder. But seen from within, they appear to be like nothing so much as a mirror-image of the Elizabethan world picture: a little world, tightly organised into its own ranks and with its own rules, as rigid in its own way as the most elaborate protocol at court or ritual in church. (*Cony-Catchers*, 13)

From the respectable view, these rogues were merely the dregs of civilization—potentially dangerous, it is true, but in no way a part of

---

[3] *Radical Tragedy*, ch. 6, 'Subversion through Transgression'.

[4] Freud's noted instance of the return of the repressed also involves the crucifixion. In an etching by Felicien Rops an ascetic monk looks to the crucifixion to banish his own temptation but in place of Christ he sees 'the image of a voluptuous, naked woman, in the same crucified attitude . . . Rops has placed Sin in the very place of the Saviour on the cross. He seems to have known that, when what has been repressed returns, it emerges from the repressing force itself' (xiv. 60). It also suggests how powerfully cathected in our culture is the image of the crucifixion.

the true social order. From another view they comprise a mirror-image of that order. But if the second view is accurate[5] do not the rogues become another clear instance of transgression contained, of a subculture which has internalized the structures and values of the dominant culture? Are they not paradoxically reproducing the laws which exclude and oppress them, even as they seem to be escaping and subverting those laws?

Not exactly, because this very mimicry of the dominant, be it a literary trope or cultural actuality, involved a scandalous inversion. In the words of one contemporary observer: 'these cheaters turned the cat in the pan,[6] giving to diverse vile patching shifts an honest and godly title, calling it by the name of law . . . to the destruction of the good labouring people' (Salgãdo, *Cony-Catchers*, 15). And feeding back through that inversion is an equally scandalous interrogation of the dominant order being mimicked; civil society is shown to be rooted in a like corruption. If this subculture imitates the dominant from below, it also thereby employs a strategy which embarrasses the dominant. Even as civil society endlessly displaces corruption from the social body as a whole on to its low life, the latter reveals both the original source and full extent of corruption within the dominant itself (pp. 16, 174). Inversion becomes a kind of transgressive mimesis: the subculture, even as it imitates, reproducing itself in terms of its exclusion, also demystifies, producing a knowledge of the dominant which excludes it, this being a knowledge which the dominant has to suppress in order to rule.

Cross-dressing

We have seen already how the most significant senses of 'perversion' in the early period do not define a sexual pathology in the modern sense. As a divergence or deviation from, perversion was also a contradiction of. Similarly, 'inversion' could signify reversal of position and/or reversal of direction, both being inimical to effective government and social control. So it is worth recalling at the outset of this discussion that it is in these senses that the female cross-dresser of the early seventeenth century could be described as an 'invert' or 'pervert', and hardly at all

---

[5] In fact, as Beier shows in *Masterless Men*, as a description of actuality it was almost as fanciful as the first. However, it concerns us here not as the truth about, but as a contemporary cultural representation of, low life.

[6] Cf. Bacon: 'There is a cunning which we in England call the turning of the cat in the pan; which is, when that which a man says to another, he says it as if another had said it to him' (cited in Brewer, *Dictionary of Phrase and Fable*, 223).

in the sense of those words as coined and popularized by the nineteenth-century sexologists and, later, psychoanalysis. We might also usefully recall that to cross is not only to traverse, but to mix (as in to cross-breed) and to contradict (as in to cross someone); also that cross-dressing potentially involves both inversion and displacement of gender binaries. Again we are confronted with a system of control in part generating the terms, the concepts, and the space of its own negation.

The female transvestite was indeed a deeply disturbing figure in the early seventeenth century.[7] Certain cultural distinctions were breaking down and in the anxiety which this provoked we can read the effects of far-reaching historical change. As Lisa Jardine has recently reminded us, in the obsession with dress and what it signified socially, we witness contemporary tensions and struggles between classes, between residual and emergent cultures, between the mercantile order and what it was actually (or seemed to be) replacing, between rank and wealth, between innate and fiscal value (*Still Harping*, 141–2, 150).[8] So before examining the challenge of the female transvestite, we need to consider the more general attitudes to dress and what it signified.

Contemporary anxieties found expression in two main kinds of attack: the one on the dress violations of the emergent (middle) class, the other on the insubordinate (female) sex. William Perkins sets out the conventional position *vis-à-vis* class. Dress, he says,

must be answerable to our estate and dignitie, for distinction of order and degree in the societies of men. This use of attire, stands by the very ordinance of God; who, as he hath not sorted all men to all places, so he will have men to fitte themselves and their attire, to the qualitie of their proper places, to put a difference betweene themselves and others . . . By which it appeares, that many in these daies do greatly offend . . . The Artificer commonly goes clad like the Yeoman: the Yeoman like the Gentleman: the Gentleman as the Nobleman: the Nobleman as the Prince: which bringeth great confusion, and utterly overturneth the order which God hath set in the states and conditions of men. (*Pioneer Works*, 210–11)

Dress underwrites not only class differences but national and racial ones also, and Perkins has harsh words for those who adopt the fashion of other countries: 'this one sinne is so common among us, that it hath branded our English people with the blacke mark of the vainest and

---

[7] This section is indebted to a number of existing and recent studies of the transvestite controversy, especially the following: Dusinberre, *Shakespeare and the Nature of Women*, esp. 231–305; Jardine, *Still Harping on Daughters*, esp. ch. 5; Woodbridge, *Women and the English Renaissance*, esp. part 2; Rose, 'Women in Men's Clothing'; Clark, '*Hic Mulier, Haec Vir*, and the Controversy over Masculine Women'; Rackin, 'Androgyny, Mimesis, and the Marriage of the Boy Heroine on the English Renaissance Stage'; Orgel, 'Nobody's Perfect'; Dekker and van de Pol, *The Tradition of Female Transvestism*.

[8] See also Whigham, *Ambition and Privilege*, 155–69.

most newfangled people under heaven' (p. 211).[9] He also castigates those who use cosmetics 'thereby making themselves seeme that which, indeede they are not', and practising what 'is most abominable in the very light of nature, and much more by the light of Gods word' (p. 214).

Accompanying the association between dress and class was that between dress and gender. This is Stubbes:

Our apparel was given us as a sign distinctive to discern betwixt sex and sex, and therefore for one to wear the apparel of another sex, is to participate with the same, and to adulterate the verity of his own kind. (*Anatomy*, sig. [F5]$^{r-v}$)

Thus the ideology of gender difference was just as fundamental as that of class in securing the social order. In fact patriarchy, class, and hierarchy all presupposed a law of gender difference which was at once divinely, naturally, and socially laid down, the law descending from the first through the second to the third. As we shall see, it is against and (again) in terms of this metaphysic that dress violation occurred. Not surprisingly then, class and gender anxieties interrelated. In a letter of 25 January 1620 Sir John Chamberlain remarks a very significant event in the contemporary cross-dressing controversy: James I's instruction to the clergy to suppress women doing it. The king is reported as having told the clergy that they must reproach the practice 'vehemently and bitterly', and if this did not succeed, he would take further measures. Chamberlain refers to this in the same breath as mentioning an argument between the Marquess Buckingham and Hamilton over 'the selling of honours and abasing ancient nobility, by new advancements'. Class and sexual disruption suggest each other, and with this conclusion: 'The truth is the world is very far out of order' (*Letters*, ii. 286–9).

Though Perkins, Stubbes, and Chamberlain hardly convey this, the controversy over dress was no less complex than the social shifts which provoked it. No simple transgression/containment model was at work. And nor can we reduce the controversy to a straightforward clash between the new and the old orders. For one thing, as Jardine points out, while on the one hand the shift of wealth to the mercantile classes was leading to the break-up of the dress code, and enabling the socially mobile to appropriate, for purposes of inclusion, what were supposed to be signs of their exclusion, it was also the case that those who had 'arrived' socially often wanted to enforce the code against those who had not. Further, Baldwin discerns in the controversy an overlap of

---

[9] Hic Mulier declares that if cross-dressing 'be not barbarous, make the rude *Scithian*, the untamed *Moore* , the naked *Indian*, or the wild *Irish*, Lords and Rulers of well governed Cities' (*Haec Vir*, sig. B^v).

class anxieties and pragmatic political considerations[10]—for example the wish to encourage home industries and discourage the buying of foreign goods (*Sumptuary Legislation*, ch. 5, 'The Reign of Elizabeth'). The situation was further complicated by those like Stubbes and Perkins who saw dress confusion as symptomatic of impending social collapse, and those like James I whose hatred of female cross-dressing introduced a misogynistic factor which antedated current social anxiety yet found a powerful focus in it.

To the modern reader the stipulated dress codes for different classes and persons of different prestige and status seem bizarre and impossibly complicated (see for instance those reprinted in Jardine, *Still Harping*, 143–4). But their very strangeness also helps us see how transgression is produced by the measures taken to contain it: the more elaborate the classifications, the more opportunity there was to transgress, and, quite possibly, the greater the attraction of transgression. Whatever, it eventually became impossible to ensure compliance.

Theatrical Transgression

A significant focus for the controversy was the theatre, which, like the transvestite, was seen both to epitomize and to promote contemporary forces of disruption in and through its involvement with cross-dressing. There was, for example, the general cultural disturbance generated by the theatrical emphasis on artifice, disguise, and role-playing. Its significance can be gauged in part by looking at the range of objections to the theatre as a place which subverted metaphysical fixity.

To begin with the players were seen to undermine the idea that one's identity and place were a function of what one essentially was—what God had made one. The idea of a God-given nature and destiny had the corollary that nothing so essentially predetermined could or should ever change. Constant change was worse still; in the words of one satirist, the scandal of the player was not so much that he disguised his real self in playing; rather he had no self apart from that which he was playing: 'The Statute hath done wisely to acknowledge him a Rogue and errant, for his chiefe essence is, *A daily Counterfeit* . . . His [profession] is compounded of all Natures, all humours, all professions.'[11] The association here of the player and the rogue is significant. Both were itinerants and masterless men, sometimes both subjected to the same vagrancy

---

[10] Such considerations were equally a factor for the cross-dressers themselves; on the different kinds of female transvestites, and their various reasons for cross-dressing, see Dekker and van de Pol, *The Tradition of Female Transvestism*.

[11] 'A Common Player' (1615), quoted from Montrose, 'The Purpose of Playing', 51 and 57.

laws (alternatively the player might be a royal servant—an interesting opposition in itself). They transgressed fixity not only because they were without fixed abode, but also because they lacked the identity which, in a hierarchical society, was essentially conferred by one's place in that society. And there was a further link between rogues, masterless men, and the players; according to some observers the theatres quite literally brought them into association, being the place 'for vagrant persons, Masterless men, thieves . . . contrivers of treason, and other idle and dangerous persons to meet together' (Chambers, *Elizabethan Stage*, iv. 322). Again we see the same anxiety: social stability depended crucially on people staying just as they were (identity), where they were (location), and doing what they always had done (calling). When the rogue meets the player two lawless identities converge.

This concern with unfixed identity was not unique to the theatre; society and politics more generally contained a theatrical dimension, what Greenblatt calls 'the theatricalisation of culture'. Renaissance courts involved theatricality in the sense of both disguise and histrionic self-presentation, while court manuals and rhetorical handbooks offered 'an integrated rhetoric of the self, a model for the formation of an artificial identity' (*Renaissance Self-Fashioning*, 162). And dissimulation was of course essential for the practice of *realpolitik*. In the theatre was a model, indeed a sustained exploration, of the role-playing which was so important for social mobility, the appropriation and successful deployment of power. It follows that the recurring emphasis within Elizabethan and Jacobean plays on life itself as a process of playing was not merely theatrical projection; the world as a stage, life as artifice, and so on; these were ideas which the theatre derived from, as well as conveyed to, its culture. Louis Montrose points out a fascinating consequence of this: 'If the world is a theatre and the theatre is an image of the world, then by reflecting upon its own artifice, the drama is holding the mirror up to nature' (Montrose, 'Purpose of Playing', 57).

Another, related, charge against the players is that in their dress violations they—again like the 'street' transvestites—transgressed the natural and fixed order of things by wilfully confusing distinctions which it was thought imperative should be kept distinct, especially within the categories of rank, class, and gender. For menials to play those of a higher rank and breeding seemed a deep violation of the principle of fixed division on which civilization rested. In Act v, Scene v, of Jonson's *Volpone* Mosca enters dressed as a gentleman; it is a moment which might be seen to mark the arrival of the urban impostor, he or she who knows that mimicry and impersonation possess the potential not just to deceive and usurp, but also to subvert social differentiation and identity itself:

MOSCA.   But what am I?
VOLPONE: 'Fore heav'n, a brave *clarissimo*; thou becomest it!
   Pity thou wert not born one.
MOSCA.   If I hold
   My made one, 'twill be well.

(V. V. 2–5)

Mosca prevaricates beautifully. It is a reply which is at once deferential and contemptuous, self-effacing and arrogant. 'Twill be well because he is not the real thing, never could be, and is not even now presuming to be; but conversely, 'twill be well because the imitation, the travesty, of the real thing can also usurp it and *to all intents and purposes* become it. What price then that metaphysical guarantee of social differentiation when it is so easily abolished in the confusion it was supposed to pre-empt and render impossible? It is a concentrated, fleeting moment of ambiguity and irony (irony and ambiguity tending to be intrinsic to transgressive reinscription and alien to humanist transgression).

It is also a moment of appropriation in which there surfaces the play's underlying knowledge, at once exhilarating, ambivalent, appalling, and violent; a knowledge which incites yet also fears that riot of the perverse, the antisocial and the anti-natural which are *Volpone*. Of course the power of superficial difference goes deep; when Volpone is discovered attempting to rape Celia he laments: 'I am unmasked, unspirited, undone' (III. vii. 277). To be unmasked *is* to be unspirited as well as undone. To lose one's cover is to lose one's soul, to be undone in the sense of socially ruined and spiritually taken apart. Can we attribute this perception entirely to Volpone's and Mosca's perversity? Not exactly, if only because it is precisely at this point that *Volpone* shows how the normal is parasitic upon the perverse. To be sure we are seeing it in a grotesquely parodied form, but what leads to Celia being nearly raped is nothing less than the prevailing structures of patriarchal and heterosexual authority: it is after all her hitherto paranoidly jealous husband who has literally dragged her to Volpone's bed.

One further aspect of dress violation associated with the theatre also contravened divine and natural law: the abomination of boys dressing as girls. For John Rainoldes the boy transvestite destroyed the fragile moral restraint containing an anarchic male sexuality; the boy incited his male audience into every kind of sexual excess.[12] Rainoldes seems to

---

[12] Rainoldes believed that the representation of sin incited sin. This is by no means necessarily a fatuous

have imagined adult male sexuality not just as anarchic, but as satanically polymorphous, capable of engaging in the forbidden with alarming ease. So, in seeing the transvestite boy, the male member of the audience might be moved to lascivious thoughts about women, which then transfer to the boy himself.[13] (In the light of which it is pleasing to discover that in 1566, when Rainoldes was a 17-year-old student at Oxford, he acted the part of a female in a play composed for Queen Elizabeth—see Paine, *The Learned Men*, 23). Rainoldes apart, the trangressions associated with the boy players, be they actual or imagined, rendered the theatrical self-consciousness surrounding transvestism complex and shifting; it provoked questions teasingly unanswerable: for example—and this is a question which remains intriguing for us today—which, or how many, of the several gender identities embodied in any one figure are in play at any one time?

There were factors at play in the association of theatrical cross-dressing and sexual transgressions. Not only did prostitutes frequent the theatre, but the street transvestite was sometimes associated with prostitution and possibly sodomy: Henriques notes a regulation dating frm 1480 forbidding prostitutes to dress as men in public, and remarks: 'This masquerading presumably would have meant an added induce-ment to sodomy' (*Prostitution and Society*, ii. 88). If he is right, then stage transgressions seemed to have spoken to immediate temptations in diverse ways.

The Roaring Girl *and Hic Mulier*

Middleton and Dekker's *The Roaring Girl* (1608–11), a play with a transvestite hero/ine called Moll Cutpurse, and the 1620 pamphlet controversy over cross-dressing both include attacks on the fraudulence of masculinity and the exploitativeness of gender inequality. In both play and pamphlet the contemporary sexual metaphysic is turned inside out: gender division is recognized not as a divinely sanctioned natural order, but as the contingent basis of an oppressive social order. Correspondingly the representation of gender inversion generates an interrogation both of the sexual metaphysic and of thé social order.

Moll Cutpurse is variously described as one who 'strays so from her kind | Nature repents she made her' (1. ii. 211–12); who some say 'is a

idea; Artaud, in *Theatre and its Double*, argues that there are powers in poetry such that a crime on stage is 'infinitely more dangerous to the mind than if the same crime were committed in life' (p. 65).

[13] *Th' Overthrow of Stage-Playes*, esp. pp. 8–9, 17–20, 108, 111, 119; see also Binns, 'Women or Transvestites on the Elizabethan Stage?', and Jardine, *Still Harping*, ch. 1.

man | And some both man and woman' (II. i. 190–1), and yet others
that she is 'a codpiece-daughter' (II. ii. 89)

> a thing
> One knows not how to name: her birth began
> Ere she was all made: 'tis woman more than man,
> Man more than woman, and (*which to none can hap*)
> The sun gives her two shadows to one shape

> (I. ii. 128–33, my emphasis)

And yet this creature who so violates the natural order and traditional
gender divisions by dressing as a man also does things better than a
man: 'I should draw first and prove the quicker man', she says (IV. i.
76)—and she does. In the process she attacks masculinity as a charade,
asserting its failure in its own sexual terms (II. i. 290 ff.), something
which the language of the play echoes elsewhere, facetiously, but
defensively too (cf. II. i. 326 ff.; II. ii. 75 ff.; III. i. 142 ff.). Moll also
offers what in this period is an exceptional awareness of the prostitute
as someone sexually exploited because of economic and other kinds of
social subjection:

> In thee I defy all men, their worst hates,
> And their best flatteries, all their golden witchcrafts,
> With which they entangle the poor spirits of fools.
> Distressed needlewomen and trade-fallen wives,
> Fish that must needs bite or themselves be bitten,
> Such hungry things as these may soon be took
> With a worm fastened on a golden hook:
> Those are the lecher's food, his prey, he watches
> For quarrelling wedlocks, and poor shifting sisters.

> (III. i. 90–8[14])

Recognizing all this, and being shown too where the power lies in this
social order, the politics of inversion become persuasive, perhaps
irresistible; this is Moll, about to thrash the predatory Laxton: 'I scorn
to prostitute myself to a man, | I that can prostitute a man to me' (III.
i. 109–10). Moll's denunciation of Laxton before she beats him up shows
that the thrashing is partly in revenge for his not untypical masculine
blend of misogyny and licentiousness (cf. II. ii. 252–5) to which of
course the prostitute can indeed testify that if these things appear
incompatible—isn't misogyny a kind of hatred, and licentiousness a
kind of love, albeit a debased one?—in reality they go hand in hand.

It is in these ways that *The Roaring Girl* begins to disclose how,

---

[14] See also Woodbridge, *Women and the English Renaissance*, 254–5.

because of the complex connections between sexuality, gender, and class, and specifically between sexual and economic exploitation, economic and political anxieties can be displaced into the domain of the sexual and, conversely, the sexual comes to possess enormous signifying power (though very different from that attributed to sexuality by the radical humanist). As I have already remarked, the king himself intervened in 1620 to try to eliminate female transvestism. He like many others at that time felt that female transvestites were usurping male authority. This is indeed exactly what Moll does throughout the play, and especially when she beats up Laxton. But perhaps more importantly the transvestite was contributing to a knowledge and a culture which undermined the discursive formations of authority itself, doing so through her perverse reinscription within those formations. Similarly in the pamphlet controversy.

Hic Mulier, the voice of female transvestites in the most interesting pamphlet, *Haec Vir* (1620), insists that gender difference is an effect of custom only. Custom becomes the cause where once it was only the effect. This inversion is also an instance of what was to become the classic move in ideological demystification: the metaphysical is displaced by, and then collapsed into, the social. Shorn of its metaphysical sanction, law in the Renaissance was always in danger of losing its prescriptive power. Nothing is more absurd, nothing more foolish, says Hic Mulier, than custom. In fact, it is 'an idiot'.[15] The radical implications of this assertion can be gleaned from an observation of Montaigne's: 'We may easily discern, that only custom makes that seem impossible unto us, which is not so' (*Essays*, trans. Florio, i. 239). Throughout the pamphlet Hic Mulier seems to be in sympathy with this remark of Montaigne's, but nowhere is her appropriation of the idea more challenging than in the way she dissolves both law and ideological fixity into a celebration of change and transformation, and, by implication, a celebration of her potential rather than her fixed nature: 'Nor do I in my delight of change otherwise than as the whole world does' (sig. B1). At a time when change was almost synonymous with evil, or at least decline, this was indeed provocative. Hic Mulier is not only shameless but, as Sandra Clark has recently pointed out, she suggests that shame itself 'is a concept framed by men to subordinate women to the dictates of arbitrary custom' ('Controversy', 175). Hic Mulier claims too that women are as reasonable as men. And then comes the crucial claim: 'We are as free born as men, have as free election, and as free spirits; we are compounded of like parts, and may with like liberty

---

[15] *Haec Vir: Or, the Womanish-Man*, sig. B2; spelling modernized.

make benefit of our creations' (sig. B3). And it is a claim whose force in this instance comes through a demystification generated across inversion.

But consider now a misgiving voiced by Linda Woodbridge and shared by many others: 'To me the one unsatisfying feature of the otherwise stimulating transvestite movement is that it had to be transvestite: Renaissance women so far accepted the masculine rules of the game that they felt they had to look masculine to be "free" ' (*Women and the English Renaissance*, 145). For understandable reasons Woodbridge seems to prefer the 'hermaphroditic vision' (p. 145 and cf. p. 317). The transvestite and the hermaphrodite: both were disturbing images; perhaps they are less so now. Potentially the hermaphrodite dissolves gender difference and, at least in its associated idea of androgyny, has become acceptable. Even in the Renaissance the figure could 'symbolise the essential oneness of the sexes' (p. 140), and, with reference back to Plato's *Symposium*, the recovery of an original lost unity (itself intrinsically sexual). The idea remains alive today, of course; I have already referred to Kaja Silverman's observation that the notion of sexual identity as an original androgynous whole, similar to that projected by Aristophanes, is central to the psychoanalytic theories of Jacques Lacan.[16]

But the transvestite? S/he is a strange and disturbing figure still, though now for different reasons from in the Renaissance. Isn't s/he a figure who has exchanged one kind of incompleteness for another? If misgivings persist they are not exactly moral. Isn't it rather that, as Woodbridge implies, the transvestite seems to be a victim of false consciousness, and by switching gender roles rather than dissolving them reinforces the very sexual division which s/he finds oppressive?[17]

---

[16] See above, Ch. 17. Jan Kott in an interesting discussion of bisexuality suggests that ambiguity (in Shakespeare's *Sonnets*) is at the same time a poetic and an erotic principle; he also sees disguise as a masquerade both erotic and metaphysical, with the hermaphrodite as the anatomical counterpart of disguise, and the androgyne as its metaphorical counterpart (*Shakespeare Our Contemporary*, 196, 213, 215). Kott offers a sensitive exploration of Renaissance challenges to gender division and sexual difference, but one which is finally and revealingly in the service of sexual unity. Here is his last paragraph: '*Coincidentia oppositorum!* The unification of all opposites! In the Forest of Arden love is both earthly, and platonically sublimated. Rosalind is Ganymede and the most girlish of girls. Constant-fickle, calm-violent, fair-dark, shy-impudent, prudent-madcap, tender-mocking, childish-grownup, cowardly-courageous, bashful-passionate. As in Leonardo, she is an almost perfect androgyny and personifies the same longing for the lost Paradise where there had as yet been no division into the male and female elements' (p. 236). Also revealing is the way changeability and antithesis are transvalued as completeness rather than evil deviation and threat, with the idealization, like the deviation and the threat, also focused in and as female desire. Demonized desire is gathered into an idealization from within which it may at any time be retriggered.

[17] Compare Dennis Altman: 'the transvestite . . . and even more the transexual, seem the ultimate victim of . . . stigma . . . so conditioned into the male/female role dichotomy that the only way they can accept their own homosexuality is by denying their bodies . . . My personal belief (hope?) is that transvestism and transexism would disappear were our social norms not so repressive of men who exhibit "feminine" traits and *vice versa*' (*Homosexual Oppression*, 149, 151).

So the transvestite fails the test of humanist transgression. But if the hermaphrodite threatens the binarism of gender through ambiguous unity, the female transvestite of the early seventeenth century positively disrupts that same scheme by usurping the master side of the opposition. To invoke again the earlier distinction between different kinds of transgression, the transvestite represents a subversive reinscription within, rather than a transcendence of, an existing order, while the hermaphrodite is often appropriated as a symbol of just such a transcendence. Essentially the assertive female cross-dresser inverted the metaphysics of difference: from being a divine law inscribed essentially in each of God's subjects and which knowledge of self would confirm, sexual identity and sexual difference are shifted irretrievably into the domain of custom, of the social, of that which can be contested. Perhaps this is the mode of transgression denied to the hermaphrodite, at least to the extent that s/he is associated with the mythological, the pre-social, the transcendent.

Containment Theory and Transvestism

What I have just offered have been partial readings of the *Haec Vir* pamphlet and *The Roaring Girl*, partial not in the sense (at least this is not what I'm confessing) of being distortions of the texts, but rather readings that focus upon textual elements which can be correlated with oppositional cultural elements within Jacobean society, and consequently possible audience positions and reading responses. But the representation of the transvestite in the pamphlet and the theatre is part of a cultural process whose complexity is worth exploring further. The complexity I am concerned with is not that supposed intrinsic property of the text which politically motivated critics allegedly distort (in biased readings) and impartial critics transparently represent (in long readings). It is the complexity which is first and foremost a social process, and within which the text was, and still is, implicated. Viewing the text in this way raises the question of the containment of transgression, since both play and pamphlet have been seen to move toward a closure which contains—even eradicates—their challenging elements.

The *Haec Vir* pamphlet ends, notoriously, with Hic Mulier declaring that women like her have only become masculine because men have become effeminate. They have taken up men's cast-off garments in order to 'support a difference' (sig. C2ᵛ)—in effect to maintain sexual difference itself. And if men revert to being masculine, the Hic Mulier figure continues, women will once again become feminine and subordinate. Actually this conclusion barely constitutes containment. To see this argument as somehow cancelling what went before is probably to interpret the pamphlet according to modern and anachronistic notions of authorial intention, character utterance, and textual unity (all three notions privileging what is said finally as being more truthful than what went before). The Hic Mulier figure (an abstraction) is a vehicle for a variety of defences of the transvestite, radical *and* conservative, and there is no good reason, given the genre, to privilege the one over the others as more truthful, more sincere, more representative, or to be dismayed that some of these arguments are incompatible with each other. Presumably if the different defences had been split between several Hic Mulier figures the problem (for us) would disappear—again alerting us to certain, not necessarily appropriate, interpretative assumptions. But it remains true that this culminating defence, conservative and apologetic as it is, still partakes of the same fundamental challenge to gender division as the other defences. To state that gender difference *can be and is being* maintained through cross-dressing and inversion is to maintain or imply the crucial claim even while apparently surrendering it: the difference in question is capable of working in terms of custom and culture (and is thereby contestable) rather than nature and divine law (which are immutable). Within this apologetic (ironic?) defence then, sexual difference is sustained by the very inversion which divine law forbids, and the fact that it can be so sustained is simultaneously a repudiation of the claim that sexual difference is itself dictated by divine or natural law. The submission ironically incorporates—contains—the original challenge.

The Roaring Girl is a stronger instance of containment. Right at the outset we are alerted to the fact that Mary Frith, the real-life cross-dresser on whom the play is based, is being given a more virtuous image than she in fact possessed (dedication, ll. 19 ff.; prologue, ll. 26–7). For sure she creates disruption, signifies abnormality, and incites lewdness in others. But she does not share the criminality of the real-life Frith who was apparently arrested several times, and variously recorded as being a bawd, thief, receiver, gang-leader, and whore; the character Moll Cutpurse definitely is not these things, and in the play-world is only falsely accused of being so.[18] So whereas the deviance of Mary Frith remained in certain respects implacably immoral and antisocial, in the figure of Moll Cutpurse that deviance is harnessed as the moral conscience of the selfsame society whose gender categories she transgresses.[19] More specifically, Frith/Moll is appropriated for a partial

[18] *The Roaring Girl*, ed. Gomme, p. xiv; see also Shepherd, *Amazons*, 74–6.
[19] This idealized rewriting of Frith is continued in a recent feminist novel *Moll Cutpurse: Her True History* by Ellen Galford. Dekker and van de Pol, *The Tradition of Female Transvestism*, usefully remind

critique of patriarchial law, sexual exploitation, and aristocratic culture. She thereby also helps regenerate society and especially its ailing patriarchal basis: 'MOLL. Father and son, I ha' done you simple service here' (V. ii. 206). At the same time she remains 'isolated from the very social structure which her courage and vitality have done so much to enliven and renew' (Rose, 'Women in Men's Clothing', 389–90). In these respects Frith/Moll is represented in the tradition of the warrior woman and the folk figure of Long Meg of Westminster, both of whom distinguish true morality from false, the proper man from the braggart, and finally submit to the former (Shepherd, *Amazons*, esp. 70–2).

What this suggests is that if the demonizing of the deviant other leads to suppression and even extermination, the colonizing of the deviant involves an assimilation which re-forms, ethically and literally, even as it re-presents. The play reconstitutes Mary Frith as Moll Cutpurse, who in turn is used to reconstitute a social order while remaining on its margins—reformed and reforming but not finally incorporated; hence Moll's stern yet haunting parting injunction to the assembled 'gentlemen' of the final scene: 'I pursue no pity: | Follow the law' (252–3).

In this case containment is not the reaction of power after, and in response to, the event of subversion. Nor is subversion the ruse of power. Rather subversion and containment are always in play, each an intrinsic dimension of social process and in a dynamic interrelationship which their binary conception misconstrues. Thus containment can effect rather than defeat change (and this does not presuppose the desirability or otherwise of that change; it might be reaction or progress or, as in this play, complex elements of both with each differently appropriated for different audience positions). Rather than seeing containment as that which pre-empts and defeats transgression we need to see both containment and transgression as potentially productive processes. *The Roaring Girl* presents a process in which containment of the deviant forms the basis of one social fraction offering a critique of, and taking power from, another. In a more radical dynamic, containment, in the very process of repressing one kind of subversive knowledge, actually produces another. It is to the latter process that I now turn.

us that this differential treatment of fictional and real-life transvestites was widespread; they conclude that although in novels and plays the transvestite might be regarded sympathetically, her real-life 'street' counterpart was usually regarded with considerable hostility (ch. 5, esp. pp. 92–8).

Transvestism and Masculinity: Love's Cure

The most interesting theatrical containment of the transvestite challenge occurs in Fletcher's little-known *Love's Cure* (1624?).[20] Indeed, one wonders if the play was written as a conservative response to the controversy, since it directly addresses the most challenging claim or implication of the radical transvestite, namely, that gender division and inequality are a consequence not of divine or natural law but of social custom. The play centres on the severe cultural disturbance generated by the fact that Clara, a girl, has been brought up as a boy and wants to remain one, while her brother, Lucio, has been brought up as a girl which he wants to remain, despite the fact that society is now demanding that both return to their normal gender ascriptions. It is a humorous situation and one played up as such. But the play also acknowledges quite clearly that what is at stake is nothing less than the legitimacy of the whole social order, hinging as it does on a 'naturally' sanctioned law of sexual difference. This is a play about the perversion of nature by culture (or 'custom'—I. ii. 47, II. ii. 95–7) with the eventual triumph of nature: 'Nature (though long kept back) wil have her owne' (IV. iv. 61–2; cf. II. ii. 248–59, IV. ii. 187–90, V. iii. 90–4).

The cultural conditioning of both Lucio and Clara seems to go deep. Parents and others try yet fail to restore the children to their natural selves; the father, Alvarez, cries angrily:

> Can strong habituall custome
> Work with such Magick on the mind, and manners
> In spight of sex and nature?
>
> (II. ii. 140–2)

The answer is, apparently, yes. But then nature succeeds where authority has failed; attraction to the opposite sex awakens the siblings' own 'true' natural instincts, and gender incongruities are resolved. Clara switches from being aggressive to being acquiescent and Lucio does the reverse. Right order prevails.

We might say that *Love's Cure* produces transgression precisely in order to contain it, and in the most insidiously ideological way: the deviant desire which initially appeared to contradict nature is reconstituted by nature in accord with her(?) order. Reconstituted, not repressed: deviant desire is effortlessly and internally transformed—not

---

[20] All quotations are from the edition by George W. Williams in *The Dramatic Works in the Beaumont and Fletcher Canon*, vol. iii. A much-needed single-volume edition of this text is in preparation by J. Marea Mitchell for the Nottingham Drama Texts series, ed. Parfitt *et al.* Mitchell also analyses the play in her D.Phil. thesis 'Gender and Identity in Philip Sidney's *Arcadia*' (University of Sussex, 1985); see also Shepherd, *Amazons*, and Clark, 'Controversy'.

forced—from the perverse to the natural. However, in the process the very masculine code of honour which is affronted by Lucio's perverse failure of masculinity is shown to border on a perversity even more excessive than his. It is as if containment, in reinstating nature over culture—that most fundamental and violent of binary oppositions—says too much about both. Thus the effect of containment resembles the unintended power of the subordinates in this play who execute the commands of the powerful and of whom the Governor complains:

> How men in high place, and authority
> Are in their lives and estimation wrong'd
> By their subordinate Ministers? *yet such*
> *They cannot but imploy*

(IV. iii. 119–21, my emphasis)

Masculine sexuality is shown to be complex and unstably implicated within the whole social domain. Either nature does not contain it or nature contains too much to be conceived any longer as natural. What is especially fascinating about this text is that a rehabilitation of masculinity coexists with an ironic repudiation of it, and a critique of what might be called masculinity's cultural unconscious. An urbane text, it nevertheless discloses a violent scenario—social, psychic, and sexual (what has sometimes been mistaken for decadence).

Most obviously and consciously there is the fact that Lucio's effeminacy, construed by Bobadillo as an affront to 'heav'n, and nature, and thy Parents' (II. ii. 22)—i.e. that powerful conjunction of divine, natural, and patriarchal law—actually embodies positive civilized virtues. Lucio would, for example, willingly renounce the savage illogic whereby a bloody family feud is being perpetuated among new generations (II. ii. 44 ff.) and also the sword as instrument and symbol of male violence (II. iv. 84 ff.). In return his father rages at him for his inability to become a 'real' man, and demands as the only acceptable proof that Lucio has regained his masculinity that he attack the very next man he sees and sexually assault the first woman (IV. iii. 37 ff.). Though conceived as an absolute, uncompromising ethical stand ('Life's but a word, a shadow, a melting dreame, | Compar'd to essentiall, and eternall honour'—V. iii. 124–5), masculine honour is also represented as straightforwardly stupid and barbaric. Also, two of masculinity's basic characteristics, sexual prowess and violence, are shown to be inextricably related, as indicated for example by the conventional but still revealingly obsessive association of sword and phallus (e.g. at II. ii. 86–90 and V. iii. 194–6) and the ambiguity of 'blood': at once sexual desire and what honour demands, literally, of the male opponent.

The internal critique is more searching still. From the punning just mentioned we see that masculine sexuality is confirmed not only by women, passively, but also by other men, actively. It is not so much that the culture of masculine honour is a sublimation of homosexuality; rather masculine honour repeatedly incites what, heterosexually, it presupposes but cannot admit. The differential status of men and women in confirming masculine sexuality is neatly demonstrated at the climax of the play, the arranged duel between Alvarez and Vitelli (seconded, respectively, by Lucio, now masculinized by falling in love, and Lamorall). As they square up to each other the spouses of the first three men 'Enter above' and implore them not to fight. Plea after plea fails. 'Are you men, or stone' cries the Governor; 'Men, and we'll prove it with our swords' replies Alvarez (v. iii. 172–3). And what honour dictates must occur between men—alliance/violence—simply overrides contrary honourable vows to women (162–4). In fact, the women's pleas for peace only intensify the men's desire to fight, and to a sexual degree. Within masculine sexuality the most significant other is the male—but it is a significance which presupposes, and is rehearsed in relation to, the female. Thus when the women stop pleading for peace and resort instead to the threat of killing themselves if the fight proceeds, it is as if the currents of sexuality and violence, circulating between the men in a way which sustains sexual difference between male and female, are suddenly switched off; the threatened self-annihilation of the women is also a breaking of the circuit. If they die, then the most necessary spectators and objects of masculine performance disappear. But also, in this *reductio ad absurdum* of masculine sexuality, men become redundant as the women threaten to perform phallic violence on themselves in the attempt to forestall male violence (Genevora to the duellists): 'The first blow given betwixt you, sheathes these swords | In one anothers bosomes' (177–8).

In an extraordinary speech masculinity is further shown to be rooted in a sexual violence performed inseparably against both men and women—(Vitelli to Clara):

> When on this point, I have pearch'd thy father's soule,
> Ile tender thee this bloody reeking hand
> Drawne forth the bowels of that murtherer:
> If thou canst love me then, I'le marry thee,
> And for thy father lost, get thee a Sonne;
> On no condition else.

(104–9)

Literally, Vitelli will kill her father and replace him with a son born of her. The object of the exercise is for Vitelli doubly to substitute himself for Clara's father: first as her husband, then as himself in, and as the father of, her son. But we can read/see much more in this speech. Again, sword and phallus substitute for each other, but in a uniquely revealing way: not only is Vitelli's violence against Clara's father erotically identified with the sexual act performed 'with' her, but the disembowelment of him is aligned with her childbirth. The hand he offers her is also the sword/phallus drawn reeking from the father's wounds. It is a supreme displacement of the rival male via the very woman whom each struggles to possess, the one as father, the other as 'lover'. Additionally, this promised disembowelment/birth will implicate Clara in Vitelli's violence without at all changing her status as its abject victim. And of course the violence against her father is as sexual as the proposed sexual intercourse 'with' Clara is violent. He fucks her and fucks him over.

This is not the first time that Vitelli has insisted to Clara that his sexual desire for her is conjoined with an equally strong desire to kill/ fuck her father (and, now, her brother):

> He, whose tongue thus gratifies the daughter,
> And sister of his enemy, weares a Sword
> To rip the father and the brother up . . .
> That my affections should promiscuously
> Dart love and hate at once, both worthily!
>
> (II. ii. 189–95)

Speaking of himself in the second person and now deploying the phallic innuendo of tongue as well as sword, Vitelli presents masculine sexuality as spectacle, again demanding and *needing* the confirmation of his masculinity by an audience even as he conceives his masculinity in terms of spontaneous, self-generating desire and autonomous honour.

The opposite of honourable antagonism between men is honourable alliance, typically affirmed in the image and name of the brother. But what are in one sense dramatically opposed kinds of relationship are in another simply alternative celebrations of masculinity. Elsewhere in Beaumont and Fletcher's work valorous males similarly oscillate between honourable antagonism and honourable alliance, in an almost erotic state of arousal. In both kinds of relationship men recognize and reinforce each other's sexuality in the triangle man–man–woman. But even as men enter into relations of honourable alliance with each other, it is with an unspoken but ever-present understanding: 'I don't desire you, I desire to be like you'. This repeated disavowal of direct desire in favour of imitative alliance is a crucial precondition of one kind of male bonding (what someone once called penises in parallel). Anticipated here is that always unstable disjunction between identification and desire upon which male bonding depends.

Strong Thighed Bargemen: The Erotics of Masculine Jealousy

Frequently in this period the representation of the man–man–woman triangle suggests that the desire which bonds men over women is as erotically invested for the men in relation to each other as for each of them in relation to the women. In Beaumont and Fletcher's *The Maid's Tragedy*, Melantius, approving his sister's marriage to his best friend, tells her: 'Sister, I joy to see you, and your choice | You look'd with my eyes when you took that man' (I. ii. 107–8). Another revealing recurrence in these plays is the way that male sexual jealousy, even as it is represented as obsessively heterosexual in its demands, produces eroticized images of the rival male which are inseparable from the denigration of the woman:

FERDINAND. . . . my imagination will carry me
  To see her in the shameful act of sin. . . .
  Happily, with some strong thigh'd bargemen;
  Or one o'th' wood-yard, that can quoit the sledge
  Or toss the bar, or else some lovely squire
  That carries coals up to her privy lodgings. . . .
                              Go to, mistress!
  'Tis not your whore's milk that shall quench my wildfire,
  But your whore's blood.
          (John Webster, *The Duchess of Malfi*, II. v. 40–9)

In *The Maid's Tragedy*, when the King becomes sexually jealous of Amintor he too evokes his rival in a way which shows that the cult of masculine honour circulating in this court is ineradicably erotic (III. i).

But should we describe this dynamic as *homo*erotic? It certainly is erotic, but is perhaps better described, following Eve Sedgwick,[21] as homosocial desire, if only, in the first instance, to avoid the easy but questionable assumption that what we witness here is the irruption of repressed homosexual desire as conceived by Freud. This seems more like an eroticism created by rather than repressed by the social bond. Even so, the question remains: why does the sexually jealous male envisage his rival so erotically? Freud argues that the man who is sexually jealous of a woman would 'not only feel pain about the woman

---

[21] *Between Men*, esp. intro. and ch. I.

he loves and hatred of the man who is his rival, but also grief about the man, whom he loves unconsciously, and hatred of the woman as his rival' ('Some Neurotic Mechanisms', x. 197–8). This may indeed sometimes be so, but, as before, the early modern period may provide grounds for some cultural distinctions within and against the psychoanalytic project.

In Jacobean drama masculine identity requires masculine ratification. At the same time, and within a heterosexual economy generally, there tends to be a profound separation between identification and desire, especially for males. Thus the male is required to identify with other males but he is not allowed to desire them; indeed, *identification with* should actually preclude *desire for*. Conversely, those whom he is supposed to desire, and always in specified ways, namely women, he is discouraged from identifying with: that would equal effeminacy; so in relation to them *desire for* precludes *identification with*.[22] *For the sexually jealous male, the separate/d objects of identification and desire—the rival man and the faithless woman—have united actually* as a distorted counterpart of the *forbidden* conjunction in the jealous subject between identification and desire. Thus his erotic imagining of the usurping male is not the eruption of repressed homosexual desire so much as the fantasized, fearful convergence of identification and desire, precipitated by an actual convergence of their respective objects.

That scenario can be distinguished from another which may nevertheless overlap and converge with it: the necessary identifications of male bonding—'I desire to be like you'—produce an intensity of admiration some of which just cannot help but transform into deviant desire for, rather than just honourable imitation of, 'man's' most significant other (i.e. man). And it occurs so easily—almost passively—requiring little more than a relinquishing of the *effort* of emulation, the erasure of '*to be like*' and the surrender to what remains: '*I desire . . . you*'; thus: 'I desire (to be like) you'. Again, we can if we like describe this second scenario as homoerotic. But it is like the first scenario in this: both kinds of eroticism are specific to male bonding, both occur within and against the very situations in which heterosexuality is most ardently pursued, and both are in part the consequence of heterosexual ardour.

To shift, as I have done in this consideration of *Love's Cure*, from the transvestite to certain wider issues of desire, the 'nature' of masculinity, sexual jealousy, and the homoerotic, is only to follow one trajectory of transvestism itself in this period: in appropriating, inverting, and

---

[22] To cite again, and from another context, John Fletcher's formulation: you cannot desire what you want to be and you cannot be what you desire (above, Ch. 12). In this scenario, incidentally, homosexuality may doubly transgress if and when desire of the male includes identification with the feminine.

substituting for masculinity, the female transvestite inevitably put masculinity itself—and sexual difference more generally—under scrutiny. Further, in the attempted containment of transvestism (*Love's Cure*) masculinity and sexual difference are put in question in a very specific way: in the containment of one hostile knowledge another is inadvertently produced; suppression of an (in)subordinate deviance discloses other, equally disturbing deviations at the heart of the dominant; erotic deviations whose repression is a condition of domination in one of its most important forms: homosocial male bonding. Finally, the transvestite challenge to masculinity and sexual difference works in terms of transgressive inversion and reinscription, not of transcendence, or the recovery of authentic selfhood. 'We [i.e. women] are as freeborn as men, have as free election, and as free spirits', says the Hic Mulier figure, *and she says it in drag.* Not then—to recall my point of departure in the previous chapter—knowing thyself, so much as knowing thy discursive formations—knowing them in the process of living but also inverting them; reinscribing oneself within, succumbing to, and demystifying them.

20 Post/modern: On the Gay Sensibility, or the Pervert's Revenge on Authenticity—Wilde, Genet, Orton, and Others

> To be really modern one should have no soul. (Wilde, 'Maxims')
>
> Will he force me to think that homosexuals have more imagination than the . . . others? No, but they are more frequently called upon to exercise it. (André Gide, *Journals*, 1931)

The Elusive Homosexual Sensibility

Separately and in different ways, Susan Sontag and George Steiner have suggested that a (or 'the') homosexual sensibility is a major influence in the formation of modern culture. In 1964 Sontag wrote that 'Jews and homosexuals are the outstanding creative minorities in contemporary urban culture. Creative, that is, in the truest sense: they are creators of sensibilities. The two pioneering forces of modern sensibility are Jewish moral seriousness and homosexual aestheticism and irony.' She seeks to substantiate this claim in the famous essay from which it is taken ('Notes on Camp', 290).

For Steiner homosexuality is if anything even more central to, and definitive of, the modern. 'Since about 1890', he believes, 'homosexuality has played a vital part in Western culture.' Whereas 'heterosexuality is the very essence of . . . classic realism', a 'radical homosexuality' figures in modernity, particularly in its self-referentiality and narcissism; indeed 'homosexuality could be construed as a creative rejection of the philosophic and conventional realism, of the *mundanity* and extroversion of classic and nineteenth century feeling'. Further, homosexuality in part made possible 'that exercise in solipsism, that remorseless mockery of philistine common sense and bourgeois realism which is modern art' ('Eros and Idiom', 115, 117, 118). Steiner's association of homosexuality with narcissism, solipsism, and the refusal of referentiality obviously suggests reservations about both modernism (as he conceives it) and the efficacy of the homosexual influence upon it,[1] and it comes as no surprise that in his most recent book he launches a strong attack on the former. Steiner now contends that two historical moments, the one epitomized in Mallarmé's 'disjunction of language from external reference', and the other in Rimbaud's 'deconstruction of the self'—*je est un autre* (I is (an)other)—splinter the foundations of the Western tradition and precipitate it into the crisis of modernity. Rimbaud would seem to be especially culpable since 'the deconstructions of semantic forms, the destabilizations of meaning, as we have known them during the past decades, derive from Rimbaud's dissolution of the self'. Compared to these two cultural moments, 'even the political revolutions and great wars in modern European history are, I would venture, of the surface' (*Real Presences*, 101, 94–6).

Steiner and Sontag are in a sense correct about the centrality of homosexuality to modern culture. But the argument of this book is that its centrality is quite otherwise than they suggest. Steiner's ludicrous generalizations stem in part from the very notion of defining cultures and history in terms of a sensibility. Even a cursory look at gay history and culture suggests that the sweep and conclusions of his argument are questionable at virtually every turn, as indeed is the very notion of a homosexual sensibility.[2]

Sontag's article at least has the virtue of tentativeness; it is in the form of notes (dedicated to Oscar Wilde), and acknowledges the difficulty of defining a sensibility, especially one as 'fugitive' as this ('Notes on Camp', 277). But still questions abound: is this sensibility transcultural, or historically rooted in the (varying) histories of the representation of homosexuality? Is it a direct expression of homosexuality, or an indirect expression of its repression and/or sublimation? Is it defined in terms of the sexuality of (say) the individual or artist who expresses or possesses it—and does that mean that no non-homosexual can possess/express it? I shall suggest that there is a sense in which the very notion of a homosexual sensibility is a contradiction in terms. I am interested in an aspect of it which exists, if at all, in terms *of* that contradiction—of a parodic critique of the essence of sensibility as conventionally understood.

Michel Foucault argues that in the modern period sex has become

---

[1] We might recall that there have been even more curious versions of this argument for the connection between homosexuality and modernity. Some in the nineteenth century thought that the modern age, bringing as it did, steam, speed, electricity, 'unnatural' city existence, and so on, encouraged decadence and degeneration, and these were in part a surrender to it. Mosse writes: 'for many physicians as well as racists, departures from the norm were caused by the surrender to modernity'; some thought the 'vibrations of modernity' led to homosexuality (*Nationalism and Sexuality*, 136).

[2] See especially Altman, *The Homosexualization of America*, ch. 5, 'The Birth of a Gay Culture'; and Bronski, *Culture-Clash, passim*.

definitive of the truth of our being (above, Chapter 14). As such, sexuality in its normative forms constitutes a 'truth' connecting inextricably with other truths and norms not explicitly sexual. This is a major reason why sexual deviance is found threatening: in deviating from normative truth and the 'nature' which underpins it, such deviance shifts and confuses the norms of truth and being throughout culture. Wilde's transgressive aesthetic simultaneously confirmed and exploited this inextricable connection between the sexual and the (apparently) non-sexual, between sexual perversion and social subversion, and does so through Wilde's own version of that connection: 'what paradox was to me in the sphere of thought, perversity became to me in the sphere of passion' (Wilde, *De Profundis*, 466).

If I had to give a single criterion of that dubious category, the homosexual sensibility, it would be this connection between perversity and paradox—if only because it suggests why that sensibility does not exist as such. As we have seen (Chapters 1 and 3), Wilde's transgressive aesthetic writes desire into a discourse of liberation inseparable from an inversion and displacement of dominant categories of subjective depth (the depth model). It is from just these categories that notions of sensibility traditionally take their meaning. Additionally for Wilde, perverse desire is not only an agency of displacement, it is partly constituted by that displacement and the transgressive aesthetic which informs it. Just as in reverse discourse the categories of subordination are turned back upon the regimes of truth which disqualify, so this 'other' sensibility is in part affirmed as an inversion and absence of sensibility's traditional criteria. Perverse desire is transvalued, socially, sexually, and aesthetically. *Dorian Gray* describes moments when 'the passion for sin, or for what the world calls sin' is utterly overwhelming

and conscience is either killed, or, if it lives at all, lives but to give rebellion its fascination, and disobedience its charm. For all sins, as theologians weary not of reminding us, are sins of disobedience. When that high spirit, that morning-star of evil, fell from heaven, it was as a rebel that he fell. (p. 210)

Law and conscience are subjected to the perverse dynamic, being made to enable and intensify the rebellion they were supposed to prevent; likewise with Wilde's transgressive aesthetic in the realm of desire and culture.

Wilde lived an anarchic and a political homosexuality simultaneously. Richard Ellmann describes him as 'conducting, in the most civilized way, an anatomy of his society, and a radical reconsideration of its ethics. . . . His greatness as a writer is partly the result of the enlargement of sympathy which he demanded for society's victims' (*Oscar Wilde*,

p. xiv). I agree, and this can stand as a cogent if incomplete description of what is meant by a political homosexuality. But Wilde also fashioned his transgressive aesthetic into a celebration of anarchic deviance, and this is yet another factor which makes it difficult to identify the sensibility involved. There is a positive desire to transgress and disrupt, and a destructiveness, even a running to one's own destruction, paradoxically creative. Though in a different way, what we have seen to be true of Gide was also true of Wilde: 'running foul of the law in his sexual life was a stimulus to thought on every subject. . . . His new sexual direction liberated his art. It also liberated his critical faculty' (Ellmann, *Oscar Wilde*, 270).

Conformity angered and bored Wilde. It is not clear which, the anger or the boredom, was thought to be the more insulting, but both were expressed as that arrogance for which he was often hated. Yeats recalls receiving a letter from Lionel Johnson 'denouncing Wilde with great bitterness'; Johnson believed that Wilde got a ' "sense of triumph and power, at every dinner-table he dominated, from the knowledge that he was guilty of that sin which, more than any other possible to man, would turn all those people against him if they but knew"' (Yeats, *Autobiographies*, 285). Maybe Johnson was paranoid; that does not stop him being correct. Gide at the end of his life remarked that Wilde only began to live after dark as it were, away from most of those who knew him (*So Be It*, 27). But the point here is that Wilde also lived in terms of the discrepancy between his 'public' and 'private' selves, and took pleasure from it—from having a sexual identity elsewhere at the same time as being socially 'here'.

The anarchic and the political, the anger and the boredom, are all active in Wilde's transgressive aesthetic, and most especially when the survival strategies of subordination—subterfuge, lying, evasion—are aesthetically transvalued into weapons of attack, but ever working obliquely through irony, ambiguity, mimicry, and impersonation.

Which brings us to camp, considered by some to be the essence of the homosexual sensibility, by others, both within and without gay culture, as virtually the opposite: the quintessence of an alienated, inadequate sensibility (above, Chapter 3). The definition of camp is as elusive as the sensibility itself, one reason being simply that there are different kinds of camp. I am concerned here with that mode of camp which undermines the categories which exclude it, and does so through parody and mimicry. But not from the outside: this kind of camp undermines the depth model of identity from inside, being a kind of parody and mimicry which hollows out from within, making depth recede into its surfaces. Rather than a direct repudiation of depth, there is a performance of it to excess: depth is undermined by being taken to and beyond its own limits. The masquerade of camp becomes less a self-concealment than a kind of attack, and untruth a virtue: many a young man, says Wilde, 'starts with the natural gift of exaggeration which, if encouraged could flourish. Unfortunately he usually comes to nothing, either falling into the bad habit of accuracy, or frequents the society of the aged and well informed' ('Decay of Lying', 294). Compare John Mitzel: 'gay people are, I have learned, in the truest sense of the word, *fabulous*. . . . The controlling agents of the status quo may know the *power* of lies; dissident sub-cultures, however, are closer to knowing their value' (cited in Bronski, *Culture-Clash*, 41).

The hollowing-out of the deep self is pure pleasure, a release from the subjective correlatives of dominant morality (normality, authenticity, etc.)—one reason why camp also mocks the *Angst*-ridden spiritual emptiness which characterizes the existential lament. Camp thereby negotiates some of the lived contradictions of subordination, simultaneously refashioning as a weapon of attack an oppressive identity inherited *as* subordination, and hollowing out dominant formations responsible for that identity in the first instance. So it is misleading to say that camp *is* the gay sensibility; camp is an invasion and subversion of other sensibilities, and works via parody, pastiche, and exaggeration.

Jack Babuscio has suggested that the homosexual experience of passing for straight leads to a 'heightened awareness and appreciation for disguise, impersonation, the projection of personality, and the distinctions to be made between instinctive and theatrical behaviour' ('Camp and the Gay Sensibility', 45). Richard Dyer remarks, in relation to Babuscio, that the gay sensibility 'holds together qualities that are elsewhere felt as antithetical: theatricality and authenticity . . . intensity and irony, a fierce assertion of extreme feeling with a deprecating sense of its absurdity' (*Heavenly Bodies*, 154). I would add that camp is often also a turning of the second set of categories—theatricality, irony, and a sense of the absurdity of extreme feeling—onto the first, such that the latter—authenticity, intensity, the fierce assertion of extreme feeling— if they remain at all, do so in a transformed state. In this respect camp, as Andrew Ross observes, anticipated many of the recent debates of sexual politics: 'in fact, camp could be seen as a much earlier, highly coded way of addressing those questions about sexual difference which have engaged non-essentialist feminists in recent years' (*No Respect*, 161).

Camp integrates this aspect of gender with aesthetics; in a sense it renders gender a question of aesthetics. Common in aesthetic involvement is the recognition that what seemed like mimetic realism is actually an effect of convention, genre, form, or some other kind of artifice. For some this is a moment of disappointment in which the real, the true, and the authentic are surrendered to, or contaminated by, the factitious and the contrived. But camp comes to life around that recognition; it is situated at the point of emergence of the artificial from the real, culture from nature—or rather when and where the real collapses into artifice, nature into culture; camp restores vitality to artifice, and vice versa, deriving the artificial from, and feeding it back into or as, the real. The reality is the pleasure of unreality. And the primacy of fantasy: as the inheritor of a religious impulse, 'modern' sexual desire seeks to universalize and naturalize itself. Camp knows and takes pleasure in the fact that desire is culturally relative, and never more so than when, in cathecting contemporary style, it mistakes itself, and the style, for the natural.

Camp is not the same as gender inversion, but it often connects with it, and with good reason. Like the cross-dressing explored in the last chapter, gender inversion remains controversial because it allegedly only inverts, rather than displaces, the gender binary. But again, in (historical) practice to invert may also be to displace. Mario Mieli quotes an unnamed gay writer: 'we [gay men] demand our "femininity", the same thing that women reject, and *at the same time* we declare that these roles are devoid of sense' (*Homosexuality and Liberation*, 46). An appropriate inversion becomes a deconstructive displacement.

So it is futile to try to define the homosexual sensibility according to the standards of conventional sensibility: first because the latter has sought to exclude the former; second because, in retaliation, the former has often worked to undermine the latter and, in the process, challenged the very nature of the aesthetic, fashioning in the process new and sometimes oppositional mutations of it. The search for the nature of the distinctively gay sensibility can be productively redirected as an exploration of the limitations of the aesthetic as conventionally understood, especially the way it is said to transcend the socio-political, and used in support of the proposition that discrimination is the essence of culture.[3] Further, rather than seeking such a sensibility in an 'inner condition', we might more usefully identify it outwardly and in relation to other strategies of survival and subversion, especially the masquerade of femininity, and the mimicry of the colonial subject. What it might be found to share with the first is a simultaneous avoidance and acting out of the ambivalence which constitutes subordination, and a pushing of

---

[3] Connecting the gay sensibility to cultural politics also invites crucial questions about whether either can operate within a reformist vision, or whether they entail a more radical vision. See Bronski, *Culture-Clash*, esp. 38–9, 197 ff., esp. 213–14.

that ambivalence to the point of transgressive insight and possibly reinscribed escape.[4] As for the colonial context, Homi Bhabha argues that here mimicry is both a strategy of colonial subjection—an appropriation, regulation, and reform of the other—and, potentially, a way of menacing colonial discourse in and through an inappropriate imitation by the native, one which reveals the normative structure of colonial control. As such, mimicry becomes, in Bhabha's memorable phrase, 'at once resemblance and menace'.[5]

Knowledge and Pleasure in Jean Genet

In so many respects utterly different from Wilde, Genet nevertheless also subverts the depth model of identity via the perverse dynamic, and perhaps more so than any other writer since Wilde. Like the latter, Genet inverts and subverts the surface/depth binary, confirming and exploiting the connections between the paradoxical and the perverse, and turning them against the regimes, heterosexual and otherwise, which outlaw the deviant. Genet, also like Wilde, produces both anarchic pleasure and subversive knowledge inseparably.

Charles Marowitz once identified a crucial characteristic of Genet's work:

In perhaps one of the most shocking hypotheses ever put forward in the drama, Genet suggests that the only thing that distinguishes the sexual pervert who masquerades as priest, king, or hero from his legitimate social counterpart, is a certain timidity. The sexual pervert lives his fantasies in private and is therefore harmless; whereas the social personages play out their roles in public. ('The Revenge of Jean Genet', 173)

This facilitates and in part constitutes the challenge of the perverse:

the highest ideal in *The Balcony* is for characters to attain that point of social definition at which others desire to impersonate them. Reality corresponds to the density of one's artifice. When a man achieves his highest reality he can serve as a fantasy for another man; and in a frightening Genetic turnabout, both then become equal. (p. 173)

They become equal because fictions of selfhood are transvalued. Genet said of himself: 'Dehumanizing myself is my own most fundamental

---

[4] On masquerade and femininity see Rivière, 'Womanliness as Masquerade'; Irigaray, *This Sex Which is Not One* (Irigaray also explores femininity in relation to mimicry); Heath, 'Joan Rivière and the Masquerade'; Modleski, 'Femininity as Mas[s]querade'; Ross, *No Respect*, ch. 5, 'Uses of Camp', esp. 161; Butler, *Gender Trouble*, esp. 46–54 (who includes a thoughtful discussion of the links between the masquerading woman and the homosexual man).

[5] 'Of Mimicry and Man', 199; see also 'Sly Civility'.

tendency' (*Our Lady*, 82). The transgressive drive in his work is not a quest for the authentic self, but almost the reverse:

The mechanism was somewhat as follows (I have used it since): to every charge brought against me, unjust though it be, from the bottom of my heart I shall answer yes. Hardly had I uttered the word—or the phrase signifying it—than I felt within me the need to become what I had been accused of being. . . . I owned to being the coward, traitor, thief and fairy they saw in me. (*The Thief's Journal*, 145)

To be sure, the characteristics of the transcendent self remain in play: to become what others saw him as being required great self-discipline 'similar to spiritual exercises'; eventually he aspires to a classical stoic independence of spirit, a kind of sainthood (p. 146). But then in *Our Lady of the Flowers* 'the gesture of solitude that makes you sufficient unto yourself' is not abstinence or retreat, but masturbation (p. 124). Inversion and substitution are intensely narcissistic; despite that—or rather because of it, since Genet also transvalues narcissism—they extend far beyond the self. Of Divine, the anti-hero/ine drag queen of *Our Lady*, it is said:

her carnal pleasures never made her fear the wrath of God, the scorn of Jesus, or the candied disgust of the Holy Virgin . . . for as soon as she recognized the presence within her of seeds of these fears (divine wrath, scorn, disgust), Divine made of her loves a god above God, Jesus, and the Holy Virgin, to whom they were submissive like everyone else. (p. 138)

Here, the figures who act as transcendent foils to a mundane inauthenticity, abjection, and subjection are themselves brought low, made to submit to what they once subjected. Notions of the freedom and autonomy of the self are at one and the same time inverted and used to pervert the ethical and metaphysical values which such a self is or was supposed to instantiate. Authentic selfhood is denied and then reconstituted in a perverse, parodic form—and then perhaps denied again, transformed from other to same and then back to a (different) other. Genet reinscribes himself within the violent hierarchies of his oppression, installing himself there relentlessly to invert and pervert them.

He writes in *Our Lady*: 'We are, after all, familiar enough with the tragedy of a certain feeling which is obliged to borrow its expression from the opposite feeling so as to escape from the myrmidons of the law. It disguises itself in the trappings of its rival' (p. 113). Such incorporation facilitates a specific kind of transgressive reinscription. As in this passage, Genet not only disguises himself in terms of the law, but internalizes the disguise. What transpires is not the sacrilege which pays testimony to the sacred (i.e. containment), but a sacrilege inscribed within the sacred. Inside the church

the [priest's] sprinkler is always moist with a tiny droplet, like Alberto's prick which is stiff in the morning and which has just pissed.

The vaults and walls of the chapel of the Virgin are white-washed, and the Virgin has an apron as blue as a sailor's collar.

Facing the faithful, the altar is neatly arranged; facing God, it is a jumble of wood in the dust and spider webs. (p. 161)

In the description of the sprinkler and the apron, and especially the altar, the internalization of law (as disguise) results in this sacrilege within reverence, an intimacy with law which can blow apart its ideological effect (revealing the hidden side of the altar)—and with a strange knowing innocence strangely inseparable from that intimacy.[6]

Orton's Black Camp

Joe Orton, so different again from Wilde or Genet, nevertheless shares their transgressive commitment to inversion and the critique of authenticity. His What the Butler Saw (1969) becomes a kind of orgy of crossdressing, gender confusion, and hierarchical inversion. It is also an angry repudiation of sexual repressiveness as enforced by the ideology of authentic, normal sexuality, now ratified by state law and the medical professions. But once again anger works through irony, parody, and pastiche, and is held together not by a unified dramatic voice but by a stylistic blankness, a kind of black camp. Here, as in his and Halliwell's notorious defacement of library books (for which they were imprisoned), and in Orton's theory of montage, there is an anticipation of that effect of pastiche which Fredric Jameson identifies as a defining criterion of the post-modern:

Pastiche is, like parody, the imitation of a peculiar or unique style, the wearing of a stylistic mask, speech in a dead language: but it is a neutral practice of mimicry, without parody's ulterior motive, without the satirical impulse, without laughter, without that still latent feeling that there exists something normal compared to which what is being imitated is rather comic. Pastiche is black parody, parody that has lost its humor. ('Postmodernism and Consumer Society', 114)

---

[6] In an elaboration of his theory of how a system is abolished only by pushing it into hyperlogic, Jean Baudrillard has spoken of how the 'masses' express 'a false fidelity to the law, an ultimately impenetrable simulation of passivity and obedience ... which in return annuls the law governing them' (In the Shadow of the Silent Majorities, 33, 46). Genet might be understood to have elaborated the potential of such a strategy and in a way which showed in advance the absurdity of its generalization in relation to the 'masses'.

The difference is that Orton's pastiche *is* comic but in a way which interrogates rather than presupposes the norm. As Jane Feuer points out, camp involves a kind of sensibility in which 'blank mimicry and a critical edge may coexist', and thereby resembles that form of postmodern parody which Linda Hutcheon defines as a 'repetition with critical distance that allows ironic signalling of difference at the very heart of similarity'.[7] Thereby camp may also, either implicitly or directly, interrogate the norm which, according to Jameson, traditional parody assumes. This is only one respect in which camp delights in the selfsame artifice which others distrust.

Orton's intention was to outrage. Had he been alive he would doubtless have been delighted at the response of the leading conservative theatre critic to *What the Butler Saw* (1969): 'Orton's terrible obsession with perversion, which is regarded as having brought his life to an end and choked his very high talent, poisons the atmosphere of the play. And what should have been a piece of gaily irresponsible nonsense becomes impregnated with evil.'[8] Perhaps Hobson spoke truer than he knew, for the play is a kind of gay non-sense:

[DR] RANCE. When Dr Prentice asked you to pose as a woman did he give a reason?
NICK. No.
RANCE. Didn't you consider his request strange?
NICK. No.
RANCE. Have you aided other men in their perverted follies?
NICK. During my last term at school I was the slave of a corporal in the Welsh Fusiliers.
RANCE. Were you never warned of the dangers inherent in such relationships?
NICK. When he was posted abroad he gave me a copy of 'The Way to Healthy Manhood'.

By insisting on the arbitrariness and narrowness of gender roles, and that they are socially ascribed rather than naturally given, Orton expresses a central motif in the sexual politics of that time. *What the Butler Saw* becomes an orgy of confused and *refused* gender identities:

GERALDINE [dressed as a boy]. I must be a boy. I like girls.
RANCE. I can't quite follow the reasoning there.
PRENTICE. Many men imagine their preference for women is, *ipso facto*, a proof of virility.

---

[7] Hutcheon is cited by Feuer in 'Reading *Dynasty*: Television and Reception Theory', 455–6.
[8] Harold Hobson, in *Christian Science Monitor*, 19 Mar. 1969, alluding to the fact that Orton was beaten to death by his lover.

Cross-dressing leads to wholesale gender confusion, while Dr Rance's precisely inappropriate assumptions about madness, the natural, and 'the order of things' discredit the claims of psychiatry:

RANCE. Were you present when Dr Prentice used this youth unnaturally?
NICK. What is unnatural?
RANCE. How disturbing the questions of the mad can be. (*To* Nick [disguised as a girl]) Suppose I made an indecent suggestion to you? If you agreed something might occur which, by and large, would be regarded as natural. If, on the other hand, I approached this child—(*he smiles at* Geraldine [disguised as a boy])—my action could result only in a gross violation of the order of things.

In the 1960s psychiatry was attacked for being a form of social policing which, with the aid of pseudo-scientific categories, mystified socially desirable behaviour as natural, and undesirable behaviour as the result of abnormal psychosexual development (a deviation from 'The Way to Healthy Manhood'). R. D. Laing wrote in *The Divided Self*:

Psychiatry can so easily be a technique of brainwashing, of inducing behaviour that is adjusted, by (preferably) non-injurious torture. . . . I would wish to emphasize that our 'normal' 'adjusted' state is too often the abdication of ecstasy, the betrayal of *our true potentialities*, that many of us are only too successful in acquiring a false self to adapt the false realities. (p. 12, my emphasis)

Orton goes further than Laing, for his plays transgress accepted norms at every point yet refuse to replace them with 'our true potentialities'; Laing is still preoccupied with the authentic self, the repressed human essence. Orton refuses that long-established kind of transgression which, in the very sincerity of its ñon-conformity, revalidates society's lapsed moral integrity. As John Milton put it centuries before: 'Men of most renowned vertu have sometimes by transgressing, most truly kept the law' (*Tetrachordon, Prose Works*, iv. 75).

A significant contemporary manifestation of that belief, and a vivid instance of how 'modern' sexuality became a surrogate religion, somewhere for an essentially religious notion of integrity to survive in a mutated and displaced form, was at the prosecution for obscenity of D. H. Lawrence's *Lady Chatterley's Lover* (1960).[9] In that trial the author was defended on the grounds that he had to transgress moral respectability in order to be moral at a deeper, more authentic level dictated by personal conscience.[10] Even the indignation of satire might

---

[9] See also Sinfield, 'Who was Afraid of Joe Orton?', 268–71.
[10] For a fuller discussion of the Chatterley trial along these lines, see my 'The Challenge of Sexuality'.

assume the same moral perspective as that of the order being challenged, or at least an alternative to it. But, as his diaries indicate, Orton's indignation was too anarchic to be recuperated in such terms. In *What the Butler Saw*, sexuality, like language, becomes decentred and therefore radically contingent: it not only escapes from, but disorientates the medical and legal attempts to define and regulate it.

Not surprisingly, Orton's anarchic irresponsibility was thought by some to go too far, not just in what he actually *did*, but in the refusal in his work to confront established morality with an earnest moral alternative. What we find instead is a kind of delinquent black camp. In the article referred to at the outset, Susan Sontag remarks that camp 'is a solvent of morality. It neutralizes moral indignation, sponsors playfulness' ('Notes on Camp', 275, 280, 290). Orton's camp is indeed constituted by playfulness and it acts as a solvent of morality—but it does this to provoke rather than disarm moral indignation. 'No first night of the sixties was more volcanic than that of *What the Butler Saw*', says Orton's biographer, John Lahr; while Stanley Baxter, who played Dr Prentice, has recalled the 'militant hate' of the audience, some of whom 'wanted to jump on the stage and kill us' (Lahr, *Prick Up Your Ears*, 333–4).

Hostile Eroticism

As a style, and even more as a politics, the transgressive reinscriptions practised by such writers have proved controversial, especially when grounded in the celebration of a perverse inauthenticity disturbingly implicated in authenticity itself, as in Genet. On the positive side there are those like Kate Millett who find in Genet's deviants a subversive inversion of dominant heterosexuality, especially its masculine component.[11] Thus inverted, these structures are shorn of their ideological legitimation; in effect the world of normality, beyond which Genet lives in exile, is ridiculed and contradicted in the very process of being imitated. Genet's femininity for instance 'is, as Sartre phrases it, a "hostile eroticism", delighted to ridicule and betray the very myth of virility it pretends to serve' (*Sexual Politics*, 18, 349). All this means that, for Millett, Genet is 'the only living male writer of first class literary gifts to have transcended the sexual myths of our era' (p. 22). Conversely, for Hans Mayer, Genet's commitment to inversion makes him deeply conservative: 'Genet's books are the exact opposite of a

---

[11] *Sexual Politics*, esp. 16–22 and ch. 8; for other feminist identifications with Genet's work see Cixous, 'Sorties', 97–8 and 255–6, and Violette Santellani's reading of a passage from Genet's *Miracle of the Rose* ('Jean Genet's *The Miracle of the Rose*', 95–7).

literature of indignation and rebellion. The author has no intention of making accusations or unmasking society. He is a true believer in the bourgeois order, not a critic.'[12] More critical still are those like Walter Heist who conclude that Genet is pervaded with fascism (cited by Mayer, *Outsiders*, 225, who dissents from the view).

Certainly there is a crucial sense in which Genet presupposes what he would challenge: 'I am steeped in an idea of property while I loot property. I recreate the absent proprietor', he says in *The Thief's Journal* (p. 129); and in a 1975 interview: 'I would like the world, and pay attention to the way I'm saying it, I would like the world not to change so that I can be against the world' (*Gay Sunshine Interviews*, 79).

There is an ambivalence in Genet which his critic always misread and his defenders often overlook. Such ambivalence often figures within transgressive reinscription, and is one reason why it rarely approximates to a straightforwardly 'correct' political attitude. Consider two kinds of ambivalent transgressive reinscription within gay culture, camp and machismo. As styles they are very different, virtual alternatives in fact. But both have been regarded as politically reprehensible, camp because allegedly insulting to women, machismo because allegedly aping the masculinity oppressive of women (lesbian and straight) and gays. Defenders of camp and machismo point out that they are parodic critiques—in the first case of what is allegedly insulted (femininity), in the second of what is allegedly aped (masculinity). Certainly both gay camp and gay machismo can and do problematize femininity and masculinity as traditionally understood. Thus Richard Dyer has argued of gay machismo that, by taking the traditional signs of masculinity and 'eroticising them in a blatantly homosexual context, much mischief is done to the security with which "men" are defined in society, and by which their power is secured' ('Getting Over the Rainbow', 61).

Throughout *Gender Trouble* Judith Butler offers—and for, rather than against, feminism—a similar defence of practices like drag, cross-dressing, and, in lesbian culture, butch/femme sexual stylization. She contests the view that these practices are 'either degrading to women, in the case of drag and cross-dressing, or an uncritical appropriation of sex-role stereotyping from within the practice of heterosexuality, especially in the case of butch/femme lesbian identities' (p. 137). Thus she reads drag as playing with a threefold distinction: anatomical sex, gender identity, and gender performance:

---

[12] *Outsiders*, 255; for a more perceptive and helpful introduction to Genet, see Adams, *The Homosexual as Hero in Contemporary Fiction*, 182–205.

If the anatomy of the performer is already distinct from the gender of the performer, and both of those are distinct from the gender of the performance, then the performance suggests a dissonance not only between sex and performance, but sex and gender, and gender and performance . . . *In imitating gender drag implicitly reveals the imitative structure of gender itself—as well as its contingency.* (p. 137)

Butler sees deviant sexualities more generally as involving this same process of denaturalizing, as parodic subversive repetitions which displace rather than consolidate heterosexual norms. The parody of deviant sex, far from presupposing and ratifying an original natural sexuality, exposes it as a fiction. Thus 'gay is to straight *not* as copy is to original, but, rather, as copy is to copy' (p. 31). Additionally, the parody encourages a 'proliferation and subversive play of gendered meaning' (p. 33). Most controversially of all, this argument has been extended to sado-masochistic sexuality which, far from ratifying the 'real' violence of society, theatricalizes and demystifies it.

In certain respects this argument replays for a post/modern politics Wilde's transgressive aesthetic and the gay (anti)sensibility which it helped inaugurate. It also resembles the strategy of the early modern female cross-dresser for whom sexual difference was not derived from natural and divine law, but produced by 'custom', that is, culture. Here then is a continuity between the early modern and the post/modern, one often overlooked when we concentrate on the differences in the way sexuality is conceptualized in the two periods. But crucial differences remain, and it was because the early modern transvestite was not conceptualized in terms of a pathological sexual subjectivity—the modern 'homosexual'—that her transgression was regarded, albeit with paranoia, as more social than sexual. The connections between gender and class were apparent enough in the early modern period, and if the transvestite was a pervert or invert it was precisely in the pre-sexological senses of these ideas; whether actually or only in the paranoid imagination of the dominant, she was regarded as upsetting the entire social domain, even when her sexual 'orientation' was not the issue.

So when it is argued today that the sexual deviant challenges sexual difference by denaturalizing it through parody, the realization of the early modern transvestite that both the deviant and the difference are effects of culture rather than nature is being revived and sophisticated. But a residual effect of the 'privatizing' of sexuality, and in particular of the construction of sexual deviance as an identity, a pathology of being, rather than a kind of behaviour in principle open to all, is that the challenge to this construction often itself remains imprisoned by the public/private dichotomy. So while the whole point of the argument, and rightly, is that when gender is understood as culture rather than nature we see that gender is implicated in all aspects of culture, in practice the argument rarely gets off the bed. As we shall see shortly, the way out of the bedroom is via the wider cultures, rather than the specific sexual acts, of transgressive reinscription—for example, the writings of Wilde, Genet, and others, the subculture from which they emerge and help to form and transform.

First there is another objection to be considered: do deviant identities and sexualities really denaturalize through theatrical parody as straightforwardly as is sometimes suggested? Leo Bersani thinks not, at least where camp and gay machismo are concerned. He concedes a potentially subversive dimension to camp, but one inseparable from a more problematic and ambivalent relation to both femininity and women:

the gay male parody of a certain femininity, which, as others have argued, may itself be an elaborate social construct, is both a way of giving vent to the hostility toward women that probably afflicts every male (and which male heterosexuals have of course expressed in infinitely nastier and more effective ways) *and* could paradoxically be thought of as helping to deconstruct that image for women themselves ... The gay male bitch desublimates and desexualizes a type of femininity glamorized by movie stars, whom he thus lovingly assassinates with his style.

Of the subversive claims for gay machismo, Bersani is even more sceptical, since he regards it as involving not a parodic repudiation of straight machismo, but a profound respect for it. But, crucially, and this reminds us of Genet, Bersani locates a challenge inseparable from a certain ambivalence: if gay males threaten male heterosexual identity, it is not because they offer a detached parody of that identity, but rather because 'from within their nearly mad identification with it, *they never cease to feel the appeal of its being violated*' ('Is the Rectum a Grave?', 208–9, his emphasis). Bersani arrives at this position because he sees gay male sexuality as enacting insights into sexuality *per se* which heterosexual culture has to repress ruthlessly (above, Chapter 17).

The cultural dynamics of transgressive reinscription suggest how both positions are correct: identification with, and desire *for*, may coexist with parodic subversion *of*, since a culture is not reducible to the specific desires of the individuals comprising it—desires which anyway differ considerably—and even less to the 'truth' of desire itself. Gay culture is in part constituted by a self-reflexive, ironic representation of desire itself, gay and straight, and of the objects of desire, again both gay and straight. This is especially so of its involvement with masculinity. In one and the same gay milieu one is likely to encounter identification with, desire for, and parodies of masculinity. Among numerous other things, gay *subcultures* (as opposed to the illusory 'truth' of a unitary homosexual *desire*) include all three, and sometimes indistinguishably. And if those subcultures discredit any notion of an essential or unitary gay desire, they also constitute a crucial enabling condition of transgressive reinscription. More than that, they help constitute it. This is why transgressive reinscription should not be understood in terms of discrete transgressive acts which 'succeed' or 'fail' in some immediate sense. Reinscription is an oppositional practice which is also a perspective and language (sensibility?) constantly interpreting and re-presenting all sections of a culture including its dominant and subordinate fractions, its conventional (e.g. heterosexual) as well as deviant (e.g. homosexual) identities. Butler remarks the importance of *repetition* in the process of resistance and transformation: 'The task is . . . to repeat and, through a radical proliferation of gender, to *displace* the very gender norms that enable the repetition itself' (*Gender Trouble*, 148). Certainly, but that displacement can only occur if it is also a struggle in and for representation—specifically, the representation of the repetition *as* re-presentation/inversion/displacement of the norm. In short, the displacing repetition still has to be culturally construed as such. In the process the transgression and the norm are both re-presented. And this, far from being a containment (transgression presupposing and thereby ratifying the norm it contravenes), is one condition of the norm's undoing.

Transgressive reinscription will always remain controversial, if only because it raises such disturbing questions about desire itself, making it profoundly social and thereby asking equally disturbing questions about culture, representation, and social process. This is even more so when, as I have argued with homosexuality, so many dimensions of a culture have been displaced and/or condensed into the identity of the transgressor. But then there is no transgression from the position of the subordinate that is not controversial; it is a virtually inevitable consequence of the disempowered mounting a challenge at all.

Thinking Transgressive Reinscription

Consider two similarities, the first between two post-structuralists whose work is in most other respects incompatible, the second between post-structuralism and the post/modern. This is Foucault:

Rules are empty in themselves, violent and unfinalized; they are impersonal and can be bent to any purpose. The successes of history belong to those who are capable of seizing these rules, to replace those who had used them, *to disguise*

themselves so as to pervert them, invert their meaning, and redirect them
against those who had initially imposed them . . . so as to overcome the rulers
through their own rules. (*Language, Counter-Memory, Practice,* 151, my
emphasis)

Elsewhere he writes:

There are no relations of power without resistances; the latter are all the more
real and effective because they are formed right at the point where relations of
power are exercised; resistance to power does not have to come from elsewhere
to be real, nor is it inexorably frustrated through being the compatriot of
power. It exists all the more by being in the same place as power. (*Power/*
Knowledge, 142)

Now compare Foucault with Derrida:

Our discourse irreducibly belongs to the system of metaphysical oppositions.
The break with this structure of belonging can be announced only through a
certain organisation, a certain *strategic* arrangement which, within the field of
metaphysical opposition, uses the strengths of the field to turn its own
stratagems against it, producing a force of dislocation that spreads itself
throughout the entire system, fissuring it in every direction and thoroughly
delimiting it. (*Writing and Difference,* 20)

And then both Foucault and Derrida with Baudrillard:

a system is abolished only by pushing it into hyperlogic, by forcing it into an
excessive practice which is equivalent to a brutal amortization . . .
     A parody and a paradox: it is by their very inertia in the ways of the social
laid out for them that the masses go beyond its logic and its limits, and destroy
its whole edifice. A destructive hypersimulation, a destructive hyperconformity
. . . that has all the appearance of a victorious challenge—no one can measure
the strength of this challenge . . '.
     There lies the genuine stake today, in this underhand, inescapable confronta-
tion between the silent majority and the social imposed on them, in this
hypersimulation reduplicating simulation and exterminating it according to its
own logic—not in any class struggle nor in the molecular hodge-podge of
desire-breaching minorities. This revolution . . . proceeds by inertia, and not
from a new and joyous negativity. (*In the Shadow of the Silent Majorities,*
46–7, 47–8, 49)

Transgressive reinscription: a *turning back* upon something and a
perverting of it typically if not exclusively through inversion and
displacement. The idea seems strange: is not transgression a liberation
from, a moving beyond; a breaking out, perhaps even a progression? As
we saw in relation to Gide, even in a secularized philosophy of
transgression, metaphors of transcendence abound. In comparison, the

idea of turning back upon, or into, seems regressive—literally reaction-ary. But transgressive reinscription appropriates reaction for resistance, thereby substituting agency for autonomy.

The early modern transvestite and the post/modern gay (anti)sensibility suggest some of the ways in which transgressive re-inscriptions have been around for much longer than post-modernism has been fashionable.[13] There are of course others: such reinscription has worked via minimalist perversion—for instance, the complete defacement via minimum change as in the street graffito which blackens one tooth of the billboard toothpaste ad, or the MLA panel paper: 'A thing of beauty is a boy forever'—a difference of barely more (or less) than a single inverted letter). Then there have been the more elaborate perversions which parody the sophistication of high art—Joe Orton's and Kenneth Halliwell's defacing of library books, Duchamp's mous-tache on *Mona Lisa*.

A principal medium of transgressive reinscription is fantasy—but again, not the fantasy of transcendence so much as the inherently perverse, transgressive reordering of fantasy's conventional opposite, the mundane. Rosemary Jackson is surely right to remind us that 'fantasy is not . . . transcendental. It has to do with inverting elements of this world, re-combining its constitutive features.' Fantastic literature 'does not introduce novelty, so much as uncover all that needs to remain hidden if the world is to be comfortably "known" . . . As the term "paraxis" has already suggested, fantasy lies alongside the axis of the real . . . This area, according to Freud, is one of concealed desire' (*Fantasy*, 8, 65; see also p. 78). Jackson quotes Freud's view that something has to be added to what is novel and unfamiliar to make it uncanny; this something is 'nothing new or alien, but something which is familiar and old—established in the mind and become alienated from it through the process of repression' (p. 66).

Fantasy may itself be a kind of transgressive reinscription, one presupposing a radical impurity in all identity, not excluding the transgressor's. It knows too the impurity of transgressive desire, and most of all perhaps the impurity of dominant forms of identity, be they white, heterosexual, whatever. The very impurity which the radical humanist seeks to transcend, only despairingly to rediscover at the very

---

[13] If transgressive reinscription emerges now as a dimension of the post/modern, it need not be contained by it, either historically or politically. Fredric Jameson for one speaks of using a kind of reinscription *against* post-modernism, of an attempt to undo it 'homeopathically' by its own methods—'to work at dissolving pastiche by using all the instruments of pastiche itself and to reconquer some genuine historical sense by using the instruments of what I have called substitutes for history' ('Regarding Postmodernism', 19).

centre of his or her being—this impurity, for the fantasies of transgressive reinscription, is not the ground of its failure but the material upon which it works. This is partly the inevitable consequence of gender being socially constructed. As many have observed, the recognition that gender is so constructed implies that it can be altered. What is less often conceded or, if conceded, considered—Bersani being a significant exception—is that if gender is socially constituted *so too is desire*. Desire is informed by the same oppressive constructions of gender that we would willingly dispense with. Desire is of its 'nature' saturated by the social. It is just this which allows subversive potential to parodic repetition but which also means that the parody will typically be inflected with the ambivalence I have described and, partly because of that ambivalence, oscillate between the political and the anarchic.

To liberate desire from oppression is not—could never be—a matter of resuming or regaining a desire/subjectivity as it existed prior to discrimination. If oppression is imagined as a distortion of the self, then the lifting of oppression might be imagined to result in the self resuming its natural undistorted form. But, even assuming, first, that the oppression has indeed been lifted, second, that we can speak of, and know, a time when that desire was ever free, and third, that we can speak meaningfully of a 'natural' or a 'liberated' desire (and my argument questions all three assumptions), even assuming all this, *liberated desire would still always be different from its pre-oppression counterpart*. It will bear the history of that oppression, not necessarily as that which disables desire (though it may), but as desire itself. All desire bears its histories, the desires of the exploited and the repressed no less than the desires of those who exploit and repress. But differently in each case. This is the subject of the next and final chapter. The proposition that the history of sexual oppression will always inhere in the sexual desire of the oppressed, most powerfully in the form of self-oppression, confesses to tragedy. There is truth in that, also in the proposition that in Western culture the 'tragic vision' has been one of the most powerful means of containing and sublimating desire. But never completely: in turning back upon his or her own desire the deviant knows how to read the history within it. Included there is a history of heterosexuality hardly known to itself.

PART 9

Beyond Sexual Difference

21 *Desire and Difference*

In Chapter 17 I considered how homosexuality has been construed within theories of sexual difference. Beholden to an anatomically derived, heterosexually structured, and all-embracing dualism, such theories could only conceive of homosexuality as a disavowal of that very difference which is assumed to be fundamental to social, psychic, and sexual organization. At the same time their insistence on otherness was found to be inseparable from a fear and disavowal of the same, or the proximate. Further, one after another these theories either over-looked or actively disallowed the erotics of other kinds of difference; as Mandy Merck observes, in such theories 'no non-genital differences (of race, class, age, etc) can signify such total Otherness, no genitally similar object can be legitimately eroticised' (Merck, 'Difference and its Discontents', 5–6). But of course such differences have always been erotically invested, not least in lesbian and gay cultures.

So perhaps then we should displace sexual difference by cultural difference? This could not exactly be a straight substitution: to attempt that would involve something like a category mistake. The suggestion to be explored is rather that to think difference culturally rather than sexually might be both more illuminating and more liberating. Attractive as that proposition has seemed in recent years, the form in which it has been pursued is fraught with difficulties. Most significantly, an ahistorical, largely theoretical, emphasis on cultural difference remains limited. As Ania Loomba puts it, in relation to colonialist studies, 'the neglect of histories surrounding native insubordination either devalues or romanticises the latter, or worse, tends to read colonised subjects through linguistic or psychoanalytic theories which, for some of us at least, remain suspiciously and problematically shot through with ethnocentric assumptions whose transfer to all subalterns is unacceptable' ('Overworlding', cited from manuscript).

Utopian Differences

No consideration of cultural and/or racial difference should ever neglect the sheer negativity, evil, and inferiority with which 'the other' has been conceived throughout history. In the shadow of that history there is all the more to appreciate about the way progressive movements in our time have turned things around, and begun positively to identify the difference of the other: 'the emphasis on discontinuity, the celebration of difference and heterogeneity, and the assertion of plurality as opposed to reductive unities—these ideas have animated almost an entire generation of literary and cultural critics' (Mohanty, 'Us and Them', 56–7). Such critics have attempted to conceive or represent the other in a way which does not replicate the repression and subjugation inherent in the traditional ways of so doing (p. 58). Just one relevant instance is Roland Barthes's celebration of difference, so much difference in fact, as eventually to subvert repression itself, producing a concept of desire wherein there would be, for instance, not homosexuality but homo-sexualit*ies* 'whose plural will baffle any constituted, centred discourse' (*Roland Barthes*, 69). Far from being an endorsement of discrimination, an excess of difference would disarticulate its very terms.

The instance of homosexuality is not incidental here since 'perverse' desire figures centrally in Barthes's influential theories of difference and textuality. Like Wilde, Gide, and others, Barthes uses perverse desire to animate and inform his aesthetic and linguistic theories, and it is in terms of language and art that such strategies would in part operate. In his inaugural lecture he imagines a utopian plurality of languages on which we would draw '*according to the truth of desire*':

This freedom is a luxury which every society should afford its citizens: as many languages as there are desires—a utopian proposition in that no society is yet ready to admit the plurality of desire. That a language, whatever it be, not repress another; that the subject may know without remorse, without repression, the bliss of having at his disposal two kinds of language; that he may speak this or that, according to his perversions, not according to the Law. (*Selected Writings*, 467)

From within such a perspective sexuality comes to be understood relationally—not as the relations within sexual difference, but the relations between the sexual and the non-sexual as these have been both imagined and as they may now be radically envisioned. To recover more for the domain of the non-sexual is related to a progressive sexual politics. But the aim now is not necessarily to liberate sexuality (the sexual drive), but to eroticize the social while at the same time releasing it from the grip of sexuality especially as manifested in the ideology of sexual difference. Such theories have been plausibly criticized for their romantic and Utopian strains, also for the way they echo and sometimes invoke a post-Freudian version of the polymorphous perverse. But again, cultural context makes the crucial difference: the appropriation of the romantic, the utopian, and the polymorphous for what has hitherto been marginal, and both demonized and repressed by the centre, and internalized as such at the margins, has quite different effects and implications from, say, a more general (post/modern?) theory that 'anything goes anywhere'. For one thing Barthes's perverse perspective on difference foregrounds a different history, one wherein there is no simple privileging of the marginal: the paradoxically perverse interrelationship between centre and margins, whereby the marginal returns to the centre in a way which disarticulates the centre/margin binary itself, is signified, in this instance, by Barthes inaugurating his professorship with a lecture on the significance of perversity *vis-à-vis* language.

Barthes's vision is sometimes aligned with the post/modern. 'Post-modern knowledge', says Jean-François Lyotard, 'refines our sensibility to difference and reinforces our ability to tolerate the incommensurable' (*Postmodern Condition*, p. xxv). This is the urbane version of how to relate to the 'other'; it is what post/modernists aspire to in contrast to the negative, paranoid, fearful way of relating to the other which produces (for instance) misogyny, homophobia, racism, and xenophobia. And as the antidote to such things it is devoutly to be wished. Except that already it is not quite that simple, since the post-modern sophisticate is also the *critic* of these other, negative ways of relating to the other; he or she is the one who diagnoses their social and psychic economies. In the process the misogynist, the racist, and the homophobe, locked into a negative fear of their own others, have *as such* become the negative others of the post-modern. Perhaps it could not be otherwise, not different. I only mean to preface this discussion of cultural difference with an awkward question: in the world we have, is it possible for us—any of us—*not* to have at least some inferior others? It is a question that needs to be asked now that, in theoretical terms, the affirmation of difference has become almost a new orthodoxy. Mohanty's warning that his celebration may involve a sentimental charity concealing a more fundamental indifference is timely.[1] So too is Homi Bhabha's scepticism about the way cultural theory uses the 'Other' to deconstruct 'the epistemological "edge" of the West'; the problem being that 'the "Other" is cited, quoted, framed, illuminated, encased in the shot-reverse-shot strategy of a serial enlightenment' while at the same time losing 'its power to signify, to negate, to initiate its

---

[1] Mohanty goes on to argue that instead of sentimentally or vaguely celebrating cultural difference, we should search for that which unites us. In this respect he argues for a conception 'of *agency* as a basic capacity which is shared by all humans *across cultures*. And in understanding the divide between "us" and "them", it is this common space we all share that needs to be elaborated and defined' ('Us and Them', 71).

"desire", to split its "sign" of identity, to establish its own institutional and oppositional discourse'. Even as otherness is being affirmed it is also being foreclosed ('The Commitment to Theory', 16).

Interestingly, homosexuality has hardly ever been rehabilitated as a positive difference within and by those heterosexual discourses which have hitherto constructed it as negative other. Progressives would willingly remove some of the stigma from homosexuality, and have often acknowledged the homosexual component within the heterosexually identified. But this is typically the at once honest and evasive acknowledgement of a troubling presence/absence. Put bluntly, to be identified positively, homosexuality usually has to be dissolved into the androgynous.[2] Or, alternatively, homosexuality might be called upon to loosen the rigid gender identities within heterosexuality: men are permitted a 'feminine' component and (though less often) women a 'masculine' one. But such acknowledgements of the 'other' gender usually make for a fuller, more rounded, heterosexual identity. Hélène Cixous is an exception in this respect, and it is interesting that she becomes so by almost reversing the psychoanalytically inspired account of homosexuality as involving a fear of difference/desire of the same. Even though homosexuality *as such* remains muted, subsumed into an 'other bisexuality', it is here nevertheless explicitly and exceptionally identified as a *creative* otherness:

This does not mean that in order to create you must be homosexual. But there is no *invention* possible, whether it be philosophical or poetic, without the presence in the inventing subject of an abundance of the other, of the diverse ... there is no invention of other I's, no poetry, no fiction without a certain homosexuality (interplay therefore of bisexuality) making in me a crystallized work of my ultra subjectivities. (Marks and de Courtivron (eds.), *New French Feminisms*, 97)

Desiring the Different

The rarity of such positive conceptions of homosexuality within, or in relation to, otherness, is the more significant given that homosexuals have been among those who have literally (rather than metaphorically or theoretically) embraced the cultural and racial difference of the 'other'.

Kobena Mercer and Isaac Julien are right to emphasize that the complexity which arises at the junction of race and sexuality is something which 'some people simply *don't want to talk* about'.[3] Of

---

[2] See above, Ch. 11 n. 10.
[3] Mercer and Julien, 'Race, Sexuality and Black Masculinity', 99.

the convergence of homosexuality and race, fewer still are prepared to speak, and those who have spoken have often done so in racist and/or homophobic terms—and that, as Mercer and Julien show, includes people in both the black and gay communities.

A constructive if brief discussion of the problematic convergence of race and homosexuality occurs in Dennis Altman's now twenty-year-old pioneering study, *Homosexual Oppression and Liberation*. Altman discerns links between the oppression of blacks and of homosexuals, in the way that both are vulnerable to an internalization of their oppression. He remarks that in America especially there has always been a strong cross-racial homosexual attraction less restrained by social barriers than its heterosexual counterpart; 'the very furtiveness and outlaw status of the gayworld has led to its greater integration across colour lines'. Yet he refuses to sentimentalize the connection, recognizing that white homosexuals are not necessarily less racist than white heterosexuals,[4] and that the cross-racial attraction in question may, for both parties, be a consequence, rather than a repudiation, of their oppression. He suggests that blacks have been 'at one and the same time both more accepting of and more hostile towards homosexuality', and that the hostility has often been extreme—as in the case of Eldridge Cleaver's notorious attack on James Baldwin (Altman, *Homosexual Oppression*, esp. 192–207). Despite this difficult history, crucial alliances have occurred. The gay movement learned greatly from black analysis and black political experience, and it was possible in 1970 for Huey Newton, joint founder of the Black Panther Party, to welcome alliance with the women's and gay movements. In this he made the Black Panthers the first significant radical group to recognize gay liberation as a valid political movement, and did so in terms which provoked hostility from some in his own party: 'maybe I'm injecting some of my prejudices by saying that "even a homosexual can be revolutionary". Quite the contrary, maybe a homosexual could be the most revolutionary' (Newton, quoted in Altman, *Homosexual Oppression*, 204; see also Genet in Leyland, *Gay Sunshine Interviews*).

The relevance of this obscure, marginal history where race and homosexuality converge is once again being recognized. Jonathan Rutherford finds something strangely relevant for cultural politics in Britain in the 1990s in the cross-racial identifications of Lawrence of Arabia some seventy years before: 'His identification with the Arabs and their culture displaced the centered position of his identity as a

---

[4] The racism of white gay male culture is both acknowledged and challenged by the contributors to Smith (ed.), *Black Men/White Men*; see especially Thom Beame's interview with Mike Smith, founder of BWMT (Black and White Men Together), and DeMarco, 'Gay Racism'.

white man. The story is a compelling image of a postmodern world that is challenging so many of our own certainties and our cultural, sexual and political identities' (*Identity*, 9). Rutherford cites Lawrence's own remark in *The Seven Pillars of Wisdom* to the effect that this identification 'quitted me of my English self, and let me look at the West and its conventions with new eyes: they destroyed it all for me'.[5] Significantly Rutherford does not mention Lawrence's homosexuality although this is, as Kaja Silverman shows, a crucial determinant in all this. Silverman explores the way Lawrence's homosexuality promotes an erotic identification which is itself crucial for his psychic participation in Arab nationalism; of how, in effect, he discovered himself within the Other. More generally the case of T. E. Lawrence becomes an exemplary reminder that we are obliged 'to approach history always through the refractions of desire and identification, and to read race and class insistently in relation to sexuality' (*White Skin, Brown Masks*, 4, 10, 12).

This is especially so with writers like Barthes and Genet, and Wilde and Gide before them, who, far from subordinating their outlawed sexuality to their radical politics or radical aesthetics, actively inform them with it. Of course, there were and are risks in doing that. From the vantage point of so-called post-liberation, we know only too well the political blindnesses of sexual desire, and how disastrous it can be to make sexuality the prime mover of a political vision. That holds true in principle for any sexuality. But, significantly, this is rarely if ever what those writers advocated. Arguably the blinder kinds of sexual radicalism, wherein sexuality is made the prime political mover, have tended to be mainly heterosexual, and in the case of Wilhelm Reich, overtly homophobic.[6] What we learn from Wilde, Gide, Barthes, and others is that a conventionally understood politics which ignores sexual desire will quite possibly be as disastrous as one which makes that desire the prime mover—even, or especially, in the age of so-called post-liberation. But also, it is not exactly that they bring sexuality to politics (it was always already there); rather deviant desire brings with it a different kind of political knowledge, and hence inflects both desire and politics differently.

---

[5] But Lawrence adds, significantly, 'I could not sincerely take on the Arab skin: it was an affectation only . . . I had dropped one form and not taken on the other . . . Sometimes these selves would converse in the void; and then madness was very near, as I believe it would be near the man who could see things through the veils at once of two customs, two educations, two environments' (*Seven Pillars*, 10).

[6] See esp. Weeks, *Sexuality and its Discontents*, 160–70.

Desire and Strangeness

In 1920 Gide recalls walking the streets of Biskra with Dr Bourget of Lausanne. The latter does not like what he sees: ' "Young men ought to be brought here to give them a horror of debauchery" exclaimed the worthy man, bursting with disgust.' Gide's response nicely if unawares repudiates the sexual-difference view of homosexuality as a solipsistic refusal of the other: 'how little he knew of the human heart!—of mine at any rate . . . Some people fall in love with what is like them; others with what is different. I am among the latter. Strangeness solicits me as much as familiarity repels' (*If It Die*, 253). Seventy years on Michael Carson, writing of his own homosexual desire for the racially other, expresses a similar sentiment though now with a revealing, probably necessary, and certainly crucial distinction: 'I have always been sexually attracted to foreigners. *Foreignness for me provided a difference that moved me in a way that sexual difference never did*' ('Home and Abroad', 44, my emphasis).

But perhaps this celebration of the exotic cultural/racial other is merely the counterpart of the racist's demonizing of the other? Very possibly, and a remark of Michael Carson's explaining what it was that took him abroad in search of the other shows how the celebration may share the stereotypes of the demonized:

what I lacked was a foreign accent, almond eyes, straight or springy black hair, a black skin, a muscular physique, a mind full of difficult alphabets, a sense of rhythm, a pitiful history of slavery and oppression, and a massive member— though not necessarily in that order. ('Home and Abroad', 44)

But Carson is also suggesting how the fantasized desire for the 'other' actually begins at home as a domestic projection; how fantasy is ineradicably social and, as such, susceptibility to stereotypes of all kinds, including racial and racist ones; how fantasy of and for the other exemplifies the mobilities of desire and identification. And that certain lack at the heart of both desire and identification: what Carson actually finds in twenty years abroad is some oppressive sexual mores epitomized in the loveless fuck over the bonnet of a Chevy Impala. And his article is about the corollary of discovering that the other begins at home, namely disenchantment: 'almost twenty years later I am not convinced that sexual love between men exists in places like Saudi Arabia' (p. 45). Gide's experience, elsewhere and seventy years earlier, was very different, but, as we shall see, he too experiences the desire of the other as finally about disenchantment. Perhaps then, and in a way which recalls Freud, Carson and Gide are also writing about the strange impossibility of desire? Whether their accounts confirm, coincide with, or can substitute for the psychoanalytic account of desire as lack is hard to say. But Gide's account especially does suggest how the vision of desire as loss is strangely inseparable from both the blindness of desire and its capacity to know more than it wants.

Taking Boys Home

I began this book with Gide's chance encounter with Wilde in Algiers and, through Wilde, that momentous sexual encounter with Mohammed which profoundly changes Gide's life and profoundly influences his art. I end it by returning to those encounters. On that same visit to Algiers Gide befriends another Arab boy, Athman, and determines that he should accompany him when he returns to Paris. Gide's mother, aided by others, fiercely resists the proposal; with unprecedented tenacity Gide rebels against his mother but eventually loses the battle. Gide contends that he was virtually blackmailed into leaving Athman behind. There is a memorable description of their parting:

When, on the third morning I looked for Athman to say goodbye to him, he was nowhere to be found and I had to leave without seeing him again. I could not understand his absence; but suddenly, as I sat in the speeding train, a long way already from El Katara, I caught sight of his white burnous on the banks of the *oued*. He was sitting there with his head in his hands; he did not rise when the train passed; he made no movement; he did not give a glance at the signs I made him; and for a long time as the train was carrying me away, I watched his little motionless, grief-stricken figure, lost in the desert, an image of my own despair. (*If It Die*, 296)

Gide had tried to persuade his mother, as he had persuaded himself, that bringing Athman to Paris was a 'moral rescue', a question of the salvation of a boy through adoption. Even so his mother was appalled; she thought 'that the desert and solitude had turned my brain' (p. 293). She told him that he would cover himself with ridicule by bringing the boy back. After much argument Gide received a letter from a trusted household servant, Marie, who 'swore she would leave the house on the day my "negro" came into it. What would become of mamma without Marie? I gave in; I had to' (p. 294).[7]

Epitomized in this struggle over Athman, and especially in Gide's

---

[7] Delay (*André Gide*, 404) suggests the arrest and trial of Wilde was also a factor, Gide now fearing the possibility of scandal if he took Athman to Paris. Delay also cites an unpublished letter of 6 Mar. 1895 where Gide says: 'My best to Marie—prepare Pauline for the idea of seeing a Negro near her' (p. 404). Although he gave in on this occasion, four years later Athman did go to Paris.

correspondence with his mother,[8] is a hesitant yet certain knowledge of how sexual discrimination relates inextricably to other kinds of discrimination. In this one episode we find interconnections with race, class, colonialism, and (cultural) imperialism, and in ironic, domestic, tragically intricate ways: witness Gide finally capitulating to the class, racial, and cultural prejudices of his own culture, *as voiced through his mother, who in turn speaks through her servant.* Discrimination descends through a hierarchy of the subordinate. Or, more accurately, *hierarchies,* including those of class, race, and gender, and within each of which each subject is situated differently. Discrimination works through the asymmetry of subject positioning, and the plurality of hierarchies, as well as the brute fact of inequality institutionalized in hierarchy itself. That is partly what it means to speak of the interconnections of race, class, and gender. It suggests too why establishing personal culpability is not the issue. But since Gide has been criticized in this respect it is something which needs to be addressed. In his personal relationships with Athman, and his political stance on colonial oppression, Gide could claim to have said and done more than most at that time. *Travels in the Congo* records his first-hand encounters with the brutalities of French colonialism. In an entry for October 1925 he states his determination to find out their full extent, and to speak out against them (*Travels,* 60). One of his biographers, Justin O'Brien, says Gide's awakening to social consciousness began here, when he saw the people of the Congo exploited, beaten, and killed by whites intent on quick profits (*Portrait,* 321). On his return to France Gide succeeded in publicizing the injustices he had witnessed, with some effect at government level. His later siding with communism was undoubtedly influenced by this journey.[9]

Against that consider the following despicable episode which occurred during that same visit. It concerned Lord Alfred Douglas who was on this occasion accompanied by Gide (but not Wilde, who had returned to England) and a boy called Ali with whom, according to Gide, Douglas was in love. On discovering that Ali was also having an affair with a prostitute, Meriem, Douglas horse-whipped him: 'his howls created a tumult among the people in the hotel'. Gide, who disliked Douglas, adds: 'I heard this uproar, but considered it wiser not to intervene, and remained shut up in my room' (*If It Die,* 291).

Gide's account is at once critical and complicit and in a way inviting reflection. In the escape from sexual oppression and sexual repression

[8] Delay cites several of the unpublished letters in ch. 42, 'Open Rebellion'.
[9] Others play down Gide's new-found political awareness; Albert Guerard remarks that his move to communism was 'indirect and hesitant' (*André Gide,* 25–6).

individuals have often, like Gide, crossed divisions of class and race. Potentially, both the experience of repression in their own culture, and the experience of cultural difference on the other side of the divides they cross, contribute to a critique of repression which includes, but also goes beyond, its sexual forms. An identification consequent on a prior dislocation can make for a creative, empathetic partiality which is then the basis of a further identification and understanding of other kinds of discrimination. I have shown how this is true of both Wilde and Gide. At the same time they remained, as we all remain, implicated in other kinds of discrimination of which they and we, originally and subsequently, are the agents rather than the victims, or maybe both agents and victims. If Douglas's brutality epitomizes racial, cultural, and sexual domination in its most callously direct form, Gide's self-description of remaining in the security of his room, considering it wiser not to intervene, becomes a resonant image of the hesitant complicities which most kinds of brutality and exploitation presuppose and in which most of us are implicated.[10]

So desire for, and identification with, the cultural and racial other brings with it a complicated history. Bronski, discussing the romanticizing of the non-Anglo by Edward Carpenter and others, declares: 'the English fascination with the non-Anglo—and therefore more "primitive" and "natural"—cultures . . . was also based in and inseparable from deeply rooted standards of white British racism and political and cultural imperialism' (*Culture-Clash*, 26–7; see also p. 15 and Bakshi, 'Homosexuality and Orientalism'). Edward Said's pioneering *Orientalism* offered a searching analysis of this phenomenon. With Gide and many others in mind, Said observes that virtually no European writer who wrote on or travelled to the Orient in the period after 1800 exempted himself or herself from a quest for sexual experience unobtainable in Europe:

What they looked for often—correctly I think—was a different type of sexuality, perhaps more libertine and less guilt-ridden; but even that quest, if repeated by enough people, could (and did) become as regulated and uniform as learning itself. In time 'Oriental sex' was as standard a commodity as any other available in the mass culture. (p. 190)

---

[10] More vindictively, there are those who, even as they suffer or flee from one kind of discrimination, become agents of others in twisted proportion to the intensity of the one (or more) being fled. Mosse describes the case of Benedict Friedländer, who defended homosexuality as manly, respectable, and necessary to any well-functioning army, and who also believed the homosexual was especially capable of 'transcending' sexuality. But Friedländer, himself a Jew, also used anti-Semitic arguments in defence of homosexuality, arguing that the attack on homosexuals was led by Jews 'determined to undermine Aryan virility and self awareness'. Mosse's comment is briskly apposite: 'the spectacle of one outsider attempting to buy his entrance ticket to society at the expense of another is common enough' (*Nationalism and Sexuality*, 41).

What makes the situation especially difficult in the case of homosexuality is that there are those who arm their homophobia by ignoring the first dimension described above—an exile which generates critique—insisting only on the second—the exile who flees one kind of discrimination only to reproduce others, and who is seen to do so in virtue of the alleged 'predatory' nature of the homosexual desire, now quintessentially defined as a desire to exploit the disadvantaged.

Decentring the Self in the Desire for the Other

For homosexuals more than most, the search for sexual freedom in the realm of the foreign has been inseparable from a repudiation of the 'Western' culture responsible for their repression and oppression. For some, as indeed for T. E. Lawrence, this entailed not just the rejection of a repressive social order, but a disidentification from it requiring nothing less than the relinquishing of the self as hitherto constituted and inhabited by that order. In other words, precisely because of the Western integration of subjectivity and sexuality, deviant desire becomes also a refusal of certain kinds of subjectivity. Of Pasolini's 'growing passion for the Third World' Enzo Siciliano says: 'He had the idea that "Negritude . . . will be the way". One might say that in him an old cultural dream—exoticism—donned progressive clothes. And it was true—progressivism was followed closely in his heart by the decadent enigmas of forgetfulness and oblivion' (*Pasolini*, 263, 265). As so often, 'decadent' is used here in a way evasive of what it gestures towards. But the connection of transgressive desire with forgetfulness and oblivion is important and follows in a long tradition: religious, mystical, or romantic or some combination of all these. It suggests too why the other of sexual fantasy may be stereotypical or two-dimensional in a way somehow at odds with the intensity and density of the desire which constructs it. It also becomes an experience which indirectly registers the resilience of the individual's own immediate cultural past: forgetfulness and oblivion are the means of its escape, but become so in a way which register its continuing presence. The case of Gide is once again exemplary. I remarked in Chapter 1 his attraction to African landscapes as places where consciousness surrenders. At the very end of his life, writing again of the importance of how his experience as a homosexual had pushed him along the path of revolt, and recalling joyfully one of his lovers, Mala, Gide adds:

My most perfect memories of sensual delight are those enveloped in a landscape which absorbs it and in which I seem to be swallowed up. In the one I have just evoked of those transports with Mala, it is not only the beautiful swooning body of the child I see again, but the whole mysterious and fearful surrounding of the equatorial forest. (*So Be It*, 42, 126–7)

Such experiences of sexual liberation bear witness to the socially constructed 'nature' of identity with respect both to its contingency and its resilience: on the one hand the self can be and is experienced as radically different in the space of the other; on the other hand if the extinction of self is the precondition of passing into the ecstasy with and through the other, it is an extinction which has to be replayed over and again as a *constitutive part of sexual ecstasy itself*. And if, as so often, ecstasy obliterates the specificity of the landscape which simultaneously enables and absorbs it, this is not only because ecstasy is of its nature blind; it is also because what we repudiate remains with us as partial blindness to what we embrace in its stead.

Those of Gide's travel journals published as *Amyntas* are even more revealing of this process whereby loss of self becomes a discovery of self; both selves, the centred and the dispersed, being kept alive, both being necessary for the lyrical, unorthodox Western narrative which Gide maps on to the African landscape and his own illicit sexuality within it.

Amyntas: *Desire and Loss*

If ecstatic union with the other entails a liberating loss of inhibition and even loss of the self, by the very same token, it is then that desire may become most unaware of the plight of the other, especially when, as here, it is powerfully mediated through the pastoral genre. *Amyntas* is a pastoral narrative of self-redemption in relation to, in the desire for, *and* in the space of, the other. But just as the loss of self is the precondition for the discovery of a more 'real' because unconflicted, unrepressed self, so the precondition for pastoral sublimity is the loss of history,[11] and once again the landscape which crystallizes desire, in such remarkable images, is also effaced by it:

I

. . . a child's laughter at the water's edge—then nothing, no misgivings, no thoughts . . .—What have I wanted until this day? What had I feared?. . .

---

[11] Many years later, in his Journal for January 1933, Gide writes that he was not unaware of the political realities of colonialism at that time; it was a feeling of incompetence that prevented him from speaking. He adds: 'It took the war to bring me to doubt of the value of "competencies", to convince myself that . . . I had just as much right as anyone else, and even the duty, to speak'. The occluded political realities of the pastoral mode have been most effectively analysed by Louis Montrose in relation to Renaissance literature, when the genre was at its height, and in ways suggestive for Gide; see especially 'The Pastoral of Power', and 'Of Gentlemen and Shepherds'.

III

... The village stays the same: no one here wants more—no effort, no novelty. Within these narrow lanes, no luxury compels such poverty to know itself.

V

... Time passing here is innocent of hours, yet so perfect is our inoccupation that boredom becomes impossible.

VI

What have I sought till this day? Why did I strive? Now, oh now I know, outside of time, the garden where time comes to rest. A tranquil country, sealed away ... Arcady! I have found the place of peace.

X

... No moving: Let time close over us like water ... over this world, let the even surface of time close once again ...

XI

... Behind us, the patch of scorching crag that blocks the north winds; sometimes a cloud passes, a white tuft; hesitates, frays out until ... absorbed by the blue air ... And ahead of us, nothing—the desert's variegated void.

XII

... Here life is more voluptuous and more futile, and death itself less difficult. (pp. 3–11)

It is not for long that death is less difficult, the histories of self and other lost, and consciousness unconflicted. As the distilled purity of pastoral and the fullness of desire give way to the absences which constitute them, so the journals move towards disenchantment, the acknowledgement of loss, and a sense of the futility of returning in order to recover an original intensity of being:

six times I have returned to that country, demanding the past from the present, flogging my emotions, requiring of them, still, that freshness they once owed to novelty, and from year to year finding in my ageing desires rewards ever less vivid ... Nothing compares to the first contact. (p. 115)

I have dreamed that I came back here—in twenty years. I passed by, and was no longer recognised by anyone; the unknown children did not smile at me; and I dared not ask what had become of those I had known, whom I feared to recognise in these bent men exhausted by life. (p. 141)

The narrative suggests a movement into time which is also a fall into knowledge and loss of innocence (p. 143). Yet there are also brief moments of recovery, moments of gratified desire and a coming to life: 'on this abandoned divan, I shall inhale for a long while still the earthy, vegetal smell which the faun left behind; then, in the morning, wakened at dawn, I shall fling myself into the delicious air' (p. 104).

Occasionally he finds a transcendence of ardour, an equilibrium beyond desire—'the disappearance of desire and the renunciation of everything', a time innocent of hours, a perfect inoccupation in which boredom becomes impossible, a coming to life which is a loss of consciousness: 'I dissolve, I evaporate into blue air'; a being alive in a world where 'death itself is less difficult' (pp. 101, 105, 107, 111). The most extraordinary moments traverse conventional divisions, occurring both in Edenic gardens (pp. 112, 146–7) and the drug-induced languor in darkened recesses of cafés: 'to linger there . . . Abd'el Kader, leaning toward me, points to the sole ornament on the white wall, hanging in the center—a hideous, shapeless, childishly daubed doll, and says in a whisper: "The Devil". Time trickled by' (p. 102).

The last travel journal ends with Gide back in Cuverville dreaming again of a loss of self—'to be rid of oneself, so that one blue breath, in which I am dissolved, might journey on . . . !—a dissolution which would redeem loss, but only by disavowing the recognition that what is most intensely desired is lost to the past. Redemption and disavowal are not compatible and the final lines suggest the yet severer knowledge that desire is of its nature the desire for what is lost:

In Normandy's autumn, I dream of the desert spring . . .
The rattle of the palm fronds! Almond trees humming with bees! Hot winds, and the sugary savor of the air! . . .
The squalling north wind beats against my windows. It has been raining for three days—Oh! how lovely the caravans were those evenings in Touggourt, when the sun was sinking into the salt. (p. 155)

There is in these travel journals a movement towards the recognition that the most acute form of nostalgia is that which, in evoking the past as lost fullness, then faces it with the knowledge that the restless incompleteness felt so acutely now, in the present, was also a part of the imaginary fullness then; the truthfulness which aims to allay nostalgia only intensifies it.

Even with such insight it has to be said: we go to the exotic other to lose everything, including ourselves—everything that is but the privilege which enabled us to go in the first place. That privilege needs to be understood in diverse ways. Gide was, at least at that time, the sexual tourist of which Said and others have written, his opportunity to come and go enhanced by what is aptly if euphemistically called independent means. His privilege and independence might further be seen to confer the trappings of a 'humaneness' which in truth was only a benign counterpart of the more brutal colonialism that appalled him. Further, what kind of indifference to (cultural) difference made Gide so confident Athman could survive in Paris? Was he really so unaware of those difficulties experienced by the person of colour in white European culture—difficulties of which Frantz Fanon was to write so compellingly fifty years later in *Black Skin, White Masks*, and in relation to France specifically? The destructive psychic and social conditions Fanon describes would have been compounded in the case of Athman. It is all too revealing that, searching through the biographical work on Gide for further references to Athman in Europe, I came across hardly anything except the occasional derogatory, passing remark. When Athman did re-emerge into visibility, it was once again as someone embroiled in the struggles of others, and, now along with Gide, subjected to the homophobic sneer. Consider, for instance, how Rupert Croft-Cooke, out to discredit Gide's account of Wilde's seduction of him (Gide) into a confirmed homosexuality (above, Chapter 1), writes of Gide that he 'picked up (among others) the Algerian boy prostitute Athman, who became known to other visiting Europeans, including Eugène Rouart and Francis Jammes and was brought to Paris by Henri Ghéon'.[12]

I would remark yet a further factor relevant to race and colonialism, one which raises again the always ambiguous status of the aesthetic, and inseparably from its achievements: Gide is in Africa as a writer discovering and nurturing a creativity of itself intrinsically exploitative. In retrospect then it is the final remark in that poignant description of Athman by the river which is the most telling: 'for a long time as the train was carrying me away, I watched his little motionless, grief-stricken figure, lost in the desert, *an image of my own despair*'. It is an image encountered by Gide, but also projected by him, familiar and unforgettable as an evocation of the sadness which pervades the history of illicit love. It is also an image which tells us that, if Gide's contribution to the liberation of the subjugated was as a writer, it is also true that he exemplified the writer's inevitably exploitative relation to the same, and that this exploitation persists as an aesthetic mode long after the blindness or impossibility of desire was acknowledged. The 'mature' writer not only survives those renunciations, they help constitute his art, an art which will always finally take priority over the plight of the other even if, as was the case with Gide, it also succeeds in mitigating it.

But I would hope to reinscribe all of this knowledge within Gide's narratives of sexual liberation without surrendering or denying their affirmations—I was about to say tenderness—and to do that in part by acknowledging that it is a knowledge implicit in or enabled by Gide's

---

[12] *The Unrecorded Life of Oscar Wilde*, 7; George Painter, *André Gide*, records that in 1904 Athman marries; in his Journal for 22 Nov. 1905 Gide writes: 'From Athman's latest letter I copy this sentence that Mardrus would not understand and that I should like not to forget: "I love her very much" (he is speaking of his very young wife) "and *yet I have been able to make her sincere* toward my mother and me; she is very good, and I only treat her very gently like how you treat a child"' (Gide's emphasis).

own transgressive crossing of some forbidden boundaries. Here the example of Frantz Fanon becomes instructive.

Fanon: Race and Sexuality

Fanon's analysis of racism and 'negrophobia', and his articulation of the predicament of the person of colour living in, or in relation to, white culture, is also instructive for understanding sexual discrimination, especially homophobia, and the predicament of the gay person living in, or in relation to, heterosexual culture. My own study is indebted to Fanon's analysis of how discrimination is internalized psychically and perpetuated socially *between* subordinated groups, classes, and races—what, in relation to the latter, he calls 'the racial distribution of guilt' (*Black Skin*, 103); also to his realization of the way the demonizing of the other is, above all, a mercurial process of displacement and condensation, so fluid yet always with effects of a brutally material, actually violent kind.

Even so, there can be no facile equation of racist and sexual discrimination, and this for three main reasons which, even as they preclude that equation, emphasize the significance of those points at which race and sexuality interconnect, and the particular importance of Fanon's work in this respect. First, as Mercer and Julien remind us, such an equivalence tends to obscure exactly those differences which need to be addressed if we are to understand not only each kind of discrimination separately but also their interconnections ('Race, Sexuality and Black Masculinity', 99–100). Second, Fanon offers a kind of cultural critique which mostly pre-empts facile politics *per se*. Homi Bhabha, in a significant essay arguing the urgent need to re-engage with Fanon in and for our own time, shows why. Bhabha writes of how Fanon 'speaks most effectively from the uncertain interstices of historical change: from the area of ambivalence between race and sexuality, out of an unresolved contradiction between culture and class; from deep within the struggle of psychic representation and social reality' (foreword to Fanon, *Black Skin, White Masks*, p. ix). It is from these uncertain interstices that there emerge Fanon's challenges to Enlightenment 'Man', and indeed to the very idea of an essential human subject; Bhabha finds in Fanon a powerful and subversive sense of identity as involving a split, precarious, contradictory relation to the Other, the upshot of which is a radical ambivalence, destructive but also potentially empowering.

The third reason why there can be no facile equation of racist and sexual discrimination via the appeal to Fanon concerns the place of sexuality, especially homosexuality, in his own writing. Fanon is surely right to stress the sexual component of racism, especially its destructive effects on (hetero)sexual relations across race. He stresses also the white person's fear of and fascination with the imagined sexual potency of the negro: 'For the majority of white men the Negro represents the sexual instinct (in its raw state). The Negro is the incarnation of a genital potency beyond all moralities and prohibitions' (pp. 159, 164, 177). Also the ways in which, as a result, the negro 'has been fixated in terms of the genital' (pp. 157, 165), and the corresponding displacement on to the person of colour of inadequacies and fears intrinsic to the *cultural* as distinct from natural formation of European sexuality (pp. 157, 165).

Despite all this, Fanon deploys some of the worst predjudices that psychoanalysis has been used to reinforce: 'All the Negrophobic women I have known had abnormal sex lives . . . And besides there was also an element of perversion, the persistence of infantile formations: God knows how [blacks] make love! It must be terrifying.' Of the white woman's negrophobic fear of rape by the black man Fanon asks: 'Basically does this *fear* of rape not itself cry out for rape? Just as there are faces that ask to be slapped, can one not speak of women who ask to be raped?'

Fanon's apparent ignorance and misrepresentation of women and feminine sexuality has been remarked before; less so his equally problematic representation of homosexuality, and the way he slides from the one to the other: 'the Negrophobic woman is in fact nothing but a putative sexual partner—just as the Negrophobic man is a repressed homosexual.' The homosexual is implicated all ways round, and according to some fairly crude psychoanalytic binaries. So, whilst in the foregoing passage *repressed* homosexuality is construed as a *cause* of a violent and neurotic racism, elsewhere Fanon regards *manifest* homosexuality as an *effect* of the same neurotic racism, though now in a *masochistic* rather than a *sadistic* form, and especially the masochistic relation of the white man to the black man: 'There are, for instance, men who go to "houses" in order to be beaten by negroes; passive homosexuals who insist on black partners' (pp. 158, 156, 177). He attributes an implied or assumed absence of homosexuality in Martinique to the absence of the Oedipus complex in the Antilles. Of certain transvestites there Fanon is anxious to assure the reader of their masculinity, and that they lead 'normal sex lives'. He adds: 'In Europe, on the other hand, I have known several Martinicans who became homosexuals, always passive. But this was by no means a neurotic homosexuality: For them it was a means to a livelihood, as pimping is for others' (p. 180). Of the 'Fault, Guilt, refusal of guilt, paranoia' which Fanon sees (surely correctly) as symptomatic of racism, he adds 'one is back in homosexual territory' (p. 183). And in the process of contesting racist representations of the negro's 'sensuality' Fanon adds: 'I have never been able, without revulsion, to hear a *man* say of another man: "He is so sensual!" I do not know what the sensuality of a man is. Imagine a woman saying of another woman: She's so terribly desirable—she's darling' (p. 201). In short, there are places in Fanon's writing where homosexuality is itself demonized as both a cause and an effect of the demonizing psychosexual organization of racism which Fanon elsewhere describes and analyses so compellingly.

Such constructions of homosexuality in relation to race and racism are not specific to Fanon. The myth that homosexuality is 'the white man's disease' persists today in some black communities, especially in certain kinds of political radicalism and nationalism. Cheryl Clarke cites from a leaflet distributed at a Black Liberation Movement meeting in 1981: 'Revolutionary nationalists and genuine communists cannot uphold homosexuality in the leadership of the Black Liberation Movement . . . Homosexuality is a genocidal practice . . . Homosexuality does not birth new warriors for liberation . . . [it] is an accelerating threat to our survival as a people and as a nation.' Clarke further remarks how here too homophobia often connects with misogyny. She also makes the crucial point that it is wrong to attribute it to the mass of black people, finding it most marked among some intellectual and political leaders, who also obscure the central roles played by lesbians and gays in black communities. By contrast, says Clarke, the poor and working class within those communities have often been more accepting of those 'who would be outcast by the ruling culture—many times to spite the white man, but mainly because the conditions of our lives have made us empathic'.[13] The point made earlier about the potential empathy of the sexual outcast is here made in reverse—about a community in relation to him or her. Those points of apparently incommensurable differences between groups, classes, nations, races, or whatever have been negotiated hesitantly and all too often anonymously by the outcasts and the deprived from either side. These are fragile empathies, too important to be either romanticized or ignored.

Another difficulty concerns the relations between politics and what has been called 'Black Macho'.[14] Again, the homosexual perspective is revealing. Jean Genet responded to an erotic charge in Arab and black masculinity inseparable from the recognition of its significance in a

---

[13] Clarke, 'The Failure to Transform', esp. 197–8, 205–6; see also Mercer and Julien, 'Race, Sexuality and Black Masculinity', 125 and 139.

[14] Wallace, *Black Macho and the Myth of the Superwoman*.

culture of resistance and fight for liberation. As we shall see shortly, this is another point of identification between the different, one which suggests that the masculinities of any culture, black, Arab, or white, cannot be grossed up as always and only homophobic. But if this 'assumption of . . . manhood' (Fanon, *Black Skin*, 41) has constituted an agency of resistance—no small achievement when one recalls the crippling effects of domination and exploitation at the subjective level, effects which Fanon himself charts—it is one which perpetuates, in terms of sexual and gender relations, the very oppression being resisted at other levels. There is an analogy here with working-class culture, black and white, where masculinity has also been a source of resistance, but once again at the expense of ratifying a larger exploitative frame-work for men as well as women.[15] As Jewelle Gomez has observed, homophobic prejudice is particularly dangerous for the black lesbian. Hers is a vulnerable yet crucial role as negotiator between difference: typically she is one who refuses to outcast herself from the black community and family, because aware of its value and importance, yet by virtue of that same fact subjected within them to sexual discrimina-tion: 'we straddle the fence that says we cannot be uplifters of the race and lesbians at the same time' ('Talking about It', 54).

Race and Humanism

The task Gomez envisages for the black lesbian returns us to radical humanism, and both Fanon and Gide as important points of reference. Homi Bhabha finds that Fanon most profoundly evokes the colonial condition not in his yearning for 'the total transformation of Man and Society', nor in his appeal to the human essence (though 'he lapses into such a lament in his more existential moment'), but in his understanding of the workings of 'image and fantasy—those orders that figure transgressively on the borders of history and the unconscious' (foreword to Fanon, *Black Skin*, p. xiii). Perhaps the two interconnect more closely than this suggests—as they did with Gide.

Gide's narrative of a development from the desire for self-redemption in the space of the other, through the loss of self at the ecstatic height of this existential quest, to the unresolved sense of desire itself as a kind of loss, is amenable to a similar analysis; in Gide's case image and fantasy do indeed figure transgressively on the borders of history and the unconscious. Even of that first ecstatic experience with Mohammed in 1895 he would write much later, 'Every time since then that I have

---

[15] Tolson, *The Limits of Masculinity*, and Willis, *Learning to Labour*.

sought after pleasure, it is the memory of that night I have pursued' (*If It Die*, 283). Nevertheless, those 'most perfect memories of sensual delight' (*So Be It*, 126–7) remained a strength, the impetus for a nonconformist humanism which, precisely because of its universalist aspirations, provides further identifications beyond sexuality. In their humanism at least Fanon and Gide may be compared. Bhabha is critical of Fanon's nonconformist humanism, especially its essentialist fantasies of the self and the yearning for total transformation which they partly enabled. On the penultimate page of *Black Skin, White Masks* Fanon declares that one of the things that he, the man of colour, wants is 'that it be possible for me to discover and to love man, wherever he may be'. And he asks:

> Why not the quite simple attempt to touch the other, to feel the other, to explain the other to myself?
>
> Was my freedom not given to me then in order to build the world of the *You*?
>
> At the conclusion of this study, I want the world to recognize, with me, the open door of every consciousness. (pp. 231–2)

Homi Bhabha finds here an 'existential humanism . . . as banal as it is beatific', adding: 'there can be no reconciliation, no Hegelian "recognition", no simple, sentimental promise of a humanistic "world of the You"' (pp. xx–xxi). He suggests that such tendencies occur here as an overcompensation for the closed consciousness or 'dual narcissism' to which Fanon attributes the depersonalization of colonial man; that 'it is as if Fanon is fearful of his most radical insights' (p. xx). I would regard Fanon's humanism otherwise. Certainly it is quite different from the timid and time-serving humanism all too familiar within 'Eng. Lit.'. More importantly, it is also utterly different from, and indeed envisioned in direct opposition to, the colonial history of humanism.

A reassessment of Fanon's humanism has become necessary for reasons similar to my reconsideration of Gide's and others' essentialism in sexual politics. Benita Parry argues that the most influential recent analysis of colonialist discourse encounters certain problems inseparable from its anti-essentialism and anti-humanism; in particular its tendency has been to obscure 'the role of the native as historical subject and combatant, possessor of an-other knowledge and producer of alternative traditions', and to 'limit native resistance to devices circumventing and interrogating colonial authority' (Parry, 'Problems', 34). Parry sees the problem which Fanon addressed as precisely that of how to constitute self-identity in a way which validates native difference, and thereby empower the native to rebel. In the process Fanon might be said to have overestimated the extent to which, from subordination, it is possible to construct 'a politically conscious, unified, revolutionary Self, standing in unmitigated opposition to the oppressor' (*Problems*, 30). Or, put slightly differently, in imagining that self, he builds into it too much of the oppressor's culture—i.e. precisely that which needs to be destroyed. Note how, in an utterly different context, we encounter again some of the same charges brought against Gide and others with their sexual essentialism. But, as with them, so with Fanon: the criticisms underestimate the extent to which an oppositional humanism transforms in the process of appropriation. Likewise with his existential emphasis, which closely relates to that humanism. If, as Kobena Mercer suggests, white, middle-class sexual politics is over-preoccupied with the 'self', and psychotherapy and psychology as its corollary (Mercer and Julien, 'A Dossier', 123), Fanon offers an alternative whereby the existential dimension is rendered inextricably social, and on virtually every page.

The same existential emphasis made Fanon acutely aware that oppositional identities emerge not simply against, but from within, the terms of their oppression. Thus Jean-Paul Sartre's dialectic relativizing of 'Negritude' (see below) is passionately reproached but not refuted. Similarly, the self-evident fact that *'the racist creates his inferior'* gives rise to a complex history, and the complex, ambivalent, conflicted identity of the subordinated (*Black Skin*, 83). So Fanon's oppositional humanism coexists with a demolition of one of the corner-stones of conventional humanism, the idea of a stable unified self. Yet, crucially, this painful awareness of the historically constituted 'nature' of oppositional identities is not disavowed but itself reconstituted *within and as* the humanist universal affirmation: 'The negro is not. Any more than the white man' (*Black Skin*, 93, 231). This is one of the several moves whereby, for Fanon, 'a native contest initially enunciated in the invader's language, culminates in a rejection of imperialism's signifying system'. As Parry adds, this is something which more recent colonialist discourse theory has not adequately considered (Parry, 'Problems', 45).

Writing the preface to Fanon's *The Wretched of the Earth* (1961) Jean-Paul Sartre remarked the violence and duplicity of European humanism in the colonial context; it had been, said Sartre, 'nothing but an ideology of lies, a perfect justification for pillage; its honeyed words, its affectation of sensibility were only alibis for our aggressions' (p. 21). In the conclusion to that book Fanon himself put it thus:

Let us waste no time in sterile litanies and nauseating mimicry. Leave this Europe where they are never done talking of Man, yet murder men everywhere they find them, at the corner of every one of their own streets, in all corners of the globe. For centuries they have stifled almost the whole of humanity in the name of a so-called spiritual experience. (p. 251)

Against Mannoni's assertion to the contrary, Fanon insists that 'European civilization and its best representatives *are* responsible for colonial racism' (p. 90, my italics). Which means that the Third World's potential for transformation is crucially conditional on *not* imitating or trying to 'catch up with Europe' (p. 252).

But, as *The Wretched of the Earth* and *Black Face, White Masks* both indicate, the social and psychic realities from which transformation will come are also those which require transformation; the dominant which the emergent contests always already informs the emergent; in short, there is no outside from which to make a totally new start. For Fanon this means that, despite Europe's crimes, which will not and cannot be forgotten, the Third World's 'new history of Man' must 'have regard to the sometimes prodigious theses which Europe has put forward' since 'all the elements of a solution to the great problems of humanity have, at different times, existed in European thought' (*Wretched of the Earth*, 253–4).

What is required in such a scenario is an insurrectionary appropriation so radical as to be also necessarily perverse: Fanon uses Hegel, Freud, and Sartre but in each case simultaneously contests and perverts fundamental principles of their thought. Thus to have application to race the theories of Hegel and Freud must undergo radical critique and transformation; with some of Freud's followers, it is even the case of first having to discredit an overtly racist psychiatry (see e.g. *Black Skin*, 63, 138, 151–2, 220; *Wretched of the Earth*, 240–50). So with humanism more generally and more radically: it is not to be imitated, not modified, not simply borrowed from or differently applied; rather, its appropriation and transformation is conditional upon its negation, the using of it destructively against itself. What emerges from the space of humanism contradicts what once defined that space; in this sense Fanon can be said to have followed the path of the perverse: a negation of the dominant is made from a trajectory that emerged from it—a deviation from, which is also, simultaneously, a contradiction of. The radical interconnectedness of culture is redeemed for a radical politics, and via transgressive reinscription.

This appropriation of European humanism was generous in a way inseparable from its shamelessness: the final manifesto of *The Wretched of the Earth* makes it clear that the vision for a new humanity which emerges from the appropriation is undertaken on behalf of Europe as well as the Third World. But perhaps the generosity is best revealed in the anecdote rather than the manifesto:

At first thought it may seem strange that the anti-Semite's outlook should be related to that of the Negrophobe. It was my philosophy professor, a native of the Antilles, who recalled the fact to me one day: 'Whenever you hear anyone abuse the Jews, pay attention because he is talking about you'. And I found that he was universally right—by which I mean that I was answerable in my body and in my heart for what was done to my brother. Later I realized that he meant, quite simply, an anti-Semite is inevitably anti-Negro. (*Black Skin*, 122)

Both *The Wretched of the Earth* and *Black Skin, White Masks* close with affirmations made in the knowledge of exactly what threatens them—that being, after all, what both books are about, and what powerfully pre-empts the charge of humanist sentimentality: 'I can already see a white man and a black man *hand in hand*' (*Black Skin*, 222).

Genet: 'Risking a Sensibility'[16]

Obviously, the demonizing of the other is often inseparable from his or her exploitation. But so too may be identification with the other, as Charles Marowitz implies when he describes Genet's *The Blacks* as a play which champions blacks 'not because they are socially down-trodden but because they personify two of [Genet's] favourite types: The Rebellious Outcast and The Splendid Primitive . . . Genet uses the blacks, the way a man who has just emptied his revolver reaches for the knife at his side' ('The Revenge of Jean Genet', 175). Possibly, except that in homosexual culture it has rarely been, and certainly was not for Genet, quite that simple. Genet speaks of his own identifications across race and culture in an interview with Hubert Fichte in 1975:

I was invited by two revolutionary movements, the Black Panthers and the Palestinians. . . . these two groups have a very strong erotic charge. I wonder if I could have belonged to revolutionary movements, even if they were as just as—I find the Panthers' movement and the Palestinians' movement to be very just—but this belonging, this sympathizing with them is at the same time dictated by the erotic charge which the Arab world in its totality or the black American world represents to me, to my sexuality.[17]

Genet joined these movements because asked by them to do so. But he made it clear that, in these identifications, desire and politics were inseparable. That might plausibly be thought to take us no further than

---

[16] The phrase is Genet's; see Leyland, *Gay Sunshine Interviews*, 76.
[17] Leyland, *Gay Sunshine Interviews*, 79–80; cf. Hocquenghem, *Homosexual Desire*, 126.

Wilde in Algiers in 1895: 'The beggars here have profiles, so the problem of poverty is easily solved' (Wilde, *More Letters*, 129). In Genet's case it produced among other things *Prisoner of Love*, a record of the time he spent with the Black Panthers[18] in the US and Palestinian soldiers in Jordan and Lebanon. He began the book in 1983 and completed it shortly before he died, in 1986. It is an extraordinary poetic meditation on desire, politics, loving, and dying.

In the same 1975 interview Genet declares that he had no choice but to identify with oppressed blacks since he too was black. What such an identification involved becomes apparent in *Prisoner* in a passage which renders the crucial difference not one of colour, yet by the same criterion reinstates the distinction between blacks and whites: 'What separates us from the Blacks today is not so much the colour of our skin or the type of our hair as the phantom-ridden psyche we never see except when a Black lets fall some joking and to us cryptic phrase. It not only seems cryptic; it is so. The Blacks are obsessionally complicated about themselves. They've turned their suffering into a resource' (p. 46).

Throughout *Prisoner* Genet again insists that his reasons for his identifications across race and culture were incorrigibly personal. He says he completely failed to understand the Palestinian revolution (p. 3), that he could never completely identify with the nation or their movement (p. 90), that he participated for fun (p. 9), that his record of what happened is inaccurate (p. 19), that writing itself is a lie (p. 27) and memory unreliable (p. 39). Even the revolution was unreal—'By agreeing to go first with the Panthers and then with the Palestinians, playing my role as a dreamer inside a dream, wasn't I just one more factor of unreality inside both movements?' (p. 149). But this is not exactly the blindness of desire, nor even the selective vision of fantasy. First because in *Prisoner* desire and fantasy seem transformed into non-sublimated social identification; as he puts it in relation to one group of black students in America, 'while I never desired any particular person, I was all desire for the group as a whole. But my desire was satisfied by the fact that they existed' (cf. pp. 178–9). Second because this is a kind of desire inseparable from an abundance of curiosity and attention; desire is curious, and attends in a way which renders desire itself an inappropriate word. Genet is inclined to speak rather of a love which alters perception and complicates judgement, especially in relation to masculinity, and relations between men in the context of war and revolution. A range of issues recur throughout Genet's book; I concentrate on masculinity only because of its problematic centrality in

---

[18] On Genet's reading of George Jackson's prison letters, see above, Ch. 7.

contemporary considerations of race, homosexuality, and gender more generally, and because Genet's reflections on it often make other recent writing about it seem by comparison the simplistic and reductive pronouncements of a banal gender politics.

Genet regards the eroticism of the Black Panthers as manifest and inseparable from their politics and the challenge they presented to white America (pp. 259–60). Moreover, despite their restraint, 'the Black Panthers couldn't throw off their mutual attraction. Their movement consisted of magnetized bodies magnetizing one another.' As for the fedayeen, they 'observed a smiling rigour. But the eroticism was palpable. I could sense its vibrations, though I wasn't bothered by it' (p. 126).

But this eroticism, and the masculinity of these men, frequently confounds the stereotypes. Thus he says of Ali, a member of Fatah, 'He knew I loved him, but it didn't make him the slightest bit arrogant. It awakened his kindness' (p. 267). Genet speaks also of the kindness of the Panthers, which 'brought me both real protection and education in affection' (p. 83). Different again is the dancing of the bedouin soldiers, at once chaste and erotic—'chaste because it takes place among men, mostly holding one another by the elbow or the forefinger ... erotic because it takes place between men, and because it's performed before the ladies. So which sex is it that burns with desire for an encounter that can never be?' In their dancing Genet detects a display, almost a confession, of the femininity that contrasted so strongly with their masculinity, and an acceptance of, even a desire for, annihilation.

Genet returns to this wish for death and martyrdom. He is admiring of the soldiers' courage but not persuaded by their beliefs: training people to sacrifice themselves produces not altruism but a fascinated following of others to death not so much to help but merely to follow (p. 88). And looking at the Palestinian revolution 'from a viewpoint higher than my own' he regards it as ultimately a revolt reaching to the limits of Islam, a 'calling for a revision, probably even a rejection, of a theology as soporific as a Breton cradle' (p. 88). Of the young Falangists, 'something halfway between monks and hoodlums', singing of the Immaculate Conception and marching towards immortality: 'I was enchanted. I could calculate their cruelty from their stupidity' (p. 32).

In others he finds both the impulse to self-sacrifice, and their masculinity, quite complex (p. 124). One of the men who most attracts him, Mubarak, is also one whose sexuality is most self-conscious, withdrawn, and complicated; Mubarak's masculinity is itself strung out across difference: he is a Sudanese African in Asia, and fighting for a people whom he does not understand and who regard him with a racist indifference (pp. 194–5); he speaks perfect French, but with a Parisian urban working-class accent. Genet describes him as 'so obviously both a pimp—a barracks or red-light district ponce—and a whore that I could never make out what he was doing among the fedayeen' (p. 153). Alternately ironic and sad, provocative and withdrawn, Mubarak shares Genet's gift for insightful reflection on the revolution and the socio-political forces at work within it and beyond. He also exhibited a flirtatiousness aimed at everyone and everything, 'a desire to charm [which] prevented him from being sufficiently implacable' (pp. 152–3). Yet later, after Mubarak's death, Genet discovers that he did not sleep with women or men; all of his sexuality was social: 'the warmth of that voice had the shy yet imperious sureness of an erect penis stroking a beloved cheek. In that too I saw him as an obvious heir to the boys of the old Paris suburbs' (p. 143). Perhaps that is also why Mubarak says, or at least why Genet recalls him saying, that if he wants his book (*Prisoner of Love*) to be read he must write it in 'a voice that's sweet but inexorable' (p. 151).

With the fedayeen, love always at once complicates and simplifies the narrative. One of his most vivid memories is of three separate groups of fedayeen, each situated on a different hill, singing to each other just before dawn; it was a polyphony, 'a great improvisation performed among the mountains, in the midst of danger', heedless of death, expressing and eliciting love (pp. 36–40). Elsewhere Genet writes of a 19-year-old, washing the clothes of his friend who is shortly to go and fight, declaring that he loves the revolution and all the fedayeen, but his friend especially: 'Yes. It is love. Do you think that at a time like this I am afraid of words? . . . if he dies tonight there will always be a gulf at my side, a gulf into which I must never fall' (p. 87). More than 200 pages later Genet writes 'out of the crowd a glance swifter than a wink reveals two fedayeen as two lovers . . . Chaste, but so close that if one of them is sad the laughter of the other immediately fills the void in him' (p. 330). These are Genet's reconstructions, and perhaps the gulf, the void, are his as well as the soldiers'.

If Genet is seduced by the magnanimity of the fedayeen, their selflessness, courage, humour, and love for each other, he is also perplexed and disillusioned by the inseparability of these qualities from an 'underlying desire for self-slaughter, for glorious death if victory was impossible' (pp. 271–2). Surfacing from that perplexity, which is to say between, and sometimes within, the lyrical meditations on love, is the sense of a truly disturbing proximity of antagonists, most powerfully articulated in Genet's angry 'fantasy' of the palace and the shanty town:

one wonders which was real and which only a reflection. Anyhow, if the Palace was the reflection and the shanty town the reality, the reflection of the reality was only to be found in the Palace, and vice versa.

Getting to know the other, who's supposed to be wicked because he's the enemy, makes possible not only battle itself but also close bodily contact between the combatants and between their beliefs. So each doctrine is sometimes the shadow and sometimes the equivalent of the other . . . What sort of beauty is it these lads from the shanty town possess? When they're still children a mother or a whore gives them a piece of broken mirror in which they trap a ray of the sun and reflect it into one of the Palace windows. And by that open window, in the mirror, they discover bit by bit their faces and bodies. (pp. 58–62)

Regarding Difference

All the foregoing texts and histories suggest why theoretical or pseudo-political gestures towards difference are inadequate. As is (another recent development) separatist or essentialist 'identity politics' wherein one group seeks its own advantage at the expense, or ignorance, of others.[19] Still, I have no intention of prescribing a correct attitude towards difference, even less a correct theory of difference; I do not even know what the latter could possibly be. My consideration of difference originated in a turn to history in order to repudiate one such theory—specifically, that which construed homosexuality as an embrace of the same because of a fear of the different. It is a history which quite quickly produces that excess of difference which discredits the theory which ignored it but which also questions the theoretically facile celebration of difference *per se*.

My task has been to reconsider some of those complicated but always significant histories wherein differences conflict and converge as desire itself. In doing so I wanted not to reduce, say, Gide's or Fanon's defence of difference to the limiting historical conditions of its articulation—the first as merely a sexual tourist, the second as developing a homophobic theory of Negrophobia. Rather, I have wanted to recover the history of each in relation to the other, finding in the process that Gide understood more than most about desire for the different, Fanon more than most about the ambivalence of difference itself. As for Genet, someone whose involvement with the different has variously been repudiated as fascist, racist, and anarchistic, his *Prisoner of Love* is nothing less than an affirmation of the love that Fanon envisaged and which has sometimes given the dissident their courage. If I risk ending this long study of sexual dissidence by speaking of love it is without apology and simply to acknowledge its inspiration.

Afterword

Gide, thirty-three years after that encounter in Algiers with which this study began:

Putting some papers in order, I recover, among old bills, the bills of the Royal Hotel of Biskra, from the time of Wilde and Douglas ... I tear them up after having noted this reference.

Dictated no fewer than fourteen letters today. (*Journals*, 4 Oct. 1928)

Bibliography

ABELOVE, HENRY, 'Freud, Male Homosexuality, and the Americans', *Dissent* (Winter 1966), 59–69.

ACHEBE, CHINUA, *Hopes and Impediments: Selected Essays, 1967–87* (London: Heinemann, 1988).

ADAMS, STEPHEN, *The Homosexual as Hero in Contemporary Fiction* (London: Vision, 1980).

ALLEN, CLIFFORD, *Homosexuality: Its Nature, Causation and Treatment* (London: Staple Press, 1958).

ALTMAN, DENNIS, *Homosexual Oppression and Liberation* [1971] (London: Allen Lane, 1974).

—— *The Homosexualization of America* (Boston, Mass.: Beacon Press, 1983).

ANDERSON, PERRY, *Considerations on Western Marxism* (London: NLB, 1976).

—— *In the Tracks of Historical Materialism* (London: Verso, 1983).

AQUINAS, ST THOMAS, *Philosophical Texts*, ed. Thomas Gilby (Oxford: Oxford University Press, 1951).

ARNOLD, MATTHEW, *Culture and Anarchy* (London: Smith Elder, [1869] 1891).

ARTAUD, A., *The Theatre and its Double*, trans. V. Conti (London: Calder, 1977).

AUGUSTINE, ST, *City of God*, Loeb Classical Library, 7 vols. with English trans. by Philip Levine (Cambridge, Mass.: Harvard University Press, and London: Heinemann, 1966).

—— *City of God*, trans. Henry Bettenson, with intro. by David Knowles (Harmondsworth: Penguin, 1972).

—— *Confessions*, trans. C. Bigg (London: Methuen, 1897).

—— *Confessions*, trans. F. J. Sheed (London: Sheed and Ward, 1944).

—— *Confessions*, trans. with an intro. by R. S. Pine-Coffin (Harmondsworth: Penguin, 1961).

—— *De libero arbitrio*, ed. W. M. Green (Brepolis: Turnholti, 1970).

—— *Enchiridion*, trans. Bernard M. Peebles, in *Writings of St Augustine*, vol. iv (Washington, DC: Catholic University of America, 1947).

BABCOCK, BARBARA, *The Reversible World: Symbolic Inversion in Art and Society* (Ithaca, NY: Cornell University Press, 1978).

BABUSCIO, JACK, 'Camp and the Gay Sensibility', in Richard Dyer (ed.), *Gays and Film* (London: British Film Institute, 1977), 40–57.

BACON, FRANCIS, 'Advertisement Touching an Holy Warre', in *The Works*, ed. J. Spedding and R. L. Ellis, vol. vii (Stuttgart: Frommann, [1857–61] 1961–3).

BAKER, MICHAEL, *Our Three Selves: A Life of Radclyffe Hall* (London: Hamish Hamilton, 1985).

BAKSHI, PARMINDER KAUR, 'Homosexuality and Orientalism: Edward Carpenter's Journey to the East', in Tony Brown (ed.), *Edward Carpenter and Late Victorian Radicalism* (London: Frank Cass, 1990).

BALDICK, C., *The Social Mission of English Criticism, 1848–1932* (Oxford: Clarendon Press, 1983).

BALDWIN, FRANCES ELIZABETH, *Sumptuary Legislation and Personal Regulation in England* (Baltimore: Johns Hopkins University Press, 1926).

BALDWIN, JAMES, *James Baldwin and Nikki Giovanni: A Dialogue*, foreword by Ida Lewis (New York: Lippincott, 1973).

—— *Giovanni's Room* [1956] (London: Corgi, 1977).

—— *The Price of the Ticket: Collected Nonfiction 1948–1985* (London: Michael Joseph, 1985).

BARKER, F., *et al.* (eds.), *The Politics of Theory* (Colchester: University of Essex, 1983).

BARRETT, MICHÈLE, 'The Concept of "Difference"', in *Feminist Review*, 26 (1987), 29–41.

BARRY, KATHLEEN, *Female Sexual Slavery* (Englewood Cliffs, NJ: Prentice Hall, 1979).

BARTHELEMY, ANTHONY GERARD, *Black Face Maligned Race: The Representation of Blacks in English Drama from Shakespeare to Southerne* (Baton Rouge, La.: Louisiana State University Press, 1987).

BARTHES, ROLAND, *S/Z* (Paris: Seuil, 1970).

—— *Mythologies*, trans. Annette Lavers (St Albans: Paladin, 1973).

—— *Roland Barthes*, trans. Richard Howard (London: Macmillan, 1977).

—— *Barthes: Selected Writings*, ed. with an intro. by Susan Sontag (London: Fontana, 1983).

BARTLETT, NEIL, *Who Was That Man: A Present for Mr Oscar Wilde* (London: Serpent's Tail, 1988).

BARTLEY, WILLIAM W. III, *Wittgenstein* (La Salle, Ill.: Open Court, 2nd edn. 1985).

BASSLER, JOUETTE M., 'The Widow's Tale: A Fresh Look at 1 Tim 5: 3–16', *Journal of Biblical Literature*, 103/1 (1984), 23–41.

BAUDRILLARD, JEAN, *In the Shadow of the Silent Majorities . . . or the End of the Social and Other Essays*, trans. Paul Foss, Paul Patton, and John Johnston (New York: Semiotext(e), 1983).

BEAME, THOM, 'Interview: BWMT Founder—Mike Smith', in Michael J. Smith (ed.), *Black Men/White Men* (San Francisco: Gay Sunshine Press, 1983).

BEAUMONT, FRANCIS, and FLETCHER, JOHN, *The Maid's Tragedy*, ed. H. B. Norland (London: Arnold, 1968).

BEIER, A. L., *Masterless Men: The Vagrancy Problem in England: 1560–1640* (London: Methuen, 1985).

BELSEY, CATHERINE, 'Towards Cultural History', *Textual Practice*, 3 (1989), 159–72.

BERGER, PETER L., and LUCKMANN, THOMAS, *The Social Construction of Reality: A Treatise in the Sociology of Knowledge* (Harmondsworth: Penguin, 1971).

BERMAN, MARSHALL, *The Politics of Authenticity: Radical Individualism and the Emergence of Modern Society* (London: Allen & Unwin, 1970).

BERNHEIMER, CHARLES, and KAHANE, CLAIRE (eds.), *In Dora's Case: Freud–Hysteria–Feminism* (London: Virago, 1985).

BERSANI, LEO, *The Freudian Body: Psychoanalysis and Art* (New York: Columbia University Press, 1986).
—— 'Is the Rectum a Grave?' *October*, 43 (1987), 197–222.
—— *The Culture of Redemption* (Cambridge, Mass.: Harvard University Press, 1990).
BHABHA, HOMI K., 'Sly Civility', *October*, 34 (1985), 71–80.
—— 'Of Mimicry and Man: The Ambivalence of Colonial Discourse', in James Donald and Stuart Hall (eds.), *Politics and Ideology* (Milton Keynes: Open University Press, 1986).
—— 'The Commitment to Theory', *New Formations*, 5 (1988), 5–23.
BHASKAR, ROY, *Scientific Realism and Human Emancipation* (London: Verso, 1986).
BINNS, J. W., 'Women or Transvestites on the Elizabethan Stage? An Oxford Controversy', *Sixteenth Century Journal*, 5/2 (1974), 95–120.
BLACKWOOD, EVELYN (ed.), *Anthropology and Homosexual Behavior* (New York and London: The Haworth Press, 1986).
BOWLBY, RACHEL, 'Promoting Dorian Gray', *Oxford Literary Review*, 9 (1987), 147–62.
BRADLEY, A. C., *Shakespearean Tragedy* (2nd edn., London: Macmillan, 1920).
BRANDON, S. G. F., *Creation Legends* (London: Hodder & Stoughton, 1963).
BRAY, ALAN, *Homosexuality in Renaissance England* (London: Gay Men's Press, 1982).
BREWER, E. C., *Dictionary of Phrase and Fable* (London: Cassell, 1894).
BRISTOW, JOSEPH, 'Homophobia/Misogyny: Sexual Fears, Sexual Definitions', in Simon Shepherd and Mick Wallis (eds.), *Coming on Strong: Gay Politics and Culture* (London: Unwin Hyman, 1989).
—— 'Being Gay: Politics, Identity, Pleasure', *New Formations*, 9 (1989), 61–81.
BRONSKI, MICHAEL, *Culture-Clash: The Making of Gay Sensibility* (Boston: South End Press, 1984).
BROOKS, CLEANTH, *The Well Wrought Urn: Studies in the Structure of Poetry* (New York: Harcourt Brace, 1947).
BROOKS, PETER, 'The Idea of a Psychoanalytic Literary Criticism', in Shlomith Rimmon-Kenan (ed.), *Discourse in Psychoanalysis and Literature* (London: Methuen, 1987).
BROWN, NORMAN O., *Life against Death: The Psychoanalytic Meaning of History* (London: Routledge, 1959).
BROWN, PAUL, 'This thing of darkness I acknowledge mine', in J. Dollimore and A. Sinfield (eds.), *Political Shakespeare: New Essays in Cultural Materialism*, (Manchester: Manchester University Press, 1985).
BROWN, PETER, *Augustine of Hippo: A Biography* (London: Faber, 1967).
BROWN, RITA MAE, *Rubyfruit Jungle* [1973] (London: Corgi, 1978).
BURFORD, E. J., *Queen of the Bawds* (London: Neville Spearman, 1974).
BURKE, KENNETH, *The Rhetoric of Religion: Studies in Logology* [1961] (Berkeley, Calif.: University of California Press, 1970).
BURTON, ROBERT, *The Anatomy of Melancholy*, ed. with intro. by Holbrook Jackson (London: Dent, 1932).

BUTLER, JUDITH, *Gender Trouble: Feminism and the Subversion of Identity* (London: Routledge and Kegan Paul, 1990).

CALVIN, JOHN, *Institutes*, trans. H. Beveridge, 2 vols. (London: Clarke, 1949).

CANGUILHEM, GEORGES, *The Normal and the Pathological*, intro. by Michel Foucault (New York: Zone Books, 1989).

CARSON, MICHAEL, 'Home and Abroad', *Gay Times*, 129 (June 1989), 42–5.

CASTLE, TERRY, *Masquerade and Civilization: The Carnivalesque in Eighteenth Century English Culture and Fiction* (London: Methuen, 1986).

CAVENDISH, RICHARD, *The Powers of Evil in Western Religion, Magic and Folk Belief* (London: Routledge and Kegan Paul, 1975).

CHAMBERLAIN, JOHN, *Letters*, ed. N. E. McClure, 2 vols. (Philadelphia: American Philosophical Society, 1939).

CHAMBERS, E. K., *The Elizabethan Stage*, 4 vols. (Oxford: Clarendon Press, 1923).

CHAPMAN, ROWENA, and RUTHERFORD, JONATHAN (eds.), *Male Order: Unwrapping Masculinity* (London: Lawrence & Wishart, 1988).

CHASSEGUET-SMIRGEL, JANINE, *Creativity and Perversion* (London: Free Association, 1985).

CIXOUS, HÉLÈNE, 'Sorties', in E. Marks and I. de Courtivron (eds.), *New French Feminisms* (Brighton: Harvester, 1981), 90–8.

CLARK, ELIZABETH A., 'Vitiated Seeds and Holy Vessels: Augustine's Manichean Past', in Karen L. King (ed.), *Images of the Feminine in Gnosticism (Studies in Antiquity and Christianity)* (Philadelphia: Fortress Press, 1988), 367–401.

CLARK, SANDRA, 'Hic Mulier, Haec Vir, and the Controversy over Masculine Women', *Studies in Philology*, 82/2 (Spring 1985), 157–83.

CLARK, STUART, 'Inversion, Misrule and the Meaning of Witchcraft', *Past and Present*, 87 (1980), 98–127.

CLARKE, CHERYL, 'The Failure to Transform: Homophobia in the Black Community', in Barbara Smith (ed.), *Home Girls: A Black Feminist Anthology* (New York: Women of Color Press, 1983).

CLEMENT of Alexandria, *Christ the Educator*, trans. Simon P. Ward (New York: Fathers of the Church, 1954).

COMTE, EDWARD LE, *A Dictionary of Puns in Milton's English Poetry* (London: Macmillan, 1981).

CONNELL, R. W., *Which Way is Up? Essays on Sex, Class and Culture* London: Allen & Unwin, 1983).

CONNOR, S., *Postmodernist Culture* (Oxford: Blackwell, 1989).

CONRAD, JOSEPH, *Heart of Darkness* [1902] (Harmondsworth: Penguin, 1973).

—— *Nostromo* (Harmondsworth: Penguin, 1963).

COOK, ANN JENNALIE, '"Bargaines of Incontinencie": Bawdy Behavior in the Playhouses', *Shakespeare Studies*, 10 (1977), 271–89.

COWARD, ROSALIND, *Patriarchal Precedents: Sexuality and Social Relations* (London: Routledge, 1983).

COWHIG, RUTH, 'Blacks in English Renaissance Drama and the Role of Shakespeare's Othello', in David Dabydeen (ed.), *The Black Presence in English Literature* (Manchester: Manchester University Press, 1985).

CRAFT, CHRISTOPHER, '"Kiss Me with Those Red Lips": Gender and Inversion in Bram Stoker's *Dracula*', *Representations*, 8 (1984), 107–33.

CRANDALL, CORYL, *Swetnam the Woman-Hater: The Controversy and the Play*, a critical edn. with intro. and notes (Lafayette, Ind.: Purdue University Studies, 1969).

CROFT-COOKE, RUPERT, *The Unrecorded Life of Oscar Wilde* (New York: David McKay, 1972).

CROMPTON, LOUIS, 'The Myth of Lesbian Impunity: Capital Laws from 1270 to 1791', *Journal of Homosexuality*, 6/1–2, (Fall/Winter 1980/81), 11–25.

CULLER, JONATHAN, *On Deconstruction: Theory and Criticism after Structuralism* (London: Routledge & Kegan Paul, 1983).

DAVIDSON, ARNOLD I., 'Sex and the Emergence of Sexuality', *Critical Inquiry*, 14 (1987), 16–48.

—— 'How to Do the History of Psychoanalysis: A Reading of Freud's *Three Essays on the Theory of Sexuality*', *Critical Inquiry*, 14 (1987), 252–77.

DAVIES, Sir JOHN, *Nosce Teipsum*, in *Poems*, ed. Robert Krueger (Oxford: Clarendon Press, 1975).

DAVIS, NATALIE ZEMON, 'Women on Top: Symbolic Sexual Inversion and Political Disorder in Early Modern Europe', in B. Babcock (ed.), *The Reversible World* (Ithaca, NY, and London: Cornell University Press, 1978).

DEKKER, RUDOLF, and VAN DE POL, LOTTE C., *The Tradition of Female Transvestism in Early Modern Europe* (New York: St Martin's Press, 1989).

DELANY, PAUL, *D. H. Lawrence's Nightmare: The Writer and His Circle in the Years of the Great War* (Brighton: Harvester, 1979).

—— 'Men in Love' [review article], *London Review of Books* (3 Sept. 1987), 21–2.

DE LAURETIS, TERESA, *Technologies of Gender: Essays on Theory, Film and Fiction* (Bloomington, Ind.: Indiana University Press, 1987).

DELAY, J., *The Youth of André Gide*, abridged and trans. by June Guicharnaud (Chicago: Chicago University Press, 1956–7).

DELEUZE, GILLES, *Masochism: An Interpretation of Coldness and Cruelty*, trans. Jean McNeil (New York: Braziller, 1971).

—— and GUATTARI, F., *Anti-Oedipus: Capitalism and Schizophrenia*, trans. Robert Hurley *et al.*, preface by Michel Foucault (New York: Viking Press, 1977).

DEMARCO, JOE, 'Gay Racism', in Michael J. Smith (ed.), *Black Men/White Men* (San Francisco: Gay Sunshine Press, 1983).

DERRIDA, JACQUES, *Of Grammatology* [1967], trans. Gayatri Spivak (Baltimore: Johns Hopkins University Press, 1976).

—— *Writing and Difference*, trans. with intro. by Alan Bass (London: Routledge and Kegan Paul, 1978).

—— *Positions*, trans. Alan Bass (London: Athlone, 1981).

—— *Dissemination*, trans. Barbara Johnson (London: Athlone, 1981).

—— *Margins of Philosophy*, trans. with additional notes by Alan Bass (Brighton: Harvester, 1982).

—— 'My Chances/Mes Chances', in J. H. Smith and W. Kerrigan (eds.), *Taking Chances: Derrida, Psychoanalysis and Literature* (Baltimore: Johns Hopkins University Press, 1984).

DOLLIMORE, JONATHAN, 'The Challenge of Sexuality', in Alan Sinfield (ed.), *Society and Literature 1945–70* (London: Methuen, 1983).

—— *Radical Tragedy: Religion, Ideology and Power in the Drama of Shakespeare and His Contemporaries* (2nd edn., Hemel Hempstead: Harvester, 1989).

DOLLIMORE, JONATHAN, 'A History of Some Importance', *Gay Times*, 119 (Aug. 1988), 44–5.

—— and SINFIELD, ALAN (eds.), *Political Shakespeare: New Essays in Cultural Materialism* (Manchester: Manchester University Press, 1985).

DONNE, JOHN, *The Sermons of John Donne*, ed. G. R. Potter and E. M. Simpson, 10 vols. (Berkeley, Calif.: University of California Press, 1953–62).

DOUGLAS, MARY, *Purity and Danger: An Analysis of Concepts of Pollution and Taboo* [1966] (Harmondsworth: Penguin, 1970)

DOWNES, D., and ROCK, P., *Understanding Deviance: A Guide to the Sociology of Crime and Rule Breaking* (Oxford: Clarendon Press, 1982).

DOYLE, B., 'The Hidden History of English Studies', in Peter Widdowson (ed.), *Re-reading English* (London: Methuen, 1982).

DRAKAKIS, JOHN, 'The Engendering of Toads: Patriarchy and the Problem of Subjectivity in Shakespeare's *Othello*', *Shakespeare Jahrbuch*, 124 (Weimar, 1988), 62–80.

DUERR, HANS PETER, *Dreamtime: Concerning the Boundary between Wilderness and Civilization*, trans. Felicitas Goodman (Oxford: Blackwell, 1985).

DUMOUCHEL, PAUL (ed.), *Violence and Truth: On the Work of René Girard* (Stanford, Calif.: Stanford University Press, 1988).

DUSINBERRE, JULIET, *Shakespeare and the Nature of Women* (London: Macmillan, 1975).

DYER, RICHARD, 'Getting Over the Rainbow: Identity and Pleasure in Gay Cultural Politics', in George Bridges and Rosalind Brunt (eds.), *Silver Linings: Some Strategies for the Eighties* (London: Lawrence & Wishart, 1981).

—— *Heavenly Bodies: Film Stars and Society* (London: Macmillan, 1987).

DYSON, A. E., and LOVELOCK, JULIAN, 'Event Perverse: The Epic of Exile', in A. E. Dyson and J. Lovelock (eds.), *Milton: Paradise Lost, A Casebook* (London: Macmillan, 1973), 220–42.

EAGLETON, T., *Walter Benjamin, or: Towards a Revolutionary Criticism* (London: Verso, 1981).

—— *Literary Theory: An Introduction* (Oxford: Blackwell, 1983).

—— 'Capitalism, Modernism and Postmodernism', in *Against the Grain* (London: Verso, 1986), 131–47.

—— 'Meaning and Material' [review article], *Times Literary Supplement* (2 May 1986), 477.

EDGLEY, ROY, 'Revolution, Reform and Dialectic', in G. H. R. Parkinson (ed.), *Marx and Marxisms* (Cambridge: Cambridge University Press, 1982), 21–38.

ELLMANN, R. (ed.), *Oscar Wilde: A Collection of Critical Essays* (Englewood Cliffs, NJ: Prentice Hall, 1969).

—— 'Corydon and Ménalque', in *Golden Codgers: Biographical Speculations* (London: Oxford University Press, 1973), 81–100.

—— *Oscar Wilde* (London: Hamish Hamilton, 1987).

EMMISON, F. G., *Elizabethan Life: Morals and the Church Courts* (Chelmsford: Essex County Council, 1973).

ERIKSON, KAI T., *Wayward Puritans: A Study in the Sociology of Deviance* (New York: Wiley & Sons, 1966).

EVANS, G. R., *Augustine on Evil* (Cambridge: Cambridge University Press, 1982).

FADERMAN, LILLIAN, *Surpassing the Love of Men: Romantic Friendship and Love between Women from the Renaissance to the Present* (London: Junction Books, 1981).

FANON, FRANTZ, *Black Skin, White Masks* [1952], trans. Charles Lam Markmann, foreword by Homi Bhabha (London: Pluto Press, 1986).

—— *The Wretched of the Earth* [1961], trans. Constance Farrington, preface by Jean-Paul Sartre (Harmondsworth: Penguin, 1967).

FELDMAN, SANDOR S., 'On Homosexuality', in S. Lorand and M. Balint (eds.), *Perversions: Psychodynamics and Therapy* (New York: Random House, 1956).

FERGUSON, MARGARET W., QUILLIGAN, MAUREEN, and VICKERS, NANCY J., *Rewriting the Renaissance: The Discourses of Sexual Difference in Early Modern Europe* (Chicago: Chicago University Press, 1986).

FERRY, ANNE, *The 'Inward' Language: Sonnets of Wyatt, Sidney, Shakespeare, Donne* (Chicago: Chicago University Press, 1983).

FEUER, JANE, 'Reading *Dynasty*: Television and Reception Theory', *South Atlantic Quarterly*, 88 (1989), 443–60.

FLETCHER, IAN (ed.), *Decadence and the 1890's* (London: Arnold, 1979).

FLETCHER, JOHN, *Love's Cure*, in *The Dramatic Works in the Beaumont and Fletcher Canon*, ed. George W. Williams, general ed. Fredson Bowers, vol. iii (Cambridge: Cambridge University Press, 1976).

FLETCHER, JOHN, 'Freud and His Uses: Psychoanalysis and Gay Theory', in Simon Shepherd and Mick Wallis (eds.), *Coming on Strong: Gay Politics and Culture* (London: Unwin Hyman, 1989).

FORSYTH, NEIL, *The Old Enemy: Satan and the Combat Myth* (Princeton, NJ: Princeton University Press, 1987).

FOUCAULT, MICHEL, *Discipline and Punish: The Birth of the Prison*, trans. Alan Sheridan (New York: Pantheon, 1977).

—— *Language, Counter-Memory, Practice: Selected Essays and Interviews*, ed. with intro. by Donald F. Bouchard; trans. Donald F. Bouchard and Sherry Simon (Oxford: Blackwell, 1977).

—— *Power/Knowledge: Selected Interviews and Other Writings 1972–1977*, ed. Colin Gordon (Brighton: Harvester, 1980).

—— *The History of Sexuality*, i: *An Introduction* (New York: Vintage Books [1978], 1980).

—— *Herculine Barbine, Being the Recently Discovered Memoirs of a French Hermaphrodite* (Brighton: Harvester, 1980).

FREEDMAN, MARK, 'Homophobia: The Psychology of a Social Disease', *Body Politic*, 24 (June 1975).

FRENCH, MARILYN, *Shakespeare's Division of Experience* (London: Jonathan Cape, 1982).

FREUD, SIGMUND, *The Pelican Freud Library*, 15 vols., general ed. Angela Richards (Harmondsworth: Penguin, 1974–86): i: *Introductory Lectures on Psychoanalysis*; ii: *New Introductory Lectures on Psychoanalysis* iii: *Studies on Hysteria*; iv: *The Interpretation of Dreams*; v: *The Psychopathology of Everyday Life*; vi: *Jokes and Their Relation to the Unconscious*; vii: *On Sexuality* (including *Three Essays on the Theory of Sexuality*; viii: *Case Histories 1* ('Dora' and 'Little

Hans'); ix: *Case Histories* 2 ('The Rat Man', 'Schreber', 'The Wolf Man', 'A Case of Female Sexuality'); x: *On Psychopathology*; xi: *On Metapsychology: The Theory of Psychoanalysis* (including *Beyond the Pleasure Principle, The Ego and the Id*); xii: *Civilization, Society and Religion* (including *Civilization and its Discontents*); xiii: *The Origins of Religion*; xiv: *Art and Literature*; xv: *Historical and Expository Works on Psychoanalysis.*

FREUD, SIGMUND, 'Analysis Terminable and Interminable', in *The Standard Edition of the Complete Works*, vol. xxiii [1937–9] (London: Hogarth, 1964).

—— *The Complete Letters of Sigmund Freud to Wilhelm Fliess 1887–1904*, trans. and ed. Jeffrey Moussaieff Masson (Cambridge, Mass.: Harvard University Press, 1985).

FROSH, STEPHEN, *The Politics of Psychoanalysis: An Introduction to Freudian and Post Freudian Theory* (London: Macmillan, 1987).

FUSS, DIANA, *Essentially Speaking: Feminism, Nature and Difference* (London: Routledge and Kegan Paul, 1989).

GABRIEL, YIANNIS, *Freud and Society* (London: Routledge and Kegan Paul, 1983).

GAGNIER, REGENIA, *Idylls of the Market Place: Oscar Wilde and the Victorian Public* [1986] (London: Scolar Press, 1987).

GALFORD, ELLEN, *Moll Cutpurse: Her True History* (Edinburgh: Stramullion Co-operative, 1984).

GALLOP, JANE, *Intersections: A Reading of Sade with Bataille, Blanchot, and Klossowski* (Lincoln, Nebr.: University of Nebraska Press, 1981).

—— *Feminism and Psychoanalysis: The Daughter's Seduction* (London: Macmillan, 1982).

—— *Thinking through the Body* (New York: Columbia University Press, 1988).

GAY, PETER, *Freud: A Life for Our Time* (New York: Norton, 1988).

Gay Black Group, 'White Gay Racism' (1st pub. *Gay News* 1982), repr. in R. Chapman and J. Rutherford (eds.), *Male Order* (London: Lawrence & Wishart, 1988), 104–10.

Gay Left Collective (ed.), *Homosexuality: Power and Politics* (London: Allison & Busby, 1980).

GENET, JEAN, *Our Lady of the Flowers* [1943], trans. Bernard Frechtman, with intro. by Jean-Paul Sartre (from *Saint Genet*) (London: Panther, 1966).

—— *The Thief's Journal* [1949], trans. Bernard Frechtman (Harmondsworth: Penguin, 1967).

—— interview with Hubert Fichte, in W. Leyland (ed.), *Gay Sunshine Interviews*, vol. i (San Francisco, Calif.: Gay Sunshine Press, 1978), 67–94.

—— *Prisoner of Love*, trans. Barbara Bray, with intro. by Edmund White (London: Picador, 1989).

GIDAL, PETER, *Andy Warhol: Films and Painting* (London: Studio Vista, 1971).

GIDE, ANDRÉ, *Journals*, 4 vols. (London: Secker & Warburg, 1947–51).

—— *Oscar Wilde*, trans. Bernard Frechtman (London: William Kimber, 1951).

—— *Correspondence between Paul Claudel and André Gide, 1899–1926*, intro. and notes by Robert Mallet, preface and trans. by John Russell (New York: Pantheon, 1952).

—— *The Correspondence of André Gide and Edmund Gosse 1904–1928*, ed.

with trans., intro., and notes by Linette F. Brugmans (London: Peter Owen, 1960).

—— *So Be It, or: The Chips are Down* [1952], trans. with intro. and notes by Justin O'Brien (London: Chatto, 1960).

—— *The Immoralist* (Harmondsworth: Penguin, 1960).

—— *Correspondence, 1890–1942: André Gide–Paul Valéry*, trans. J. Guicharnaud, cited here from the abridged version, *Self-Portraits: The Gide/Valéry Letters* (Chicago: University of Chicago Press, 1966).

—— *If It Die* [1920, private edn. 1926], trans. Dorothy Bussy (Harmondsworth: Penguin, 1977).

—— *Travels in the Congo* [1927/8], trans. Dorothy Bussy (Harmondsworth: Penguin, 1986).

—— *Amyntas: North African Journals* [1906], trans. Richard Howard (New York: Ecco Press, 1988).

GILBERT, ARTHUR N., 'Sexual Deviance and Disaster during the Napoleonic Wars', *Albion*, 9 (1977), 98–113.

GILMAN, SANDER L., 'Sexology, Psychoanalysis, and Degeneration: From a Theory of Race to a Race to Theory', in J. Edward Chamberlain and Sander L. Gilman (eds.), *Degeneration: The Dark Side of Progress* (New York: Columbia University Press, 1985).

GIRARD, RENÉ, *Deceit, Desire and the Novel: Self and Others in Literary Structure* (Baltimore: Johns Hopkins University Press, 1965).

—— *Things Hidden since the Foundation of the World* (Stanford, Calif.: Stanford University Press, 1987).

GOLDBERG, JONATHAN, 'Sodomy and Society: The Case of Christopher Marlowe', *Southwest Review* (Autumn 1984), 371–8.

GOMEZ, JEWELLE, and SMITH, BARBARA, 'Talking about It: Homophobia in the Black Community', *Feminist Review* (*Perverse Politics: Lesbian Issues*), 34 (Spring 1990), 47–55.

GOODHEART, EUGENE, *The Utopian Vision of D. H. Lawrence* (Chicago: Chicago University Press, 1963).

GOODMAN, JONATHAN, *The Oscar Wilde File* (London: W. H. Allen, 1988).

GORDON, JAN B., 'Decadent Spaces: Notes for a Phenomenology of the *Fin de siècle*', in I. Fletcher (ed.), *Decadence and the 1890's* (London: Arnold, 1979).

GRAMSCI, ANTONIO, *Selections from Cultural Writings*, ed. David Forgacs and Geoffrey Nowell-Smith, trans. William Boelhower (London: Lawrence & Wishart, 1985).

GREENBERG, DAVID F., *The Construction of Homosexuality* (Chicago: Chicago University Press, 1988).

GREENBLATT, STEPHEN, *Renaissance Self-Fashioning from More to Shakespeare* (Chicago: University of Chicago Press, 1980).

—— *The Power of Forms in the English Renaissance* (Norman: Pilgrim Books, 1982).

—— 'Invisible Bullets: Renaissance Authority and its Subversion', in J. Dollimore and A. Sinfield (eds.), *Political Shakespeare* (Manchester: Manchester University Press, 1985).

—— *Shakespearean Negotiations: The Circulation of Social Energy in Renaissance England* (Oxford: Clarendon Press, 1988).

GREENFIELD, MEG, 'Heart of Darkness', *Newsweek* (4 Dec. 1978), 132.

GUERARD, ALBERT J., *André Gide* (2nd edn., Cambridge, Mass.: Harvard University Press, 1969).

HALL, MARGUERITE RADCLYFFE, *The Well of Loneliness* [1928] (London: Falcon Press, 1949).

HALL, STUART, *et al.*, *Policing the Crisis: Mugging, the State, and Law and Order* (London: Macmillan, 1978).

HARRIS, F. J., *André Gide and Romain Rolland: Two Men Divided* (New Brunswick: Rutgers University Press, 1973).

HASELKORN, ANNE M., *Prostitution in Elizabethan and Jacobean Comedy* (New York: Whitston, 1983).

HASSAN, I., 'Pluralism in Postmodern Perspective', *Critical Inquiry*, 12/3 (1986), 503–20.

HAWKES, TERENCE, *That Shakespeherian Rag: Essays on a Critical Process* (London: Methuen, 1986).

HAYWARD, JOHN (ed.), *The Penguin Book of English Verse* (Harmondsworth: Penguin, 1956).

HEATH, STEPHEN, *The Sexual Fix* (London: Macmillan, 1982).

—— 'Joan Rivière and the Masquerade', in Victor Burgin, James Donald, and Cora Kaplan (eds.), *Formations of Fantasy* (London: Methuen, 1986).

HEBDIGE, DICK, *Subculture: The Meaning of Style* (London: Methuen, 1979).

HENRIQUES, FERNANDO, *Prostitution and Society*, 2 vols. (London: Mac-Gibbon and Kee, 1962–3).

HICK, JOHN, *Evil and the God of Love* (Glasgow: Collins, 1968).

Hic Mulier: Or, the Man-Woman and Haec-Vir: Or, the Womanish-Man [1620], facsimile (The Rota at the University of Essex, 1973).

HILL, CHRISTOPHER, *The World Turned Upside Down: Radical Ideas during the English Revolution* (Harmondsworth: Penguin, 1975).

HOCQUENGHEM, GUY, *Homosexual Desire* [1972], trans. Daniella Dangoor, with preface by Jeffrey Weeks (London: Allison & Busby, 1978).

HODGDON, BARBARA, 'Kiss Me Deadly, or the Des/Demonized Spectacle', forthcoming.

HOLLERAN, ANDREW, *Dancer from the Dance* [1978] (London: Jonathan Cape, 1979).

Homily against Disobedience and Wilful Rebellion, in *Certain Sermons or Homilies: Appointed to be Read in Churches* (London: Society for Promoting Christian Knowledge, 1890).

HOOKER, RICHARD, *Of the Laws of Ecclesiastical Polity*, 2 vols., intro. by C. Morris (London: Dent, 1969).

HOWARD, JEAN, 'Crossdressing, the Theatre and Gender Struggle in Early Modern England', *Shakespeare Quarterly*, 39 (1988), 418–40.

HUGHES, PAUL L., and LARKIN, JAMES L. (eds.), *Tudor Royal Proclamations*, 3 vols. (New Haven, Conn.: Yale University Press, 1964–9).

HULME, PETER, *Colonial Encounters* (London: Methuen, 1986).

HUME, DAVID, *Dialogues concerning Natural Religion*, in *Classics of Western Philosophy*, ed. Steven M. Cahn (Indianapolis: Hackett, 1977).

HUNT, WILLIAM, *The Puritan Moment: The Coming of Revolution in an English County* (Cambridge, Mass.: Harvard University Press, 1983).

HUNTER, WILLIAM B., *et al.* (eds.), *A Milton Encyclopedia* (Lewisburg: Bucknell University Press, 1970).

HYDE, H. M., *The Trials of Oscar Wilde* (London: William Hodge, 1948).

—— *Oscar Wilde: A Biography* (London: Methuen, 1982).

IGNATIEFF, MICHAEL, 'State, Civil Society and Total Institutions: A Critique of Recent Social Histories of Punishment ', in S. Cohen and A. T. Scull (eds.), *Social Control and the State* (Oxford: Robertson, 1983).

The Interpreter's Bible, ed. G. A. Buttrick *et al.*, 15 vols. (New York: Abingdon Press, 1954).

IRIGARAY, LUCE, *This Sex Which is Not One*, trans. Catherine Porter with Carolyn Burke (Ithaca, NY: Cornell University Press, 1985).

IZARD, THOMAS C., *George Whetstone: Mid-Elizabethan Gentleman of Letters* (New York: Columbia University Press, 1942; repr. New York: AMS Press, 1966).

JACKSON, GEORGE, *Soledad Brother: The Prison Letters of George Jackson*, intro. by Jean Genet (Harmondsworth: Penguin, 1971).

JACKSON, ROSEMARY, *Fantasy: The Literature of Subversion* (London: Methuen, 1981).

JAMESON, FREDRIC, *The Political Unconscious: Narrative as a Socially Symbolic Act* (London: Methuen, 1981).

—— 'Postmodernism and Consumer Society', in H. Foster (ed.), *The Anti-Aesthetic: Essays on Postmodern Culture* (Washington, DC: Bay Press, 1983).

—— 'Postmodernism, or the Cultural Logic of Late Capitalism', *New Left Review*, 146 (1984), 53–92.

—— 'Regarding Postmodernism: A Conversation with Fredric Jameson', in Andrew Ross (ed.), *Universal Abandon* (Edinburgh: Edinburgh University Press, 1988).

—— 'Marxism and Postmodernism', in Douglas Kellner (ed.), *Postmodernism/ Jameson/Critique* (Washington, DC: Maisonneuve Press, 1989), 369–87.

JARDINE, LISA, *Still Harping on Daughters: Women and Drama in the Age of Shakespeare* (Brighton: Harvester, 1983).

JAY, MARTIN, 'Hierarchy and the Humanities: The Radical Implications of a Conservative Idea', *Telos*, 62 (Winter 1984–5), 131–44.

JONES, ELDRED, *Othello's Countrymen: The African in English Renaissance Drama* (Oxford: Oxford University Press, 1965).

JONSON, BEN, *Works*, ed. C. H. Herford and P. Simpson, 11 vols. (Oxford: Clarendon Press, 1922–52).

—— *Volpone, or: The Fox*, ed. R. B. Parker (The Revels Plays) (Manchester: Manchester University Press, 1983).

JOURNET, CHARLES, *The Meaning of Evil*, trans. Michael Barry (London: Geoffrey Chapman, 1963).

KARRAS, RUTH MAZO, 'The Regulation of Brothels in Later Medieval England', *Signs: Journal of Women in Culture and Society*, 14/2 (1989), 399–433.

KELLY, J. N. D., *Early Christian Doctrines* (5th edn., London: Black, 1977).

KERMODE, FRANK, *History and Value* (Oxford: Clarendon Press, 1988).

KHAN, M. MASUD R., *Alienation in Perversions* (London: The Hogarth Press, 1979).

KIBERD, DECLAN, *Men and Feminism in Modern Literature* (London: Macmillan, 1985).

KINSEY, A. C., et al., *Sexual Behavior in the Human Male* (Philadelphia: Saunders, 1948).

KITZINGER, CELIA, *The Social Construction of Lesbianism* (London: Sage, 1987).

KOHUT, HEINZ, 'Death in Venice: A Story about the Disintegration of Artistic Sublimation', in H. M. Ruitenbeek (ed.), *Psychoanalysis and Literature* (New York: Dutton, 1964).

KOTT, JAN, *Shakespeare Our Contemporary*, trans. Boleslaw Taborski, preface by Peter Brook (London: Methuen, 1967).

KRAMER, LARRY, *Faggots* (London: Futura, 1980).

KRISTEVA, JULIA, *The Kristeva Reader*, ed. Toril Moi (Oxford: Blackwell, 1986).

KRUPNICK, M. (ed.), *Displacement: Derrida and After* (Bloomington, Ind.: Indiana University Press, 1983).

KUNZLE, D., 'World Turned Upside Down: The Iconography of a European Broadsheet Type', in Barbara Babcock (ed.), *The Reversible World: Symbolic Inversion in Art and Society* (Ithaca, NY: Cornell University Press, 1978).

LACAN, JACQUES, *Écrits: A Selection*, trans. Alan Sheridan (London: Tavistock, 1977).

—— *Feminine Sexuality: Jacques Lacan and the École freudienne*, trans. Jacqueline Rose with intros. by Rose and Juliet Mitchell (London: Macmillan, 1982).

—— *The Seminar of Jacques Lacan*, i: *Freud's Papers of Technique 1953–54*, trans. with notes by John Forrester (Cambridge: Cambridge University Press, 1988).

—— *The Seminar of Jacques Lacan*, ii: *The Ego in Freud's Theory and in the Technique of Psychoanalysis 1954–55*, ed. Jacques-Alain Miller, trans. Sylvana Tomaselli, notes by John Forrester (Cambridge: Cambridge University Press, 1988).

LACTANTIUS, *The Minor Works*, trans. Sister Mary Francis McDonald (Washington, DC: The Catholic University of America Press, 1965).

LAHR, JOHN, *Prick Up Your Ears* (Harmondsworth: Penguin, 1980).

LAING, R. D., *The Divided Self* (Harmondsworth: Penguin, 1965).

LAMMING, GEORGE, *The Pleasures of Exile* (London: Michael Joseph, 1960).

LAPLANCHE, JEAN, *Life and Death in Psychoanalysis*, trans. with intro. by Jeffrey Mehlman (Baltimore: Johns Hopkins University Press, 1976).

—— and PONTALIS, J. B., *The Language of Psychoanalysis*, trans. D. Nicholson-Smith (London: Hogarth, 1983).

LAQUEUR, THOMAS, 'Orgasm, Generation, and the Politics of Reproductive Biology', *Representations*, 14 (1986), 1–41.

—— *Making Sex: Body and Gender from the Greeks to Freud* (Cambridge, Mass.: Harvard University Press, 1990).

LATIMER, D., 'Jameson and Postmodernism', *New Left Review*, 148 (1984), 116–28.

LAURITSEN, JOHN, and THORSTAD, DAVID, *The Early Homosexual Rights Movement (1864–1935)* (New York: Times Change Press, 1974).

LAWRENCE, D. H., *Selected Essays*, intro. by Richard Aldington (Harmondsworth: Penguin, 1950).

—— *Phoenix: The Posthumous Papers of D. H. Lawrence*, ed. with intro. by Edward D. McDonald (London: Heinemann, 1936).

—— *Phoenix II: Uncollected, Unpublished and Other Prose Works*, collected and ed. with intro. and notes by Warren Roberts and Harry T. Moore (London: Heinemann, 1968).

—— *A Selection from Phoenix*, ed. A. A. H. Inglis (Harmondsworth: Penguin, 1979).

—— 'Pornography and Obscenity', in *A Selection from Phoenix*, ed. A. A. H. Inglis (Harmondsworth: Penguin, 1979).

—— Introduction to *Pansies*, in *A Selection from Phoenix*, ed. A. A. H. Inglis (Harmondsworth: Penguin, 1979).

—— Review of *The Social Basis of Consciousness* by Trigant Burrow, in *A Selection from Phoenix*, ed. A. A. H. Inglis (Harmondsworth: Penguin, 1979).

—— *Women in Love* [1921] (Harmondsworth: Penguin, 1977).

—— *Aaron's Rod* [1922] (Harmondsworth: Penguin, 1968).

—— *The Plumed Serpent* [1926] (Harmondsworth: Penguin, 1968).

—— *Lady Chatterley's Lover* [1928] (Harmondsworth: Penguin, 1960).

—— *Studies in Classic American Literature* [1924] (Harmondsworth: Penguin, 1971).

—— *The Complete Poems of D. H. Lawrence*, collected and ed. with intro. and notes by Vivian de Sola Pinto, 2 vols. (London: Heinemann, 1967).

—— *The Letters of D. H. Lawrence*, ii: *1913–16*, ed. George J. Zytaruk and James T. Boulton (Cambridge: Cambridge University Press, 1981).

LAWRENCE, T. E., *Seven Pillars of Wisdom* [1926] (London: Cape, 1976).

LEAVIS, Q. D., *Fiction and the Reading Public* (London: Chatto, 1932).

LENTRICCHIA, FRANK, *Ariel and the Police: Michel Foucault, William James, Wallace Stevens* (Brighton: Harvester Press, 1988).

LEVINE, LAURA, 'Men in Women's Clothing: Anti-theatricality and Effeminization from 1579–1642', *Criticism*, 28 (1986), 121–43.

LEWES, K., *The Psychoanalytic Theory of Male Homosexuality* (London: Quartet, 1989).

LEYLAND, WINSTON (ed.), *Gay Sunshine Interviews*, vol. i (San Francisco: Gay Sunshine Press, 1978).

LICHTMAN, RICHARD, *The Production of Desire: The Integration of Psychoanalysis into Marxist Theory* (New York: The Free Press, 1982).

LIEB, MICHAEL (ed.), *Achievements of the Left Hand: Essays on the Prose of John Milton* (Amherst: Massachusetts University Press, 1974).

LOOMBA, ANIA, *Gender, Race, Renaissance Drama* (Manchester: Manchester University Press, 1989).

—— 'Overworlding the "Third World"', *Oxford Literary Review*, forthcoming.

LORDE, AUDRE, *Zami: A New Spelling of My Name* [1982] (London: Sheba, 1984).

—— *Sister Outsider: Essays and Speeches* (New York: The Crossing Press, 1984).

LYONS, B., *Voices of Melancholy: Studies in Literary Treatments of Melancholy in Renaissance England* (London: Routledge and Kegan Paul, 1971).

LYOTARD, JEAN-FRANÇOIS, *The Postmodern Condition: A Report on Knowledge*, trans. G. Bennington and B. Massumi, foreword by Fredric Jameson (Manchester: Manchester University Press, 1984).

MACCABE, COLIN, *Theoretical Essays: Film, Linguistics, Literature* (Manchester: Manchester University Press, 1985).

MACCLEAN, IAN, *The Renaissance Notion of Woman* (Cambridge: Cambridge University Press, 1980).

McCLOSKY, H. J., *God and Evil* (The Hague: Martinus Nijhoff, 1974).

MACCUBBIN, ROBERT PURKS (ed.), *'Tis Nature's Fault: Unauthorised Sexuality during the Enlightenment* (Cambridge: Cambridge University Press, 1988).

MAILER, NORMAN, 'The Homosexual Villain' and 'Advertisement for "the Homosexual Villain"', in *Advertisements for Myself* [1954] (London: André Deutsch, 1961), 197–205.

—— *The Prisoner of Sex* (London: Weidenfeld & Nicolson, 1971).

MANN, THOMAS, *Death in Venice* [1912], trans. H. T. Lowe-Porter (Harmondsworth, Penguin, 1971).

—— *Letters 1889–1955*, selected and trans. by Richard and Clara Winston (New York: Alfred Knopf, 1971).

—— *Diaries 1918–1939*, trans. Richard and Clara Winston (London: André Deutsch, 1983).

MARCUS, S., *Freud and the Culture of Psychoanalysis* (London: Allen & Unwin, 1984).

MARCUSE, HERBERT, *Eros and Civilization: A Philosophical Inquiry into Freud* [1955] (Boston: Beacon Press, 1966).

MARIENSTRAS, RICHARD, *New Perspectives on the Shakespearean World*, trans. Janet Lloyd (Cambridge: Cambridge University Press, 1985).

MARITAIN, JACQUES, *St Thomas and the Problem of Evil* (Milwaukee, Wis.: Marquette University Press, 1942).

MARKS, ELAINE, and DE COURTIVRON, ISABELLE (eds.), *New French Feminisms: An Anthology* (Brighton: Harvester, 1981).

MAROWITZ, CHARLES, 'The Revenge of Jean Genet' [1961], in Charles Marowitz *et al.* (eds.), *The Encore Reader: A Chronicle of the New Drama* (London: Methuen, 1965).

MARX, KARL, *Selected Writings in Sociology and Social Philosophy*, ed. with intro. and notes by T. B. Bottomore and Maximilien Rubel; texts trans. T. B. Bottomore (Harmondsworth: Penguin, 1969).

—— and ENGELS, FREDERICK, *Selected Works*, in 1 vol. (London: Lawrence & Wishart, 1968).

MAYER, HANS, *Outsiders: A Study in Life and Letters*, trans. Denis M. Sweet, (Cambridge, Mass.: MIT Press, 1982).

MERCER, KOBENA, 'Welcome to the Jungle: Identity and Diversity in Postmodern Politics', in Jonathan Rutherford (ed.), *Identity: Community, Culture, Difference* (London: Lawrence & Wishart, 1990), 43–71.

—— and JULIEN, ISAAC, 'Race, Sexuality and Black Masculinity: A Dossier', in R. Chapman and J. Rutherford (eds.), *Male Order: Unwrapping Masculinity* (London: Lawrence & Wishart, 1988), 97–164.

MERCK, MANDY, 'Difference and its Discontents', *Screen*, 28/1 (1987), 2–9.

MEYERS, JEFFREY, *Homosexuality and Literature 1890–1930* (London: Athlone, 1977).

MIDDLETON, THOMAS, and DEKKER, THOMAS, *The Roaring Girl*, ed. A. Gomme (New Mermaid edn.) (London: Benn, 1976).

—— and ROWLEY, WILLIAM, *A Fair Quarrel*, ed. R. V. Holdsworth (London: Benn, 1974).

MIELI, MARIO, *Homosexuality and Liberation: Elements of a Gay Critique* [1977], trans. David Fernbach (London: Gay Men's Press, 1980).

MILLER, CHRISTOPHER L., *Blank Darkness: Africanist Discourse in French* (Chicago: University of Chicago Press, 1985).

MILLETT, KATE, *Sexual Politics* (London: Virago, 1977).

MILTON, JOHN, *Complete Prose Works*, general ed. Don M. Wolfe (New Haven, Conn.: Yale University Press, 1953–82).

—— *Poetical Works*, ed. Douglas Bush (Oxford: Oxford University Press, 1969).

—— *Paradise Lost*, ed. Alastair Fowler (London: Longman, 1971).

MITCHELL, JULIET, *Psychoanalysis and Feminism* (London: Allen Lane, 1974).

—— *Women: The Longest Revolution: Essays on Feminism, Literature and Psychoanalysis* (London: Virago, 1984).

MOBERLY, ELIZABETH R., *Psychogenesis: The Early Development of Gender Identity* (London: Routledge & Kegan Paul, 1983).

—— 'New Perspectives on Homosexuality', *Journal of the Royal Society of Health*, 105/6 (1985), 206–10.

MODLESKI, TANIA, 'Femininity as Mas[s]querade: A Feminist Approach to Mass Culture', in Colin MacCabe (ed.), *High Theory/Low Culture: Analysing Popular Television and Film* (Manchester: Manchester University Press, 1986).

MOHANTY, S. P., 'Us and Them: On the Philosophical Bases of Political Criticism', *Yale Journal of Criticism*, 2/2 (1989), 1–31; repr. in and cited from *New Formations*, 8 (1989), 55–80.

MOI, TORIL, 'Representation and Patriarchy: Sexuality and Epistemology in Freud's Dora', in C. Bernheimer and C. Kahane (eds.), *In Dora's Case* (London: Virago, 1985), 188–99.

—— *Sexual/Textual Politics: Feminist Literary Theory* (London: Methuen, 1985).

MONTAIGNE, MICHEL, *Essays*, ed. D. M. Frame (Stanford, Calif.: Stanford University Press, 1958).

—— *Essays*, trans. John Florio, 3 vols. (London: Dent, 1965).

MONTROSE, LOUIS, 'The Purpose of Playing: Reflections on a Shakespearean Anthropology', *Helios*, NS 7 (1980), 51–74.

—— ' "Eliza, Queene of shepheards", and 'the Pastoral of Power', *English Literary History*, 10 (1980), 153–82.

—— ' "The Place of a Brother" in *As You Like It*: Social Process and Comic Form', *Shakespeare Quarterly*, 32 (1981), 28–54.

—— 'Of Gentlemen and Shepherds: The Politics of Elizabethan Pastoral Form', *ELH* 50 (1983), 415–59.

MOORE, SUZANNE, 'Getting a Bit of the Other: The Pimps of Postmodernism', in Rowena Chapman and Jonathan Rutherford (eds.), *Male Order: Unwrapping Masculinity* (London: Lawrence & Wishart, 1988).

MOSSE, GEORGE L., *Nationalism and Sexuality: Respectable and Abnormal Sexuality in Modern Europe* (New York: Howard Fertig, 1985).

MULLANEY, STEVEN, *The Place of the Stage: Licence, Play and Power in Renaissance England* (Chicago: University of Chicago Press, 1988).

NALBANTIAN, SUZANNE, *Seeds of Decadence in the Late Nineteenth Century Novel: A Crisis in Values* (London: Macmillan, 1983).

NASHE, THOMAS, *The Unfortunate Traveller and Other Works*, ed. J. B. Steane (Harmondsworth: Penguin, 1972).

NASSAAR, CHRISTOPHER S., *Into the Demon Universe: A Literary Exploration of Oscar Wilde* (New Haven, Conn.: Yale University Press, 1974).

NESTLE, JOAN, *A Restricted Country: Essays and Short Stories* (London: Sheba Feminist Publishers, 1987).

NEWMAN, KAREN, '"And Wash the Ethiop White": Femininity and the Monstrous in *Othello*', in Jean Howard and Marion F. O'Connor (eds.), *Shakespeare Reproduced* (London: Methuen, 1987).

NEWTON, ESTHER, 'The Mythic Mannish Lesbian: Radclyffe Hall and the New Woman', in Estelle B. Freedman *et al.* (eds.), *The Lesbian Issue: Essays From Signs* (Chicago: Chicago University Press, 1985).

NIXON, ROB, 'Caribbean and African Appropriations of *The Tempest*', *Critical Inquiry*, 13/3 (1987), 557–78.

NORDAU, MAX, *Degeneration*, trans. from 2nd edn. (New York: Appleton and Co., 1895).

NUSSBAUM, FELICITY, and BROWN, LAURA (eds.), *The New Eighteenth Century: Theory, Politics, English Literature* (London: Methuen, 1988).

O'BRIEN, JUSTIN, *Portrait of André Gide: A Critical Biography* (New York: Alfred Knopf, 1953).

OKRI, BEN, 'Leaping out of Shakespeare's Terror: Five Meditations on *Othello*', in Kwesi Owusu (ed.), *Storms of the Heart: An Anthology of Black Arts and Culture* (London: Camden Press, 1988), 9–18.

ORGEL, STEPHEN, 'Nobody's Perfect, or: Why Did the English Stage Take Boys for Women?', *South Atlantic Quarterly*, 88/1 (1989), 7–29.

—— 'The Boys in the Backroom: Shakespeare's Apprentices and the Economics of Theater' (forthcoming).

ORKIN, MARTIN, *Shakespeare against Apartheid* (Craighall: Ad. Donker, 1987).

ORTON, JOE, *What the Butler Saw*, in *The Complete Plays*, intro. John Lahr (London: Eyre Methuen, 1976).

—— *The Orton Diaries*, ed. John Lahr (London: Methuen, 1986).

OTTO, W. F., *Dionysus: Myth and Cult*, trans. R. B. Palmer (Bloomington, Ind.: Indiana University Press, 1965).

OWENS, CRAIG, 'Outlaws: Gay Men in Feminism', in Alice Jardine and Paul Smith (eds.), *Men in Feminism* (London: Methuen, 1987).

PAINE, GUSTAVUS S., *The Learned Men* (New York: Thomas Y. Crowell, 1959).

PAINTER, GEORGE D., *André Gide: A Critical and Biographical Study* (London: Baker, 1951).

PARKER, HERSCHEL, *Flawed Texts and Verbal Icons: Literary Authority in American Fiction* (Evanston, Ill.: Northwestern University Press, 1984).

PARKER, PATRICIA, *Literary Fat Ladies: Rhetoric, Gender, Property* (London: Methuen, 1987).

PARRY, BENITA, 'Problems in Current Theories of Colonial Discourse', *Oxford Literary Review*, 9 (1987), 27–58.

PATTERSON, ORLANDO, *Slavery and Social Death: A Comparative Study* (Cambridge, Mass.: Harvard University Press, 1982).

PEARSON, GEOFFREY, *The Deviant Imagination* (London: Macmillan, 1975).

PEQUIGNEY, JOSEPH, *Such is my Love* (Chicago, Ill.: University of Chicago Press, 1985).

PERKINS, WILLIAM, *William Perkins 1558–1602: English Puritanist: His Pioneer Works on Casuistry: 'A Discourse of Conscience' and 'The Whole Treatise of Cases of Conscience'*, ed. with intro. by Thomas F. Merrill (Nieuwkoop: B. De Graaf, 1966).

PFISTER, MANFRED, *Oscar Wilde: The Picture of Dorian Gray* (Munich: Wilhelm Fink, 1986).

PHARR, SUZANNE, *Homophobia: A Weapon of Sexism* , illustrations by Susan G. Raymond (Inverness, Calif.: Chardon Press, 1988).

PLANT, RICHARD, *The Pink Triangle: The Nazi War against Homosexuals* (Edinburgh: Mainstream Publishing, 1987).

PLUMMER, KENNETH (ed.), *The Making of the Modern Homosexual* (London: Hutchinson, 1981).

—— 'Homosexual Categories: Some Research Problems in the Labelling Perspective of Homosexuality', in K. Plummer (ed.), *The Making of the Modern Homosexual* (London: Hutchinson, 1981), 53–75.

PROUST, MARCEL, *Remembrance of Things Past*, trans. C. K. Scott Moncrieff and Terence Kilmartin, 3 vols. (Harmondsworth: Penguin, 1983).

PUIG, MANUEL, *Kiss of the Spider Woman* [1976], trans. Thomas Colchie (London: Arrow Books, 1984).

PUTTENHAM, GEORGE, *The Arte of English Poesie*, ed. Gladys Willcock and Alice Walker (Cambridge: Cambridge University Press, 1936).

RACKIN, PHYLLIS, 'Androgyny, Mimesis, and the Marriage of the Boy Heroine on the English Renaissance Stage', *PMLA* 102 (1987), 29–41.

RADFORD, JEAN, 'An Inverted Romance: *The Well of Loneliness* and Sexual Ideology', in Jean Radford (ed.), *The Progress of Romance: The Politics of Popular Fiction* (London: Routledge and Kegan Paul, 1986), 97–111.

RAINOLDES, JOHN, *Th' Overthrow of Stage-Playes* (including texts by William Gager and Alberico Gentili, and with a preface for this edition by Arthur Freeman) (New York: Garland, 1974).

RAPAPORT, HERMAN, *Milton and the Postmodern* (Lincoln, Nebr.: University of Nebraska Press, 1983).

RECHY, JOHN, *The Sexual Outlaw: A Documentary* [1977] (London: W. H. Allen, 1978).

—— *Rushes* (New York: Grove Press, 1979).

REED, T. J., *Thomas Mann: The Uses of Tradition* (Oxford: Clarendon Press, 1974).

REICH, WILHELM, *The Sexual Revolution: Toward a Self-Governing Character Structure* [1936] (London: Vision, 1969).

REIK, THEODOR, *Masochism in Sex and Society*, trans. Margaret H. Beigel and Gertrud M. Kurth (New York: Grove Press, 1962).

RENAULT, MARY, *The Charioteer* (London: New English Library, 1977).

RICHARDS, ANGELA, intro. to Freud's *Three Essays on the Theory of Sexuality* in *The Pelican Freud Library* (Harmondsworth: Penguin, 1974–86), vii. 34–8.

RICKS, CHRISTOPHER, *Milton's Grand Style* (Oxford: Clarendon Press, 1963).

RIMBAUD, ARTHUR, *Collected Poems*, intro. and prose trans. by Oliver Bernard (Harmondsworth: Penguin, 1962).

RIVIÈRE, JOAN, 'Womanliness as Masquerade', in Victor Burgin, James Donald, and Cora Kaplan (eds.), *Formations of Fantasy* (London: Methuen, 1986).

ROCHLIN, GREGORY, *The Masculine Dilemma: A Psychology of Masculinity* (Boston: Little, Brown & Co., 1980).

ROLPH, C. H. (ed.), *The Trial of Lady Chatterley* (Harmondsworth: Penguin, 1961).

ROPER, LYNDAL, 'Discipline and Respectability: Prostitution and the Reformation in Augsburg', *History Workshop Journal*, 19 (1985), 3–28.

—— 'Will and Honor: Sex, Words and Power in Augsburg Criminal Trials', *Radical History Review*, 43 (1989), 45–71.

ROSE, JACQUELINE, *Sexuality in the Field of Vision* (London: Verso, 1986).

ROSE, MARY BETH, 'Women in Men's Clothing: Apparel and Social Stability in *The Roaring Girl*', *English Literary Renaissance*, 14 (1984), 367–91.

ROSS, A. (ed.), *Universal Abandon: The Politics of Postmodernism* (Edinburgh: Edinburgh University Press, 1988).

—— *No Respect: Intellectuals and Popular Culture* (London: Routledge and Kegan Paul, 1989).

ROUSSEAU, G. S., and PORTER, ROY (eds.), *Sexual Underworlds of the Enlightenment* (Manchester: Manchester University Press, 1987).

ROWBOTHAM, SHEILA, *Woman's Consciousness, Man's World* (Harmondsworth: Penguin, 1973).

RUBIN, GAYLE, 'The Traffic in Women: Notes on the "Political Economy" of Sex', in Rayna R. Reiter (ed.), *Toward an Anthropology of Women* (New York: Monthly Review Press, 1975), 157–210.

RUEHL, SONJA, 'Inverts and Experts: Radclyffe Hall and the Lesbian Identity', in Rosalind Brunt and Caroline Rowan (eds.), *Feminism, Culture and Politics* (London: Lawrence & Wishart, 1982).

RULE, JANE, *Lesbian Images* (London: Davis, 1975).

RUSSELL, JEFFREY BURTON, *The Devil: Perceptions of Evil from Antiquity to Primitive Christianity* (Ithaca, NY: Cornell University Press, 1977).

—— *Satan: The Early Christian Tradition* (Ithaca, NY: Cornell University Press, 1981).

—— *Lucifer: The Devil in the Middle Ages* (Ithaca, NY: Cornell University Press, 1984).

—— *Mephistopheles: The Devil in the Modern World* (Ithaca, NY: Cornell University Press, 1986).

RUTHERFORD, JONATHAN (ed.), *Identity: Community, Culture, Difference* (London: Lawrence & Wishart, 1990).

RYAN, KIERNAN, *Shakespeare* (Harvester New Readings) (Hemel Hempstead: Harvester Wheatsheaf, 1989).

SAID, EDWARD, *Orientalism* [1978] (Harmondsworth: Penguin, 1985).

SALGĀDO, GĀMINI (ed.), *Cony-Catchers and Bawdy Baskets* (Harmondsworth: Penguin, 1972).

—— *The Elizabethan Underworld* (London: Dent, 1977).

SAMAHA, JOEL, 'Gleanings from Local Criminal Court Records: Sedition among the Inarticulate in Elizabethan Essex', *Journal of Social History*, 8 (1975), 61–79.

SANTELLANI, VIOLETTE, 'Jean Genet's *The Miracle of the Rose*', in S. Sellers (ed.), *Writing Differences* (Milton Keynes: Open University Press, 1988).

SCOTT, JOAN W., 'Gender: A Useful Category of Historical Analysis', *American Historical Review*, 91 (1986), 1053–75.

SCOTT, ROBERT A., 'A Proposed Framework for Analyzing Deviance as a Property of Social Order', in R. A. Scott and Jack D. Douglas (eds.), *Theoretical Perspectives on Deviance* (New York: Basic Books, 1972), 9–35.

SCREEN, 28/1 (1987) (issue on *Deconstructing 'Difference'*).

SCRUTON, ROGER, *Sexual Desire: A Philosophical Investigation* (London: Weidenfeld & Nicolson, 1986).

—— *The Philosopher on Dover Beach: Essays* (Manchester: Carcanet, 1990).

SEDGWICK, EVE KOSOFSKY, *Between Men: English Literature and Male Homosocial Desire* (New York: Columbia University Press, 1985).

—— 'A Poem is Being Written', *Representations*, 17 (1987), 110–43.

—— 'Epistemology of the Closet' (1), *Raritan* (Spring 1988), 39–69.

—— 'Across Gender, Across Sexuality: Willa Cather and Others', *South Atlantic Quarterly*, special issue *Displacing Homophobia*, 88/1 (1989), 53–72.

SEGAL, HANNA, 'Hanna Segal Interviewed by Jacqueline Rose', *Women: A Cultural Review*, 1 (1990), 198–214.

SELLERS, SUSAN (ed.), *Writing Differences: Readings from the Seminar of Hélène Cixous* (Milton Keynes: Open University Press, 1988).

SENNETT, RICHARD, *Authority* (London: Secker, 1980).

SHAKESPEARE, WILLIAM, *Othello*, ed. Alvin Kernan (Signet Classic Shakespeare) (New York: New American Library, 1963).

—— *Measure for Measure*, ed. J. W. Lever (London: Methuen, 1965).

—— *Antony and Cleopatra*, ed. M. R. Ridley (London: Methuen, 1965).

—— *Twelfth Night*, ed. J. M. Lothian and T. W. Craik (London: Methuen, 1975).

—— *Henry V*, ed. Gary Taylor (Oxford: Clarendon Press, 1982).

—— *The Tempest*, ed. S. Orgel (Oxford: Oxford University Press, 1987).

SHARPE, J. A., *Crime in Seventeenth-Century England: A County Study* (Cambridge: Cambridge University Press, 1983).

SHARPE, KEVIN, and ZWICKER, STEPHEN, *Politics of Discourse: The Literature and History of Seventeenth Century England* (Berkeley, Calif.: California University Press, 1987).

SHEEHAN, BERNARD, *Savagism and Civility: Indians and Englishmen in Colonial Virginia* (Cambridge: Cambridge University Press, 1980).

SHEPHERD, SIMON, *Amazons and Warrior Women: Varieties of Feminism in Seventeenth Century Drama* (Brighton: Harvester, 1981).

SHEPHERD, SIMON, *Marlowe and the Politics of Elizabethan Theatre* (Brighton: Harvester, 1986).

—— and WALLIS, MICK (eds.), *Coming on Strong: Gay Politics and Culture*, (London: Unwin Hyman, 1989).

SHIERS, JOHN, 'Two Steps Forward, One Step Back', in Gay Left Collective (ed.), *Homosexuality: Power and Politics* (London: Allison & Busby, 1980).

SHUGG, WALLACE, 'Prostitution in Shakespeare's London', *Shakespeare Studies*, 10 (1977), 291–313.

SICILIANO, ENZO, *Pasolini: A Biography*, trans. John Shepley (London: Bloomsbury, 1987).

SILVERMAN, KAJA, *The Subject of Semiotics* (New York: Oxford University Press, 1983).

—— 'Masochism and Male Subjectivity', *Camera Obscura*, 17 (May 1988), 31–66.

—— 'White Skin, Brown Masks: The Double Mimesis, or with Lawrence in Arabia', *Differences*, 1/3 (1989), 3–54.

—— 'A Woman's Soul Enclosed in a Man's Body', forthcoming in *Male Subjectivity in the Margins* (New York: Routledge and Kegan Paul, 1991).

SINFIELD, ALAN, 'Power and Ideology: An Outline Theory and Sidney's *Arcadia*', *ELH* 52 (1985), 259–77.

—— 'Who's for Rattigan?', *Gay Times*, 120 (Sept. 1988), 44–6.

—— *Literature, Politics and Culture in Post-War Britain* (Oxford: Blackwell, and Berkeley, Calif.: California University Press, 1989).

—— 'Who was Afraid of Joe Orton?', *Textual Practice*, 4/2 (1990), 259–77.

SMITH, ANNA MARIE, 'A Symptomology of an Authoritarian Discourse: The Parliamentary Debates on the Prohibition of the Promotion of Homosexuality', *New Formations*, 10 (1990), 41–65.

SMITH, MICHAEL J. (ed.), *Black Men/White Men: A Gay Anthology* (San Francisco: Gay Sunshine Press, 1983).

SNITOW, ANN, STANSELL, CHRISTINE, and THOMPSON, SHARON (eds.), *Powers of Desire: The Politics of Sexuality* (New York: Monthly Review Press, 1983).

SNODGRASS, CHRIS, 'Swinburne's Circle of Desire: A Decadent Theme', in I. Fletcher (ed.), *Decadence and the 1890's* (London: Arnold, 1979).

SOLTAN, MARGARET, 'Night Errantry: The Epistemology of the Wandering Woman', *New Formations*, 5 (1988), 108–19.

SONTAG, SUSAN, 'Notes on Camp ', in *Against Interpretation* (New York: Farrar, 1966).

SPENSER, EDMUND, *The Faerie Queene*, ed. Thomas P. Roche (Harmondsworth: Penguin, 1978).

SPIVAK, GAYATRI, preface to J. Derrida, *Of Grammatology*, trans. G. Spivak (Baltimore: Johns Hopkins University Press, 1976).

STALLYBRASS, P., and WHITE, A., *The Politics and Poetics of Transgression* (London: Methuen, 1986).

STANNARD, D. E., *Shrinking History: On Freud and the Failure of Psychohistory* (Oxford: Oxford University Press, 1980).

STARKIE, ENID, *André Gide* (Cambridge: Bowes, 1953).

STEAD, C. K. (ed.), *Shakespeare: Measure for Measure: A Casebook* (London: Macmillan, 1971).

STEIN, ARNOLD, *Answerable Style: Essays on 'Paradise Lost'* (Minneapolis: University of Minneapolis Press, 1953).

STEINER, GEORGE, 'Eros and Idiom', in *On Difficulty and Other Essays* (Oxford: Oxford University Press, 1978).

—— *Real Presences: Is There Anything in What We Say?* (London: Faber, 1989).

STIMPSON, CATHARINE R., 'Zero Degree Deviance: The Lesbian Novel in English', in Elizabeth Abel (ed.), *Writing and Sexual Difference* (Brighton: Harvester, 1982).

STONE, LAWRENCE, *The Family Sex and Marriage in England 1500–1800* (London: Weidenfeld & Nicolson, 1977).

—— *The History of Sex* (2 parts), *National Times* (19 July–1 Aug. 1985), 9–14, 9–12.

STUBBES, PHILLIP, *Anatomy of Abuses* [1583] (repr. New York: Garland, 1973), STC 23376.

SULLOWAY, F. J., *Freud, Biologist of the Mind* (London: Deutsch, 1979).

SUMNER, COLIN, *Reading Ideologies: An Investigation into the Marxist Theory of Ideology and Law* (New York: Academic Press, 1979).

SUNDELSON, DAVID, 'Misogyny and Rule in *Measure for Measure*', *Women's Studies*, 9/1 (1981), 83–91.

SURIN, KENNETH, *Theology and the Problem of Evil* (Oxford: Blackwell, 1986).

TANNER, TONY, *Adultery in the Novel: Contract and Transgression* (Baltimore: Johns Hopkins University Press, 1979).

TATCHELL, PETER, *The Battle for Bermondsey*, preface by Tony Benn (London: Heretic Books, 1983).

TAYLOR, BARRY, *Vagrant Writing* (Hemel Hempstead: Harvester Wheatsheaf, 1991).

TAYLOR, CHARLES, 'Logics of Disintegration', *New Left Review*, 170 (1989), 110–16.

TAYLOR, MARK C., *Erring: A Postmodern A/theology* (Chicago: Chicago University Press, 1984).

TENNENHOUSE, LEONARD, *Power on Display: The Politics of Shakespeare's Genres* (New York: Methuen, 1986).

TERDIMAN, R., *Discourse/Counter Discourse: Theory and Practice of Symbolic Resistance in Nineteenth-Century France* (Ithaca, NY: Cornell University Press, 1985).

THEWELEIT, KLAUS, *Male Fantasies*, i: *Women, Floods, Bodies, History*, foreword by Barbara Ehrenreich, trans. Stephen Conway in collaboration with Erica Carter and Chris Turner; ii: *Male Bodies: Psychoanalyzing the White Terror*, foreword by Jessica Benjamin and Anson Rabinbach, trans. Chris Turner and Erica Carter in collaboration with Stephen Conway (Cambridge: Polity, 1987 and 1989).

TOLSON, ANDREW, *The Limits of Masculinity* (London: Tavistock, 1977).

TRIPP, C. A., *The Homosexual Matrix* (London: Quartet, 1977).

TUCKER BROOKE, C. F., *The Life of Marlowe and the Tragedy of Dido Queen of Carthage* (London: Methuen, 1930).

VAUGHAN, ALDEN T., 'Shakespeare's Indian: The Americanization of Caliban', *Shakespeare Quarterly*, 39 (1988), 137–53.

WALLACE, MICHÈLE, *Black Macho and the Myth of the Superwoman* (Dial Press, 1978).

WALVIN, JAMES, *Black and White: The Negro and English Society* (London: Allen Lane, 1973).

WATNEY, SIMON, 'The Banality of Gender', in *Oxford Literary Review*, 8/1–2 (1986), 13–21.

—— *Policing Desire: Pornography, Aids and the Media* (London: Methuen, 1987).

WATTS, CEDRIC, '"A Bloody Racist": About Achebe's View of Conrad', *Yearbook of English Studies*, 13 (1983), 196–209.

—— *The Deceptive Text: An Introduction to Covert Plots* (Brighton: Harvester, 1984).

—— *Measure for Measure* (Penguin Masterstudies) (Harmondsworth: Penguin, 1986).

WEBER, SAMUEL, *The Legend of Freud* (Minneapolis: University of Minnesota Press, 1982).

WEBSTER, JOHN, *The Duchess of Malfi*, in *Selected Plays*, ed. Jonathan Dollimore and Alan Sinfield (Cambridge: Cambridge University Press, 1982).

WEEKS, JEFFREY, *Coming Out: Homosexual Politics in Britain, from the Nineteenth Century to the Present* (London: Quartet, 1977).

—— *Sex, Politics and Society: The Regulation of Sexuality since 1800* (London: Longman, 1981).

—— *Sexuality and its Discontents: Meaning, Myths and Modern Sexualities* (London: Routledge, 1985).

—— *Sexuality* (London: Tavistock, 1986).

WEINBERG, GEORGE, *Society and the Healthy Homosexual* (New York: Anchor, 1973).

WELCH, DAVID, *Propaganda and the German Cinema 1933–45* (Oxford: Clarendon Press, 1983).

WELLS, ROBIN HEADLAM, *Shakespeare, Politics and the State* (London: Macmillan, 1986).

WHIGHAM, FRANK, *Ambition and Privilege: The Social Tropes of Elizabethan Courtesy Theory* (Berkeley, Calif.: University of California Press, 1984).

WHITE, EDMUND, *States of Desire: Travels in Gay America* [1980] (London: Pan Books, 1986).

WHITE, HAYDEN, *Tropics of Discourse: Essays in Cultural Criticism* (Baltimore: Johns Hopkins University Press, 1978).

WILDE, OSCAR, *The Artist as Critic: Critical Writings of Oscar Wilde*, ed. R. Ellmann [1968] (London: W. H. Allen, 1970) ('The Decay of Lying' [1889]; 'Pen, Pencil and Poison' [1889]; 'Mr Froude's Blue Book' [1889]; 'The Critic as Artist' [1890]; 'The Soul of Man under Socialism' [1891]; *Phrases and Philosophies for the Use of the Young* [1894]).

—— *The Picture of Dorian Gray* [1890/1] (Harmondsworth: Penguin, 1949).

—— *The Importance of Being Earnest* [1894/9], ed. R. Jackson (London: Ernest Benn, 1980).

—— *The Letters of Oscar Wilde*, ed. Rupert Hart-Davis (New York: Harcourt Brace & World, 1962).

WILDE, OSCAR, *More Letters of Oscar Wilde*, ed. Rupert Hart-Davis (London: Murray, 1985).

—— *De Profundis* [1897], in *The Letters of Oscar Wilde*, ed. Rupert Hart-Davis (New York: Harcourt Brace & World, 1962).

—— 'A Few Maxims for the Instruction of the Overeducated, in *The Complete Works*, with intro. by Vyvyan Holland (London: Collins, 1948), 1203–4.

WILDEN, ANTHONY, *System and Structure: Essays in Communication and Exchange* (London: Methuen, 2nd edn. 1980).

WILLIAMS, RAYMOND, *Modern Tragedy* [1966] (rev. edn. London: Verso, 1979).

—— *Marxism and Literature*, (Oxford: Oxford University Press, 1977).

—— *Problems in Materialism and Culture: Selected Essays* (London: Verso, 1980).

WILLIS, PAUL, *Learning to Labour* (Farnborough: Saxon House, 1977).

WINSTON, RICHARD, *Thomas Mann: The Making of an Artist 1875–1911*, with afterword by Clara Winston (New York: Alfred A. Knopf, 1981).

WITTIG, MONIQUE, *The Lesbian Body* [1973], trans. David Le Vay (London: Owen, 1975).

—— 'Paradigm', in E. Marks and G. Stambolian (eds.), *Homosexualities and French Literature* (Ithaca, NY: Cornell University Press, 1979), 114–21.

—— 'One is Not Born a Woman', *Feminist Issues*, 1 (1981), 47–54.

—— 'The Category of Sex', *Feminist Issues*, 2 (1982), 63–8.

—— 'The Point of View: Universal or Particular?' *Feminist Issues*, 3 (1983), 63–9.

—— 'The Mark of Gender', *Feminist Issues*, 5 (1985), 3–12.

—— 'The Straight Mind' [1980], in Sarah Lucia Hoagland (ed.), *For Lesbians Only: A Separatist Anthology* (London: Onlywoman Press, 1987), 431–9.

WOODBRIDGE, LINDA, *Women and the English Renaissance: Literature and the Nature of Womankind, 1540–1620* (Brighton: Harvester, 1984).

WOODCOCK, GEORGE, *The Paradox of Oscar Wilde* (London: Boardman, 1949).

WOODS, GREGORY, *Articulate Flesh: Male Homo-Eroticism and Modern Poetry* (New Haven, Conn.: Yale University Press, 1987).

WUTHROW, R., et al., *Cultural Analysis: The Work of Peter L. Berger, Mary Douglas, Michel Foucault, and Jürgen Habermas* (London: Routledge and Kegan Paul, 1984).

YEATS, W. B., *Autobiographies* (London: Macmillan, 1955).

YOUNG, ROBERT, 'The Same Difference', *Screen*, 28/3 (1987), 87–9.

Index

DATE DUE

JUN 21 1994	
JUN 2 0 1994	
MAY 1 8 1998	
JUN 0 4 2008	

DEMCO, INC. 38-2971